MADRONA

THE
PLAZA

THE
PLAZA

THE SECRET LIFE OF AMERICA'S
MOST FAMOUS HOTEL

JULIE SATOW

TWELVE

New York Boston

Twelve
Hachette Book Group
1290 Avenue of the Americas, New York, NY 10104
twelvebooks.com
twitter.com/twelvebooks

First Edition: June 2019

Twelve is an imprint of Grand Central Publishing. The Twelve name and logo are trademarks of Hachette Book Group, Inc.

The publisher is not responsible for websites (or their content) that are not owned by the publisher.

The Hachette Speakers Bureau provides a wide range of authors for speaking events. To find out more, go to www.hachettespeakersbureau.com or call (866) 376-6591.

Library of Congress Cataloging-in-Publication Data

Names: Satow, Julie, author.
Title: The Plaza : the secret life of America's most famous hotel / Julie Satow.
Description: First edition. | New York ; Boston : Twelve, 2019. | Includes bibliographical references and index.
Identifiers: LCCN 2018048170 | ISBN 9781455566679 (hardcover) | ISBN 9781549175930 (audio download) | ISBN 9781455566662 (ebook)
Subjects: LCSH: Plaza Hotel (New York, N.Y.)—History.
Classification: LCC TX941.P58 S28 2019 | DDC 917.47/106—dc23
LC record available at https://lccn.loc.gov/2018048170

ISBNs: 978-1-4555-6667-9 (hardcover), 978-1-4555-6666-2 (ebook)

Printed in the United States of America

LSC-C

10 9 8 7 6 5 4 3 2 1

For Stuart

Contents

TIMELINE

1890: The first Plaza opens its doors on the site of a former ice-skating pond; it is demolished fifteen years later.

1907: A new, second Plaza, which still stands today, opens and is immediately hailed as New York's most opulent and expensive hotel. Alfred Gwynne Vanderbilt, the dashing millionaire, becomes the Plaza's inaugural guest, while outside the hotel's entrance, the ubiquitous New York taxicab makes its debut.

1909: Princess Vilma Lwoff-Parlaghy becomes one of a long line of colorful guests to check into the Plaza, bringing with her a private zoo that includes a falcon, a family of alligators, and a pet lion who lives in her bathtub.

1920: Prohibition and the Jazz Age arrive, and the Plaza becomes renowned for private parties, tea dances, and F. Scott Fitzgerald, who famously jumps fully clothed into the Pulitzer Fountain.

1930: The Great Depression takes hold, leading to the ruination of the Plaza's mercurial owner, Harry S. Black, who dies soon after from a self-inflicted gunshot wound.

1943: Amid wartime rationing and the draft, Conrad N. Hilton acquires the Plaza. He is met with a chilly reception from its blue-blood fans, particularly Clara Bell Walsh, the supposed inventor of the cocktail party and the most famous of the hotel's eccentric dowagers.

1955: The mischievous six-year-old Eloise becomes the Plaza's most famous resident, flooding the hotel lobby with diminutive devotees desperate for a chance to glimpse the fictional heroine. The Plaza's young fan base grows when, a decade later, the Beatles check in and are greeted by a mob of screaming teenyboppers and a nervous hotel staff.

1966: Truman Capote hosts the Black and White Ball at the Plaza's ballroom, and the likes of Gloria Vanderbilt and Frank Sinatra mingle with the doorman from the author's apartment building.

1975: With New York City facing fiscal ruin and near bankruptcy, Westin Hotels acquires the Plaza. It soon confronts bomb scares, armed robberies, and a sanitation strike that leaves a seven-foot-high pile of garbage next to the hotel's front door.

1988: Donald J. Trump buys the hotel for a record price, using entirely borrowed funds. He installs his wife Ivana as the Plaza's president, promising to pay her $1 and all the dresses she can buy.

1992: The Plaza, unable to pay down the debt that Trump has saddled on the hotel, files for Chapter 11 bankruptcy protection for the first time in its history.

1995: The Plaza comes under foreign ownership when Saudi Prince Alwaleed bin Talal and a Singaporean billionaire purchase the hotel from Trump's lenders. A Trump lieutenant spies on the negotiations from a hidden room at the Plaza, but fails to sabotage the deal.

2005: In its biggest transformation ever, the Plaza is carved into multimillion-dollar condominiums, a boutique hotel, and retail stores. Preservationists, politicians, and the powerful New York hotel union stage a vociferous resistance, with New York mayor Michael Bloomberg negotiating a compromise.

2008: The first apartment owners move into the Plaza, with a roster of buyers that includes Hollywood executives, Russian oligarchs, and anonymous shell companies with questionable links as far afield as Kazakhstan and the Pacific islands.

2012: Subrata Roy, a colorful Indian business tycoon, purchases the Plaza Hotel without ever sleeping in one of its rooms. Under investigation, Roy is eventually sentenced to two years in jail in Delhi and is barred from traveling abroad.

2017: The Plaza suffers from the indignities of an absentee owner, while Roy entertains offers for the hotel from a cast of characters of dubious repute. A series of fiascos ensues, replete with lawsuits, a fistfight in the Palm Court, and a journalist who is sent to the same jail where Roy himself was imprisoned.

2018: In a surprise move, Roy's tenure comes to a sudden end when the hospitality arm of the Qatar Investment Authority emerges as a stealth bidder, successfully acquiring the hotel. Longtime Plaza aficionados are optimistic that the new stewards will restore the property to its former glory.

The Ground Floor of the Plaza in 1907

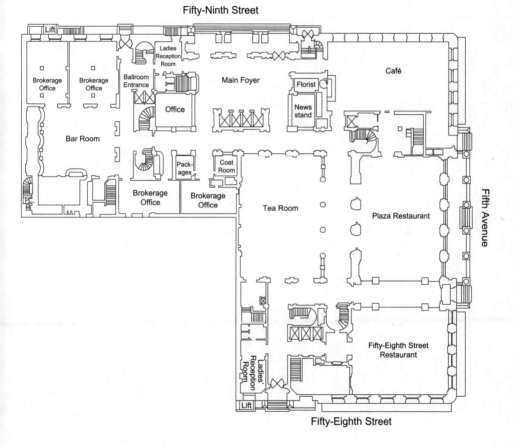

Fifty-Ninth Street

Fifth Avenue

Lift

Brokerage Office

Brokerage Office

Ballroom Entrance

Ladies Reception Room

Office

Main Foyer

Café

Florist

News stand

Bar Room

Packages

Coat Room

Brokerage Office

Brokerage Office

Tea Room

Plaza Restaurant

Ladies' Reception Room

Lift

Fifty-Eighth Street Restaurant

Fifty-Eighth Street

The Ground Floor of the Plaza in 2007

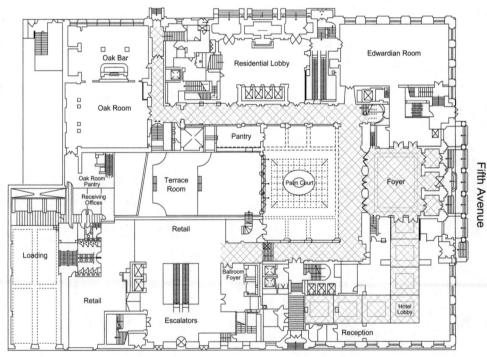

Fifty-Ninth Street

Oak Bar

Oak Room

Oak Room Pantry

Receiving Offices

Loading

Retail

Retail

Escalators

Residential Lobby

Pantry

Terrace Room

Palm Court

Ballroom Foyer

Reception

Edwardian Room

Foyer

Hotel Lobby

Fifth Avenue

Fifty-Eighth Street

INTRODUCTION

Subrata Roy was reclining on a sofa in a pink shirt, orange pocket square, and plaid blazer, his outfit contrasting sharply with the sparse, all-white living room. It was a steamy August afternoon in New Delhi in the summer of 2017, but inside it was hushed and cool, a world away from the honking and beggars' cries ringing out from the crumbling streets below. Roy, his hair and mustache dyed the same black as his shiny shoes, sipped water from a glass handed to him by a uniformed servant carrying a silver tray. After a pause, Roy looked at me and declared, "Such lovely history it has!" I waited for him to expound further, answering my question on why he loved the Plaza, his prized New York hotel. But Roy seemed to have nothing more to add.

Perhaps it wasn't surprising that the sixty-nine-year-old fallen mogul had little to say about the historic property. After all, Roy had visited the Plaza just once, and then only for a brief tour. That was back in 2012, just before he shelled out $570 million to buy the hotel.[1] A few weeks later, the Indian Supreme Court issued a devastating decision, ordering Roy to repay more than $3 billion, plus interest, to tens of millions of poverty-stricken Indians who had invested in his company's bonds. Roy scrambled to refund the money, and was eventually arrested after failing to appear at a court-mandated hearing. He spent two years behind bars in one of Southeast Asia's most notorious prisons.[2] In 2016, Roy was released on parole, but while freed from his cell, he remained prohibited from traveling abroad. Roy never had a chance to lay his head on a Plaza pillow, let alone relish his newest toy.

When envisioning the Plaza, most people don't conjure up visions of an absentee owner stuck in India, plagued by investigations and billions of dollars in debt. They think of Eloise, the impish guest who pours water down the mail chute, or lavish weddings in the gold-and-white ballroom. Maybe for some, the Plaza conjures up images of men in top hats riding horse-drawn carriages, or the writer F. Scott Fitzgerald frolicking in the Pulitzer Fountain. These are all accurate depictions. But today, so is Subrata Roy.

How did we get from the glory of what the Plaza once represented to its current state? What does this say about historic institutions and changes in America and the moneyed class? This book is a history of the 1 percent, of celebrity, of pop culture and gossip. It also examines how the Plaza is ground zero for the increasing globalization of money and the slow decoupling of pedigree from wealth.

Hotels straddle the public and private spheres, making them uniquely positioned to explore matters of history, money, and class. This is especially true of the Plaza, with its fame and longevity. Hotels are owned by those seeking profit and prominence and peopled with thousands of employees. And anyone—from a guest who rents out the largest suite, to a tired tourist who stops in for tea, to a prostitute who works the bar—can enjoy them. "To many people the fact that the Plaza is in private ownership is merely a technicality," the former *New York Times* architecture critic Paul Goldberger once wrote. "They look upon it as if they themselves were the owners, as surely as they own Central Park or the Brooklyn Bridge."[3]

When I started this project three years ago, I, too, harbored a more simplistic vision of the Plaza. It was a hotel that epitomized New York in its heyday, the site of Neil Simon's comedy *Plaza Suite*, and where Roger Thornhill was abducted in Hitchcock's classic *North by*

Northwest. Or where the spaghetti strap on Marilyn Monroe's dress broke as she gave a press conference, much to the joy and excitement of the gaggle of photographers who hungrily snapped away.

Growing up, many spring afternoons were spent in Central Park, with the Plaza's white marble tower looming over Sheep Meadow, a backdrop to my childhood. When my grandmother visited from her small town in Pennsylvania, the Plaza was her hotel. We would often meet for tea at the Palm Court before walking across the street to gawk at the rows of stuffed animals at FAO Schwarz. In 2009, when I was planning my wedding, like many brides before me, I chose to stand among the elegant balustrades, mirrors, and coffered ceiling of the Terrace Room to take my vows.

But as I dug deeper into my research, my view of the hotel shifted. I interviewed retired Plaza bellmen who had spent their careers at the hotel, and frustrated managers who quit after a few short months. I spoke with chefs who oversaw the kitchens, and lawyers who sued management. I traveled from Israel to India to meet with the Plaza's owners, and if they were no longer alive, I met with their spouses or children. The likes of Eric Trump, President Trump's middle son, and Robert Kraft, owner of the New England Patriots, shared with me their memories of the hotel. I spent days buried in the stacks of hotel archives in search of new material. And thanks to recently digitized newspapers and magazines, I sifted through tens of thousands of articles dating from as far back as 1890. I saw the fashions, vanities, and class politics of the rich shift over time, and the impact of union battles, lawsuits, and financial failures. In the end, my idealized version of the Plaza gave way to a deeper, nuanced perspective.

I discovered that the Plaza is a mirror that has reflected the country's cultural narrative, from era to era, for over a century. The hotel's first guests were the country's richest citizens, such as Alfred Gwynne Vanderbilt and John "Bet-a-Million" Gates, who ushered in a new vogue among the elite for apartment living. The Plaza's first owner, Harry S. Black, basked in the success of his creation, an expression of his ambition and drive, becoming the first to helm a skyscraper conglomerate. But there was also a darker side to the glamour and wealth. The construction workers erecting the hotel would commit murder before the building was complete. And Harry Black would ride the stock market of the 1920s to its pinnacle, until the 1929 Wall Street crash would find him, pistol in hand, the victim of ruin.

During the Great Depression, it was the steely will of hundreds of wealthy dowager widows that sustained the hotel, their bizarre antics notwithstanding. There was the Kentucky horsewoman who reportedly invented the cocktail party and the princess who arrived with a menagerie that included guinea pigs and a pet lion. She fled without paying her bill, and turned out not to be the only Plaza guest of dubious royal distinction. In fact, one purported baron was unmasked as a huckster who, wooing an heiress, wreaked havoc of Shakespearean proportions.

The Plaza has existed in periods of plenty, in financial depressions, during times of vice and licentiousness, and when the country was pulled apart by politics. The Great War was accompanied by union campaigns and African American strikebreakers, while Prohibition brought bellman bootleggers and F. Scott Fitzgerald. World War II ushered in the rationing of bread rolls and elevator parts, as well as a new Plaza owner, the archetype hotelier Conrad Hilton. With the 1950s came the postwar baby boom, and, suddenly, the deprivations of the previous decade were replaced with a roaring economy and the birth of modern-day consumerism. As usual, the Plaza epitomized the times, housing the author whose six-year-old alter ego, Eloise, also lived at the hotel, spurring one of the largest publishing juggernauts of the era.

The increasing turbulence of the 1960s and 1970s was marked by the Beatles, bomb scares, and the feminist Betty Friedan. As

New York's finances devolved into near bankruptcy, the city itself seemed to be coming apart. At the Plaza, guests faced down gun-wielding robbers, an incursion of prostitutes, and a seven-foot-high oozing pile of garbage next to its front door.

In the 1980s, at the peak of his real estate prowess, Donald Trump bought the Plaza, gilding its rooms in gold leaf and putting his wife Ivana in charge. Then the Trump empire crumbled, and not even a desperate attempt to spy on his enemies could prevent the inevitable. The Plaza filed for bankruptcy—its first and only time—before a Saudi Arabian prince and a billionaire from Singapore took the hotel off Trump's hands. An increasingly international cast of characters took central stage, with an Israeli developer eventually selling the hotel to India's Subrata Roy. The summer of 2018 saw the Plaza's latest handoff, when a hospitality company controlled by the Gulf state of Qatar acquired the building.

Inside, the Plaza's original 800-odd hotel rooms have shrunk to less than 300, the most coveted views facing Central Park and Fifth Avenue converted into a series of multimillion-dollar condominiums. The hotel's once-grand lobby has been halved so that Russian oligarchs, South Pacific politicians, and Hollywood executives can have their own private entrance. Everyone from the creator of *American Idol*, to a disgraced Spanish businessman, to the owner of Jose Cuervo tequila has had a home there. But few, if any, visit. The residents' lobby is often empty, and upstairs is a series of darkened hallways and mostly unused penthouses. Some apartments serve as anonymous bank accounts, where the world's wealthiest citizens park, and in some cases launder, their money.

The changes at the Plaza were inevitable. Large-scale New York City luxury hotels don't make as much sense today. The cost of upkeep for a historic building, the expense of wages for thousands of employees, and the price of operating dozens of public rooms and restaurants is simply too high. Land in Manhattan is far too valuable, and the vagaries of the hotel industry too unstable to justify it. Today, visitors who pass nattily dressed doormen to walk up the carpeted front steps are confronted with the news that the famed Oak Room is shuttered and that aside from the Palm Court, the only place to dine is in a basement-level food hall. There, a warren of subterranean kiosks serve everything from cupcakes to sushi in windowless rows. It's a far cry from dinner at the Edwardian Room, where tuxedoed waiters once tossed Caesar salad table-side, mixing the creamy dressing with dramatic flourish. In fact, the Edwardian Room is now a vacant storefront.

Throughout its history, the men who owned the Plaza—yes, they were all men, except for Ivana Trump, the closest thing to a woman owner—exploited the hotel's status for self-aggrandizement and legitimacy. From Harry Black, to Conrad Hilton, to Donald Trump, and, finally, to Subrata Roy, the Plaza has been a means to an end, a pathway to fame. Like the story of *The Giving Tree* by children's poet Shel Silverstein, each subsequent owner took what they needed from the hotel, leaving the Plaza further diminished until, at last, what remained was mostly memories. With the new Qatari owners who arrived last summer, it's possible that finally, this cycle may be reversed, and a flood of investment could return the Plaza to its former stature.

Why has all of this occurred here? What makes the Plaza so uniquely desired? The answer is in part geography. The hotel's location at the southeastern corner of Central Park, where Fifth Avenue meets Fifty-Ninth Street, is the crossroads of New York's high streets, where the wealthiest have congregated since the time of the Astor 400. It is also the physical midpoint of Manhattan island, the hub of New York City, which, in many ways, is the center of America and the world. What better way to announce yourself than by purchasing a piece of the Plaza? It is, as one of Subrata Roy's executives once told me, the ultimate global calling card.

Despite periodic raids from the robber barons of various eras, the Plaza has also benefited from countless good fortunes. There was the owner who rebuffed entreaties to tear down the hotel and replace it with a lucrative office tower. And, in later years, there was the mobilization of employees and preservationists to protect the Plaza's interiors from demolition. The Plaza's longevity has also added to its myth. With every decade it survives, it becomes more unusual, more historic, more emblematic of a passing time.

Over its 111 years, the Plaza has extolled beauty on the surface and grit behind the scenes. It has been a story of aspiration and of base instincts, of the moneyed class and those who serve them. It has played host to the country's most famous Hollywood starlets, Washington politicos, and Wall Street financiers. It has weathered the Jazz Age, the Great Depression, two World Wars, a new millennium, and an influx of billionaire foreigners. It began in an era before radio and exists in the time of Facebook. Like a white marble mountain rising in the center of the city, the Plaza stands weathered, permanent, and implacable. My hope is that this book will memorialize the hotel's contributions to many of the country's greatest characters and moments, and answer the question of how we got here.

—*Julie Satow, New York City, August 2018*

THE

PLAZA

PART ONE

Chapter 1

PARADE OF MILLIONAIRES

"Great hotels have always been social ideas, flawless mirrors
to the particular societies they service."
—*Joan Didion*

On the morning of October 1, 1907, the hotel bellmen and front
desk staff were scurrying about the marble lobby, smoothing their uniforms and making final preparations. Upstairs, maids
in starched white aprons checked the sumptuous suites, fluffing
feather pillows and straightening the damask curtains. As the hotel
manager barked orders, a troop of nervous doormen, dressed in
black satin breeches and jackets inlaid with yellow braid, filed outside the Plaza's bronze revolving door, arraying themselves along the
entryway's red-carpeted steps.

Along Fifty-Ninth Street, crowds had been gathering since the
early hours. At 9 a.m., a shiny black carriage finally pulled up in
front of the entrance and out stepped Alfred Gwynne Vanderbilt,
one of the country's wealthiest men. The excitement grew palpable as
onlookers jostled one another for a glimpse of the New York princeling, while newspapermen called out for a quote. Wearing a top hat
and a wide grin, the dashing Vanderbilt strode past the spectators, up
the hotel's grand staircase, and through the revolving door.

Once inside, Vanderbilt headed straight for the front desk. But instead of meeting the clerk, he was confronted by a young Irish girl perched atop the counter, absentmindedly clicking her heels. Mary Doyle was meant to be minding the Plaza newsstand, but while her fellow employees were busily preparing for the grand opening, she had aimlessly wandered over to the desk when she saw the clerk momentarily leave his post. It was at that exact moment that Vanderbilt made his entrance.

"I suddenly realized that the newsstand, where I was supposed to be on duty, wasn't even in sight from where I sat," Doyle recalled in her memoir, *Life Was Like That*. "But, not knowing what else to do, I remained where I was." As the debonair millionaire looked on bemusedly at the young girl with thick blond hair and a snub nose, there was "a slightly strained moment of silence." Then, "with a barely perceptible trace of sarcasm," Vanderbilt inquired if he might not check in. "Still sitting on the desk, I reached out casually, swung the brand-new register pad around in front of him, and dipped and handed him a pen."[1] Vanderbilt bent over the large book and on the first line of the first page signed, "Mr. and Mrs. Vanderbilt and servant," forever inscribing himself as the Plaza's inaugural guest.

Vanderbilt's entrance presaged the fact that nothing at the Plaza was quite as it first appeared. While it should have been a ceremonial and formal process, his check-in was anything but. And Vanderbilt himself had agreed to move into the hotel only after insisting that he be its first guest. The Plaza had willingly agreed, leaking the gossip to the papers, which promptly heralded the news to sell that morning's edition. It was an elaborate staging meant to draw attention to the hotel and indelibly impress it into the New York canon of myth and fantasy. Even Vanderbilt's "Mr. and Mrs." hotel inscription was a bit of smoke-and-mirrors: Mrs. Vanderbilt was nowhere to be found.

Vanderbilt's wife, in fact, was back in the family's Newport, Rhode Island, cottage, convalescing following a minor car accident the day before. Her absence augured a larger split that would take place in several months' time, when she filed for divorce in a scandal that led to the tragic death of Vanderbilt's paramour. But that dark cloud was still months away. For now, attention was wholly focused on the stream of millionaires and celebrities who arrived throughout the morning.

There was "Diamond Jim" Brady, with one hand on a diamond-and-ruby-encrusted cane and the other on the arm of his companion, the actress Lillian Russell. Mr. and Mrs. George Jay Gould followed, with several children in tow, as did John Wanamaker of Philadelphia and Benjamin N. Duke, the tobacco industrialist. The newspapers detailed the new Plaza guests in all their minutiae, one outlet even providing readers a handy diagram showing which millionaire was renting which floor.[2] The socialite Mrs. Oliver Harriman, for instance, was to occupy a suite overlooking Central Park; while two floors below were the rooms of Cornelius Kingsley Garrison Billings, famed for throwing an elaborate dinner party where guests sat upon horses, dined off trays attached to their saddles, and drank champagne from bottles nestled into their saddlebags.[3]

John "Bet-a-Million" Gates was moving into one of the hotel's most palatial suites, stretching across sixteen rooms, for which he was paying the unheard-of sum of $46,000 a year,[4] or the equivalent of $1.2 million today. The barbed-wire magnate was relocating from the Waldorf-Astoria, leaving what had been New York's greatest hotel for its newest one. Gates's presence at the Plaza wasn't a surprise, considering that he had invested in the hotel and was given free rein to customize his suite. Gates had decorated it with gusto, down to a pink-and-yellow bathroom that featured an oversized tub large enough to submerge his mammoth frame, and to which he reportedly retired at least twice a day.[5]

As the parade of new Plaza residents continued unabated for hours, there may have been a handful of those in the crowd who recalled the headlines that ran the previous summer, when the Plaza was still under construction. Those who remembered would have known that as Vanderbilt, Gates, and the other guests crossed the threshold of their new home, they were traipsing through a battle-field littered as much with violence and bloodshed as the trappings of glamour and riches.

It was on a warm morning back in July 1906, when the hotel was only partially constructed up to its eighth floor, that a deadly fight broke out. Michael Butler, a forty-one-year-old retired cop, had just arrived at work that morning, stepping off the top rung of a ladder and onto the wooden planks that served as the building's temporary floor-ing. Sweating from nerves and exertion, Butler struggled to balance on the treacherous, narrow boards, tentatively pushing past a leaning tower of steel rebar as he surveyed the laborers.

If Butler was uncomfortable at such heights, the brawny iron-workers who were busily erecting the steel girding of the hotel were sure-footed. Up here, hundreds of feet above the traffic, was the world of the rivet gangs, the ironworkers whose exertion and indus-try built the skyscrapers that were just then taking form across the Manhattan skyline. Before there was Rambo, or the Terminator, it was these "cowboys of the sky"[6] who, working with neither helmets nor harnesses for safety, epitomized brute male strength.

The rivet gangs practiced a complex, heavy-metal ballet. Some wielded enormous tongs, while others muscled pneumatic-powered jackhammers, while still more flung white-hot metal across yawn-ing gaps of sky as easily as if they were tossing a baseball. It took an experienced gang just minutes to complete the series of moves, which they repeated, tens of thousands of times, as they finished the steel girding.[7] To construct the Plaza required ten thousand tons of steel, with ironworkers completing two stories every six days.[8]

That July morning, as Butler commenced his rounds, he turned a corner, showing his back to the ironworkers. Just then, a heavy metal bolt soared through the air and struck him in the head. Butler swayed, trying to regain his balance, but before he could get his footing, ten workers pounced, raining down blows on the ex-patrolman. When Butler fell unconscious, the men grabbed his limp arms and legs and tossed his body through a hole in the unfinished flooring, where it fell two stories and landed with a thud.

Nearby, John J. Cullen saw the eruption of violence. A former policeman like Butler, Cullen moved unsteadily across the wavering planks to come to his colleague's defense. But before he could reach Butler, a second gang of furious workmen began assaulting Cullen with their heavy tools, nearly tearing his right eye from its socket. Cullen, too, fell unconscious, and the attackers briefly contemplated throwing him off the side of the unfinished building, but reconsidered after envisioning the horrified reactions from the pedestrians who milled about the Fifth Avenue sidewalk below. Instead, they left him bleeding and slumped against a pile of metal.

A third ex-patrolman, William O'Toole, was by now trying to proceed as quickly as he could to the scenes of violence, but before he was able to help his fallen comrades, O'Toole also was attacked. Beaten with monkey wrenches, he suffered a broken nose and jaw before he passed out. Then, as suddenly as the violence had erupted, it stopped. The workmen on the eighth floor turned their backs on the injured men and resumed quietly and studiously attending to their various activities.

The ironworkers' assault on Butler and the other ex-patrolmen was the culmination of months of rising tension. The men had been angling for a pay raise, from $4.50 to $5.00 a day, eventually negotiating a compromise of $4.80.[9] These were highly skilled union ironworkers, and the Plaza's owners needed them to erect the steel skeleton of the hotel. But to make up for having to pay the higher wages, the Plaza's owners decided to contract out simpler ironwork jobs to cheaper, lesser-skilled nonunion laborers.[10] The presence of these nonunion workers infuriated the union men. So as the union ironworkers toiled on the construction of the hotel, moving higher up the building as they completed each subsequent floor, they began "accidentally" dropping hot molten metal from their charcoal forges at the feet of their nonunion competitors.

Such harassment wasn't unusual during the first decade of the twentieth century, and would prove the first of many union battles at the Plaza. The labor movement was in its infancy, and it would take another thirty years before laws were instituted to protect the rights of workers to unionize. Until then, laborers often viciously protected their turf, with frequent and violent growing pains. Ironworkers were notorious for being one of the bloodiest of these early unions, carrying out frequent strikes and employing severe methods to intimidate nonunion workers and the builders who dared hire them.

At the Plaza, as the bouts of violence continued and the number of injuries increased, the hotel's owners decided to hire Butler and his fellow ex-patrolmen to guard the peace. But far from calming matters, their presence only further riled up the workers. "As a union man, a free born American citizen and a hard-working man, I did not believe my employers had any right to hire men to watch me," William Betty, a union member, would later testify.[11]

O'Toole, who had been the least injured of the three, soon awoke from his stupor. Seeing Butler and Cullen lying there, he slid unnoticed down a steel girder and, once safely on firm ground, screamed for the foreman to fetch the police.[12] Before long, twenty-five policemen surrounded the building, the sirens on their patrol wagons blaring. They began making their way up the half-built tower, but the ironworkers had booby-trapped the ladders and progress was slow. Eventually, the police reached the eighth floor. Drawing their revolvers, they compelled the ironworkers to descend to the ground.

The critically injured Butler was taken to the hospital, where he awoke long enough to identify four perpetrators before slumping once more into unconsciousness and, eventually, succumbing to his injuries. An autopsy revealed he suffered from fractured ribs, a broken breastbone, and severe internal hemorrhaging.[13] O'Toole and Cullen also managed to identify a few attackers, and soon seven ironworkers had been rounded up, charged with homicide, and locked up in the Tombs Prison. The following morning, newspaper headlines blared "Murder in Mid-Air."[14] "I think this was the most brutal murder I ever heard of," a magistrate remarked to reporters. "It would be a reversion to barbarism if such atrocities should be tolerated."[15]

A little over a year later, as Mary Doyle, the newsstand girl, handed Vanderbilt the hotel registry, the gruesome attack on the patrolmen had been seemingly forgotten. The Plaza's grand opening was celebrated with lavish abandon, the violence that undergirded the building's construction as concealed behind its lustrous white facade as the ironworkers' steel beams. There was much to celebrate, as the Plaza was the most expensive hotel in the city's history, its looming eighteen stories dominating the surrounding skyline. Its arrival was so monumental that it ushered in new behaviors that would leave their mark on New York for generations.

The Plaza's opening, for instance, coincided with the debut of one of the city's most enduring symbols, the modern taxicab. On that first day, those in the crowd who ventured to the Fifth Avenue side of the hotel discovered a fleet of twenty-five bright red cars. These vehicles, imported from France, featured gray interiors with long bench seats and two facing single seats that could be turned up when not in use. The drivers were decked out in matching uniforms made of a similar gray-blue as the interiors. To generate publicity and entice wealthy fans on this first day of business, these prototypes for today's ubiquitous yellow cabs were being offered free of charge to Plaza guests.

In 1907, cars were still novelties—it would be thirteen more years before the first traffic light graced Fifth Avenue. New Yorkers who didn't own carriages often depended on two-wheeled hansom cabs to get around town. But these new taximeter cars, with their decidedly faster pace and clearly marked odometers—charging 30 cents for the first half mile and 10 cents for every quarter of a mile after—quickly replaced horse-drawn hansom cabs as popular transport. "The hansom cabbies were curious at first" about the cars, remembered Tom Clifford, a Plaza doorman who was there that first day, "but it was plain to see that trouble was coming."[16]

In only a few short years, the calls of "Cab, cab, cab!" from hansom drivers perched high upon their platforms were replaced with insistent honking and belching from the new red cars.[17] In 1912, when a *New York Times* reporter stood outside the Times Square newsroom to count traffic, he found that of the forty-eight vehicles that passed by, just five were driven by horses, while nearly one-quarter were taxis.[18] Ironically, today the only place one can find horse-drawn cabs is directly across from the Plaza, where the New York City taxis that marked their death knell were first introduced.[19]

The advent of the Plaza ushered in other new behaviors, besides the use of modern taxis. In the wake of the hotel's opening, for instance, wealthy New Yorkers began embracing a wider public life. Those who had long maintained enormous Manhattan mansions, with their large staffs and expensive upkeep, began moving instead into hotels. The term "hotel" is a bit of a misnomer, since the terms "apartment" and "hotel" were often used interchangeably. Guests like Vanderbilt, Gates, and 90 percent of those who checked in that day were permanent residents with plans to stay indefinitely; some would remain for a lifetime. By living in hotels, these new apartment dwellers avoided what was dubbed the "servant problem," or finding and keeping affordable, well-trained help. The *New York Times* marveled at "the large number of suites to be occupied by people who have hitherto had their own private residences."[20]

There was also the draw of the Plaza's unsurpassable modern amenities. Guests could order exotic dishes like turtle soup and enjoy the ease of such conveniences as thermostats, telephones, and automatically winding clocks. "Certainly, no private house, however expensively equipped can, as yet, show the appliances for making life not only comfortable and easy, but also hygienic," the fashion magazine *Vogue* wrote in an early review of the hotel.[21] Guests didn't have to hire decorators, as every one of the Plaza's eight hundred rooms came replete with the most elegant of furnishings, including dark wood armoires and sofas upholstered in rich brocade. There were three-button panels that allowed guests to call for a bellboy, maid, or waiter, who were stationed on every floor. And room service was delivered through an elaborate system of pneumatic tubes and dumbwaiters, so it would arrive still warm from the cavernous kitchens below.[22]

Of course, not every guest appreciated the modern conveniences. When the famed tenor Enrico Caruso first moved into his suite at the Plaza, the loud ticking emanating from the automatic clock in his room interrupted his vocal training. In a fit of pique, he put the annoyance out of commission with a blow. But he failed to realize that each clock was connected to a master clock, and the destruction of one machine ruptured the entire system. Sleepy guests who awoke "to glance at the room clock, discover[ed] that the day evidently was standing still," noted a dispatch in the *Baltimore Sun*.[23] "Those who had luncheon engagements were assailed by ennui as they waited for the hour that came not."

Irate guests began hounding the front desk, and a manager was dispatched to investigate. When he arrived at the door of Caruso's suite, he was told by the tenor's servant that "Chevalier Caruso" could not be interrupted since "such annoyance was disconcerting to the aesthetic soul." The manager insisted, and when he eventually won entrance, he was confronted with the necessary proof. There, "beneath the embarrassed face of the clock in the Caruso suite hung a mass of broken and twisted wires."

The opening of the Plaza also influenced fashion and social patterns. Since the 1890s, the elite of society had paraded their finery along Peacock Alley, a three-hundred-foot marble corridor that ran the length of the fashionable Waldorf-Astoria hotel. It was a grand spectacle that epitomized the excesses of the Gilded Age. But now, with the Plaza, this behavior became a broader phenomenon. It became popular to go out to restaurants and eat among strangers, and to spend evenings ballroom dancing to an orchestra with hundreds of other couples. The Plaza and its compatriots became preeminent places to show off, enjoy one's wealth, and cement one's status in high society.[24] At the Plaza, you could march through the lobby in the latest fashion and be assured of appearing in the society column, the hotel hallways being clogged with reporters in search of gossip to fill the next day's papers.

The Plaza also offered new levels of celebrity, a precursor to reality stars like the Kardashians. For instance, when one of New York's wealthiest society matrons, Mrs. Stuyvesant Fish, arrived at the Plaza one evening dressed in a broadtail fur cloak fastened with a conspicuous diamond brooch on the outside of her coat, it caused a flurry of copycats. "In a flash this innovation had sunk deep into the hearts of other women," detailed one columnist, in a piece titled "Jewels Outside Your Furs."[25]

Even those with less wealth could successfully leverage the publicity offered by a hotel. As one reporter archly noted, all you had to do was host a relatively inexpensive party, "amounting to no more than afternoon tea," and you would find yourself the exalted subject of an item such as: "Mrs. So-and-So entertained 50 guests at luncheon at the Plaza Hotel, the company afterwards playing bridge."[26]

And long before the Beatles drew frenzied fans to the Plaza, highly anticipated celebrity sightings were attracting crowds. A year after the Plaza opened, word leaked out that Miss Gladys Vanderbilt, sister of Alfred Gwynne Vanderbilt, and her betrothed, the Count Laszlo Szechenyi, would be having tea at the Plaza's Palm Court. They were to arrive at the same time as Miss Theodora Shonts and her fiancé, the Duc de Chaulnes, and the public, anxious to catch a glimpse of the titled royalty, began swarming the hotel.

"Within half an hour the corridors were impassible. Visitors took possession of bellboys' benches and every available chair," noted the *New York Times*. The hotel closed the Palm Court's glass doors against the throngs, but "the crowd was undismayed and courteously stormed" the room, forcing the maître d'hôtel to use his "broad shoulders" to "resist the advances of a flying wedge of well-dressed women." In the end, when the famous guests arrived, one couple was surreptitiously escorted to their table by way of the hotel's ground-floor pantry, while the other snuck in through a lobby brokerage office.[27]

Another draw of hotel life was the dining. It was from hotels that Parker House rolls, Waldorf salad, and the Manhattan cocktail originated.[28] The Plaza's popular subterranean Grill Room, located beneath the lobby, featured a glass refrigerator from which patrons could pick their own steak or pork chop. As an added bonus, the restaurant unexpectedly offered ice-skating during the warm summer months. As June rolled around, the hotel flooded the Grill Room's tile floor with water they then froze, so that customers could while away the time between courses skating, a full orchestra dressed in white tuxedos providing the musical accompaniment.

As notable as ice-skating in the summer was, the service that the Grill Room offered to patrons who had pets was even more astounding. The restaurant featured a "dog check room," presided over by a French maid who provided her pampered pooches with a selection of large and small padded baskets, pans filled with water, and an unending supply of dog biscuits.[29] In fact, at any one time, the Plaza was home to nearly three dozen dogs, "many of them imported and virtually every one of them well pedigreed," according to *Life* magazine, which later published a multipage feature on the phenomenon.

"Like their owners, Plaza dogs tend to be exceptionally well dressed and well fed. They find life at the hotel unhurried and pleasant," the magazine noted.[30] There was Nana, a French poodle who boasted her own room featuring a miniature bath, a dog tutor, a dog nurse, and, of course, a specially designed dog-food menu. There was also Pelleas, a chic Pekingese owned by a famous Belgian author; and Bonzu, who at thirteen was the hotel's oldest canine inhabitant. Given the wealth of its residents and the life of ease many enjoyed, it made sense that the Plaza was known for its dogs. As Thorstein Veblen, the economist who coined the phrase "conspicuous consumption," noted, the dog, unlike the mouse-chasing cat, "commonly serves no industrial purpose." A dog is merely "an item of expense," its "unquestioning subservience and a slave's quickness in guessing his master's mood" making it an ideal showpiece for the rich.[31]

Not all dogs, however, were showpieces. A tiny Pomeranian named Digi would prove Veblen wrong when he accomplished what even a New York City police detective could not. Digi's mistress, Patricia Burke, a socialite visiting from Los Angeles, had lost a diamond-and-pearl ring somewhere in the vast reaches of the hotel. Employees were dispatched to look for it, and a detective was called. But it wasn't until Digi, who had been following his mistress about the hotel all day, began making strange noises that she finally paid him some heed. "Miss Burke looked at Digi, and there, to her amazement, was the ring gripped tightly in the teeth of the Pomeranian," reported the *Washington Post*.[32] Another useful dog was Captain, a bulldog who belonged to Plaza resident Mrs. Benjamin Kirkland. Every evening, Captain appeared at the front desk to collect a leather case filled with valuable jewels, which he would then carry—"never did anyone touch the bag in the Boston bull's mouth"—to Kirkland's room in time for her to dress, according to one retelling.[33]

A multitude of employees was needed to care for these pets and serve the Plaza's exacting guests. If a team of ironworkers striving in unison was necessary to erect the hotel, then a collaboration of hundreds of staff was critical to the Plaza's operations. When it came to dining, for instance, the heart of the enterprise was the subterranean kitchen, a maze of white-tiled rooms located in the building's lower reaches. It was overseen by Monsieur Lapperraque, a French master chef, the "Grand Poo-bah in this underground land of saucepans," who surveyed eighty-three cooks from a glass-enclosed office "like a watchful spider in the midst of his web."[34] There were separate rooms for storing meat, fish, dry goods, and green groceries, and in what sounded almost like a nursery rhyme, each cook was tasked with a specialty, including a bread baker, an ice cream maker, and a candy creator. It wasn't unusual for the kitchen to prepare such fare as kangaroo meat or to string up giant game or oversized tortoises on racks to ready them for the ovens.

Even the Plaza's air was rarefied. The hotel used an elaborate ventilation system to purify the oxygen pumped into the building, and a network of thermostats ensured "there is no annoyance with furnaces that will not burn, with steam radiators that refuse to be hot, or that persistently compel us to endure either a tropical heat or dangerous draughts from windows opened in despair," *Vogue* wrote approvingly.[35] The refrigeration equipment was also a modern wonder, used not only to produce ice for tea and cocktails, but to circulate brine all the way up to the hotel's seventeenth floor, above the guest rooms. There, it was used to cool a storage room for guests' fur coats.

On these upper floors, where the mansard roof created sloped ceilings and dormer windows, there was also the housekeepers' department and the maids' dormitories. On the eighteenth floor was a carpenters' workshop, a valets' room with electric heated irons, and a tailors' studio with a battery of sewing machines.[36] These upper floors, in later decades, would be repurposed as exclusive "penthouses," tempting billionaire Russian oligarchs and fashion moguls.

The staff necessary for running a hotel of this size totaled roughly 1,500, including 50 each of chambermaids, housemaids, and bellboys; plus 200 waiters, 75 laundresses, and 25 porters. There were also 20 bartenders, 10 wine cellar men, 15 barbers, and, in later years, two men whose sole job was dusting the chandeliers, and another who patrolled the hallways stamping ashtrays with the double-P Plaza logo.[37] To get one of these coveted jobs wasn't an easy feat. George, the head waiter at the Ritz in London, for instance, was making a special effort for his new stint at the Plaza. Known among his society clientele by his single moniker, George had curly hair, a cherubic face, and the polished manners expected of a man in his position. But he also spoke in a strong English clip, and was "strenuously cultivating a New York accent" to better fit in.[38]

Many of the new employees were poached from the Waldorf-Astoria, the Plaza's chief competitor. While the Waldorf was the grandest of establishments, the Plaza was something new, a more refined version of glamour. Its location, "many blocks farther north on Fifth Avenue than anyone had gone before—more than a mile above the still-unchallenged Waldorf—was a venture of no little daring," wrote Doyle, the newsstand girl. She, like many of her colleagues, had come from the Waldorf. That hotel's "colored marble, its gilding and red velvet, palms, and marble statues, had seemed to all America the last word in luxurious magnificence," Doyle recalled in her memoir. "But even the older generation felt dimly the superiority of the Plaza's cool green and white marble, its greater spaciousness, with no more than judicious touches of crystal and silver to relieve its corridors from severity."

Doyle, who was among the first Plaza employees to be hired, described the mood in the months leading up to the hotel's opening. "Cooped up as we were in that big, still bare and raw-edged structure, with only ourselves for company, the newly assembled Plaza staff was not unlike a band of colonists new-landed on a promising but still unproved coast." The man who would captain these new colonists was Frederick Sterry, the Plaza's first manager, who "made every one of us, down to the humblest, feel that we had an active share in it," wrote Doyle.

Sterry's strategy for success was to convince the wealthiest guests who resided at the Waldorf-Astoria to come instead to the Plaza. "To do this, the Plaza, he had determined, must from the first strike a much more exclusive and correct, a more expensively restrained note than the gaudy old place it was to supersede," Doyle wrote. "Our management had little or no precedent to guide it in its efforts to cultivate that precise degree of snobbery which should prove most profitable," she noted, but "it was becoming plainer every day that the Plaza had 'caught on.'" The Plaza's elegant if demure decor, the soft tones of the harpsichord wafting from the Palm Court, the air suffused with hints of floral perfume, gave visitors "a sense in which the opening of the Plaza was the first intimation that an age was passing—the age of the Waldorf and of all that it typified."[39]

Doyle's conjecture was soon proven true. The ornate Waldorf-Astoria and the Gilded Age that it exemplified were coming to a close. Since the mid-1890s, the American economy had been growing at a rapid clip, producing numerous robber barons, copper

kings, and railroad magnates.[40] But just as the first Plaza guests
unpacked their steamer trunks and explored their sumptuous suites,
a few miles to the south, in the banks and brokerage houses of
Wall Street, the mood was far less celebratory. The markets had
been shaky for weeks, and shortly after the Plaza opened its doors,
stocks went into a tailspin. There was a run on the banks, and what
became known as the Panic of 1907 set in.[41]

Yet, inside the Plaza, guests seemed mostly isolated from the
troubles. The Panic did create a dip in the number of arriving
guests—about $300,000 worth of bookings were canceled[42]—but
the impact was muted. On that first Christmas, Santa Claus skipped
over a multitude of Americans suffering from the Wall Street fall-
out, but he dropped down every chimney at the Plaza. "In the new
Plaza particularly, it was a merry Christmas, without a suggestion
of hard times," wrote the *New York Times*.[43]

Millionaire guests wanting to tip their favorite hotel staff that year
requested so much money from the Plaza's cash box that the hotel suffered from a "money famine," forcing several guests to postpone their
gift-giving until the hotel could refill its coffers. Mrs. C. H. Strong of
Erie, Pennsylvania, handed out a dozen gold watches to her favorite
Plaza employees; while Vanderbilt shelled out $1,000 in $5 and $10
bills. The tenor Caruso gave away several of his artworks (crayon trac-
ings of magazine illustrations—of questionable artistic value); and a
maid received a lace handkerchief "fit for a Queen." Doyle and the
other newsstand girls were gifted a five-pound box of candy.

As the Plaza stood largely isolated from the troubles of the Panic
of 1907, its refined sophistication and modernity heralded the start
of a new era. With the Plaza came New York taxis, apartment living,
room service, celebrity culture, and even pampered pets—hallmarks
of high society that still hold true today. The hotel's heyday was set
to begin. But before it could start in earnest, a murder had to be
solved.

Chapter 2

A Typical French House

"Edifices of this order have been unknown to past
generations. They have no prototypes."
—*Henry Janeway Hardenbergh, architect of the Plaza*

O n the top floor of the Criminal Courts Building in Lower
Manhattan, seven accused men were lined up along the western wall, their rough hands resting on thick thighs, tanned faces
turned toward the gallery. It had been ten days since Michael Butler
died, and an inquiry into his alleged murder was set to begin. "The
ironworker on the spider web framework of a skyscraper is graceful
and inspiring in spite of his thick shoes and his uncouth attire,"
wrote a reporter for the *World*, who sat in the courthouse that day.
"Dressed up and on solid ground, with a charge of murder against
him, he is not so engaging."[1]

As the case got underway, more than fifty ironworkers who had
been stationed just feet from the violent scene were called to the
witness stand. With their wives and girlfriends looking on, the men
testified, one after another, that they hadn't noticed a thing. "Did
you see anything of the trouble which happened within fifteen
feet of your post?" asked the chief coroner who was overseeing the
hearing.

"No, I didn't see anything of it," replied Daniel McTammany in a typical ironworker response.

"You were attending to your work; you always attend to your work?"

"Yes, sir."

"You wouldn't notice it if there was an earthquake or anything like that?"

"No, I wouldn't."[2]

As the obfuscations continued, one newspaper quipped, "Union ironworkers, deep of chest, strong of limb, and active as squirrels, are, nevertheless, shortsighted and hard of hearing." Despite being "confined within a radius of 60 feet or so," the workmen "were all so busy that a fight offered no attraction whatever to them to delay their labors even for a moment."[3]

Following the ironworkers' testimonies, O'Toole, one of the ex-patrolmen, his head still wrapped in bandages from the beating, took to the witness stand. He positively identified his attackers, even recounting a damning conversation he'd had just a few days prior to the fight: "What are you fellows doin' up here anyhow?" one ironworker had aggressively inquired of him. "We're sent up here to see that you fellows stop dropping sledge hammers and red-hot bolts," O'Toole replied. "Beat it!" the ironworker answered. "If you know your business you'll skiddoo." The ironworker concluded by warning him, "Get off the job or we'll get you."[4]

During the hearing, the chief coroner who was tasked with unbiasedly presiding over the case, gave a series of press interviews that indicated he was anything but impartial. "Michael Butler was not murdered," he declared to a *New York Sun* reporter, who happened upon the coroner at a saloon, as the coroner nursed a beer during a break in the proceedings. Butler had fallen accidentally, the coroner continued, and it was really Butler's employer, the Plaza's builders, who were to blame. The George A. Fuller Construction Company that was erecting the hotel had failed to sufficiently warn Butler of the job's perilous dangers, the coroner maintained. The construction firm was "plainly culpable under the employers' liability act," he concluded.

As the *New York Sun* reporter dutifully recorded the conversation, he wondered aloud whether the coroner, who was soon up for reelection, wasn't more interested in securing the ironworkers' union support for his political aspirations than he was in uncovering the truth. "I do not owe my present position to union labor," the coroner replied, "but I'd rather be reelected by union labor votes than by a campaign contribution from the Fuller Company."[5]

Several weeks later, the case finally went to the jury. After thirty minutes of deliberation, they filed back into the courtroom with a verdict. Butler, the jury declared, had indeed fallen by accident, and the ironworkers were blameless in the death. The question of how Butler's two colleagues also happened to come by their bruises and broken bones remained unanswered. Whooping cheers rang out as the accused's families ran forward to hug the newly freed men.

But if inside the courtroom the mood was buoyant, outside the verdict was greeted with disillusionment. The ironworkers had committed "defiant perjuries," wrote the *New York Times*, calling the attacks "murder in the first degree." It assailed "the inherent asininity of Coroner's inquest procedure," and declared, "A community that would stand this sort of brutal defiance of law and decency would stand anything."[6]

While controversy swirled around the downtown courthouse, uptown, at the edge of Central Park, a white tower continued rising without pause. The day after the attack, the George A. Fuller Construction Company had replaced the troublesome ironworkers with nonunion laborers, paying them thirty cents less a day. It also hired eighteen new security guards to patrol the site and installed a telephone, so any trouble could be immediately reported to the police.[7] Construction remained on schedule—so much so, in fact, that when the Plaza was completed twenty-seven months after breaking ground, it set a New York record.[8]

This Plaza was not actually the first building on the site; it was not even the first Plaza. Long before ironworkers or Michael Butler, a bucolic pond had occupied the corner of Fifty-Ninth Street and Fifth Avenue. This was the home of the New York Skating Club. There, men in peacoats and wool trousers and women in beribboned caps and fur muffs enjoyed a wintry thrill surrounded by expansive country views, blissfully unaware of the changes that were to come.[9]

In 1882, two builders paid $850,000, or $21 million in today's dollars, for the land, with ambitions to construct a family apartment hotel, a hybrid popular at the time.[10] But two years later, the hotel was still incomplete, and the troubled builders were facing a mountain of unpaid bills. The New York Life Insurance Company foreclosed on the site and hired McKim, Mead & White, the architecture firm who designed the original Pennsylvania Station and the Washington Square Arch, to finish the building. Finally, in 1890, the first Plaza opened its doors.

This initial building was considered a palatial establishment, "one of the grandest hotels in the world," *King's Handbook of New York City*, the preeminent guidebook of the era, declared in 1892.[11] "Rising majestically . . . to the height of eight full stories," its facade was "brick and brownstone, diversified, but not overladen, with terra cotta and polished marble, balconies and cornices." The Plaza, the handbook continued, "shows rich and tasteful effects on all sides and the simple beauty of Italian Renaissance architecture."[12]

Inside, the hotel was equally elegant, with four hundred oversized guest rooms, wide corridors, and heavy red-velvet carpeting. Facing Fifth Avenue were two parlors, a pink one and a blue one, furnished with onyx tables, frescoed ceilings, and walls covered in embossed silk drapery. The hotel's coat of arms was the lion, and the imposing figure was emblazoned on the mosaic flooring of the hotel's entryway and woven into its lace curtains. Framed vivid likenesses of animals created by Massachusetts painter Alexander Pope Jr. decorated the rooms, including his painting of a regal lion that hung under the hotel's staircase. The lion painting was an attraction, and New Yorkers who were strolling on a Sunday afternoon through Central Park would often stop in to see it.

Explorer Sir Henry Morton Stanley and journalist and financier Henry Villard were frequent guests of this original Plaza. Villard was famous for holding court in the smoking room, where he would sit at a six-foot-long table made from the root of a mahogany tree.[13] The hotel's sumptuous gold-and-white dining room was constantly booked with glamorous affairs, such as the reception for Philippe d'Orléans, Comte de Paris, who served in the Union Army during the Civil War. Attended by one hundred of the count's former comrades, including General W. T. Sherman, the men dined at a horseshoe-shaped table surrounded by a bed of roses, upon which "Army of the Potomac" was inscribed in white flowers.[14]

In 1890, the year that this Plaza opened, the economy, driven by expansions in industries like railroads and steel, was surging, and New York's population was exploding. Millionaires were being minted at an unprecedented pace, and mansions to house them were being erected almost as frenetically. Along Fifth Avenue, where once there had been a country pond and a dusty footpath, there were now rows of elegant edifices featuring private ballrooms and art galleries, with residents named Astor and Vanderbilt. In 1898, *Munsey's Magazine* called Fifth Avenue "the backbone of New York," with "more wealth than can be found in any other residential two miles of any city of the world."[15]

Three years into the original Plaza's existence, the ornate Waldorf Hotel opened on Fifth Avenue and Thirty-Fourth Street. It was followed four years later by the Astoria Hotel, and soon the two adjacent buildings were connected to create the famed Waldorf-Astoria.

More new hotels followed suit, and in comparison, the old Plaza began to appear increasingly dowdy. As it lost its allure and its popularity waned, the Plaza's owners looked to sell. Now considered in an unrivaled location, at the crossroads of Fifth Avenue and Central Park South, the Plaza was bombarded with a multitude of bidders who lined up for a chance to buy the hotel.

The eventual winners agreed to pay $3 million, or the equivalent of $88 million today, for the property—shattering all previous records in the annals of New York real estate.[16] But while the price tag made headlines, what really set tongues wagging was the fact that the new owners intended to demolish the twelve-year-old structure to replace it with something new. Critics decried the move, complaining the Plaza was to be "leveled to the ground as ruthlessly as though it had been a horse shed."[17] Asked one journalist, bewilderedly, "What manner of hotel can be erected that will justify the destruction of the old one?"[18]

Two men were busy fashioning an answer to this query. Bernhard Beinecke and Harry S. Black were the originators of the Plaza that we know today, hoteliers who set the mold for all the owners who followed. In most ways, the men were opposites. Beinecke was a portly, bespectacled German émigré who, at fifty-six, was one of the city's largest, and richest, meat butchers. The Plaza offered Beinecke a chance to make a genteel investment, to create a private club for his circle of friends. Black, on the other hand, was a thirty-nine-year-old rakish adventurer for whom the Plaza represented a stepping-stone on his career path, a means for realizing his grand ambitions.

Beinecke had arrived in New York City in 1865 from a small industrial town in Germany, one of millions carried by the historic wave of immigration then crashing against the city's shores. The nineteen-year-old landed on the Lower East Side and soon began wheeling a meat delivery wagon through the packed chaos of the tenement district. He saved his money and bought his own butcher shop, selling it two years later at a profit. He used the proceeds to start a wholesale meat business, Beinecke & Co., with a storefront on Chrystie Street. As the proprietor, Beinecke was driven by his oft-repeated phrase, "Earn it, if you want to own it."[19]

Ten years after landing in New York, Beinecke had a burgeoning business and solid prospects. He married Johanna Elisabeth Weigle, with whom he would stay wedded until his death. The industrious couple moved to East Ninth Street, a cramped neighborhood known as Little Germany. Beinecke spent the next several decades methodically growing his wholesale meat operation, providing steaks and chops to the city's top restaurants and hotels. The family's wealth increased, and the Beineckes, now with six children in tow, abandoned the huddled masses living downtown and relocated to a spacious town house on West Seventy-Sixth Street, designed by John H. Duncan, who also designed Grant's Tomb.

In 1890, the year the original Plaza opened, Beinecke was forty-four years old. With his stiff manners, dark, formal suits, and the staccato trace of an accent, Beinecke projected an old-world air. He had been in the meat business for close to thirty years, but even as he clung to vestiges of his native Germany, he embraced the American ideal of reinvention. That April, he sold his meat concern and, within days, jumped into a new venture.

Beinecke partnered with four others to create what would become one of the first national hotel chains. One of its first moves was to pay $127,500 a year to lease and manage the original Plaza. Beinecke would eventually partner with Black to redevelop the hotel. "Born of his experience in supplying meat to hotels was a decision to invest in hotels," wrote Eve Brown, the publicity director of the Plaza in the 1960s, in *The Plaza, 1907–1967: Its Life and Times*, her breezy history of the hotel.[20] Like subsequent Plaza owners, Beinecke used the proceeds from his butchering business to invest in a hotel that would confer on him legitimacy and status.

Black traveled quite a different path to arrive at the Plaza. Born on the coast of Lake Ontario in Canada to an impoverished major in the British army, Black's first job was minding the general store in his small town. A restless youth, Black soon joined a surveying party that was embarking for the Northwest and the Pacific Coast. He then became a traveling salesman for a wool wholesaler. With the short, sturdy build of a fighter, Black had a handsome face accentuated by bright blue eyes, a cleft chin, and a mop of dark hair.[21] A natural salesman, he leveraged his looks and charisma into a successful business career, eventually opening several banks and stores.[22]

In 1893, Black traveled to Chicago for the World's Fair. It was there, among the crowds gawking at the first Ferris wheel and the first moving sidewalk, that Black's destiny with the Plaza would begin.[23] At the fair, Black met George A. Fuller, a wealthy Chicago real estate developer. Fuller was famous for building the first-ever tower without load-bearing curtain walls, an architectural feat that was accomplished with the use of a steel skeleton. Before, buildings used thick curtain walls on the lower floors to bear the weight of the stories that rose above. But this limited a building's height, since the ground-floor walls could only be so thick. With a steel skeleton, such walls became unnecessary, revolutionizing the industry and allowing for the construction of skyscrapers.

Fuller was a dozen years older than Black and took an immediate liking to the ambitious young businessman. "I'd been thinking of my man in skyscraper terms, and in Harry, I got what looked like a one-story and a basement," Fuller would later joke, belying his affection.[24] Fuller's teenage daughter Allon Mae was equally enamored, and the two soon fell in love. In 1895, seventeen-year-old Allon Mae Fuller and thirty-two-year-old Harry S. Black were married. Black soon began working at his father-in-law's real estate firm. In 1900, when Fuller became sick and died, it fell to Black to run the business.

Nepotism may have gained Black entry into the George A. Fuller Construction Company, but he soon proved himself worthy. Black began methodically growing the business, aggressively bidding for large construction jobs and strategically acquiring smaller firms. Soon, Harry and Allon had moved to New York and the Fuller Construction Company was erecting such iconic structures as the triangular-shaped Flatiron Building and the flagship Macy's Herald Square.

There is no record of how Beinecke and Black met, but the fact that the men would have known one another is not surprising, considering the former was a nascent investor in hotels and the latter was a major builder. When the Plaza was finally put up for sale, Beinecke convinced Black that the George A. Fuller Construction Company should buy the property. The two men then set about re-envisioning the hotel. The key would be how to finance their ambitions, since such an unrivaled property as the one they hoped to build would be exorbitantly expensive, more than the two men could personally afford. The pair cast about for a solution to their financing gap. It wasn't long before an answer materialized in the form of one of the most deep-pocketed, colorful business titans of the day.

According to lore, Beinecke and Black were lunching at the St. Regis, a hotel built by Colonel John Jacob Astor just a few blocks south of the Plaza on Fifth Avenue. The men were deep in conversation when John "Bet-a-Million" Gates approached. A friend and frequent business partner of Black's, Gates never looked like much, with a short and wide frame, but his personality more than made up for it. Gates was a hustler, a poor Illinois farm boy who had made it rich selling barbed wire to Texas ranchers. As his moniker declared, Gates enjoyed speculating and hosted high-stakes poker games at his suite of apartments at the Waldorf-Astoria. It was on a rainy evening during one of those games that Gates earned his nickname, betting the enormous sum of $1 million on which raindrop would slide down the windowsill first.

When Gates saw Beinecke and Black huddled together at the St. Regis, he walked over to say hello. The men told Gates what they were planning for the Plaza, and of their financial needs. Gates listened to the men, then boomed in his commanding voice that he would happily finance the endeavor. He had just one request: They must hire Gates's favorite hotel manager, the young Frederick Sterry. "I'll wager my fortune on his hotel ability," Gates said. As long as Sterry was on board, "you can count on me for all you need."[25]

Sterry was an obvious choice for the Plaza. He had grown up near Saratoga Springs, a favorite resort destination for the wealthy, particularly avid horse-racing fans. At age twenty-three, Sterry began working at one of the area's top hotels, and by age twenty-seven he was the manager of a hotel in Hot Springs, Virginia. Noted for his tact and skillful handling of sensitive issues that often arose when dealing with wealthy hotel guests, Sterry soon moved on to Palm Beach, Florida.[26] There, he was a key architect in the creation of the town as a playground for the rich, managing two of its best-known hotels, the Royal Poinciana and the Breakers.[27] Quickly, Beinecke and Black hired Sterry, and, by extension, Gates and his millions were secured.

With their financing in hand, Beinecke and Black could finally begin their project. Their first step was to demolish the existing structure. It was on a warm June evening in 1905 that the first Plaza was to celebrate its final night in existence. C. B. Tedcastle, who had stayed at the hotel on its inaugural evening in 1890, intended to close out the era by being the last person to sign the Plaza's hotel registry. Alas, another patron, Frederick Gardner Moore, thwarted his plans when he swooped in, signing the registry with a melodramatic flourish that read "The Last of the Mohicans."[28]

The next morning, most of the remaining guests were ushered out and the patter of the hotel's hallways and humming of its elevators was silenced. The only sounds to echo across the empty rooms came from four obstinate guests, who had refused to vacate.

As the day progressed, the holdouts stubbornly sat, not budging from the remaining couches and chairs, even as auctioneers arrived and began selling the doomed hotel's furnishings out from under them.[29] Eventually, no longer able to postpone the inevitable, the guests filed out of the building. Now that it was finally emptied, the Plaza's demolition began. Inside of eight weeks, the old Plaza had disappeared, and a white gleaming tower began rising in its place.

The man designing this new Plaza, where ironworkers would soon battle in midair during its construction, was Henry Janeway Hardenbergh. He was, appropriately enough, also the architect of the original Waldorf-Astoria (the hotel would be demolished in 1929 to make way for the Empire State Building, and was later rebuilt farther uptown). Hardenbergh remains a mercurial figure, with scant historical facts available about him. It is known he was born in New Jersey to a prominent Protestant family whose ancestors arrived from Holland in 1644. Hardenbergh's great-great-grandfather was a founder of Rutgers College, and he was married, although his wife soon died, and the couple was childless.[30]

The dearth of biographical details is surprising, given that Hardenbergh was a success during his lifetime. He designed not only the Waldorf-Astoria but several other notable structures, including the Dakota apartment building on West Seventy-Second Street. While his other work was celebrated, it was for hotels that he was best known. Hardenbergh was "the pioneer hotel builder," wrote the *Architectural Record* upon his death at age seventy-one, "the first to develop the esthetic problem of hotel design and the mechanical problem of hotel planning for safety and convenience."[31]

The *Architectural Record* interviewed Hardenbergh in the spring of 1906, just as the plans for the new Plaza were coming together. The article described him as "Napoleonic in stature, but of wiry build, with a shrewd, worldly-wise expression in his eyes." During the interview, Hardenbergh spoke of finding harmony between the interior of a building and its exterior. "In a hotel all tastes have to be satisfied, and one must know pretty well how the space is going to be utilized before one can realize the artistic vision of the outward appearance of a building," he said. "The architect has to deal with three factors, all of equal importance," Hardenbergh declared. "First, the artistic element; second, construction; and third, interior decoration. It is just as in music, a certain *Leitmotif* should run through everything. Otherwise, it would be merely a collection of miscellaneous details."[32]

At the Plaza, Hardenbergh harnessed the site's most unique characteristic, one that remains a defining aspect of the hotel even today. The Plaza is situated on a corner that has two setbacks, Central Park and Grand Army Plaza, creating one facade on Fifty-Ninth Street and the other on Fifth Avenue, that can be clearly apprised from a distance. If hotels are public spaces by their very definition, then the Plaza is doubly so, with its twin exposures making the building even more conspicuous than most.

Hardenbergh took advantage of the Plaza's visibility, constructing a classical column. The first three stories were finished in rusticated Vermont marble to form the column's base, and the remainder in cream-colored enameled terra-cotta brick to form the column's shaft. The sloping mansard roof, with its ornate dormers and gables made from copper and slate, echoing the green of Central Park, formed the column's capital.[33] It was a French Renaissance château, executed in skyscraper proportions.

During the interview with the *Architectural Record*, Hardenbergh pulled out his sketches of the Plaza. The publication, comparing the Plaza design to the Waldorf-Astoria, noted, "There seems to be a striking tendency in this latest of his work, to abandon the picturesqueness and irregularity of his former style, and to arrive at a simpler, and at the same time more pleasing effect." The architectural historian Robert A. M. Stern would later put it even more succinctly: "The owners of the Plaza surpassed the Waldorf-Astoria by hiring the Waldorf's architect to design his masterpiece."[34]

Hardenbergh placed the Plaza's main entrance on Fifty-Ninth Street, across from Central Park, not on Fifth Avenue, where it was later moved. Visitors entering the lobby were greeted with an elaborate marble foyer furnished in the rococo style, with brocades in tints of rose and green and walls accented with marble half columns topped with capitals of gilt bronze. There was a large jardiniere with seats around the base, and behind that, a battery of four elevators featuring glass doors, through which the mechanical pistons could be seen. Called "plungers," the elevators, technologically advanced for the time, stood on enormous shafts that descended deep into the city's bedrock. The elevators would remain a noted feature of the hotel for decades, long after other buildings had replaced the manned plunger cars with automated electrical versions.

The lobby also featured the front desk and a ladies' reception room, which was to the right of the elevator banks, as well as the newsstand and a florist shop that stood to the left. A mezzanine, at the top of a set of carpeted stairs, housed several stockbrokers' offices, as well as telegraph, telephone, and writing rooms. The Café, later the Edwardian Room, took up the coveted corner of Fifty-Ninth Street and Fifth Avenue, with walls of paneled dark oak wainscot and featuring an Aubusson tapestry frieze made in France. Over the years, the space would be reimagined countless times, as a romantic dining spot, a condominium sales center, and, eventually, a clothing store hawking $1,000 dress shoes.

Another male refuge was the Bar Room, with oil frescoes featuring German castles and a chandelier laden with grapes and a barmaid hoisting a stein. Later known as the Oak Room, it would become famous as the site of New York's first "power breakfasts," where politicians would gab with businessmen over bacon and eggs. It was also a regular hangout for George M. Cohan, the composer known as "the man who owned Broadway" and the subject of the tune "Yankee Doodle Dandy." When Cohan died, his favorite table was declared "Cohan Corner," replete with a commemorative bronze plaque.

At the far end of the Oak Room, between two imposing columns, was an enormous wooden bar for which the Oak Bar was later named. That, too, would be displaced over the years, with the bar removed during Prohibition to make way for a brokerage office, where throngs of desperate investors would crowd in 1929 to watch the stock ticker plummet as they begged bewildered brokers for answers.

The ground floor also featured a second ladies' reception room by Fifty-Eighth Street, as well as a tearoom, later called the Palm Court. The garden-like space was known for its ceiling, called a laylight, through which sunlight filtered, giving the room a soft, outdoorsy ambience. A wall of mirrors and large casement windows added to the effect, as did a forest of oversized palm trees and rubber plants. A low marble balustrade divided the room from the lobby, while female figurines, supposedly taken from an Italian palace, looked down from above. The furniture was made from green and white enamel, and a thick French moquette carpet finished off the design.[35]

Just a month after opening, British actress Mrs. Patrick Campbell caused a historic scene at the Palm Court. She appeared, at the height of the tea hour, "in all her statuesque beauty," and, "having inevitably drawn all eyes to her, calmly produce[d] and [lit] a cigarette," recalled Mary Doyle, the Plaza newsstand girl, who was there that day. "A cigarette publicly displayed in a lady's mouth marked her definitely as a fallen woman," she continued, noting that at the Palm Court, it was "a horror unthinkable." The staff looked on aghast. "I don't remember which intrepid soul it was who, after a series of whispered conferences in which dismay mounted rapidly toward panic, finally volunteered to approach the lady." In response to the rebuke, Mrs. Campbell stood up imperiously, extinguished the offending cigarette, and stomped from the room. She soon checked out of the hotel.[36]

Hardenbergh's Plaza also featured two dining rooms divided by sliding doors that could be removed at will. One area was set aside for permanent guests who lived at the hotel, the other for transient guests and visitors. Situated at the Fifth Avenue and Fifty-Eighth Street corner, the Rose Room, as it was later known, featured outsized arched windows overlooking Grand Army Plaza and the Vanderbilt mansion—a 130-room behemoth, the largest private residence ever built in Manhattan—next door. There were fourteen-foot columns covered in gilt panels, mirrors overlaid with chiseled bronze, and hundreds of electric bulbs that gave the room an inviting glow.[37] Over the next century, the space would become, variously, a car dealership, a luggage closet, a nightclub, storage rooms, and, finally, the site of the current lobby.

Upstairs, Hardenbergh had designed a ballroom, a panoply of white and gold, with walls of yellow brocade and enormous crystal chandeliers. With views of Central Park, the ballroom could serve six hundred people and featured balconies on three sides. The fourth wall was an architectural marvel, with a stage that could be raised or lowered with the push of a button. This floor also housed the State Suite, a private residence boasting a drawing room, a dining room, and a novel system of private hallways that enabled the hotel to expand the suite to encompass as many additional bedrooms and baths as needed. The State Suite would be occupied over the years by US presidents and celebrities, as well as a war widow, an insurance tycoon, and a convicted felon.

To furnish such a hotel was no small task. The decorator E. F. Pooley made a buying trip to Europe to handpick furniture and commission original pieces. In Belfast, more than $2.7 million was spent in today's dollars on Irish linen; in Switzerland, embroidered organdy curtains were purchased for the equivalent of $3,900 each; glassware was bought at the famed Baccarat shop in France. Back in New York, the largest single order in history was placed

for gold-encrusted china at L. Straus & Sons. There were 1,650
chandeliers to light the hotel; and the flat silver, featuring the hotel's
insignia of two P's back-to-back, totaled four thousand pieces and
cost the equivalent of $8 million today.[38]

"Building a house like this is much like making a woman's dress,"
Sterry told journalists as he gave them a preview tour of the hotel on
the eve of its opening. "Everything is specially made and specially
fitted for a purpose. I will venture to say there is not a stock thing in
the decorations. Even the border for the mosaic floor was designed
for this room, and that open circle in the bronze work was made
for a clock, in turn made for that particular space, and so with the
carpets, furniture and tapestries." It was, added Pooley with under-
statement, "a typical French house."[39]

Despite the money lavished on its design and interiors, the new
Plaza was considered restrained. It was "rich, but not gaudy," wrote
the *Hotel Monthly* trade magazine in a review. "The furnishings
invite to rest. The decorations, while of the costliest type, are not
obtrusive."[40] In the end, the new Plaza shattered records and drew
broad applause. The price of construction was unrivaled, running
to an unheard-of $12.5 million, or $340 million in today's dollars.
"It is the opinion of hotel men, architects, builders and capitalists
that with the Plaza the climax has been reached in the size and cost
of hotels," declared the magazine *Architecture*. "It is unlikely that
more than $12,500,000 will ever be invested in the ground, struc-
ture and plant cost of a single hotel."[41]

Even the most jaded observers gazed in awe. "One stood in the
park at nightfall and marveled," wrote one besotted tourist who
came to see the Plaza one evening, looking up at the thousands
of chandeliers that cast a soft yellow warmth across the cold pavement. "The tiers of irregular light and shade make one think of all
humanity living in one building. It is surely one of the most moving
sights in New York."[42]

Chapter 3

A GREEK TRAGEDY

"In Hungary von Arkovy is what we call a 'Hochstapler.' In
France they call it a 'Chevalier d'Industrie.' Over here the
term would be 'soldier of fortune.'"
—New York Times

It was around 6 p.m. on a Wednesday evening in March 1911
when the Hungarian baron Richard von Arkovy paused by the
Plaza's front desk to check for messages on his way to dinner. As he
waited to talk with a clerk, a man gently tapped him on the shoulder.
Speaking in a hushed tone so as not to arouse the suspicion of the
fashionable guests nearby, the man informed the baron that he was
a detective, and he was placing him under arrest for grand larceny.

Von Arkovy, who cut a dashing figure in a brown suit and spats,
a dark mustache, a monocle, and a cane, stiffened his slender frame.[1]
The thirty-one-year-old dandy then turned to look the detective
over haughtily and began walking toward the dining room where
his dinner guests were waiting. But the detective grabbed his shoulders in an attempt to steer him to the exit instead, and soon the two
were skirmishing. The din of the lobby quieted as people turned
to stare, and, just as suddenly as the scuffle had started, the baron
dropped his hands from around the detective. "Very well my good

man," he said, laughing good-naturedly. "I will go with you gladly, but it is such a joke, this charge, such a very comical joke."[2]

Von Arkovy strode out of the Plaza behind the detective and sat mutely in the car as it made its way to police headquarters in Little Italy. There he was processed and charged with stealing two platinum crucibles, or bowls, worth $900 from a Cuban diplomat and illegally pawning them. As the detectives searched the baron, they found in his suit pockets $3,000 in cash and several diamond-studded tiepins that he had planned to hand out as party favors to his dinner companions that evening. A search of his fur-lined overcoat turned up something more nefarious: a pair of heavy brass knuckles, deadly inch-long spikes protruding from each joint. Laughing as he had a few hours earlier, von Arkovy assured the detectives that despite their ferocious appearance, brass knuckles were "quite the thing" for European gentlemen, nearly as common as the monocle.[3] The skeptical detectives added carrying a concealed weapon to his list of charges and threw the Hungarian nobleman into a jail cell.

At the time of the baron's arrest, the Plaza had been open for four years. The hotel was a vortex of money and glamour, attracting the country's richest citizens, politicians, business titans, diplomats, and society doyennes. It was also invariably a magnet for those who lacked the requisite cash or pedigree but still desired to be in this orbit of wealth. The baron was one such person, a man whose entire energies were depleted chasing the lifestyle espoused by the Plaza, with eventually calamitous results.

Despite his dapper trappings, the baron's origins were less exalted than first impression indicated. He was born in Budapest in 1880 as Richard Arnstein, the only son of Dr. Aaron Arnstein, a well-known Jewish dentist who counted Hungarian nobility among his clientele. To accept a teaching post at the University of Budapest, his father converted to Christianity and adopted the surname Arkovi.[4]

The dentist gave his son an expensive education, and after the baron graduated from university, he published a well-reviewed book on political economy at the tender age of twenty-three. It wasn't long, however, before his early promise faded, replaced with an insidious addiction to gambling fed by a seemingly infinite reservoir of charm.

Around the time that the new Plaza was opening in New York City, the dentist's son found himself embroiled in a major card scandal in Budapest. Buried under a pile of debts he couldn't possibly pay, he fled to England.[5] In London, the baron shed his pedestrian identity, rechristening himself Baron Richard von Arkovy (the addition of "von" and the replacing of "i" with "y" both connote nobility in Hungarian). Armed with his self-appointed title, he circulated among British high society, and soon began wooing the daughter of a wealthy British aristocrat. In a misplaced gesture of largesse, the baron invited the girl's father on a hunting trip to his fictitious ancestral lands in Hungary. When, much to his chagrin, the girl's father accepted the invitation, von Arkovy was forced to scramble.

The baron wrote to old acquaintances in Budapest, begging to visit and promising to bring with him an esteemed British friend. A wealthy Hungarian nobleman, Count Zichy, finally acquiesced. The count spoke no English and the wily von Arkovy schemed, telling the British aristocrat that Count Zichy's estate was his own, and casting the count as only the superintendent hired to maintain the property. But while the count may not have spoken English, he wasn't stupid. Count Zichy soon grew suspicious of his guests and, upon further investigation, learned the true state of affairs. There followed a stormy scene between the baron and the count, and, his deception discovered, von Arkovy fled once more. This time he came to America.[6]

Von Arkovy arrived in New York City, penniless and friendless. He moved into a boardinghouse and found work as a clerk in a cigar store and as an occasional writer. He was barely scraping by, and, perhaps in a dramatic bid for attention, or in a moment of true desperation, the twenty-seven-year-old attempted suicide. Von Arkovy propped up on his bedside table a thirty-page memoir he had written, in which he fabricated friendships with various members of the Social Register, detailed how he had lost his noble fortune in the Wall Street Panic of 1907, and added, for good measure, that he had just 75 cents to his name. Then he removed the tube from the gas fixture in his dingy third-floor room, pulled it toward his bed, lay down, and inhaled.

Luckily, a neighbor at the boardinghouse found the baron before it was too late, saving his life. Credulous newspaper reporters covered the story, writing headlines like "Baron Ruined on Wall Street, Attempts to Die."[7] Dr. Arkovi, hearing of his son's dire straits and near death, quickly wired him money. A recovered von Arkovy, his coffers newly replenished, immediately returned to his cunning ways.

One day, attending a matinee vaudeville show on Broadway, the baron noticed a young "beautiful girl of the blonde Teutonic type," accompanied by her governess.[8] He managed an introduction, and discovered that she was seventeen-year-old Elsa Schroeder, an heiress whose maternal grandfather had been Jacob Hoffman, the wealthy president of the Hoffman Brewing Company.[9] Betting that this conquest would prove an easier victory than the British aristocrat's daughter had been, von Arkovy set his trap. He began regularly calling on Elsa, and it wasn't long before the dashing European charmed the young girl as well as her mother, the two women lapping up the Hungarian suitor's tales of princely palaces.[10]

Elsa's father was far more skeptical. He hired a private detective to investigate von Arkovy's backstory and forbade the suitor from calling at the home. But over her father's objections, Elsa continued to secretly correspond with von Arkovy, passing letters to her lover with her mother's assistance. In short order, the two lovers eloped. When the father found out about his daughter's secret marriage, "there was a stormy scene between Schroeder and his wife in which Mrs. Schroeder was accused of having been a party to the match," reported the *New York Times*. The mother admitted as much but insisted that her new son-in-law's claims to noble bloodlines were genuine. "Mr. Schroeder then produced proofs that the daughter's husband was an imposter, and Mrs. Schroeder collapsed."[11]

When Mrs. Schroeder learned that she had helped engineer the marriage of her daughter to a pauper and an impostor, she was inconsolable. She refused to leave her room for an entire week. Finally, the despondent mother dragged herself to her upstairs bathroom and, locking the doors and windows, filled it with gas to asphyxiate herself. Where her son-in-law had failed, she was victorious. In her will, Mrs. Schroeder bequeathed her entire $250,000 fortune, or more than $6.5 million in today's money, to her daughter. Elsa's inheritance was to be disbursed when she turned twenty-one, two years hence. In the interim, Elsa would be given a lucrative allowance equivalent to more than $26,000 a month in today's dollars.

Elsa and her husband left for Europe, spending the next two years living lavishly off the allowance. In February 1911, the month of Elsa's fateful twenty-first birthday, they returned, checking into a seventh-floor suite at the Plaza. There, the couple hosted dinner parties and whiled away the time, waiting for her birthday, and the moment when Elsa's father would be forced to turn over the bulk of the inheritance.

Finally, the appointed day arrived. Elsa promptly—and against the beseeching advice of her lawyer—handed her new wealth to her husband for safekeeping. A few days later, the newspapers reported that Elsa had left the couple's Plaza suite and sailed back to London, alone. No reasons were cited for Elsa's travel or the couple's apparent split, but von Arkovy, now in full control of his wife's money, remained behind. It was just a short time later that von Arkovy was arrested while standing in the Plaza lobby. Why the baron would stoop to stealing $900 bowls, when he controlled a multimillion-dollar inheritance, remains a mystery, but maybe theft was simply his habit.

Von Arkovy spent a few uncomfortable hours in a prison cell before he made bail and returned to his cushy Plaza suite. Two days later, he once again exited the Plaza, but this time he was prepared. Decked out in his customary monocle, his black mustache carefully curled up at the ends, he strode out of the hotel's revolving doors, graciously greeting the crowd of reporters and spectators anxious to get a glimpse of the Hungarian nobleman on his way to court. He shook hands and even handed out sepia-toned photographs of himself to fans. Then, disregarding the by-now-commonplace taxicab, the baron stepped into a hired limousine car to whisk him away.[12]

At the Jefferson Market Courthouse in Greenwich Village, the first person to take the stand in the case against the baron was the Cuban diplomat who had first accused him of thievery. "While it is true," said Julio S. Jarron, the Cuban vice-consul, "that von Arkovy pawned the crucibles without my consent...I am convinced the baron didn't intend to do me out of the money, and I want to withdraw the complaint." The magistrate was indignant. "I would like to know just why you changed your attitude toward this fellow," he inquired. "Didn't you come to me the other day and tell me that this man was a well-known crook; that he had stolen the crucibles, and that you were anxious to press the complaint?" The Cuban stammered, and the magistrate continued to push: "How much was offered you to drop this case?"

The Cuban denied any payout, but eventually did acknowledge that he had spent the prior evening having dinner with von Arkovy's lawyer. As the baron stood yawning and looking bored, the frustrated magistrate finally snapped, "Discharged!" Von Arkovy smiled in satisfaction as he strode out of the courtroom, stepping into his hired limousine and speeding back to his Plaza suite.

But while von Arkovy fared well in court, Lady Luck didn't follow him to the hotel. There, he received an upsetting notice. In the wake of the controversy, the hotel simply could no longer shelter him, the Plaza had written, giving its apologies. Plaza management was scandalized by the unwanted attention and anxious to be rid of the nobleman of dubious distinction. "The 'baron' was plainly annoyed yesterday when he was notified in writing that his rooms were needed," reported the *New York Times*. So, three days after being first escorted from the lobby by the detective, von Arkovy was once again ushered unwillingly from the hotel. As his valet scrambled to pack up numerous trunks, von Arkovy dismissed the eviction as just "another insult," although he later insisted he had left the Plaza of his own accord.[13]

Standing on the pier, awaiting the ocean liner that would take him back to Europe, the baron spent the time before sailing "in abusing the United States in six languages—English, French, German, Hungarian, Italian and Spanish—changing from one to another when at a loss for a word," a reporter who was there recounted.[14] While von Arkovy made his way back to Europe, Elsa would not be there to greet him. The now wised-up wife was sailing in the opposite direction, heading back to New York to return to her estranged, long-suffering father. The daughter and father reunited, but it was insufficient salve to heal the wounds that her ill-fated marriage had wrought.

Mr. Schroeder's life had been difficult since the scandal. Not only had his wife died tragically, but also her inheritance, which made up the bulk of the family's money, was now in the hands of the baron. Mr. Schroeder had struggled to make ends meet, and it may have been the financial duress, or his wife's untimely death, or his daughter's ruined reputation—or likely a combination of the three—that finally proved too much.

Two years later, Mr. Schroeder lugged a fur rug and pillows from his parlor up to the same second-floor bathroom where his wife had met her fate, then dragged in a small gas heater and, closing the windows and locking the door, lay on his ad hoc deathbed and inhaled the poison. When her father didn't come down for breakfast the following morning, Elsa and a servant went upstairs to check. They detected the smell of gas and found the bathroom locked. The servant climbed up the fire escape and entered through a window, where she discovered Mr. Schroeder's body half-dressed and prostrate.[15]

As for the baron, after leaving New York he resurfaced in France, where he continued to make a big impression with the help of his wife's money. In the resort town of Dieppe, the baron stayed in an expensive suite at the Hotel Royal, drove around in a large motorcar, and tipped "like a Pittsburg millionaire," according to reports. The crowds were in awe of the mysterious, dashing gambler, who was rumored to be a diplomat in the Austrian embassy, and was referred to in the press as "the sensation of the Dieppe season," or simply, "the Austrian." Aside from his big suite, his big car, and his big tips, von Arkovy had two talismans always with him at the casinos: "a carved jade figure of a Chinese baby which he carefully strokes before touching the card" and "a pretty and plump Englishwoman, who always occupies a chair behind him at the gaming table."[16]

At the end of the season, the baron left Dieppe for London, where he took a room at the Carlton, continuing his reckless tour of the world's top hotels. He spent the next two years gambling at a nearby baccarat house (he lost a staggering $900,000 in today's money in a single night at the tables) and consuming large quantities of morphine. Three months before Mr. Schroeder decided he could no longer stand to take another breath, the baron lay down, high on morphine, in his hotel bed. During the night, the young man's heart stopped beating. The newspapers called his death a suicide, although whether the overdose was purposeful or not will never be known.[17] As for what became of Elsa, no longer a wealthy heiress, her trail fades away.

Just as the tale of Baron von Arkovy and his tragic wife, Elsa, was coming to its sad conclusion, back at the Plaza, Harry Black was celebrating the opening of the Champagne Porch. A narrow outdoor patio, the restaurant once unfurled along the hotel's Fifth Avenue side, where today the front entrance is situated. It was early June 1913, and the staccato sounds of laughter and clinking glasses permeated the night air. The guests were enjoying their repose, surrounded by trellises of spring flowers and views of the Pulitzer Fountain, the recently opened spectacular featuring flowing water surrounding a graceful statue of Pomona, the goddess of abundance.

The Social Register set had turned out in droves for the opening, and every table was filled with women in graceful columnar dresses and men in crisp tuxedos and waistcoats. Yet, the group "that commanded the eyes of the whole assemblage was Harry Black's crowd—the biggest party present and made up of practically the crème de la crème of New York society," chronicled the erstwhile society paper *Town Topics*.[18] In the six years since he had developed the Plaza, Black had managed to transform himself from a Canadian upstart, the mere son-in-law of skyscraper pioneer George A. Fuller, to a noted real estate magnate and key player in New York's social and business scenes.

It had not been a smooth transition. In 1905, Harry Black had suffered from a self-inflicted, but devastating nonetheless, split from Allon. The beautiful young daughter of his mentor had divorced Black amid rumors of his unfaithfulness. *Town Topics* had a field day with the breakup, its front page littered with gossip and innuendos. "Black is known about town as a very liberal man," it mused, adding that "of course there is a woman—one specified woman—in the case. Lots of guesses have been made as to her identity, for Mr. Black is very popular."[19] The divorce records were sealed, and, during their lifetimes, the identity of the other woman was cloaked in secrecy. But a century later, Alice Sparberg Alexiou, in her book *The Flatiron*, revealed that Black was carrying on with the nurse hired to care for Allon's mother. At one point, even John "Bet-a-Million" Gates had gotten involved, helping Allon to confront her husband's mistress.[20]

It was a messy split, and in the end, Black agreed to a generous settlement. He gave Allon the equivalent of $170 million in today's money, the amount representing her fortune plus the profits Black had earned. Black also maintained his close relationship with George Allon Fuller, his ex-wife's young nephew. George's mother had tragically jumped from a hotel window to her death when he was a baby, and his father was largely absent. Childless, Black and Allon had unofficially adopted the boy. When the Plaza opened, Black had even outfitted the hotel's basement with a speedway that ran one-seventh of a mile, and given eight-year-old George a miniature electric automobile. It could run up to twelve miles an hour, presumably to the annoyance of the hotel staff, who had to look both ways before crossing.[21]

The divorce was a social blow for Black, who was considered the chief beneficiary of the union. "It does look as if Harry Black was guilty of great ingratitude, since he owes his wealth entirely to his late father-in-law," *Town Topics* wrote rather pointedly.[22] Black managed a social rehabilitation of sorts by taking up with Tessie Oelrichs, a buxom brunette and the daughter of a Nevada silver miner who had struck it impossibly rich. The widowed Oelrichs, along with Mrs. Stuyvesant Fish and Mrs. Alva Belmont, were known as the "Newport triumvirate," matrons who ruled New York and Newport society. A departure from the much younger Allon, Oelrichs was the same age as Black, on the cusp of fifty, and intimately knowledgeable about the pitfalls of social climbing.

Black and Oelrichs became inseparable—strolling arm in arm through the lion house at the Bronx Zoo on a Sunday afternoon;

cavorting at a concert at the Ritz; and riding Black's private Pullman car to a resort in Bretton Woods or Palm Beach.[23] "In many ways Harry Black is just the sort of a man Mrs. Oelrichs might be expected to choose for a husband," speculated *Town Topics*. He "is not a society man, and knows nothing of the social politics," it noted, continuing, "Mr. Black, however, seems ambitious to learn."[24] Despite this coupling, Black, ever a ladies' man, remained aloof to the idea of remarrying. The society paper was more hopeful:

> *The maids and widows cry "Alas!" and also cry "Alack!"*
> *They roll their eyes and set their caps at handsome Harry Black.*
> *He casts his smiles on that one, and he casts his smiles on this,*
> *He's lovely to the Mrs. and he's lovely to the Miss.*
> *But nonetheless I doubt not that again he will be caught.*
> *And that a hand in marriage will by Harry then be sought.*
> *And when that time at last arrives, and honeymooning starts,*
> *There will be in this town of ours full many aching hearts!* [25]

While Black's social life was in full swing, the Plaza, too, found itself in secure standing. There was dinner dancing in the Rose Room and tea dancing in the Grill Room, couples spending their afternoons doing the bunny hug or the turkey trot. The now-famous Plaza had also become more than just society's chief gathering spot; it was also the foundation of a powerful real estate empire, the likes of which had never been seen.

In 1902, shortly after Black and Beinecke had purchased the old Plaza, Black proved his financial genius by creating the first-ever skyscraper trust. Similar to the railroad and steel monopolies of the time, the United States Realty & Improvement Company consisted of several subsidiaries, including the George A. Fuller Construction Company and the Plaza Operating Company, which owned the controlling interest in the Plaza.

The United States Realty & Improvement Company enabled Black to not only build skyscrapers, but also to buy, sell, and manage buildings. A publicly traded trust valued at $66 million, or close to $2 billion today, it boasted New York properties like the Flatiron Building and the Trinity Building, as well as real estate stretching from Atlanta to Toronto. Its board of directors was a who's who of Wall Street, including James Stillman, president of the National City Bank, the forerunner to today's Citibank; Charles M. Schwab, president of the large trust U.S. Steel; and Henry Morgenthau, the German-Jewish financier. John "Bet-a-Million" Gates owned a major share of the company and also sat on its board. The trust "unquestionably occup[ies] a unique position among industrial combinations," wrote the *Wall Street Journal*, adding, "It is recognized as the pioneer consolidation of realty and construction concerns."[26]

As the Plaza, and Black himself, reveled in success, few would have known that behind the scenes, the hotel had recently emerged from its most severe labor unrest since Butler's murder on the hotel's unfinished eighth floor. The first decades of the twentieth century were a period of rapid industrialization, with factory workers spending long hours in cramped, filthy, and even dangerous work environments. The Triangle Waist Company factory fire in 1911, which caused nearly 150 deaths, many of the victims young girls, led to sweeping efforts to organize workers and improve conditions. While institutions like the Plaza were a world away from the sweatshops of the Garment District, hotel employees were not unionized and there was certainly enough for them to grumble about.

In these years, hotel pay was often dismal, with some employees earning as little as 83 cents a day. There were no paid days off, and shifts could last as long as eighteen hours. And to make it at one of the grand hotels like the Plaza, employees had to be highly skilled. "Do you know what they expect of a waiter who works in one of the swell hotels in this city?" one Plaza waiter rhetorically asked a reporter. "He's got to be able to speak four languages. He needs French, so that he can talk to the chef; he needs Italian so that he can talk to his 'omnibus,' who is a cheap boy who takes away the dishes and fills the glasses with water; he needs German, so that he can talk with his family, and he needs English, so that he can speak to the customers."

Hotel waiters were often forced to rely on tips to make ends meet, but these were so variable that it could be hard going. "The other day a man with a forty-dollar check gave me a one-dollar-and-a-half tip," recounted the Plaza waiter. "The cook wanted his share, the head-waiter wanted his share, the hat boy wanted his share, I had promised my 'omnibus' a quarter, and where did I come in?"[27]

While there was griping at the Plaza, it was at the nearby Hotel Belmont, at the corner of Forty-Second Street and Park Avenue, where the real trouble started. The waiters there worked for a tyran-nical boss—who had once been employed at the Plaza—and who penalized them for the most minor of infractions. According to a list that hung from the kitchen pantry, waiters at the Hotel Belmont were charged $1 for smiling or laughing, $2 for drinking leftover coffee, and $5 for giving the cashier leftover cakes. There were fines for having dirty shoes or long fingernails, tardiness, dropping silver, or talking too much.[28]

Eventually, in May 1912, the workers had had enough. Three hundred Hotel Belmont waiters walked out en masse, spurring one of the first widespread waiters' strikes across the city. Soon, 150 waiters quit the Vanderbilt Hotel, 130 walked out of the Hotel Savoy, and another 50 left the Hotel Brevoort. Waiters at the city's top eateries also joined in, quitting fashionable establishments like Delmonico's, Sherry's, and the Elks Club.

At the Plaza, the workers were treated somewhat better than at the Hotel Belmont—waiters earned $1 for dinner service and there were fewer fines—but it was far from perfect. A couple of weeks after the Hotel Belmont workers quit, Frederick Sterry, the Plaza manager who had been hired at the behest of John "Bet-a-Million" Gates, tried to circumvent trouble. Sensing there may be unrest among his employees, he assembled two hundred Plaza waiters shortly before the lunch service was to start.

"You are all quite well acquainted with me," Sterry said. "Many of you have been with me a long time. Some of you were employed in the old Plaza," he told them. "Until very recently I never knew that any of you harbored a grievance. Now I have a question to ask and that is, 'Do you men think more of your union than you do of your job in this hotel?'" No man spoke a word. "All right then. I will put the matter in another way," said Sterry. "Are you with the Plaza or against it?" There was a mumbled acquiescence as most men declared loyalty. But when Sterry asked whether the men would feel compelled to strike if the nascent hotel union asked them to, some nodded. "Very well," he said. "Those who feel that they would obey the union rather than remain loyal to the hotel had better quit right now."[29] At that, forty men took off their aprons, turned on their heels, and filed out of the room.

"I do not think this thing is settled," Sterry confided later that day to a reporter. "These men may walk out on me tonight, for all their protestations of loyalty."[30] Sterry's fears were borne out. At 7:15 that evening, just as the soup course was being served in the dining room, one hundred Plaza waiters and cooks simultaneously walked off their posts, leaving diners without waiters and kitchens deserted of staff. The men, filing quietly out of the hotel and onto Fifth Avenue, joined throngs of other striking waiters who had also just left their places of employ and were marching down the avenue.

But Sterry was resourceful. While other restaurants and hotels had been caught unawares, scrambling to find replacements when their workers went on strike, Sterry had installed a backup measure. Ensconced in several rooms upstairs at the hotel were experienced waiters Sterry had invited up from the winter resort hotels in Florida and elsewhere in the South. It now being spring, the men were currently out of work and happy for the chance at employment. This group was a decided departure from the mass of waiters who were typically employed at the Plaza. The bulk of the Plaza's waiters, chambermaids, room service attendants, and other employees came from the ranks of white European immigrants who were plentiful in New York City. But the men Sterry had brought up from the South were African American.

In the nineteenth century in New York City, black servants and waiters were a sign of prestige and were often employed in the city's exclusive hotels. By the first decade of the twentieth century, however, the mass influx of white immigrants from Europe had changed this balance, and hotels began hiring white employees over their black counterparts. Between 1900 and 1910, the number of African American servants and waiters remained virtually unchanged, while the number of white workers nearly doubled.[31] In 1911, an investigation by the *New York Age*, a leading black paper in the city, found that three hundred black hotel and restaurant workers had been fired from their jobs and replaced with whites.[32]

When the fledgling Hotel Workers Union, which was exclusively white, called the Plaza employees to strike, it was a complete shock when Sterry replaced them with African American waiters who had been waiting at the ready in the rooms upstairs. "Within five minutes it was said, service was going on again as usual," reported the *New-York Tribune*.[33] Sterry wasn't necessarily an equal opportunity employer or a champion of civil rights. His strategy was driven by logic: "From our hotels in the South we could within twenty-four hours bring up 2,000 colored waiters who are not only skillful and polite, but who would be glad of the opportunity," he told the *New York Times*. "It is only because we do not believe in mixing our help that we have made no attempt in the past to bring the colored waiters up North."[34]

The *New York Age* reported the story with glee. As other hotels followed the Plaza's lead, the newspaper relished the reappearance of "these dusky knights of the tray," noting how "Manhattan is being treated to a spectacle of bygone days." These new Plaza employees did not consider themselves strikebreakers. They were simply "working for managers who see fit to hire them at Palm Beach, Saratoga and other winter and summer resorts," wrote the *New York Age*, and now they "feel it their duty to help a friend in need."[35]

The white waiters on strike took the news bitterly. They called the Plaza's decision to hire African American waiters "a sinister and ugly move."[36] The white strikers tried to rectify matters by reaching out to the Colored Waiters Association, asking them to become allies, and by trying to recruit black waiters and cooks into their all-white Hotel Workers Union. They also attended an editorial board meeting with the *New York Age*, and spoke with black preachers, begging them to give sermons urging their congregants not to break the strike.[37]

Some of the preachers took to the white workers' cause. They were likely motivated in part out of fear that the presence of African American waiters at the hotels would incite racial violence. There was also concern that the hoteliers would discard the strikebreakers once the white waiters returned, leaving them destitute and reliant on public assistance. "It has been shown that negro waiters are not wanted in the first-class hotels here under ordinary circumstances, and I think they would make a mistake in accepting temporary occupation to break a strike," the Reverend Dr. George H. Sims, a popular black pastor in New York, told the *New-York Tribune*. "Such of my race as will be imported will be used as cat's paws during the strike, and are likely to become public charges when it is all over."[38]

Despite the hiring of black replacements, the strike spread, with some 2,500 waiters walking off their jobs, joined by 1,000 cooks and 3,000 other hotel employees. Among their demands were one day off every week, limiting the workday to ten hours, and a pay increase to $10 a week. They also requested sanitary lockers and toilets, spacious and well-ventilated dining rooms where they could eat wholesome food, and overtime pay.[39] For their part, the Hotel Men's Association, which represented hotel owners, said it would consider some concessions, but they were unified in their absolute refusal to recognize the right of the workers to unionize. In defiance, they declared they "would close the doors of their hotels entirely before they would open them to the union."[40]

Faced with the immovable position of the hotel owners, the striking waiters' determination began to waver. The Hotel Workers Union didn't have a large treasury to pay the men who had left their places of employ, and the strikers began to feel the pinch. Where once thousands of men felt compelled to leave their work and take to the streets, their numbers began dwindling into the dozens. The *New-York Tribune*, in writing of the strikers' emotional state, noted that "desperation and anger at the continued obduracy of the hotel men were turning their fervor...into the desperation of self-preservation."[41]

In the end, the strike was something of a draw. Before the waiters had gone on strike they were earning just $25 a month. The hotel owners now offered a compromise, with many hotels, including the Plaza, increasing the waiters' pay to $30 a month, and agreeing to give them half a day off every week or one full day off every two weeks. They also banned the punitive fines. With this compromise in hand, some seven weeks after it had started, the strike was finally declared over. It would take numerous additional strikes—and another twenty-six years—before hotel workers in New York City successfully unionized. And one day, nearly a hundred years after this first strike, it would be the very existence of a hotel union that would secure the Plaza's survival.

As for the strikers, many tried to get their old jobs back, with varying degrees of success. In some cases, the hotels and restaurants rehired their old ranks, while others considered them persona non grata. At the Plaza, the *New York Times* reported, the decision was that "not a man had been taken back and that no men would be."[42] As for the Southern waiters who had been wooed northward by the promise of jobs, very few continued on once the strike was over. According to the *New York Age*, many New York establishments, including the Plaza, were willing to keep on their replacement staff, but black waiters chose to leave because they could earn more at the summer resorts in the South just then reopening for the season.[43]

At the Plaza and the other New York City grand hotels, the owners' stubborn refusal to entertain efforts by their workers to unionize had paid off. Profits were up, and costs were down. As could be seen by the smash opening of the Champagne Porch and the soaring value of Black's skyscraper trust, the waiter strike created little lasting impact.

But just as the faux Baron von Arkovy's luck had not held, so the Plaza's fortunes would soon be turning. Across the Atlantic, Europe was headed for war, and even though it would take several more years before America entered the fray, the conflict damaged the pocketbooks of many Plaza guests. Meanwhile, the temperance movement, once seen as a fringe effort to block the sale of alcohol, was quickly gaining steam.

Chapter 4

THE WET AGE

"America was going on the greatest, gaudiest spree in history
and there was going to be plenty to tell about."
—*F. Scott Fitzgerald*

O n an October morning in 1914, a reporter for the *New-York
Tribune* was walking down Third Avenue when he spotted
an unusual sight. Shuffling along the sidewalk was a Skye terrier,
but the pet's fur wasn't cream or black; rather, it was a peculiar
shade of baby blue. When asked, the dog walker said the pet didn't
suffer from any malady but was what's known in Latin as a "mutt
ultramarinus," the latest fad among the fashionable set. The dog
walker was bringing the crazily colored pooch to the Plaza, where
a woman, bedecked in a dress of the exact same hue, was anxiously
expecting him. Think she would stroll the avenue "in a blue dress
and with a black dog in her arms? Not by several shades," the journalist reported. "Introducing, then, the Skye blue terrier. He is not
a myth, nor an idea, nor yet the product of a disordered cerebellum.
He is a product of the times."[1]

These times were, like the blue dog, or like Harry Black enjoying himself on the Champagne Porch, marked by exuberance

and excess. "Alexander's Ragtime Band" by the young, relatively unknown composer Irving Berlin was a hit, the new Woolworth Building was the tallest tower in the world, and automobiles were being manufactured at a fast clip thanks to Henry Ford's assembly lines.

At the Plaza, Mrs. Alva Belmont organized a two-day bazaar to raise money for the suffragette cause, while Margaret Sanger held a three-day conference on birth control. The Women's Motoring Club of New York hosted an endurance race from the Plaza to Philadelphia,[2] and Mrs. Emily Ladenburg made headlines when, hours after being awarded the equivalent of $16 million from her dead husband's estate, she used $1 million to throw herself a party at the Plaza.[3] Down in the restaurants, crowds were dancing the kangaroo dip, while up in the rooms, guests ranged from the Prince of Serbia to a shogun from Japan.

Yet despite all this headiness, a World War was looming. Fighting had already broken out in Europe, and the torpedoing of a luxury ocean liner would shift America's attention from frivolity to the battlefield. In a matter of a few short years, Liberty bonds and Prohibition would dominate the headlines, and guests at the Plaza would be far more concerned with blue laws than blue dogs.

In May 1915, a German U-boat torpedoed the *Lusitania*, sinking the ocean liner and killing most of the 1,962 people aboard. One of the passengers on the doomed ship was Alfred Gwynne Vanderbilt, the debonair society figure who helped usher the fashionable crowd into the Plaza as its first, lauded guest. Vanderbilt had enjoyed an eventful few years since arriving at the Plaza, helming his family's railroad business and spending time on hobbies, like riding and sports. Vanderbilt's wife, the former Elsie French, who had stayed behind recuperating in Newport, Rhode Island, that first day at the Plaza, had filed for divorce just six months after the couple moved in. The separation was the result of the millionaire's rakish tendencies, particularly his affair with Mary Agnes O'Brien Ruiz.

The daughter of a Missouri farmer, Ruiz was a former actress and the current wife of the Cuban attaché. She had been out riding on the Central Park bridle path one morning when her saddle buckle jammed and Vanderbilt came to her aid. In the weeks that followed, Ruiz was observed taking frequent, extended rides through the park, followed by suspiciously long hours spent in a nearby Turkish bath. Rumors began to spread, reaching a fevered pitch when Ruiz was seen driving around town in an automobile that cost the equivalent of $300,000 today.[4]

As Vanderbilt began spending more time with Ruiz and less time with his wife, Vanderbilt's mother, Mrs. Cornelius Vanderbilt Sr., grew increasingly scandalized. She urged her son to visit and discuss his marriage troubles, sending a barrage of messages to his Plaza suite. The messages didn't have far to travel, as the Vanderbilt mansion was next door, on the site of today's Bergdorf Goodman department store. The society matron was forced to watch from her perch at an upstairs bedroom window as her son repeatedly left his hotel and drove past her front door without pause, willfully ignoring her pleas.

One morning it looked as if Vanderbilt might finally stop in. "His big red racing car swerved from the avenue to the curb directly in front of the Vanderbilt mansion entrance," reported the *Cincinnati Enquirer*, but "while the mother gazed in astonishment, the young multimillionaire who was driving gave the wheel a wrench and sent the big car in a circle and to the opposite curb." Instead of knocking on his mother's door, Vanderbilt paid his friend Harry Payne Whitney a visit.[5]

Eventually, the infatuated Ruiz secured a divorce and moved to London, hoping that Vanderbilt would be similarly emancipated and the two would finally marry. The couple did make a handful of appearances in London and Paris society, but by then the novelty of Vanderbilt's affair had worn off. Ruiz grew suspicious that her paramour had taken another lover and she stopped eating, becoming increasingly thin and despondent. The frequency of Vanderbilt's visits decreased, and when he stopped making appearances altogether, the jilted lover shot herself through the chest with a revolver.

Ruiz's death went unreported for weeks, as journalists were bribed by unnamed men to keep the news quiet. One reporter later admitted to withholding the story "because a lawyer representing a wealthy American mentioned in the case made it worth his while" to do so.[6] After a month of silence, however, the salacious news trickled out, and eventually papers were running stories with headlines like "Loss of Vanderbilt's Love True Cause of Ruiz Suicide" and "Loving Vanderbilt, She Killed Herself."

By the time Vanderbilt bought his transatlantic ticket on the *Lusitania*, the Ruiz scandal had long since passed and the wealthy scion was remarried to Margaret Emerson, a divorcée and heiress to the Bromo-Seltzer fortune. After boarding the ship, Vanderbilt, who was traveling without his wife, checked into one of the *Lusitania*'s elegantly appointed suites. As his valet unpacked his many trunks, there was a knock at the door. Vanderbilt answered, greeting a reporter who had come in search of a quote before the ship departed. Instead of a quote, Vanderbilt shared with him a telegram he had just received. "The Lusitania is doomed. Do not sail on her," it read. The note was signed, ominously, "Mort." Vanderbilt shrugged off the warning, reassuring the reporter that it was "probably somebody trying to have a little fun at my expense."[7]

But it was hardly a joke. War was raging, and the *Lusitania* was crossing waters that were rife with deadly German submarines. As it sailed off the coast of Ireland, the ship was targeted, the enemy's torpedo striking with deadly accuracy. As the *Lusitania* slid to the watery bottom, witness accounts hold that Vanderbilt, looking calm, handed his life jacket to a young woman, even though he himself did not know how to swim. Vanderbilt then ordered his valet to help him round up the children who were scrambling around the deck in a panic, searching for their parents. The men ran repeated laps to the few available lifeboats, carrying their screaming cargo to safety. Despite a $5,000 reward, Vanderbilt's body was never recovered.[8]

The sinking of the *Lusitania* helped turn American sentiment away from isolationism and toward the war effort. Although it was not until April 1917, two years later, that America officially entered the fray. When diplomatic relations between America and Germany were finally severed that spring, guests at the Plaza happened to include the German ambassador and his wife, the Count and Countess von Bernstorff. The couple were staying at the hotel while attending the annual horse shows at Madison Square Garden. They quickly hightailed it back to Germany, with "little honor, social or otherwise."[9]

It was fitting that the German ambassador had been at the Plaza when America officially declared war. It would soon be discovered that in the months preceding, Count von Bernstorff had been plotting with a spy who was living at the hotel. In February 1916, Paul Bolo Pasha, a French national on the German payroll, checked into the Plaza with a mission to whip up support for a peace deal between France and Germany. To fund his efforts, the Germans had given Pasha the equivalent of more than $150 million in today's money.[10] But Pasha failed to muster enthusiasm for such a peace, his major success limited to befriending and gaining support from William Randolph Hearst, the famed publisher. In the end, Pasha returned to France, where he was arrested as a traitor.[11]

As the war got underway, the Plaza's hallways and lobby, its ballroom and restaurants, reflected the new reality. Liberty bond rallies were held in the sprawling Grand Army Plaza just outside the hotel, while the Grill Room and ballroom were awash with American, Italian, French, and Belgian uniforms as soldiers traveled back and forth from the front. "White tie and tails gave way to Sam Browne belts and spiral leggings; the playboy gave way to the doughboy, and the flowing headdress of the Red Cross replaced the chic chapeau of the debutante and the tiara of the dowager," Eve Brown wrote in *The Plaza*.[12]

On the European continent, farmland was transformed into battlefields and farmers were conscripted into fighting. Food production slowed, and a number of America's allies faced near starvation. To alleviate the shortages, President Woodrow Wilson appointed Herbert Hoover to oversee the federal Food Administration. Under Hoover's supervision, the government implemented campaigns such as "Meatless Mondays" and "Wheatless Wednesdays." Households were urged to do the same with less, and recipes for sugarless desserts and slogans like "Food will win the war" were plastered across the country's newspapers.

Hotel patrons did their part, hosting war bond drives and charity fund-raisers. Some efforts were more successful than others. In one account, a Plaza guest approached the hotel's manager to inquire about a "'war luncheon'—something simple and unpretentious." As the manager nodded his head, he was mentally rolling his eyes at the guest's concept of thrift. Among her requirements were costly brut champagne and a healthy serving of caviar. When he told her that it would cost the equivalent of $190 a plate, she feigned shock. "Oh, dear! Isn't food becoming almost prohibitive!" Then the tone-deaf hostess, without missing a beat, ordered "plates for twenty. Please have everything as simple as possible."[13]

The hotel also made sacrifices. In what the *New York Times* called "the most radical changes ever attempted in the menus of the big hotels,"[14] the Plaza joined with several others to agree to complete food overhauls. This included serving so-called war bread—tough, mealy bread baked from scraps and stale pieces—and substituting wheat flour with alternatives like potato and rye flour. The Plaza agreed to measure the size of its bread rolls to keep them uniformly small, and to feature one beefless day a week on its menu. The hotels even agreed to eliminate frying food so as to conserve fats like butter and lard.

While they mostly adhered to these restrictions, there were some slipups. For example, the Plaza, along with the St. Regis and a handful of other luxury New York establishments, was found to have blatantly flouted the rationing of sugar. The Plaza hoarded 11,800 pounds of the sweetener, enough for a three-month supply rather than the one-month supply it was allowed. As its punishment, the government ordered the Plaza to suspend the baking of bread or pastry, and the making of ice cream, for thirty days.[15] The restrictive menus had unintended consequences, namely, smaller tips, as guests who longed for soft bread and a second lump of sugar took out their frustrations on the waiters who had the unfortunate job of telling them no. "Men and women who pose as patriots demand that waiters violate the rules of the Food Administration by serving additional portions of sugar and bread," reported the *New York Times*. "When the waiter explains the portions are limited the diners become enraged."[16]

In November 1918, only eighteen months after America joined the fight, the First World War was won. As news of the armistice agreement broke at 3:30 a.m., Sterry, the Plaza's manager, corralled a brass band to march through the hotel corridors in celebration. "Startled guests responded with frenzied enthusiasm" and "the consumption of champagne to celebrate the Allied victory reached an all-time high," wrote Brown.[17] But the celebration was to be brief. Troops returning from the battlefields were soon marching in parades down Fifth Avenue, their bandaged heads and missing limbs a sobering sight. Then something even more momentous occurred to further tamp down the festivities—the swift passage of the Eighteenth Amendment.

The precursor to national Prohibition had been the Wartime Prohibition Act, which barred the manufacturing of beer and wine and prohibited the sale of beverages with more than 2.75 percent alcohol. It was a temporary measure, meant to conserve grain for the war effort, but its intention was questionable since it was enacted ten days after the armistice agreement was signed.[18] Still, Americans became acclimated to weak "war beer" and watered-down wine, and advocates for Prohibition grew ever more numerous. "Prohibition seems to be the fashion, just as drinking used to be," noted the *New York Times* in a snarky editorial. "Let's adopt it, not because we want it, but because we 'want to be on the winning side.'"[19]

In what seemed inevitable to many, in January 1919, Congress ratified the Eighteenth Amendment to the Constitution, prohibiting the production, transport, and sale of alcohol. Woodrow Wilson, halfway through his second term as president, tried to stop the effort by vetoing the Volstead Act, which outlined the particulars of how Prohibition was to be enforced. His objections were overridden, and the amendment passed that October.

Like many foes of Prohibition, the hotel industry had mounted a tepid and disorganized campaign to combat the new restrictions. In his book about the 1920s, *Only Yesterday*, the journalist Frederick Lewis Allen wrote, "Half-hearted and ineffective were the forces of the opposition, so completely did the country as a whole take for granted the inevitability of a dry regime."[20] The Hotel Association of New York, of which the Plaza was a prominent member, attached to paychecks a notice warning employees that Prohibition "would affect your business as well as ours: you might not have this check and those of many other concerns."[21] The Plaza and several other hotels also agreed to give up 5 percent of their gross receipts from the sale of alcohol to fund their lobbying efforts.[22] The hotel even helped form the Association Opposed to National Prohibition, which published politically charged advertisements, with headlines such as "Will Bolshevism Come with National Prohibition?" But in the end, their efforts had little impact.

Within a few months of these sweeping new strictures, illegal speakeasies popped up in basement hideouts and brownstones across the city. Waiters looked the other way when restaurant patrons pulled out hip flasks, and small clubs began offering "tea service" that failed to include sugar cubes or a side of milk, the liquid pouring from their kettles an intoxicating, syrupy brown. It was illegal to sell liquor, but in one of the nonsensical provisions of the amendment, it wasn't illegal to drink alcohol. In other words, if you had it, you could consume it.

While there was much drinking in the speakeasies and smaller restaurants in New York, it was another story for major institutions like the Plaza. Large hotels were too conspicuous, too high-profile to flout the new amendment. "It has been suggested that if the country goes 'dry' there will be plenty to drink. If there is, it will not be in the hotels," Thomas D. Green, the president of the Hotel Association of New York, told reporters.[23] Hotels like the Plaza risked immediate censure: "Prohibition gave many of New York's highest-profile gastronomic institutions the choice of a quick death or a slow death," wrote Michael A. Lerner in his book *Dry Manhattan*. "Economically, they were doomed to fail without the revenue derived from alcohol sales, but if they defied the dry law, the authorities were bound to catch up with such high-profile defectors."[24]

As if an ax had been swung, dividing the period before and after Prohibition began, the effect on hotels was immediate. "At 5 o'clock and on to the dinner hour, not so long ago, these places were packed with men," wrote one newspaper. "There was often a long wait and a hard shove, all together, to reach the rail and give the order to the fast-flying bartenders."[25] Now, these same places were "models of decorum and sobriety."[26]

While speakeasies like the 21 Club were packed with thumping jazz music, cigarette smoke, and tipsy, loose-pocketed patrons, at the hotels there were vast, empty chambers, devoid of people save for a lonely guest or two, sipping soda and bemoaning what once was. The bar had been "the altar around which hotel life revolved," wrote the *New York Times* magazine in a 1932 piece that reflected on the impact of Prohibition. Without the bar, "hotel life as Americans had known it since the days of Andrew Jackson suddenly ceased to exist."[27]

The hotels tried their best to keep up. Many converted their bars into soda fountains and began offering colorful nonalcoholic drinks, such as the Boston Cooler (two ounces cream, one bottle sarsaparilla, stir well) and the Philadelphia Cockade (half teaspoon powdered sugar, good dash of apple cider, half teaspoon Worcestershire sauce and milk, well frapped).[28] Others offered "bone-dry rooms" that boasted wholesome entertainment like bowling alleys and swimming pools.[29] Hotels also touted the privacy of their guest suites, where socializing (and drinking) could be done freely, without the prying eyes of dry agents. And they began leasing out their bars for other uses. At the Plaza, after the bar in the Oak Room was removed, the brokerage firm E. F. Hutton and Company took over the space, while the Plaza's Rose Room was eventually converted into an automobile showcase for the Studebaker Company.

Hotels also began looking for new ways to raise revenues. One strategy was to increase their room rates—in New York the cost of renting a hotel room shot up by an average of 35 percent during the years of Prohibition.[30] The higher room prices provided some alleviation for hotel owners, but soon a ceiling was reached, and hotels could not charge more for their rooms without risking losing guests.[31] "Before and during the war a hotel man did not worry greatly about what his exact room costs were," wrote the trade publication *Hotel World*. "Now that they must depend almost entirely upon their room revenue for their profit, they find that the rates which were raised to care for increased war and post-war costs cannot come down if they are to make a profit and stay in business."[32]

Despite their best efforts, the lack of liquor was devastating to hotels' bottom lines. "With the wine card may also vanish the peacock alleys, the cascades, the marble facades, and much of the pomp that has made New York hotels famous all over the world," wrote the *New York Times*.[33] Some hotels even shuttered. One of the first to close was the luxurious Hotel Knickerbocker in Times Square, the birthplace of the dry martini.[34] It was converted into an office building, although some of the tenants who populated the revamped Knickerbocker weren't actually office workers. In an ironic twist, the businesses in several of these new "offices" were actually beer runners, including the infamous bootlegger Waxey Gordon, who had his headquarters there.[35] The Manhattan Hotel, home of the Manhattan cocktail, and the Eastern Hotel, New York's oldest hotel at the time, where Commodore Vanderbilt and P. T. Barnum once slept, also shut their doors.[36]

As Prohibition wreaked havoc on hotels, it also spurred a crime wave, with illegal bootleggers driving up rates of thievery, homicide, racketeering, and assault. Grand hotels, where wealth congregated, were increasingly targeted. At the Plaza, for example, a Woolworth heiress was the victim of a brazen jewel heist. Mrs. James P. Donahue, the daughter of the five-and-ten store magnate Frank W. Woolworth, had moved into a six-room suite at the Plaza with her husband in the fall of 1925. One afternoon, Donahue was at her Plaza suite, luxuriating in a hot bath. She had absentmindedly left her key in the door, and a thief brazenly walked into her rooms. Rifling through her dresser, he found a long strand of Cartier pearls, as well as a ten-carat diamond ring, and absconded with the treasure. Donahue was oblivious of the theft, following her bath with a visit from her personal masseuse. It was only when she began dressing for dinner that Donahue realized she had been robbed.[37]

Mrs. Donahue's insurance company quickly dispatched a detective to recover her valuables, which had been appraised at the equivalent of $10.5 million today. The detective arranged a ransom payment, successfully returning the items to the heiress. But in a perplexing turn, the perpetrator of the crime remained at large, his identity a continued mystery. Since the thief was never found, the detective himself was charged, only to be eventually acquitted of the crime.[38]

With Prohibition now in full effect, everyone wondered what would happen on New Year's Eve. That first year, hotels fielded calls from anxious patrons, but the question burning up the phone lines wasn't how much a table would cost, but rather, "What about 'bringing our own?'"[39] Hip flasks were all the rage and eventually became de rigueur. "A true New Yorker is known by the Bootlegger he keeps and not by any other sign," quipped the *New Republic* magazine.[40]

Entrepreneurial hotel employees took advantage of this new appreciation for surreptitious drinking, selling thirsty guests rye or whiskey at $15 a quart.[41] Occasionally the employees were caught. One Plaza headwaiter was arrested after a quart of Scotch, a quart of red wine, and a pint bottle of claret were found in the Grill Room. The waiter admitted to the Scotch, but claimed he was keeping the wine and claret for a guest. Despite his denial, he was summarily dismissed.[42]

Prohibition did allow doctors to prescribe alcohol for medicinal purposes, and Dr. Donald McCaskey, a frequent Plaza guest, employed his license to its full capacity. In fact, just before Christmastime in 1920, he prescribed a pint of whiskey to thirty-three different hotel employees. Authorities questioned what illness would necessitate such medicine, and the good doctor testified that while he "could not recall whether more than one of the 'patients' came to his office," he did remember that "all had been examined with his eye, voice and judgment."[43] In the end, the authorities revoked the doctor's permit.

The Plaza's Grill Room, the least formal of its dining rooms, had been hosting afternoon tea dances since it launched the trend in 1912. During Prohibition, guests, sated from their hidden libations, helped drive these parties to new heights of popularity. Debutantes thronged the room in crepe and velvet dresses in dark hues of black or soft gray, topped by karakul coats with contrasting fur, and cloche hats tilted to the side.[44] The Grill Room was, wrote Brown, "the gayest, most fashionable rendezvous for New York's younger set."[45] Every weekend, "the lads from Princeton and New Haven congregated at the Biltmore and Plaza," the *Chicago Daily Tribune* reported. "At the latter, even weekday afternoons saw the lesser lights of Columbia standing three and four deep about the dance floor waiting for a chance to cut in."[46]

One frequent patron often found among the crowd at the Plaza was a young, struggling writer whose work and persona would soon become synonymous with the hotel. F. Scott Fitzgerald, a Princeton dropout, was living in a cramped room uptown, spending his days toiling at an advertising firm and his nights writing stories. During his free time, he was drinking with friends at the Plaza or pining for Zelda, a judge's daughter he had met while serving as a second lieutenant in the US Army infantry, stationed in Alabama.

"New York had all the iridescence of the beginning of the world," Fitzgerald wrote of this period. "The returning troops marched up Fifth Avenue and girls were instinctively drawn east and north toward them—we were at last admittedly the most powerful nation and there was gala in the air." Yet, "as I hovered ghost-like in the

Plaza Rose Room of a Saturday afternoon...I was haunted always by my other life—my drab room in the Bronx, my square foot of the subway, my fixation upon the day's letter from Alabama."[47]

In 1920, Fitzgerald's life shifted dramatically when his novel *This Side of Paradise* was published to rave reviews, labeling the young author "a hero of his generation."[48] The story of Amory Blaine, who, like Fitzgerald, was a Midwesterner with literary leanings and romantic hopes, indelibly entwined the author with the "Jazz Age," a term he popularized. "For this role he appeared to be almost ideally equipped," wrote Arthur Mizener in *The Far Side of Paradise: A Biography of F. Scott Fitzgerald*. "Strikingly handsome, gracefully casual and informal, he loved popularity and responded to it with great charm."[49] Zelda, whom Fitzgerald soon married, was equally as appealing. "In no way a professional beauty, or, like some Southern girls, consciously feminine, she had with her striking red-gold hair an 'astonishing prettiness.'"

For Fitzgerald, the Plaza was a sort of shorthand, a symbol to which he often returned in his work to connote wealth and frivolity. A Plaza guest room, for instance, is the backdrop for the bacchanalia that leads to the climactic face-off between Jay Gatsby and Tom Buchanan in *The Great Gatsby*; while Gloria Gilbert, the beautiful, tragic protagonist in *The Beautiful and Damned*, lives at the hotel before marrying. The line between Fitzgerald's work and his personal life was often thin, and while he never lived at the hotel, it held import for him personally. When flush with cash, it was to the Plaza he often went. Most famously, in an anecdote that may be apocryphal, the author jumped fully clothed into the Pulitzer Fountain, a youthful, almost adolescent display that both celebrated the Plaza's grandeur and poked fun at its conservative strictures.

"Why, once when I'd just arrived in New York with a lot of money to spend," Fitzgerald said, according to his friend Edmund Wilson's retelling of the episode, "I came back to the Plaza the first night and

I looked up and saw that great creamy palace all blazing with green and gold lights and the taxis and the limousines streaming up and down the Avenue—why, I jumped into the Pulitzer fountain just out of sheer joy! And I wasn't boiled either."[50] Of Fitzgerald's passion for the hotel, another friend, Ernest Hemingway, once joked, "If you really feel blue enough, get yourself heavily insured and I'll see you can get killed . . . and I'll write you a fine obituary . . . and we can take your liver out and give it to the Princeton Museum, your heart to the Plaza Hotel."[51]

For Fitzgerald, the poster boy of the era, to be fixated on the Plaza was somewhat eyebrow-raising. The Jazz Age was known for its embrace of modernity, yet by this time, the Plaza was an institution. The hotel was occupied by wealthy dowagers, not youthful flappers, and its rooms sagged under the weight of heavy Louis XVI oak furnishings, not the sleek, silver lines of art deco design. "It was better to be modern, everybody wanted to be modern, and sophisticated, and smart, to smash the conventions and to be devastatingly frank," wrote the journalist Frederick Allen in his history of the 1920s. "Up-to-date people thought of Victorians as old ladies with bustles and inhibitions, and of Puritans as blue-nosed, ranting spoilsports."[52] When it first opened, the Plaza was considered refined modernity, a change from the oppressive opulence of the Gilded Age of the Waldorf. But it was no longer at the vanguard.

When, for example, a pretty young thing dared to order a sandwich at the Palm Court while decked out in the latest accessory—a bare leg that revealed her tawny skin rather than the modest sheen of a silk stocking—she was quietly asked to leave. "But it's being done, sir," she insisted indignantly. " 'Not here,' replied the waiter. 'This is the Plaza Hotel.' "[53] It was the same at the Plaza ballroom. Tea dances in the Grill Room may have been popular among the college set, but the ballroom orchestra strictly adhered to the waltz. "Champagne and fine liquors always urged people on to dance themselves breathless. Now that the Eighteenth Amendment seems to be fairly under way, everyone has settled back to take things more comfortably," declared the Plaza's stodgy entertainment manager. "The waltz and the old time gliding steps are here to stay."[54]

While Fitzgerald personified his generation, he was also a master of nostalgia, which may have been the root of his love for the hotel. The Plaza, with its history and elegance, evinced an earlier, simpler time, when wealth meant marble mansions and manservants, not stocks and margin calls. Fitzgerald eventually soured on the Roaring Twenties, writing later, "The city was bloated, glutted, stupid with cake and circuses." In those years, he wrote, "the buildings were higher, the morals were looser and the liquor was cheaper but all these benefits did not really minister to much delight."[55]

It was this truth that would come back to roost at the Plaza. Harry Black, the ambitious owner of the hotel, had, like Fitzgerald, drunk the Kool-Aid and was filled with the ethos of the age, relishing its frenzy and moneymaking. But while Fitzgerald eventually understood that the Jazz Age, for all its alcohol-fueled adventures, wasn't as shiny and optimistic as it first seemed, Black would never enjoy the benefit of such hindsight.

Chapter 5

THE BIG LANDLORD

" 'Bigger and bigger' was his watchword. Bigger and bigger
was the spirit of the time."
—*Paul Starrett,* Changing the Skyline

During the prolonged period of official national abstinence,
Harry Black spent the colder months in Florida. There, he
whiled away many nights in careless repose, a whiskey in one hand
and a woman in the other. One night in March 1921, a year after
Fitzgerald had published *This Side of Paradise,* a watchman saw a
truck loaded with crates leaving a train depot in Coconut Grove.
This was the station where Black's Pullman sleeper, the favored
method of travel for the überwealthy, was parked. Suspicious of
what cargo needed to be moved at such a late hour, the guard called
in federal Prohibition agents. The agents burst into Black's train car,
rummaged through the contents, and discovered $8,000 worth of
contraband liquor squirreled away in hidden compartments.

Jubilant with their haul, the agents went to Black's hotel room
to arrest him. It was 2 a.m., and he was still out. They returned at
6 a.m., roused the hungover Black, and dragged him to the station.
By then, word had spread that a New York millionaire had been
nabbed by Prohibition agents. During these years, high society could

drink mostly with impunity, hidden in private party rooms or speak-easies. The fact that Black had been caught was notable, and temperance advocates cheered. William Jennings Bryan, the perennial presidential candidate, even held a rally celebrating the arrest.[1] Black insisted that he was innocent, claiming, somewhat improbably, that he had asked his porter to buy him grapefruit, but the porter had misheard, stocking Black's Pullman car with liquor instead.

During the ensuing court case, the jury was urged to try Black's liquor themselves, "in order that they might determine whether or not it was intoxicating," wrote the *New York Herald*.[2] As the court inquiry proceeded, "bottle after bottle of various rare vintages was uncorked, the jurors holding the glasses up to the light and sipping the contents like connoisseurs."[3] The jury—by then quite inebriated—retired to consider the facts. In only a handful of minutes they returned, delivering a unanimous verdict of not guilty.

Black had little time to relish his victory, as the swashbuckling businessman was needed back in New York. By now, Black had built a sprawling real estate empire that consisted of constructing, managing, and buying properties across the country. His real estate trust was seeing its profits soar, reaching nearly $2.5 million in 1921, compared with less than $900,000 the year before.[4] As business was booming, Black decided that an expansion of his most famous flagship hotel, the Plaza, was in order. It was an idea that had been percolating for several years.

When the Plaza first opened its doors in 1907, the neighborhood that spread east of Fifth Avenue to the river was riddled with tenements, small repair shops, and waterfront oyster shacks. But as the century's third decade got underway, Midtown Manhattan was rapidly transforming, and the streets around Madison Avenue and Park Avenue were becoming one of the city's most exclusive shopping and residential districts.[5] The Plaza Operating Company, the subsidiary of U.S. Realty that owned the Plaza, perhaps in anticipation of the neighborhood's eventual improvement, had been acquiring properties adjacent to the hotel's Fifty-Eighth Street side as they became available. In 1920, the owners secured the last two contiguous parcels they needed to build an extension. The move would allow them to more than double the hotel's frontage on Fifty-Eighth Street and create an additional space on Fifty-Ninth Street.

During the time Black was acquiring the sites for his expansion, civic forces were advocating to protect light and air in the rapidly developing metropolis. Five years earlier, in 1916, the nation's first citywide zoning code was passed. It included height restrictions on West Fifty-Eighth Street, where the Plaza hoped to build its annex. To comply, the hotel was made to apply for an exemption.

In its review of the Plaza's proposal, *American Architect* magazine advocated for the expansion with one caveat: the small brownstones that lined Fifty-Eighth Street across from the hotel must never be torn down and replaced with a tower. If that were to occur, "it would seem that the tall hotel structure would not only have less light than the law intended, but that the new building opposite would also be deprived of that light and air which the zoning ordinance sought to guarantee."[6] Half a century later that is exactly what occurred, when a builder bought up the low-slung properties on Fifty-Eighth Street and redeveloped them as part of a forty-nine-story behemoth. Nine West Fifty-Seventh Street, as the skyscraper is known, is one of New York's most expensive office towers, and the predicted loss of light and air failed to curtail demand, or rents. Despite the possible future threat of an alleyway-like Fifty-Eighth Street, the city voted in favor of enlarging the Plaza.

With its approval in hand, the hotel began preparatory work on the $5 million project, hiring Warren & Wetmore, the architecture firm that designed Grand Central Terminal. The firm's plans closely adhered to Hardenbergh's original creation, seamlessly blending the new spaces into the existing hotel. There were some changes, most notably relocating the hotel's entrance from Fifty-Ninth Street to Fifth Avenue, where it remains today. The new extension included an additional 350 hotel rooms; a terraced restaurant; and an updated ballroom, which still exists, large enough to accommodate 1,000 guests for a dance or 800 at a seated dinner.[7]

In a nod to the private gatherings that had become so integral to nightlife under Prohibition, the Plaza carved out three floors devoted entirely to private entertaining, with individual dining rooms and separate event spaces. The rooms were accessed by their own entrance on West Fifty-Eighth Street, which allowed patrons to come and go as they pleased without garnering attention from the main hotel. When the extension opened in 1921, "it was really almost like the original opening of the great hotel itself," dished *Town Topics*. "Nothing more beautiful than the vista from the imposing new entrance on the Fifth Avenue side... has been disclosed to society in a long, long time."[8]

Just as the Plaza's new extension was rising, so was the stock market, the beginning stages of what would become an unprecedented upward trajectory. Harry Black's real estate trust had stopped issuing dividend payments on its stock in 1914, as the war and Prohibition took its toll. Now, dividends began flowing once more. In 1922, they were 1½ percent, and by the following year, they had increased to 7½ percent. By 1925, they were raised again, to 10 percent.[9] The trust's stock price, meanwhile, traded from a high of 69¾ in 1920, all the way to a high of 184½ in 1925.[10] The company's assets—and its principals—were also doing well. By 1923, the Plaza was New York City's most valuable hotel, and Black found himself in the same tax category as Solomon R. Guggenheim and Frederick W. Vanderbilt.[11]

While the Plaza and Black's businesses were performing

exceptionally well, Black still had his detractors. In 1924, several members of the U.S. Realty & Improvement Company's board tried to unseat Black as chairman and take control of the company. It was the second time that Black had faced a revolt from his board—and won. Twenty years before, in 1904, a group of board members had similarly connived to remove Black from his chairmanship. In both instances, Black outmaneuvered his opponents by surreptitiously buying up stock to emerge as his company's majority shareholder. He then ousted his enemies before they could oust him.

In 1924, the shares that Black bought in order to retain majority control of his trust belonged to the estate of the late John "Bet-a-Million" Gates. Gates, one of the original Plaza investors and Black's staunch backer, had died in 1911. In what was the first, and perhaps only, funeral at the Plaza, his coffin was laid out in the ballroom surrounded by a profusion of flowers and more than one thousand mourners. Black had been an honorary pallbearer. Before Gates died, he had instructed his wife, "Do not sell a share of United States Realty under $100—Harry Black is bound to make it worth more than that."[12]

In 1918, Gates's widow also died at her suite in the Plaza, and the stock remained unsold—having not yet broken the three-digit barrier. So when Black faced being ousted, it was to Gates's estate that he turned, buying up his old friend's stake in the trust to become its single largest shareholder. As the major owner, Black then voted out those who had opposed him, consolidating his control of the real estate conglomerate. The company was now worth $90 million, or the equivalent of $1.3 billion today. "For the second time in twenty years, Harry Black . . . has been called on to fight strong financial interests seeking to wrest control of his company, and for the second time he has emerged victorious," wrote the *New York Herald*.[13]

Black, as the unopposed head of a powerful real estate trust, constantly graced the society and news pages. Even the fashion bible

Vogue dedicated space to his birthday party, regaling their readers with a list of his illustrious dinner guests, including the queen of Romania. Yet for all the ink spilled over Black, he remained a mercurial presence, even for those who knew him best. Paul Starrett, a senior executive at Black's real estate trust, had met his boss when he was in his early thirties and Black was just a few years older. The two had been colleagues for decades, yet, despite their closeness, Starrett struggled to paint a portrait of Black.

"It isn't easy to picture him," Starrett wrote in his memoir, *Changing the Skyline*. "He was a business genius, a gambler, a financial juggler. He had a smile that would charm the birds off the tree. He ignored anyone in whom he was not interested. He had a contagious sense of humor and told anecdotes illustrating his points effectively. He was big-hearted and selfish and, according to my standards, rather unscrupulous. His contradictions had me baffled."[14]

Black could sometimes express views that seemed contradictory or controversial. In 1929, the Canadian native addressed employees at the George A. Fuller Construction Company, a subsidiary of his trust. During the talk, Black decried "the foreign element" in real estate. "I think it all wrong," he declared, "for a foreigner to be able to acquire a good old New England name for instance, because the one he bears when he comes to this country he finds detrimental to him in business."[15] It was a seemingly veiled reference to Jews who changed their names to appear less ethnic.

New York City during this time had grown increasingly diverse: When the original Plaza had opened in 1890, the city was 48.8 percent Protestant, 39.2 percent Roman Catholic, and 12 percent Jewish. By 1920, the population of Protestants and Catholics had each dropped to 34.6 percent, while the Jewish community had exploded to 29.2 percent.[16] In real estate this was even more pronounced. By 1927, fully 80 percent of the speculative builders in the city were Jewish.[17]

Black's diatribe to his employees was even odder, given the fact that his beloved nephew, whom he had unofficially adopted, had done exactly the thing that Black was criticizing. George Allon Fuller had actually been born Fuller Chenery, Chenery having been the name of his father. When he was a teen, Black's nephew legally changed his name, adopting that of his famous grandfather. Black may have found this acceptable, however, since his nephew was merely swapping one "good old New England name" for another. Black's speech was made into pamphlets and distributed to company stockholders, according to an article in the *Jewish Advocate*.[18]

As capricious as Black could be, perhaps it shouldn't have surprised friends when the longtime bachelor, now nearing age sixty, suddenly remarried. His new wife was Isabelle May, a young debutante from a well-heeled Washington, DC, family. Like Allon, Black's first wife, May was much younger than her husband and a far cry from Tessie Oelrichs, the middle-aged society matron whom Black had dated in the wake of his divorce.

"In the way of surprise engagements in New York, nothing has surpassed that of Harry Black and Miss Isabelle May," wrote *Town Topics*. "That the redoubtable Harry Black should succumb at last after the many onslaughts that have been made upon him," it wrote, "proves that even he, like Achilles, has a vulnerable spot."[19] The new couple's home was to be of unrivaled glamour, a penthouse on the roof of the Plaza's new extension. It was a gilded duplex in the sky, offering expansive views of Central Park and the surrounding city.

It was around the time Harry and Isabelle moved into their grand penthouse that the frenzy that would become known as Coolidge Prosperity took hold. The Roaring Twenties was a decade of firsts: the first time women could vote, the first flight across the Atlantic, and the first Hollywood "talkie." Millionaires were being minted at an astonishing pace, with the number of Americans paying taxes on income of more than $1 million a year soaring 277 percent between

1924 and 1927.[20] Automobile ownership nearly quadrupled, while sales of radios leapfrogged 1,300 percent.[21]

America went crazy for flappers, the Charleston, and, especially, stocks. Everyone was in on it. "The rich man's chauffeur drove with his ear laid back to catch the news of an impending move in Bethlehem Steel; he held fifty shares himself on a twenty-point margin," wrote Allen in *Only Yesterday*. There was the broker's valet who made almost a quarter of a million dollars, the nurse who cleaned up by gathering tips from grateful patients, and "a Wyoming cattleman, thirty miles from the nearest railroad, who bought or sold a thousand shares a day—getting his market returns by radio and telephoning his orders to the nearest large town to be transmitted to New York by telegram."[22]

Like everyone else, Black was caught up in the ballyhoo. He had enlarged his father-in-law's firm into one of the biggest construction companies in the country, epitomizing the era's hunger for expansion. "Black, my boss, had a Napoleon complex," wrote Starrett. "Like Napoleon and those other Napoleons of my day, Harriman, Jim Hill and J.P. Morgan, Black loved to amalgamate and expand."[23] Despite his short stature, the *Wall Street Journal* dubbed Black "The Big Landlord," noting, "He believes in doing everything in a big way."[24]

For instance, when news broke that Chicago was about to see the largest and grandest hotel in the country, Black, in typical fashion, was determined to beat it. The new Stevens Hotel was a three-thousand-room behemoth that boasted a bowling alley, a hospital, and even a miniature golf course on its roof. Black was "depressed at the blight put on his famous Plaza" by the much-larger Stevens, and was determined to "go them one better."[25]

Black set his sights on the Savoy Hotel, a building that was across Fifth Avenue from the Plaza. He wanted to tear it down and replace it with a larger hotel that could trump the Chicago newcomer. The Childs Company, which ran the popular Childs restaurant chain, owned the Savoy, so Black partnered with them to redevelop the building. Black—who later ousted the Childs Company to take over the project himself—hired the architecture firm McKim, Mead & White to design the new structure. The Savoy-Plaza, as it was to be called, would be New York's most valuable hotel, taking up the entire block on the east side of Fifth Avenue, between Fifty-Eighth and Fifty-Ninth Streets. And it would rise twenty-nine stories—one more than the Stevens, his Chicago rival.

While it may have been the city's best new hotel, the Savoy-Plaza faced plenty of competition. During these years, New York City was in the grip of a massive building boom. Between 1927, when the Savoy-Plaza opened, and 1933, a staggering eighty-four new hotels opened across New York, creating a 66 percent increase in the number of guest rooms.[26] As F. Scott Fitzgerald put it, the city was "bloated." Hotels were a $5 billion industry, employing thousands and making their owners millions. At the time, hotels, in fact, were the nation's seventh-largest industry in terms of capital invested, ranked just behind steel.[27]

As the new Savoy-Plaza began rising floor-by-floor, Harry Black's old partner, Bernhard Beinecke, who had no involvement in this latest project, watched out the windows of his twelfth-floor Plaza suite. He may have sensed a coming doom, or at least the grim knowledge that what goes up must eventually come down. For as he stood there, observing the work of his old partner, Beinecke shook his head with dismay.[28] During the intervening years, as Black rode the markets upward like Icarus tempting the sun, Beinecke adhered to a grounded path focusing on steady investments, slowly growing his wealth and raising his extended family of children and grandchildren. A century later, there would be a lasting legacy to his stable hand, with the Beinecke Rare Book & Manuscript Library at Yale University, the Beinecke Scholarship, and surviving generations to carry the name. While Black would also have a fund set up in his name, that is where the similarities ended.

Eschewing his old partner's conservatism, Black embraced Coolidge Prosperity with both hands. Nothing symbolized this more than Black's relationship with Charles E. Mitchell, the personification of the speculative and inflated stock market of the 1920s. Mitchell, who ran National City Bank, one of the country's largest, was "a genial extrovert with a talent for headlines," wrote the economist John Kenneth Galbraith in his book *The Great Crash, 1929*, "known to one and all as a leading prophet of the New Era."[29]

Mitchell's bank had ties to Black's real estate trust dating back to when the U.S. Realty & Improvement Company was first formed, and the bank's then president, James Stillman, joined the company's board. Now, in the spring of 1928, Black's skyscraper trust had seen its stock price soar to 90. Under Mitchell's guidance, the bank acquired a large stake in Black's firm; a month later, Mitchell and two others affiliated with the National City Bank joined Black's board. "The National City Bank further tightened its grip on United States Realty and Improvement," wrote the *New York Herald Tribune*.[30]

As the irrational exuberance on Wall Street reached a peak, these new partners announced a joint venture to fund real estate projects using—what else?—stocks. Traditionally, developers borrowed money from banks or insurance firms in the form of mortgages to construct or buy buildings. Black and Mitchell were proposing doing away with that, and to raise money by issuing stocks instead. It was a "radical departure," where "the issuance of mortgages against real estate operations will be entirely eliminated and preferred and common stock will be issued in their stead, thus offering a substitute for a system that has been in vogue for centuries."[31] The move symbolized the "1929 investment styles," wrote the *New*

York Herald Tribune, adding that it "emphasized more than could reams of statistics the recent rise in popularity of stocks."[32] Truly, Harry Black had immersed himself in the quagmire of Wall Street speculation.

Soon Coolidge was gone, replaced with Herbert Hoover. It seemed as if the raging bull market would run on forever. During this time, both Black's trust and the Plaza were experiencing heady success. U.S. Realty & Improvement had a surplus of more than $12 million, while the Plaza was one of the company's top income producers. It was considered New York City's third-most-valuable hotel, with an assessed value of $13.8 million, or almost $200 million in today's dollars. Black's Savoy-Plaza was the most valuable at $17.5 million, or $250 million today.[33] Even though it no longer commanded the top spot, "the Plaza is doing the best business in its history and has the highest percentage of permanent rentals," wrote the *Wall Street Journal* in August 1929.[34]

But eventually, there had to be a break. The following month, in September 1929, there were rumblings of a downturn as the once-sparkling stock market lost some luster. There were an increasing number of days when stock prices reversed their long-held course and trended downward. One plucky investment firm even ran an ad with the hair-raising headline: "OVERSTAYING A BULL MARKET."[35] Soon, brokers began making margin calls, meaning that the stocks being held in lieu of payment had declined to the point where they were no longer sufficient collateral, and borrowers were being asked to put in more cash. Not everyone had the money. At the Plaza, for example, Frederick Beinecke, a son of Bernhard, was working as the hotel's treasurer when he discovered a discrepancy in the books. When he pulled out a drawer in his auditor's desk, he found it stuffed with margin calls. The auditor, who had been taking money from the Plaza and doctoring the books to meet his debts, was summarily fired.[36]

As things began to slip toward what would eventually be a historic run on the markets, certain stock boosters continued to spew their optimistic rhetoric. One of the most notable was Mitchell, the bank president and Black's business partner. "The markets generally are now in a healthy condition," he insisted, adding, "Nothing can arrest the upward movement."[37] Mitchell would be proven categorically wrong, and as the stock market crashed, his name quickly receded from the headlines. That is, until 1933, when Mitchell was arrested for tax evasion. He was acquitted, but his reputation never recovered.

On Friday, October 18, the market proceeded as it had for weeks, with signs that things might improve, only for those hopes to be dashed. In the morning the stock ticker rose, but "before the day was over, the fall in prices had been resumed with considerable violence," wrote the *New York Times*. "At the close there was hardly any exception to the roster of losses."[38] Black's U.S. Realty stock was trading at around 88, having lost more than a quarter of its value from its high of 119½ in February.

Black spent the afternoon lunching at the Manhattan Club with his old associate Paul Starrett. "He had a private dining room and a most elaborate layout," wrote Starrett, who recalled being "amazed" at how well Black seemed. "He was in his sixties, but he abounded with youth, his eyes sparkled, his smile and laugh had all their old magic."[39] But Black was always charismatic, and his enthusiasm perhaps belied a premonition that the good times were nearing an end. Black returned that evening to a lonely penthouse atop the Plaza, his wife having gone out to dine with friends. Black retired to take a bath, but when his valet failed to hear anything from him for some time, he went to the bathroom to check.

Black didn't answer his knock, and so the valet put his ear to the door. He heard a disturbing gurgling sound, and quickly forced himself inside, only to find Black lying face down in the tub, water overflowing onto the floor. The valet pulled his unconscious boss out of the bath and laid him on the bed; then he called the Plaza house physician. The doctor phoned the Consolidated Gas Company for a pulmotor crew, which employed an emergency breathing apparatus that was used to resuscitate victims of gas asphyxiation or poisoning. The fact that the doctor failed to first call the police—or even an ambulance—was likely an attempt to hush up the troubling incident.

The pulmotor crew arrived close to 9 p.m. and found Black unconscious. They pulled his body onto the floor and began applying CPR and the inhalator in constant intervals. As the pulmotor crew worked, the hotel finally called the police, telling them J. M. Black, age sixty-six, a manager of the hotel, had been found unconscious in the bath. Curious guests and nosy reporters, who saw the pulmotor crew's emergency vehicle parked in front of the Plaza, were told a similar story.

It was hard to keep it quiet, however, and eventually the hotel house doctor was forced to revise his story. The victim was in fact Black, who had suffered from "an attack of acute indigestion, probably brought on by the hot water of the tub, which caused a fainting spell," the doctor dubiously posited.[40] Finally, in the early hours of Saturday morning, after the pulmotor crew had been working on Black for a total of nine hours, he was pronounced conscious and out of danger. "The life of Harry S. Black, the 'world's greatest landlord,' was saved today by a gas company inhalator squad," reported the *Washington Post*.[41]

While Black was physically revived, he never mentally recovered. Black was a consummate gambler with a savvy sense of when to exit a bet, but the happiness and vigor he had shown during his lunch that day with Starrett may have been his best poker face. The rough seas bashing the stock market would soon become a tidal wave, drowning Black's precious trust in debt and failure.

The following week, on October 24, panic tore through Wall

Street. In what became known as Black Thursday, the market plummeted 11 percent. Like all stocks, Black's U.S. Realty & Improvement's shares bottomed out. On November 13, the real estate trust's shares reached a low of 50½. Fearful crowds stuffed themselves into the old Oak Room bar, now the E. F. Hutton brokerage offices. Stunned onlookers watched the frantic ticker, its numbers falling so fast and the volume of trading so great that its quotes lagged hours behind the real-time trades.[42]

The lows kept coming and the Great Depression replaced Coolidge Prosperity as the shorthand for the age. By Friday, July 18, 1930, U.S. Realty's stock was trading at anemic levels, stuck in the low to mid-50s. The construction industry was at a standstill and the outlook was grim. Black had spent his entire professional life battling challenges and beating the odds, but it seemed as if "The Big Landlord" had finally tired of the fight.

The following morning, Black was at Allondale, his Long Island mansion named for his first wife. His second wife, Isabelle, was away in Ireland. Black awoke and thumped loudly on the floor to tell the servants to turn down the radio set. But by 11 a.m., Black had failed to emerge from his room or call for breakfast. His valet, the same one who had found him in the tub, went to check. As he tiptoed into the darkened room, it was immediately clear that something was awry.[43]

The valet found sixty-seven-year-old Black, propped up in bed, his head sagging unnaturally forward, still in his pajamas. In his right hand was a pistol. He was bleeding and it was clear that this time, not even a pulmotor crew could save him. Black's nephew George was summoned from Southampton, Long Island. He rushed to his uncle's side, where Black, with a gunshot wound to his right temple, remained unconscious for the rest of the day. At 8:15 that evening, Black died.[44]

Two months after nearly drowning in the tub, and seven months before he shot himself, Black wrote a will. In it, he divided his estate equally between his second wife, Isabelle, and his nephew. If either passed without children, the money was to be placed in the Harry Black and Allon Fuller Fund. The fund, which continues to give out grants today, was instructed to allocate 60 percent of the estate to New York City charities and 40 percent to those in Chicago because, Black explained, his fortune was started in Chicago and finished in New York.

At around the time Black wrote his will, he also gifted his wife and nephew ten thousand shares each of U.S. Realty & Improvement stock, valued at nearly $1 million. And he transferred to his wife ownership of the Long Island estate, Allondale, insisting that Isabelle maintain the home out of income from his stock gift.[45] Black also bequeathed money to his brothers and sister, and allocated between $3,000 and $5,000 to numerous longtime servants, like Mary Daly, a Plaza laundress who for years had ironed his shirts.

The real estate magnate left no note, and no diary has been uncovered, but there are clues to Black's mental state. Before the market took a nosedive, there had never been any indication that Black suffered from depression or had attempted death by his own hand. In the spring of 1929, before the stock market began its rapid decline, Black's assets were valued at more than $15 million, or $215 million today. When he died, his wealth was roughly one-third of what it had been, or just over $5 million.[46] By the time Black's assets were sold and his estate disseminated, his holdings had shrunk even further, to barely more than $194,000.[47]

The image persists that following the 1929 crash, desperate bankers and businessmen hurled themselves from windows and rooftops, forcing pedestrians to step gingerly across Wall Street to avoid the bodies of fallen financiers. In truth, there was no such rash of suicides. In New York during 1929, there were 17 suicides per 100,000 people; by 1930, the number was 18.7 per 100,000; and in 1932, the total ticked up to 21.3.[48] It was not an epidemic, yet Black was numbered among them.

Fourteen months after Black died, his thirty-two-year-old nephew George also tragically passed away in his sleep of heart disease. The two men are buried in the same plot, at the high point of a grassy knoll in a cemetery in Valhalla, a town in Westchester County that is thirty-five miles north of bustling Midtown Manhattan and Black's beloved Plaza. It's a lonely place, two small ground stones marking the men's names, enigmatically placed at opposite ends of the large plot. Neither Black's widow nor Fuller's are buried there, and the only reminder of Black's outsized accomplishments is a sandy, oblong headstone that towers over the hillside, its shape reminiscent of a skyscraper, the singular BLACK inscribed atop in large letters.

PART TWO

Chapter 6

THE THIRTY-NINE WIDOWS OF THE PLAZA

"The Plaza Hotel announces for tonight
a 'Poverty Party.' Paper tablecloths will be
used... Costumes will be plain."
—New York Herald Tribune

Clara Bell Walsh was a broad-shouldered Southern belle turned
Manhattan social arbiter. She was famous for her living arrangements, legendary for her entertainment skills, and renowned as the
Plaza's most ardent booster. "Clara Bell Walsh is almost entirely
known for her residence in the Plaza," wrote the gossip columnist
Lucius Beebe, "as though one's address were a dominant personal
characteristic."[1] If Harry Black was the man who built the hotel,
then Clara Bell Walsh was the woman who sustained it.

A noted horsewoman and an avid consumer of Kentucky bourbon, Walsh's earliest accomplishment was the supposed invention
of the cocktail party. "Positively the newest stunt in society is the
giving of 'cocktail parties,'" wrote the *Washington Post* in 1917, noting that "Mrs. Walsh introduced it recently with the first cocktail
party in society's history."[2] The most notorious of her soirees was

one she hosted with a "kindergarten" theme, where guests dressed up as poor little rich girls and sailor boys. One strapping six-foot-tall male guest wore a pink romper, while another heavy-set fellow dressed as "a big fat Mammie" in a kinky wig and white apron. The hostess herself was less risqué, donning white lingerie, with a blue bow in her curly locks, while her husband was resplendent in the black velvet suit and lace collar of Little Lord Fauntleroy. Guests had to maneuver through an obstacle course, climbing up a ladder and sliding down a board to reach the bartender, who served them Sazeracs and martinis in baby bottles.[3]

It would be several years after Walsh gave her kindergarten-themed event that she would move into the Plaza. But once she arrived, she remained—part den mother, part head cheerleader—until her death. While Walsh kept her exact age a mystery, it is known that she was born Clara Bell, the only child of one of Kentucky's wealthiest families, her grandfather Henry Bell having been an associate of multimillionaire merchant A. T. Stewart.[4] In 1905, Clara Bell married Julius Walsh Jr., who owned a streetcar line and a share of the Royal Typewriter Company. The wedding ceremony was held at Bell Place, her family's estate, now a public park, beneath an enormous bell made from white and yellow flowers. Two rooms were filled from floor to ceiling with gifts, including the deed to a farm and a case of silver from her in-laws.

Despite the lavish trappings, Walsh refused to follow convention. After her wedding, the bride climbed into a plain one-horse carriage and, taking the reins herself, drove through town to thank well-wishers and stop at a nearby hospital to deliver the floral bouquets from her ceremony.[5] Less than a year later, when her husband was arrested after getting into a fistfight with a railroad conductor, it was Walsh who hunted down the mayor, dragged him to the police station, and convinced him to free her husband.[6] She was as acclaimed for her abilities with a horse as she was for her pluck.

"Few women in America are her equal as a rider and driver," wrote the *Detroit Free Press*.[7] The *St. Louis Post-Dispatch* called her "a fine example of the picturesque type of Bluegrass belle."[8]

By 1922, Walsh's seventeen-year marriage was dissolving, and life in St. Louis, where the couple lived, was increasingly dull. So she left her husband and the Midwest, decamping for the Plaza in New York. A year later, Walsh officially filed for divorce, a matter that was dispatched with quickly. "A brief three hours after Clara Bell Walsh, of St. Louis, had filed suit for divorce from Julius Walsh, and thirteen minutes following her entrance into the courtroom, she was awarded a decree," noted *Town Topics*.[9] Walsh would always insist, despite evidence to the contrary, that she checked into the Plaza on opening day in 1907. She also claimed to be a widow—technically true, but only six years after her divorce was finalized.[10]

Once at the Plaza, Walsh held court in her suite, swathed in enormous ermine wraps, her nails painted to match her dress.[11] Her guests, who included theater stars and singers, lolled on brocade Edwardian sofas among tables crammed with Chinese lamps and tiny animal figurines.[12] "Clara Bell Walsh, I think, has the best time of any local matron," wrote columnist and frequent visitor Ed Sullivan, who would go on to host his eponymous television show. "She lives at the Plaza, year after year, and you can generally find Amos 'n' Andy, the Lawrence Tibbetts and other interesting celebs in her company."[13] Drinks flowed, and her food consumption, or the lack thereof, was a source of constant fascination. "Clara Bell Walsh would like to live on a diet of Kentucky products but finds a lack of necessary vitamins in ham and bourbon exclusively," wrote Beebe, who often chronicled her in his column, "This New York."[14]

While friends would come and go, Walsh's constant companion was Skippy, a small terrier who "had four movie offers" and was even given his own obituary when he died. Skippy was "a button-eyed midget Sealyham with comic whiskers and the grand and grave manners of a patriarch," wrote society reporter O. O. McIntyre in his eulogy of the pooch. He "had no truck with anyone save his mistress and her chauffeur, but he sat up in bored dignity for all who approached."[15]

When not hosting celebrities, Walsh was at the theater. She was such a Broadway fixture that the *Tex and Jinx Show* booked her on their radio program, billing Walsh as "the oldest resident of the Plaza Hotel."[16] When a production of *Frederika* opened on Broadway, advertisements featured Walsh's pull quotes just beneath those from actor and performer Clifton Webb.[17] Walsh also frequented the Persian Room, the Plaza's nightclub. She was so notable a presence in the front row that Kay Thompson, the performer who would later write the Eloise books, co-opted several of her idiosyncrasies. For instance, when Thompson's six-year-old alter ego had her hair done in an *Eloise* book, it was at the men's-only barbershop in the Plaza's lobby, as was also Walsh's wont. Thompson even liked to go out with two red dots on her eyelids, creating a "subliminal flash-of-red effect," a nod to Walsh's habit of attending dinner parties with fake eyes painted on her eyelids.[18]

Walsh was one of the Plaza's best-known guests, but she was far from the only wealthy woman living at the hotel. Over the years, hundreds of dowagers, with their diamonds and dogs, private nurses and palatial suites, called the Plaza home. Their presence was so notable, in fact, that they became a meme of sorts. Dubbed "the thirty-nine widows of the Plaza"—the origin of the phrase is murky—these permanent guests were all single, mostly older, and every one rich.

One of the earliest of the widows was a member of a noble bloodline, or at least claimed to be. Princess Vilma Lwoff-Parlaghy was, like Baron von Arkovy, a Hungarian of murky royal lineage. But whatever her heritage, she was indisputably wealthy. In 1909, she moved into a dozen-room suite on the second floor of the Plaza, bringing with her a retinue that included three French maids; a first, a second, and a third attaché; a marshal; a courier; a butler; and a chef. "And that's not all. With her also is one small yappy, white woolly dog, a pair of guinea pigs badly in need of a haircut, a couple of young wolves, an ibis, a falcon, several owls and a family of alligators. And that's not all. With her also are several drays of the gaudiest luggage that any local hotel has ever sheltered. It is all printed red, white and green, the Hungarian colors," wrote one amazed reporter.[19]

Despite her extensive, and excessive, trappings, Parlaghy was an occasional target of disdain. When she arrived, she also brought along a chasseur, or private bodyguard, who wore a cocked chapeau adorned with a torrent of feather plumes and an ornamental sword. "For a private person such as Mme. Parlaghy, who is a woman of the most obscure and lowly Magyar origin, to travel about with a chasseur, is extremely ridiculous, and would excite the utmost derision were it to be known in Europe," wrote the Marquise de Fontenoy, a royal watcher and columnist for the *Washington Post*.[20] With such a retinue, and being of questionable pedigree, Parlaghy struggled to find appropriate housing. The Waldorf-Astoria, for example, turned up its nose at the forty-two-year-old. The Plaza, however, welcomed her staff, private zoo, and forty-three pieces of luggage.

Parlaghy was also a child prodigy and noted portrait painter. Beautiful, with a curvy bodice and reddish-gold hair, she had had her own studio as a young woman in Berlin, where she did a brisk business with a stream of European aristocracy. Her most famous client was the German kaiser Wilhelm II, and the relationship spurred much gossip. "Sneers were cast at her work and at her personally," reported the *New York Times* in a profile it published of Parlaghy when she was not yet thirty. It also called her "a talent decidedly above the commonplace."[21]

By the time Parlaghy arrived at the Plaza she was twice divorced, most recently to a minor Russian prince. She leveraged her ex's title, forevermore insisting she be called Princess Lwoff-Parlaghy or, simply, Her Serene Highness. As soon as she moved into the hotel, Parlaghy began advertising her portraiture services. One of her first clients was Major General Daniel E. Sickles, age ninety-two, one of the few surviving veterans of the Civil War. (He lost a leg fighting at Gettysburg, later sending the limb to the Army Medical Museum in Washington to be displayed.)

One day, soon after Parlaghy finished painting a portrait of Sickles, she attended the Ringling Brothers Circus at Madison Square Garden. While there, she fell in love with a baby lion. Sickles shelled out $250 to buy her the pet, and she named her newest animal General Sickles, in honor of her benefactor.[22] The lion cub, which she usually called Goldfleck for short, lived in the bathtub of Parlaghy's Plaza suite, until he outgrew both his porcelain home and the Plaza's patience. Goldfleck was then taken to the Bronx Zoo, and when he died, Parlaghy had him buried in a pet cemetery in Westchester, just ten minutes from Harry Black's final resting place.

Parlaghy courted controversy wherever she went, even in the Plaza elevators. When she had first arrived at the hotel, she gave strict orders that no one could ride in the same elevator car with her. One day, Parlaghy returned from a drive in Central Park and, accompanied by her footman, swept through the lobby and into the elevator. Just then, the Duchess of Manchester also stepped into the car. "The Princess whispered to the footman, the footman whispered to the elevator boy, and the Duchess was asked to vacate," the *New York Times* tittered. "The Duchess was left standing alone, with the gate closed in her face, while the Princess sped up to her extensive suite on the second floor."[23] The duchess was outraged at the insult, and soon departed the hotel in disgust, taking refuge with Mrs. Frederick Vanderbilt at her Long Island mansion. But not before the story had spread, adding "a good deal of zest to the apathy of the waning social season."[24]

No one knew where Parlaghy's wealth came from; she seemed "to have found Aladdin's lamp or a Midas wand," marveled the *Los Angeles Times*. She struggled to spend her money and "almost tearfully admitted that she had not succeeded in spending a million a year, as she had hoped," the paper reported. "The best she could do was $250,000."[25] Her rooms at the Plaza cost $36,000 a year and she claimed it was impossible to dress for less than $6,000 a year.[26]

But in 1914, when war broke out in Europe, her once-abundant wealth suddenly vanished. Parlaghy began charging for her paintings—after previously claiming that to paint for money was vulgar—and struggled to pay her mounting bills. Her lawyer, banker, and the stables where she boarded her horses sued for nonpayment. There was even a lawsuit from a Fifth Avenue jeweler over a $250 imitation diamond tiara, and she owed the Plaza $12,000.[27] In desperation, she fled the hotel, leaving her paintings, bronzes, and tapestries behind. "Managers of the Plaza Hotel profess to be absolutely ignorant of the whereabouts of the princess," reported the *New-York Tribune*.[28] When she didn't return, they put her belongings in storage.

In 1916, Parlaghy reappeared in the press. By then, she had moved to East Thirty-Ninth Street, "far away from the hateful, menacing shadows of the Plaza Hotel." The occasion for her reemergence was an event in her honor, celebrating a portrait she had completed of the reclusive inventor Nikola Tesla. At the party, the "much toned down" princess talked "with plain folk" as she ate thinly sliced boiled tongue and other everyday Russian dishes. "I have moved from the Plaza long, so long ago," Parlaghy said at the event. "My bills have been all paid and now I am of conscience free."[29]

But Parlaghy was not free of her debts, despite her statements to the contrary. By 1923, as the Jazz Age raged around her, the menagerie and numerous staff that had once accompanied Her Serene Highness were gone. Parlaghy lay dying inside her home, its walls crammed with her unsold artworks, only a single maid left for company. Outside, a line of creditors gathered. To keep the debt collectors at bay, someone had tacked a white sheet of paper to a dusty pane on her front door. In pencil was scrawled "Out of Town." Parlaghy died destitute, although at her funeral, her few remaining friends scrounged up a plush robe of blue and gold and a crown of silver in which to dress the body. As the mourners reminisced about her past glory, a deputy sheriff stood impatiently waiting for the proceedings to end, so he could take possession of what meager assets remained.[30]

Over the decades, the legend of the Plaza widows grew. The women (and a few men) became a tourist attraction in their own right, visitors flocking to the hotel as much to glimpse a quirky widow as to visit the Pulitzer Fountain or have tea at the Palm Court. When the Great Depression set in, it was these permanent residents who became a financial lifeline, providing a steady stream of annual rent for the hotel when transient guests were hard to come by.

For instance, Mrs. Charles O. Maas moved into the State Suite, the most sumptuous rooms at the Plaza, during the Great War. Her husband had been an aide to President Woodrow Wilson, but he died while serving in France. Maas paid over $200 a month for her rooms overlooking Central Park and Fifth Avenue, remaining there until her death in 1954.[31] Ella Peterson Tuttle Freeman was the Plaza's oldest resident, arriving in 1932 and not checking out until her death at the age of 103 in 1960.[32] The most cantankerous of the widows was undoubtedly Fannie Lowenstein. The ancient widow was so litigious that Donald J. Trump once told the *National Enquirer* she was tougher to handle than Ivana or Marla Maples. Today, employees still recount how Lowenstein, in a fit of pique, relieved herself on the rug in the Palm Court in front of a shocked Sunday brunch crowd.

Several older men also lived at the Plaza. There was the architect Frank Lloyd Wright, who occupied "Diamond Jim" Brady's old suite while designing the Guggenheim Museum.[33] The Hungarian playwright Ferenc Molnar took refuge in a small one-bedroom at the Plaza after escaping Nazi persecution during World War II. Mr. Rosenbloom, whose first name is lost to history, also arrived at the Plaza after fleeing the horrors of war. A rich banker in Berlin, Rosenbloom showed up one day in the hotel lobby "dressed in a shaggy old bath robe, a towel wrapped around his head, unshaven and in bedroom slippers." Despite his disheveled appearance, he had deep pockets, checking into a three-bedroom suite where he stayed for years, refusing to talk to any Plaza staff save for Birdie, the woman who did his laundry.[34]

While there were many widows, it was Clara Bell Walsh who personified their ilk. In 1957, in honor of Walsh's birthday and her supposed half-century spent living at the hotel, the Plaza threw her a lavish party. Guests ranged from musical star Ethel Merman to retired head Plaza waiter Jack Koch. When a photographer asked her to pose for pictures, Walsh quipped, "What do you want us to do, swing through the trees?" She said that the bouquets of yellow snapdragons that filled the room were "more appropriate at a gangster's funeral," and told an inquiring reporter that her age was "none of your business."[35]

At the party, Walsh was described as "a tall Junoesque figure," and, echoing earlier commentators, the *New York Times* noted, "Her health is so good she never gives it a thought, eating whatever and as much as she likes and drinking only pure, Kentucky bourbon."[36] But talk of Walsh's strong constitution was more fiction than fact. Five months later, just a few weeks shy of the Plaza's half-century mark, Walsh suffered a cerebral hemorrhage in her suite and died.[37]

The thirty-nine widows rose to prominence just as the men who had created the hotel passed away in quick succession. In 1933, three years after Harry Black's suicide, Frederick Sterry, the Plaza's

first manager, died. Sterry's death came on the heels of Bernhard
Beinecke's, who passed away the year before. Beinecke was age
eighty-six when he died in his Plaza suite, surrounded by his wife of
more than fifty years and his extended family.[38]

Beinecke's widow continued to live at the hotel, as did several of
his children. Edwin J. Beinecke rented Black's old penthouse atop
the Plaza, moving into the glamorous twenty-two-room apartment
with his wife and daughter just three months after Black ended his
life. Edwin's sister, Theodora, also lived at the hotel, although in
later years she suffered from acute depression, brought on by the
death of her husband, followed just three weeks later by the death
of their only child. In 1940, Theodora jumped from the window of
her parents' twelfth-floor Plaza suite, clad only in a blue satin dinner dress. Her note read, "Please forgive me. I seem to be sick most
of the time."[39]

Just as these Plaza founders passed away, so the Plaza they had
envisioned faded from view. Following the 1929 crash, the Great
Depression took hold and factories closed, skyscrapers emptied of
workers, and the jobless hawked apples in the street. In 1930, the
year of Black's suicide, 26,000 businesses failed, and more than four
million Americans were unable to find a job. In 1933, the year that
Frederick Sterry died, President Herbert Hoover was voted out of
office and Franklin Delano Roosevelt replaced him.

The new president immediately began implementing his New
Deal to shore up stressed financial institutions and get the unemployed back to work. But despite President Roosevelt's best efforts,
the Great Depression persisted, and with it, the country's hotel
rooms, ballrooms, and restaurants remained mostly vacant, devoid
of paying guests. Parents stopped holding lavish coming-out parties
for their debutante daughters, while young couples opted against
extravagant weddings, or, in some cases, marriage at all.

At the Plaza, the taxis lining the front entrance stood idle as customers took the subway or walked, and the hansom cab drivers across Fifty-Ninth Street dozed off in boredom. The Pulitzer Fountain was crumbling; the limestone pedestal on which Pomona, the goddess of plenty, welcomed Plaza guests, was chipped and the fountain lip so cracked that water stopped shooting from its spigots.[40] Central Park became home to squatters, who built shelters from cardboard and brick, their makeshift village, known as a Hooverville, so complete that the post office began delivering mail to them there.[41]

With the economy in shambles, the nation's hotel industry, the Plaza included, slipped into the red. The average hotel occupancy rate—the ratio of occupied guest rooms to the total number of rooms—went from around 70 percent in 1929, to 51 percent by 1932.[42] In other words, hotels were just barely half full. This trend was exacerbated by the sheer number of hotels that were competing with one another, many built in the heyday of the 1920s, such as Black's Savoy-Plaza. To attract guests and increase their occupancy, hotels began to slash their prices. "Desperate attempts were made to retain old customers and attract new ones from other hotels by reducing rates," wrote the *Harvard Business Review.* "The other hotels countered with sharper reductions, and the practice continued with rates going down and down."[43]

Between 1929 and 1933, the cost of hotel rooms dropped an average of 30 percent, but at the same time, hotels struggled to cut their operating costs. Just because there were fewer guests, and those who did check in paid a lower rate, did not mean that hotels could curtail their food service, shut off their heat, or stop paying what remained of their skeletal staff. This mix of an oversupply of rooms, lower room prices, and numerous fixed costs was a toxic brew. "Few industries in the United States suffered more severely than the hotel business in the depression," wrote the *Harvard Business Review*. In 1932, at the depths of the downturn, an astounding 81 percent of the nation's hotels filed for bankruptcy.[44]

The Plaza was not immune to the same economic ills. In 1933, the Plaza Operating Company, the subsidiary of the U.S. Realty & Improvement Company that owned the Plaza, posted a net loss of nearly $708,000.[45] With little money for maintenance, the Plaza's facade grew dingy, its white marble turning gray from pollution and grime. Inside, the Plaza's tapestries became threadbare, its oak paneling dulled and pockmarked. The hotel's mechanical under-pinnings, once so cutting-edge that the *New York Times* described them in minute detail, began breaking down.[46] Staff sometimes waited weeks for their paychecks, and transient guests were occasionally forced to carry their own luggage.

In a bid to save on costs, the hotel closed many of its once-fashionable gathering places. The downstairs Grill Room, the favored hangout of F. Scott Fitzgerald, became a storage closet. The Rose Room was rented out to the Studebaker Company for an automobile showroom; when the car company left, the Rose Room, too, was shuttered. On most evenings there was just one lonely Plaza restaurant for guests to choose from, the Fifth Avenue Café, at the spot that would later become the Edwardian Room. Still, the thirty-nine widows of the Plaza remained, a steady presence helping to shore up the hotel's increasingly precarious financials. By the 1930s, the number of permanent residents, who had once made up 90 percent of the hotel's guests, had dwindled to four hundred, or about half of the rooms. Their presence was critical, as they paid regular rent on which the hotel could depend, with some permanent residents shelling out as much as $27,500 a year, or the equivalent of $280,000 today.[47]

But even the widows couldn't stop the bad news from piling on. One pressing issue was the cost of labor. The early 1930s saw major upheavals among workers across the country, with some two thousand strikes taking place in 1934 alone. In 1935, the government passed the Wagner Act, which outlawed unfair labor practices. New York hotel workers had been trying to unionize for years, with failed attempts in 1912, 1918, 1929, and 1934.[48] This time, however, the city hotel workers would be successful.

Ten months of intense negotiations concluded in the early morning hours of December 28, 1938, when, after a raucous meeting that stretched more than five hours, a contract between hotel employees and owners was reached. Among the stipulations was the agreement to set minimum weekly wages for hotel workers at $9 for waiters, $7.50 for waitresses, and $18 for telephone operators.[49] It was just a starting point, since over the next nine years, hourly average earnings for hotel workers would more than double.[50]

The union contract covered 60,000 hotel workers across 160 New York hotels, but some employees were excluded from the deal. In 1939, there were more than 5,000 African American hotel workers in New York, but just 2,000 were members of the union.[51] "It is common knowledge throughout the country that there are countless unions which, despite official resolutions and pronouncements, either openly bar Race workers from membership in their lily white unions by clauses in their constitutions, by-laws or rituals—or else covertly practice discrimination," wrote the *Chicago Defender*, an African American newspaper.[52] To combat this, the CHENY Cultural League, which stood for Colored Hotel Employees of New York, was established in Harlem. Its purpose was "to make Negro hotel workers more aware of the principles underlying trade unionism as well as to promote the general welfare of the Negro hotel workers," wrote the *New York Amsterdam News*.[53]

The color barrier wasn't a hurdle just for hotel employees. Unsurprisingly, guests, too, were victims of discrimination. The *Afro-American*, which was started by a former slave, wrote about the experiences of black guests at the large hotels in New York:

" 'We have orders to direct all colored people to the freight elevator,' is a refrain that will greet you upon entering eight out of ten hotels in the City of New York," it reported. "You might be a servant, you see, and they cannot take any chances." The newspaper added that "the average New Yorker does not know and the individual outside of New York would never believe to what extent the Negro is discriminated against in America's biggest and most cosmopolitan city." The Plaza, noted the *Afro-American*, was not exempt: "Many hotels will not permit a tenant to employ colored servants. Such a case came to light only recently," it noted, when the Plaza refused to allow a young African American girl to attend to her white boss.[54]

Even as racial discrimination persisted among both hotel workers and guests, some managed to squeeze through the color barrier. Emmita Casanova was an African American beauty and a showgirl in the famous Ziegfeld Follies. Adventuresome from the start, Casanova ran away from college with the football team's star quarterback. She then moved to Europe, where she "gave the Continentals a treat, leaving behind a hubby with two children."[55] When Casanova returned to New York, Florenz Ziegfeld took notice of her and cast her in his theatrical revue. She was "the most exotic girl," whose eyes had "the sensuousness of the lotus flower," rhapsodized Walter Winchell, the famous Broadway columnist, in a review that claimed the light-skinned Casanova hailed from Cordova, Spain.[56]

While Casanova was performing at the Follies, she met the son of the African American composer and violinist Clarence Cameron White, and the couple married at the Plaza. "Emmita Casanova, show girl in 'A Night in Venice,' is authority for the statement that she will marry William White, a lawyer, today at the Hotel Plaza," read a notice in the *New York Herald Tribune*.[57] Days later, the couple's race was revealed, causing an apparent scandal. "Married in the Plaza hotel, news of the couple's wedding 'broke' on the first pages of metropolitan daily newspapers, which were totally unaware that they were Negroes," reported the *New York Amsterdam News.*[58]

While racism remained a persistent problem, one barrier that hotels faced would soon be removed. During these years, the will to overturn Prohibition gained steam as proponents of repeal argued that the law was not only unenforceable, but it had given rise to violent gangsters and bootleggers. In 1933, thirteen years after it was instituted, Congress ratified the Twenty-First Amendment, repealing Prohibition. Despite the ongoing economic downturn, or perhaps because of it, guests needed a respite from the doom and gloom. Now that serving alcohol was legal, hotels quickly offered it up as a salve.

Immediately following Prohibition's repeal, the Plaza converted a shuttered corner of the hotel at Fifty-Eighth Street and Fifth Avenue into the Persian Room. The nightclub was decked out with a twenty-seven-foot bar, and the hotel lavished nearly $1 million in today's dollars on designs. Joseph Urban, a Viennese painter who had made a name creating sets for Ziegfeld's Follies, designed the interior, with window drapes made from rich red velvet, upholstered chairs in a brighter shade of the same hue, and room accents in the unusual color of Persian blue. The painter Lillian Gaertner Palmedo heightened the ambience with five wall murals, portraying "in luminous colors the pleasures of dancing, singing, hunting, eating and drinking in Persian fashion."[59]

This was the start of "Café Society," with crowds flocking to small nightclubs, paying 55 cents for a sip of gin and $3 for a full dinner to forget about their troubles. The Persian Room, where guests could watch Tony and Renee DeMarco ballroom dance while listening to the handsome bandleader Eddy Duchin, proved to be a major money-earner for the Plaza.[60] It was also a hit with the fashion crowd. On the Persian Room's opening night, photographers snapped the socialite Lucile Harris in a turban headpiece, a nod to the room's theme, and soon turbans were all the rage in the Fifth Avenue boutiques. The department store B. Altman & Co. rolled out dresses "in colors taken from the murals in the new Persian room of the Plaza Hotel," while reporters from *Women's Wear Daily* duly noted how dresses of black velvet and silver lamé, fur stoles, and short hair crowded the club. One daring guest attracted gasps when she slid across the Persian Room's dance floor in a dress "slit about six times and irregular in length so that the longest slit on one side revealed the leg right up to the knee."[61]

During this period, the Plaza's ballroom also continued hosting glamorous parties, albeit in smaller numbers than it had before the Depression. Many events were charity fund-raisers, such as the oddly named "Fun and Frolic" benefit for "crippled children."[62] A popular series of lunches benefited families devastated by the Depression, with wealthy Plaza patrons "adopting" families for $15 a week. One needy family of six, who counted four children ranging in age from five months to four years, lived together "in a cold flat with hardly any food in the house," reported one newspaper. "Because of their previous comfortable standard of living, both parents are on the verge of a nervous breakdown. The gas has been discontinued and the babies have milk only when relatives, who are doing all they can to help, give a few cents." The luncheons raised more than $3 million in today's dollars.[63]

Eventually, the economy began to dig itself out of the doldrums, pulling the Plaza along with it. While in 1933, the Plaza posted a loss of almost $708,000, by 1935 that loss had shrunk to $562,000, and by 1936, the hotel showed a loss of less than $135,000.[64] As the years went on, it looked more and more likely that the Plaza would be one of just 19 percent of the country's hotels to make it through the Great Depression without declaring bankruptcy. Yet, while it now appeared the Plaza was a survivor, its parent company could not claim the same.

FIFTH AVENUE SKATING POND.

SEASON TICKET.

NOT TRANSFERABLE under any CIRCUMSTANCES.

Admit *Miss Isabel Place*

Members have the privilege of bringing friends with them, who can be admitted on payment of 25 cents at the Gate. No person will be admitted unless in company with a Regular Subscriber.

J. L. Brown

BUCOLIC ORIGINS: The site of the Plaza Hotel was once a skating pond, where New York's social elite enjoyed a wintry thrill surrounded by rolling hills and fields. Here is a season pass for the exclusive Fifth Avenue Skating Pond, circa 1863. *Credit: Museum of the City of New York*

FIRST PLAZA: The first Plaza Hotel was an eight-story structure with a brick-and-brownstone facade, four hundred guest rooms, and a famous painting of a lion by the Massachusetts artist Alexander Pope Jr. It was, for a time, considered one of New York's grandest hotels. Here is how it appeared in 1894. *Credit: H.N. Tiemann & Co. / Museum of the City of New York*

DEMOLITION: A dozen years after opening, the first Plaza was torn down in the space of just eight weeks. In its place, a new white marble edifice, which still stands today, began rising. Here, workers in 1905 remove the foundation of the original Plaza. *Photo by Museum of the City of New York / Byron Collection / Getty Images*

DEBONAIRE BLACK: A rare photo of a young Harry S. Black, the man who spearheaded the building of the current Plaza Hotel. It may have been taken when Black attended the 1893 Chicago World's Fair, where he met George A. Fuller, the inventor of the modern skyscraper and his future father-in-law. *Courtesy of Beth Pringle*

SKYSCRAPER TYCOON: Over the years, Black transformed himself from a young, ambitious builder to a real estate titan, helming the country's first-ever skyscraper trust. As owner of the Plaza, Black was a charismatic risk-taker who both confounded and fascinated those who knew him. *Courtesy of the Ralph Corey Family*

HUMBLE START: Bernhard Beinecke was a German emigre who arrived in New York as a penniless teenager. Starting off pushing a meat cart through the Lower East Side, Beinecke eventually became one of the city's wealthiest butchers. In middle age, he transformed himself once more, turning into a hotelier and partnering with Harry Black to build the Plaza. Here he is, circa 1904. *Credit: Beinecke Family Records. General Collection, Beinecke Rare Book and Manuscript Library, Yale University*

PLAZA MASTERMIND: Henry Janeway Hardenbergh, the architect of the original Waldorf-Astoria and the Dakota apartment building, designed the Plaza as his masterpiece. While well-known during his lifetime, he remains a mercurial figure, with few surviving biographical details. *Credit: Canadian Centre for Architecture*

WHITE BEACON: The Plaza was designed as a French chateau in skyscraper proportions, with a facade of marble and white terracotta, and a copper mansard roof that reflected the green of nearby Central Park. Here it is in 1920, dominating the skyline. *Credit: Byron Company (New York, N.Y.) / Museum of the City of New York*

PLAZA ON PARADE: On the Plaza's opening day, October 1, 1907, a stream of New York's wealthiest citizens arrived to check in to the hotel. None was more celebrated than the dashing Alfred Gwynne Vanderbilt, who remains indelible as the hotel's inaugural guest. Here he is with his first wife, Elsie French, whom he divorced shortly after moving into the Plaza. *Credit: Interim Archives / Archive Photos / Getty Images*

QUINTESSENTIAL NEW YORK: On the Plaza's opening day, not only was the iconic hotel introduced to New Yorkers, but so was another indispensable city accoutrement. Here, the first-ever New York City taxicabs line up along the Fifth Avenue side of the Plaza, awaiting their first passengers. It wasn't long before these taxis displaced horse-drawn hansom cabs as New Yorkers' transportation of choice. *Courtesy of the National Automotive History Collection, Detroit Public Library*

PLUNGERS: Inside its doors, the Plaza was sumptuously outfitted with lavish furnishings in brocades of rose and green, more than one thousand crystal chandeliers, and elevators featuring glass doors through which the mechanical pistons could be seen. Called "plungers," these elevators were a technological feat, and remained in use well into the 1970s. Here, an image of the lobby as it appeared on opening day 1907. *Credit: Byron Company (New York, N.Y.) / Museum of the City of New York*

TEA TIME: The tea room, later named the Palm Court, featured a curved ceiling made of colored glass that let in daylight, and oversized palm trees and rubber plants, lending the room a garden-like ambience. It was here that the British actress Mrs. Patrick Campbell scandalized patrician patrons by lighting up a cigarette shortly after the hotel's opening. *Credit: Byron Company (New York, N.Y.) / Museum of the City of New York*

PENTHOUSE APPEAL: In 1921, Harry S. Black built an extension on the Plaza, and created for himself a sprawling penthouse on the eighteenth floor, replete with Tiffany chandeliers, a walk-in wine vault, and views that stretched across Manhattan. Here are some images of his library and living room, taken between 1923 and 1925. *Credit: Beinecke Family Papers. Beinecke Rare Book and Manuscript Library, Yale University*

REPEAL: In 1920, the country went dry under Prohibition, and crowds shunned hotels like the Plaza in favor of illegal speakeasies. In 1933, when the dry laws were finally repealed, the Plaza celebrated by turning a shuttered corner of the hotel into the Persian Room, a swank nightclub that boasted a twenty-seven-foot bar and Persian murals by the painter Lillian Gaertner Palmedo, pictured here. *Credit: Bettmann/Getty Images*

CAFE SOCIETY: In the 1940s, as World War II raged and the Plaza was inundated with soldiers, Hildegarde often held court at the Persian Room. A beautiful chanteuse, Hildegarde was famous for singing for her many military fans, kissing them on the cheeks or bald spots between tunes. Here she is in 1946. *Photo by Eileen Darby / The LIFE Images Collection / Getty Images*

COWBOY CONNIE: In 1947, Conrad Hilton became the hotel's second owner, and Plaza blue bloods immediately marked him as an uncouth Westerner who would upend their beloved institution. Despite being treated with disdain, Hilton lavished millions of dollars on the aging hotel, eventually quelling his critics' fears and earning their begrudging respect. *Photo by Yale Joel / The LIFE Picture Collection / Getty Images*

DOWAGER DOYENNES: The Plaza was known for many years as home to a number of rich, eccentric residents, collectively known as the thirty-nine widows of the Plaza. They could often be found congregating in the hotel lobby, taking up positions on a favorite chaise lounge or settee, where they would while away the hours listening to the harpsichord wafting from the Palm Court or lobbing a string of complaints at the hotel staff. *Photo by Jerry Cooke / The LIFE Images Collection / Getty Images*

ROYAL ECCENTRIC: Princess Lwoff-Parlaghy was one of the most famous thirty-nine widows of the Plaza. Of murky royal lineage, she was a portrait painter and an animal lover, causing quite a scene when she arrived at the Plaza with owls, alligators, and eventually, a pet lion who lived in her bathtub. Here she is in *New Broadway Magazine* in 1908, in an article titled "Prominent People in Picture and Paragraph." *Credit: General Research Division, The New York Public Library*

FANCY PANTS: Kay Thompson was a singer and dancer who performed regularly at the Persian Room. She was the main focal point of the act, with the four Williams Brothers in dark matching suits moving in choreographed unison behind her. The fact that Thompson was the star, superseding the men, was notable, as were her trademark pants and her tiny, twenty-three-inch waist. Here she performs with her act in 1951. Andy Williams is second from right. *Credit: NBC / Photofest*

SKIPPERDEE: While Kay Thompson was a notable performer, it was in book publishing that she achieved true fame. Joining with a young illustrator, Hilary Knight, the pair published *Kay Thompson's Eloise: A Book for Precocious Grown Ups* in 1955. It was an immediate blockbuster, and the Plaza, grateful for the publicity, gave Thompson a free suite, where she lived, off and on, for years. Here, Thompson hams it up with a young actress playing her diminutive alter ego. *Credit: CBS Photo Archive / CBS / Getty Images*

BEATLEMANIA: In 1964, four mop-haired musicians from Liverpool descended on New York, and mass frenzy gripped the city. The Beatles stayed at the Plaza for their first New York visit, and the staid hotel was inundated for days by hordes of hysterical teenyboppers. Here, fans run in front of the Plaza to meet the arriving musicians. *Credit: NY Daily News Archive / New York Daily News / Getty Images*

MCCARTNEY MOMENT: While countless young fans tried to sneak up the Plaza's back staircase into the Beatles' twelfth-floor suite, Gregg Salomone, whose father managed the hotel, strolled through the front door of the musician's rooms. Here, a six-year-old Gregg stands with Ringo, Paul, and George, as well as his sister Lourdes and her friend Bunny Castalano. Gregg's hand is hovering over his crotch because moments earlier, Paul had pointed out that his fly was open. *Courtesy of Gregg Salomone*

ODD COUPLE: In 1966, Truman Capote was reveling in the runaway success of his true-life crime thriller *In Cold Blood*. To celebrate, he decided to throw himself the "party of the century" in the Plaza's Grand Ballroom. Realizing it was uncouth to have the fete in his own honor, he picked Katharine Graham, the publisher of the *Washington Post*, to be the honoree. Here, the diminutive author arrives with his date. *Credit: Bettmann / Getty Images*

CULTURE WARS: By 1969, the Vietnam War, civil rights, and women's equality were dominating the headlines. The Plaza's old-fashioned Oak Room, an all-male bastion that prohibited female diners, soon came under fire from the National Organization for Women. Here, feminists, including Betty Friedan, picket the hotel before entering the restaurant hoping to be served. *Credit: New York Daily News Archive / Getty Images*

CITY ON THE BRINK: In the 1970s, New York City was plagued by drugs, a soaring crime rate, and the possibility of bankruptcy. During two days in July 1977, a citywide electricity blackout struck and the city's residents were plunged into mayhem, with looting and arson across many neighborhoods. Here, guests at the Plaza's Palm Court are forced to dine by candlelight. *Credit: AP Photo/Calvin C. Cook*

OOZING STENCH: Throughout the 1970s, sanitation workers went on multiple strikes, including one in 1975 that resulted in the Plaza's basement being filled to capacity with rotting garbage. Finally, with no room left inside the building, the hotel began dumping its waste outside, creating enormous garbage piles on the sidewalk beside its Fifty-Eighth Street entrance. *Credit: J. Michael Dombroski/Newsday*

REBRANDING: Faced with the challenges of the 1970s, the Plaza tried to shed its reputation as an old-age home for rich ladies and to refashion itself as a destination for the hip crowd. Here, an advertising insert in the Sunday *New York Times* features psychedelic swirls, pop star acts like Dusty Springfield, and a new, democratic tagline, "The Plaza is something for everybody." *Credit: New-York Historical Society*

GO-GO EIGHTIES: With the advent of the 1980s came shoulder pads, hairspray, and Donald Trump. At the peak of the decade of excess, the real estate magnate paid a historic sum to acquire the Plaza, a hotel he had long coveted. Trump had a direct view of the hotel from his office on the twenty-sixth floor of Trump Tower, and would often stare at the building, which he dubbed "the Mona Lisa," as he mapped out a strategy to acquire it. *Photo by Joe McNally / Hulton Archive / Getty Images*

PRESIDENTIAL FIRST: As soon as he acquired the Plaza, Trump appointed his wife Ivana as the hotel's president—the first and only time a woman has held the position. In a press conference announcing her new job, Trump famously quipped that he would pay her "$1 and all the dresses she can buy." *Credit: Norman Parkinson / Iconic Images / Premium Archive / Getty Images*

GROUND ZERO GAFFE: After Trump bankrupted the Plaza, the Saudi Prince Alwaleed bin Talal and his billionaire partner, Singaporean Kwek Leng Beng, swooped in to purchase the hotel. On October 11, 2001, the one-month anniversary of the World Trade Center attack, Alwaleed visited Ground Zero to hand then-mayor Rudolph Giuliani a $10 million check to help with the rebuilding efforts, seen here. Hours later, comments made by the Saudi owner of the Plaza drew immediate censure, prompting Giuliani to return the money. *Credit: AP Photo / Stan Honda, pool*

HAND-OFF: By 2004, the owners of the Plaza were ready to offload the hotel. An ambitious Israeli-born condominium developer, Miki Naftali, flew to Singapore and convinced Kwek Leng Beng to sell him the historic property. Here, at the closing ceremony celebrating the sale, Naftali stands next to his boss, Isaac Tshuva, as well as Kwek Leng Beng and his son Sherman (R-L). The men hold a check representing the Plaza's price tag, and this time, unlike with Prince Alwaleed and Mayor Giuliani, no one returned the money. *Credit: Steve Friedman*

PLAZA PROTESTS: In 2005, the Plaza was set to close for a multi-year renovation that would transform the hotel into exclusive condominiums for the very wealthy, as well as a small boutique hotel. The labor union that represented hundreds of middle-class doormen, bellmen, and housekeepers who stood to lose their jobs, decided to fight back. Here, workers begin gathering for one of many protests they held in front of the hotel. *Courtesy of the New York Hotel Trades Council, AFL-CIO*

HOTEL ACCORD: In the end, after months of difficult negotiations, the hotel workers and the Plaza ownership struck a deal. Negotiated with the help of Mayor Michael Bloomberg, seen here celebrating with workers, the Plaza agreed to retain 282 hotel rooms and 350 hotel jobs. *Credit: AP Photo / Kathy Willens*

BIRTHDAY PARTY: The Plaza's centennial was in October 2007, and even though the building was closed for renovations, the owners celebrated with lavish abandon. The party included a twelve-foot cake replica of the hotel, an original song performance by Paul Anka, and what may have been the largest-ever pyrotechnic display attempted from atop a building. *Credit: Konrad Tho Fiedler / New York Sun*

OSTENTATIOUS OWNER: In 2012, a new hotelier took over the Plaza. Subrata Roy was a colorful Indian tycoon who claimed to employ more workers than any other company in India, save for the Indian railroad. A regular on the celebrity circuit, Roy was known for partying with Bollywood stars, cricketers, and politicians, and for grand displays. Here, thousands of his employees stand in nearly 100-degree heat to break the Guinness World Record for the greatest number of people singing the national anthem. *Credit: Bloomberg / Getty Images*

SCANDAL: Just a month after Roy acquired the Plaza, the Indian Supreme Court ordered him to repay $3 billion plus interest to nearly thirty-one million poor Indians who had bought his company's bonds. Here, as Roy made his way to the country's Supreme Court in New Delhi, he was attacked by a critic who splattered him with black ink and called him a thief. *Credit: AP Photo*

Harry Black's U.S. Realty & Improvement Company, the first skyscraper trust, had cut its stock dividends in 1914, but resumed payments during the heady Jazz Age. In 1931, it once again began slicing its stock dividends, until it finally stopped issuing them altogether. The Savoy-Plaza, which Black built at the peak of the Roaring Twenties, causing Bernhard Beinecke to shake his head in dismay, went bankrupt. Other U.S. Realty & Improvement properties soon followed suit. "The condition of the hotels of the country, in general, shows that they have ceased to be profitable ventures," R. G. Babbage, a faithful deputy to Black and his successor at U.S. Realty & Improvement, wrote in a letter to shareholders.[65] Investors were fleeing the company as its stock traded at just a fraction of its high, the share price now fluctuating between the teens and the single digits.

In 1936, R. G. Babbage retired as the company's president and Edwin Beinecke, Bernhard's son, who had worked over the years in various roles at the company, succeeded him. It was perhaps fitting that Edwin, who had moved with his family into Black's penthouse at the Plaza, should now take over his real estate trust.[66] But while Edwin may have been a logical heir, he was unable to stem the company's losses. On the day he took the helm of the U.S. Realty & Improvement Company, the stock was trading at $9 a share—three years later it had hit a low of $1.[67]

By 1942, with the national economy rebounding, U.S. Realty was in worse shape than ever. The company began shedding its assets, dismantling the skyscraper trust that Black had so carefully erected. It sold buildings and subsidiaries and, finally, offered up the George A. Fuller Construction Company to bidders. The sale of the original firm, which had been started by Black's father-in-law and was the foundation on which Black had built his unprecedented real estate conglomerate, was a moment of brutal defeat. It was also the final blow for U.S. Realty's most prized property.

The Plaza had always been under the same ownership, stretching for more than three decades. But thirty-six years after Vanderbilt walked through the doors to become its first hotel guest, the Plaza was finally sold. This would be the beginning of a journey that would see the hotel pass from owner to owner as if in a game of hot potato. Over the next century, famous and ambitious men would try leveraging the Plaza's name for their own gain, slowly chipping away at the institution's once-impervious facade, incrementally damaging it until it was almost irreparable.

For this first handover, Conrad N. Hilton, an up-and-coming hotel magnate, took ownership of the Plaza. Hilton paid a measly $7.4 million to U.S. Realty, a 40 percent discount off the Plaza's original $12.5 million price tag.[68] By then, Edwin Beinecke had resigned, relocating to England to serve as an executive at the Red Cross.[69] As for the once-great U.S. Realty & Improvement Company, it retreated to a small headquarters in the village of Flemington, New Jersey. In 1944, with just four properties to its name, the original skyscraper trust filed for bankruptcy.[70]

Chapter 7

WARTIME

"To hell with domesticity and living at home. Anybody's a
fool who doesn't live in a hotel."
—*Lillian Hellman*

From the start, Conrad N. Hilton, a six-foot-two Westerner with
a movie star wife and a mansion in Los Angeles, struck fear in
the hearts of Plaza traditionalists. This would be the first time an
outsider was in charge of the hotel, and it would not be an easy
transition.

When Hilton, known as "Connie," strode through his newly
purchased hotel, admiring his latest acquisition, the thirty-nine
widows stationed themselves at their regular spots on the lobby's
settees, glaring in resentment. When Hilton wrote them each a
personal letter, trying to reassure them that he would be a good
steward of their home, the permanent residents tossed his missives
aside. When Hilton dared update the breakfast menu, Clara Bell
Walsh made "impassioned threats to leave the premises," and when
he tried enlivening the Palm Court with new potted shrubbery, she
was apoplectic.[1] "With the coming of Hilton they anticipated the
glitter of the dime store," wrote Thomas Ewing Dabney in *The Man
Who Bought the Waldorf: The Life of Conrad N. Hilton*. "In some

small way, the feeling was comparable to the apprehension in Rome on the approach of Attila the Hun."[2]

It was not just the prickly widows with which Hilton was forced to contend. In 1939, World War II had broken out in Europe, and with the bombing of Pearl Harbor in December 1941, America joined the fighting. Across the country, factories that had been idle during the length of the Great Depression once again turned on their conveyor belts, churning out tanks and army uniforms for the war effort. Members of the labor force, meanwhile, began to awaken as if from a long slumber, finally rejoining the ranks of the fully employed.

In New York, however, it was another matter. The city's manufacturing sector was not equipped to handle the machinery and other industrial equipment needed in wartime. So even as other parts of the country were resurgent, New York remained in abysmal shape. As late as mid-1942, there were fifty thousand more people registered as unemployed in New York City than there had been in 1939.[3]

It was just as bleak for New York's hotel industry. The 1920s hotel boom had left a glut of oversupply, which kept downward pressure on hotel room rates. There was also a shortage of supplies resulting from the war effort, and the grim realities of wartime rationing. In 1944, the year that Harry Black's U.S. Realty & Improvement Company filed for bankruptcy and a year after it had sold the Plaza to Hilton, wartime prosperity was peaking across much of the country. Yet, in New York, the rates that hotels were charging guests for rooms were still below the highs that were reached during the heyday of the 1920s.[4]

At the Plaza, for instance, when Hilton took over, just 61 percent of its rooms were occupied, and many of its public areas remained shuttered.[5] Just as during World War I, "conservation" and "restraint" were the watchwords. Housekeepers were ordered to limit the amount of stationery they inserted into desk drawers and the number of coat hangers they hung in the closets. No extra rolls of toilet paper were stacked in bathrooms, and even complimentary face soaps were reduced from ¾-ounce to ½-ounce portions.[6] Napkins were made smaller to save on linen, and if they remained untouched by guests, they were reused before washing. With wartime foodstuffs being diverted to feed troops, waiters were barred from offering mints or petits fours gratis to diners at the close of a meal. Jam and marmalade weren't offered either, unless requested; free coffee refills were halted; and hotel managers were urged to use smaller dippers for ice cream scoops.

Just as it had been during the last war, sugar was an especially rare commodity. Articles such as "Cooking and Baking without Sugar" were popular, as were advertisements for "sugar-server envelopes," which promised to "put an end to the irritating monotony of asking every customer if he or she wants sugar," while simultaneously diminishing the risk of spillage or waste. Hotels even hired guards to protect their supplies. "Sugar is being placed in the control of a designated person and all supplies allotted thru one source," *Hotel Monthly* wrote of one hotel's practice.[7]

Meat rations were instituted, and the Plaza began searching for alternatives. There was "roast larded Dakota bison," which "rather surprises" diners, the chef admitted,[8] and once again, Meatless Mondays became a matter of patriotism.[9] The Plaza also began serving more cold entrees, like "ham printaniere," which involved whipping together boiled ham, cream sauce, and lukewarm meat jelly, then adding heavy cream and chilling the concoction in the refrigerator before serving.[10] Lamb stew also was on offer, and as the *New York Times* noted, "If the great Plaza, known for dignity plus glamour makes a to-do over lamb stew, why should any housewife feel apologetic over serving such a dish to her family?"

Hotels, in addition to struggling with food rationing, had to contend with a shortage of critical machinery to fix equipment like elevators and laundries, as the tools and parts were diverted over-seas for the war effort. There was also the constant threat of blackouts, air-raid drills, and extreme shortages in staffing. Like many male-dominated industries, hotels were having trouble hiring employees, having to compete with the draft and high-salaried factory jobs.

Plaza bellboy Michael J. McKeogh, for instance, was drafted to be the chauffeur for Dwight D. Eisenhower. He spent the war years driving the commander in chief of the Allied forces to vari-ous meetings, including to No. 10 Downing Street to strategize the Normandy invasion.[11] For other Plaza employees, the hotel became a refuge. The Sachs family, for instance, came to the Plaza after escaping Nazi Germany. Herman Sachs had been an associate judge in the ministry of justice there, and he now operated the Plaza's ser-vice elevator, while his wife, Marta, worked in the kitchen.[12]

As hotels struggled to find workers, they began searching outside their typical applicant pool. Just as Rosie the Riveter inspired women to work in factories, so hotel kitchens, long the domain of men, were suddenly occupied by female chefs, or "cheferrettes." Discussions abounded on whether the term "bellmen" should be replaced with "bellwomen"[13]; and one hotelier in Yakima, Washington, invented a lightweight baggage cart with rubber wheels to help his female staff more easily lug guests' baggage.[14] The Plaza even had a female credit manager, Sheila B. Lee, who was so notable that she made guest appearances on local radio shows and received fan mail.[15] "Women who have replaced men at the front office desk are doing a good job," reported *Hotel Monthly*. "Several hotel men said that except for the night shift, they would keep the fair sex on after the war."[16]

It wasn't only women who benefited from the dearth of available workers. Just as with the waiter strike of 1912, African Americans were hired for jobs that had previously been closed to them. "Thou-sands of competent colored women [are] prepared to serve as wait-resses, dieticians, cooks, elevator operators, maids, clerical helpers, and in other capacities," noted the Tuskegee Institute, calling them "forgotten daughters of democracy. Like her dark-skinned brother, the colored woman worker desires and requests an opportunity to contribute her share in the battle for what we believe is our right and our heritage."[17]

It was in this challenging atmosphere, with its rationing and staffing shortages, that Hilton took over the Plaza. The new owner had much in common with his predecessor, Harry Black; both men were characterized by outsized ambitions and busy social calendars. Hilton, like Black, had also come to the Plaza from humble beginnings, and for both men, the hotel represented a means for establishment, a currency that could be used to turn mere wealth into pedigree and social status.

Hilton was born on Christmas Day 1887 in San Antonio, Texas, a town of dirt horse paths and farmland so inconsequential that it wasn't even included in the census.[18] His parents were pioneers, and Hilton grew up in an adobe bungalow in what was still the New Mexico Territory. It was an upbringing as far removed from the East Coast power center of New York City as one could be without leaving the confines of the United States. Like Black, Hilton, too, began his career at a general store. It was owned by his father, and it sold everything from dress fabrics to wagon wheels. There, Hilton honed his negotiating skills, and, despite a sporadic education, he displayed a talent for numbers, uncannily tallying up large figures in his head.

When Hilton was a young man, just a few weeks after the Plaza's grand opening in New York, the 1907 Panic that roiled Wall Street upended the Hilton family in faraway New Mexico. Just as Vanderbilt, Gates, and the other hotel residents were reveling in their luxurious new surroundings, the Hilton family's general store saw business drop precipitously. To make ends meet, Hilton's father converted part of the store into an inn and put his son in charge. It was then that a young Hilton had his first taste of running a hotel.

After some years, Hilton chose to strike out on his own. He ran for state legislature when New Mexico was voted into the Union in 1912 and, at age twenty-four, became the state's youngest assemblyman. But Hilton grew sick of the backroom dealings that dominated local politics and returned to business. He opened a bank, with the goal of opening a string of New Mexico banks, but the outbreak of World War I thwarted his efforts. Hilton became a second lieutenant and was sent first to San Francisco for training, then to France, where he was posted to Paris. Hilton's experience in the gilded, if besieged, City of Lights forever changed him, widening his worldview and whetting his appetite for adventure.

After the war, Hilton was thirty-one and casting about for his next move. As a boy, a New Mexico railroad baron had told him, "If you want to launch big ships, you have to go where the water is deep." Hilton now heeded that advice and left New Mexico for Texas. This was during the Coolidge Prosperity of the 1920s. More people had money to spend on travel, automobiles were becoming ever more common, and the nation was experiencing a hotel construction boom. Hilton hungrily partook of that expansion, opening first one, and then a string of hotels throughout the Lone Star State. By 1929, Hilton owned eighteen hundred hotel rooms in Texas, with deals to expand to Wichita, Kansas, and Mobile, Alabama.

Like Harry Black, and later owners such as Donald Trump, Hilton's ambition led him to constantly build up his business. But unlike these other men, Hilton adhered to mostly conservative financing strategies, including during the heady 1920s. "Even in the midst of this uproar he managed to keep his head and insist on two fundamentals: always deal with banks of the highest standing and always subscribe as much personally in any venture as any other single member of the syndicate," wrote his biographer, Dabney.[19]

Despite his conservatism, Hilton was no match for the disruption posed by the stock market crash in 1929, and the ensuing Great Depression. The hotelier's businesses grew ever more precarious until, finally, his lawyer suggested that Hilton file for bankruptcy. "Like hell I will!" Hilton replied. "Don't be silly," the lawyer responded. "The way you're going now you can't work this out in a thousand years. You haven't any choice." Hilton was bitter. "That sounds fine now, but how would it be later on? I'm in the hotel business and I want to stay in it. With a record like that who would ever trust me again?"[20] In the end, Hilton was forced to file for bankruptcy protection, but only for a single property. "It was no disgrace," wrote Dabney, because "most of the country was in the same boat."[21]

Hilton emerged from those brutal years with two-thirds of his hotel rooms still in his possession.[22] As the Depression began to dissipate, and the war economy began to churn, Hilton set about rebuilding his hotel empire. By the spring of 1943, he owned some of the country's most valuable properties, from the luxurious Dallas Hilton to the Town House in Los Angeles, where Hilton often stayed and where he soon moved his corporate headquarters. The next logical step was the East Coast.

Hilton zeroed in on New York, even though the city's economy remained sluggish and its hotels were unprofitable. Hilton was confident that it was only a matter of time before the prosperity that the rest of the country was experiencing would reach Manhattan. Wall Street investors greeted Hilton's optimism with ridicule, raising cynical brows as the newcomer began buying up hotel mortgage bonds at a deep discount. As late as 1942, New York "was half empty and hotel bondholders had long since employed their certificates for papering the rumpus room," Dabney wrote. "Hotels were new, gigantic, and hopelessly busted... Nobody seemingly perceived the possibility that there might be another turn in fortune."[23] Despite these naysayers, Hilton persisted. "I've never gambled on the stock market in my life," Hilton told a friend who questioned his investment strategy. "I'm not gambling now. I know hotels. They're getting healthy. This is the chance of a lifetime."[24]

Then, in June 1943, Hilton went beyond just buying hotel bonds and bought an actual New York City hotel.[25] The Roosevelt was in Midtown, adjacent to Grand Central Station. He liked it, Hilton wrote in his autobiography, *Be My Guest*, because it had "twenty-three stories, a thousand seventy-nine rooms, [and] a lobby that reminded me of the vast open spaces around San Antonio."[26]

As soon as Hilton's purchase of the Roosevelt was announced, the New York business elite solidified its attitude toward this uncouth cowboy from the West, treating Hilton with disdain. "It was scarcely flattering to have everyone assume that I would ride my horse into the lobby or install spittoons in the famous Roosevelt Grill," Hilton wrote. One New York State politician even put it into verse: "From what we hear it would appear there's been some changes made, / That great hotel, the Roos-e-velt, is mixed up in a trade. / Some bird named Connie Hilton from his California nest / Is gonna show New Yorkers how they do it in the west."[27]

Hilton's unusual moves—buying up hotel bonds when no one else wanted them and purchasing the Roosevelt when the industry was in the doldrums—were largely dismissed as the actions of a novice. But some contrarians on Wall Street were intrigued. Specifically, the Atlas Corporation, a conglomerate with stakes in businesses ranging from railroads to department stores. Atlas had money to invest but knew little about the hotel industry. The corporation approached Hilton about joining together to purchase the Plaza, and Hilton jumped on the opportunity. "For the first time the Big Money I'd prayed for, that I needed for expansion, made a move in my direction," Hilton recalled.[28] "It would be ridiculous to say that such subtle tribute to my talents left me unmoved after my initial welcome to the hotel business in New York."

So, four months after acquiring the Roosevelt, in October 1943, Hilton made an even bigger splash when he acquired 60 percent of the Plaza, with Atlas taking the remaining 40 percent stake. (Atlas would later exchange its ownership in the Plaza for a stake in Hilton's hotel chain.)[29] The purchase price for the Plaza was a bargain, at $7.4 million. U.S. Realty, on the verge of filing for bankruptcy, was so grateful for a buyer that it willingly accepted the deeply discounted number. The deal, which Hilton financed with $600,000 in cash and a mortgage, was "a master stroke," wrote Dabney. It proved "to the financial world that his ability to command money and his managerial success had made him Big Business."

The hotelier from the West wasn't finished conquering New York. Hilton followed up his Plaza purchase with a deal to acquire the Waldorf-Astoria, putting an exclamation point on his New York domination. In fact, Dabney's biography of Hilton had been called *The Man Who Bought the Plaza*, until the Waldorf acquisition forced the publisher to destroy dust jackets and reprint them with the amended title of *The Man Who Bought the Waldorf*. Hilton loved the Waldorf, keeping a picture of it on his desk with the phrase "The Greatest of Them All" scribbled on the image. But "in the most fundamental sense, the purchase of the Plaza was more important to Hilton's reputation," Dabney wrote.[30]

The Plaza that Hilton acquired was riddled with the battle scars of the Great Depression and wartime struggles. Hilton would eventually spend $6 million—nearly the hotel's full purchase price—to refurbish the property.[31] The Plaza, now under the Hilton banner, became part of a well-oiled national hotel operation that excelled at increasing efficiencies and, more importantly, squeezing out profits. One of Hilton's first moves was to reopen the Oak Bar, adjacent to the Oak Room. The space was converted following Prohibition into an office for the brokerage firm E. F. Hutton. The Wall Street brokerage was paying a minuscule $416 a month in rent,[32] so it was shunted upstairs to the mezzanine level.

Hilton outfitted the Oak Bar with murals by Everett Shinn, an American realist painter and a member of the Ashcan school. The works depicted early scenes from the hotel, including the old Vanderbilt mansion that had once been next door, and a moody rendering of the Pulitzer Fountain cloaked in moonlight. He built a bar that stretched thirty-eight feet, and installed sofas upholstered in what was described as "crimson novelty fabrics."[33] Guests were enamored with the space, and the Oak Bar was soon grossing $225,000 a year.[34]

Hilton's other improvements included refurbishing the Fifth Avenue lobby with two small sitting rooms on each side of a new arched entranceway, featuring a seventeenth-century Savonnerie rug. To generate more revenue, Hilton built glass display cases around the lobby and rented them out for between $500 and $2,000 a year; Plaza employees were offered a commission if they could secure a tenant.[35] In the Fifty-Ninth Street lobby there was a new flower shop, visible from the street, as well as an enlarged newsstand and a theater ticket desk. On the Fifty-Eighth Street side of the building, an outpost of the Bonwit Teller department store was opened.[36]

Keeping an ever-vigilant focus on reducing costs, Hilton also invested in new laundry equipment that enabled the hotel to cut in half the number of laundresses it employed,[37] and he created a safety program to help eliminate costly hotel accidents. He even instituted a ten-week training course to teach employees the principles of hotel management.[38] Hilton also leased out Harry Black's former home, the sprawling penthouse that had been mostly empty since Edwin Beinecke left, to a prestigious all-girls school. Later, the food magazine *Gourmet* would take over the space for its New York headquarters.

Hilton also asked various famous fans of the Plaza to decorate guest rooms that would be named for them, so-called designer suites, a marketing strategy that would be copied by later owners such as Donald Trump. Cecil Beaton, a British photographer and dandy who once showed up at a press conference wearing a leopard-skin robe and blue pajamas, was given free rein to choose what he wished for the suite. Beaton plumbed the depths of the Plaza's subbasement, where the hotel kept many of its original furnishings, draperies, and lights, and which, he said, rated "high on the list of the world's fascinating places." He chose red velvet chaises, terra-cotta cupids, and light fixtures made from "rose-colored Tiffany glass that look like clusters of opening tulips." The suite also featured extra-rococo gilt-framed mirrors, curtains appliqued with gold-thread birds, and a hallway covered with green billiard cloth studded with brass nailheads.[39]

One decision that Hilton made, which would later be considered a travesty of landmark proportions, was the removal of the graceful dome ceiling of the Palm Court. The laylight was dismantled to make way for the height of modernity—air-conditioning units and fluorescent lighting. Hilton replaced the graceful colored lead glass with "a flat, oddly perforated ceiling that doesn't look much like the French Renaissance to *us*," the *New Yorker* magazine complained.

In fact, Hilton's many renovations rankled the ever-discriminating chorus of Plaza observers. "Having been brought up on the works of F. Scott Fitzgerald, in which the Plaza Hotel, like Long Island and Skull and Bones, is made to stand for the visible splendor of life," the *New Yorker* wrote, "we have been upset lately by the sound of carpenters scurrying back and forth behind the Oak Room's opulent woodwork."[40] Plaza chronicler Lucius Beebe was similarly agitated. The lobby had been turned into a construction zone, he bemoaned, and travel from the Fifth Avenue entrance to the Fifty-Ninth Street elevator required "the services of native guides." Various staff "almost disappeared in a forest of scaffoldings," and one unlucky manager was stuck behind a glass divider "like a peculiarly deadly reptile in the zoo."

Hilton was taken aback by the level of resistance to his attempts to prop up the aging dowager hotel. "The Plaza dwellers, much more bound up in tradition, much more conservative, truly seemed to think my connection with their hotel might mark the end of their world," Hilton wrote in his autobiography. He was taking so much flak that at one point Hilton said to his staff, "Why, I oughta just let the hotel just fall apart at their knees. Because that's what's going to happen to it if we don't do something. The place is a wreck." When an executive responded, "Who cares what anyone thinks?" Hilton raised his voice. "Public relations is important. I can't have those New Yorkers spreading the word that Conrad Hilton is a country hick."[41]

To minimize complaints, Hilton's staff took to working at night. They repaired tapestries, scrubbed marble finishes, polished wood, and wiped grime off the decorative ceilings, all while guests slept. One day toward the end of the renovation, Hilton stood in the lobby as two of the widows passed by. They gave Hilton "a firm nod, a direct look, and a grimace approximating a smile." It was proof, Hilton insisted, that he had finally won over his toughest critics.[42]

Hilton would also convince the business establishment, who had thought him crazy to expand into New York hotels, that it was, in retrospect, a brilliant move. As World War II continued, business in New York finally followed the rest of the country and began improving, just as Hilton had posited. Soldiers traveling to and from the front began passing in droves through New York and the Plaza. On any given day, the lobby would be awash in army khaki and sailor white, with guest rooms filled to capacity with women in the starched blue uniforms of the Naval Reserve, or volunteers wearing the Red Cross insignias.

By 1945, two years into Hilton's tenure as owner of the Plaza, the average occupancy rate for hotels across the country was a record

91 percent.[43] While for several years New York had lagged, now the city surpassed the national average, posting an occupancy rate of 98 percent, or almost full capacity.[44] With so much demand for hotel rooms, the Plaza was forced to limit stays, imposing a five-night maximum on guests and even setting up cots in the Grand Ballroom and the hotel's executive offices to handle the overflow.[45]

All this demand wasn't as profitable as it might have been, however. That's because the government, in an effort to prevent price gouging, instituted caps on the rates that hotels could charge. These restrictions would eventually pave the way for New York City rent control legislation, which would apply to much of the housing stock in the city. In the coming years, rent control would prove a massive headache for landlords, including at the Plaza, where the hotel's widows would turn from financial boosters to major fiscal drags. It was rent control that would enable the prickly Fannie Lowenstein, for instance, to pay absurdly low rent for one of the Plaza's most valuable suites, without ever having to face eviction. But for now, it meant that hotels couldn't raise their room rates, limiting profit.

On the plus side, all this business did translate into packed restaurants and nightclubs. Particularly popular was the Plaza's Persian Room, and its most famous act was the chanteuse Hildegarde. "She pinches young soldiers on the cheeks and kisses old soldiers on their bald spots," read one press clipping. "You can't forget her playing the piano primly, with her gloves on, telling her naughty jokes with the air of a youngster who has been eavesdropping."[46]

In her cheeky autobiography, *Over 50—So What!* Hildegarde wrote of the era, "War money flowed. So did champagne. And I drew a champagne crowd, thank God!" After her shows, Hildegarde, whose full name was Hildegarde Henrietta Sell, would retire to her Plaza suite, where she hosted everyone from the actress Helen Hayes to the industrialist Henry J. Kaiser. "In those days my suite at the Plaza, with its pink marble fireplace, glistening chandelier, and

lovely quilted chintzes, always filled with flowers, was an exciting
and wonderful scene," she recalled.

The hotel stayed busy hosting tea dances for Allied officers and
war bond drives for civilians. Debutantes filed into the Plaza's ballroom wearing "warsages," or corsages of flowers made from 25-cent
war stamps, and every Sunday, Mrs. Charles O. Maas, one of the
thirty-nine resident widows, entertained a handful of servicemen at
her home in the State Suite. "She did not import girls for the boys,
and she discouraged war stories. Those lucky enough to get an invitation were content to dine with her in the elegant Persian Room
and return to her apartment to wander, as in a museum, gazing at
paintings and antiques," wrote Eve Brown. When the war ended,
Maas would often take out and peruse a cherished book "in which
the boys had inscribed their names and expressed their thanks."[47]

Business was finally picking up, and Hilton was successfully
navigating his hotel renovations and his critics. His personal life,
however, was in trouble. Hilton was on his second marriage, to the
movie star Zsa Zsa Gabor. His first marriage had been to a Kentucky teenager he met when he was still in Texas building his hotel
chain. Like Harry Black, Hilton was much older when he met his
first wife. In the Roaring Twenties, Hilton was thirty-seven, and
busy buying up hotels, when he crossed paths with nineteen-year-
old Mary Barron, who was in town visiting family. A courtship
ensued, followed by marriage and three sons, born in quick succession. But when the market collapsed in 1929, Hilton became con-
sumed with saving his hotel chain, to the detriment of his marital
union. Hilton and Mary divorced after a decade together, and, as
a lifelong practicing Catholic, Hilton vowed to remain a bachelor.

Hilton maintained that promise until one night in December 1941, the same month that Pearl Harbor was attacked. Hilton was living in Los Angeles and was invited to attend a dinner
party. When he arrived, he was seated next to a Hungarian beauty,

Sari Zsa Zsa Gabor, runner-up for Miss Hungary 1933.[48] She was "blonde, witty, vivacious, and just off the boat," Hilton recalled of their initial meeting. "Sitting next to me at dinner, she suddenly did one of those fascinating tricks women do with their eyes and announced: 'I theenk I am going to marry you.'"[49] Four months later, the budding actress's premonition became fact.

Gabor, who would go on to marry a total of nine husbands, was known as much for her extravagant lifestyle as for her movie roles. One day, bedridden with the flu, Hilton watched in amazement as his new bride went about her day. At ten o'clock in the morning Gabor sat at her dressing table and began layering creams and oils on her face, as if participating in "the rite of an ancient Aztec temple," Hilton recalled. He asked his wife what she was doing. "'I am dressing for lunch, seely,' she replied casually, as if everyone knew that the time to commence dressing for lunch was directly after breakfast. Then she held up a brooch, discarded it, tried another, sniffed this perfume, that perfume, tried on a gay scarf, frowned and tried on another. 'You like thees?' she demanded." The ritual repeated itself throughout the day as she returned to the dressing table directly from lunch to begin dressing for afternoon tea. It was repeated once more that evening when she prepared for the main event, dinner. "Glamour, I found, is expensive and Zsa Zsa was glamour raised to the last degree," Hilton wrote.[50]

But just as the courtship and wedding was a quick affair, so was the realization that the pair were ill-suited. "Our marriage was doomed before it started," Hilton conceded. Being married to Gabor "was a little like holding on to a Roman candle, beautiful, exciting, but you were never quite sure when it would go off." They separated, and, in 1945, Gabor announced plans to divorce the hotel magnate, demanding "that he give her ten million dollars, which she said she intended to turn over to European refugees—'All of them,' one cynic remarked, 'named Zsa Zsa Hilton.'" Accusations flew, including the charge that Gabor, suffering a nervous breakdown, had been kept in "continuous slumber" for six months through the injections of some "mysterious" drug and downing eighteen sleeping pills a day. In the end, Hilton gave her $35,000 in cash, a $2,000 monthly allowance, and six months' free stay at the Plaza.[51]

As the Hilton-Gabor divorce was playing out, in August 1945, World War II ended in victory. Just as had occurred following the Armistice some three decades before, the Plaza was the site of "a frenzy of joyous celebration from cocktail hour long into the dawn of another day, when the last newspaper was on the streets and the confetti was swept out of the lobbies." A few weeks later, on Navy Day, when forty-seven warships gathered along the Hudson River, Hildegarde opened the fall season at the Persian Room. Dressed in red, white, and blue, she dedicated her performance to "our boys."[52]

With the end of World War II came a new world order. The United Nations, a body whose mission was to negotiate disputes through diplomacy, opened in New York City. It firmly established the hometown of the Plaza as a global capital. In those years, international guests flocked to the hotel as they conducted statecraft. "Hindus with diamonds in their foreheads" and "Arabian military chiefs in flowing desert robes" were a common sight in the plush hotel corridors, while "nobody in the gangways of the Plaza Hotel bats an eye nowadays if an Australian bushman attired in a breechclout and silk top hat swims into his ken," wrote Beebe with his characteristic flair.[53] Over the ensuing decades, the Plaza would maintain its standing among an international clientele, although in later years, it would be foreign businessmen looking to park their wealth, not diplomats on missions, who would seek out the hotel in greatest number.

In 1946, the Soviet ambassador made the Plaza his home while attending the UN Security Council. It was tradition that when foreign dignitaries visited, the Plaza hung the country's flag on its awning. "No New Yorker ever dreamed he would live long enough to see the Soviet flag flying over the Plaza Hotel, long a symbol of die-hard capital," wrote the *Atlanta Constitution* in a piece titled "What Goes On? Hammer and Sickle Fly Over Capitalistic Plaza."[54] The Plaza, as it always had, straddled the contradiction with aplomb. The hotel was no doubt the epitome of capital aspirations, but it was equally comfortable in its role as global ambassador.

On the advent of its fortieth birthday on October 1, 1947, the Plaza, thoroughly nipped and tucked thanks to Hilton, was ready for its close-up. Magazines and newspapers extolled its virtues. "Instead of being a novelty, it has achieved the status of an institution," declared the *New York Herald Tribune*.[55] To mark the day, a ball was held featuring dances from each of the Plaza's four decades, including a Gibson Girl of 1907, who danced a turn-of-the-century waltz; and Adele Astaire, who performed choreography by her brother Fred.[56] Longtime Plaza employees, including Tom Clifford, a doorman since opening day, lit an enormous birthday cake. The following night, Hilton held court at the Baroque Room. Among those in attendance was Edwin Beinecke, Bernhard's son, who had returned from England following his stint with the Red Cross.[57]

The Plaza had proven that even as owners came and went, the building would maintain its sense of permanency. "This then is the Plaza, a repository and trustee of many things to many people, a microcosm of immutability in a changing world, a bond between the storied past and opulent present," wrote Beebe in an essay published in the Plaza's gilt-edged birthday brochure. "It is this continuity with the past, more than anything else, which lays hold upon the imagination at mention of the Plaza, this quality of intactness from a time that is even now, to a whole generation of Americans, only a wistful souvenir of an age of graciousness and glamour."

Chapter 8

THE REAL ELOISE

"If you don't know who Kay Thompson is, please
turn the page. You just flunked pizazz."
—*Rex Reed*

Kay Thompson was in her suite at the Plaza, obliging a reporter
with an interview. In the midst of the conversation, she suddenly had a hankering for a coffee. "Please give me room service,"
Thompson said into the receiver. "As she held the telephone, she
lit a cigarette, did a couple of dance steps, hummed, pulled on a
lock of her hair and finally flung herself on the couch, two long,
slim legs over the back," the journalist reported. "From here she
leaped up again, sang a few bars in a deep, throaty voice, and then,
her voice changing entirely to a childish prattle, said, 'Hello, room
service? This is me, Eloise. Here's what I want. Hot coffee. Hot,
hot, hot. Here's what I don't want. To wait for it. So you skibble
right up here, will you please? Otherwise I feel as if I might sklonk
someone.'"[1]

In the decade of the 1950s, Thompson, a choreographer, musical
arranger, actress, and, most famously, author, would be the Plaza's
unlikely saving grace. But long before Eloise appeared, with her
plucky persona and wiry hair, or even before Kay Thompson herself,

there was Kitty Fink. A pencil-thin, red-haired radio performer with a prominent nose, Fink was a native of St. Louis, Missouri, where Clara Bell Walsh had once lived in boredom with her husband. Just as Hilton was buying the Plaza, Fink arrived in Hollywood, dreaming of movie stardom. She bleached her hair blond, underwent the first of countless rhinoplasties, and rechristened herself Kay Thompson in order to fit the part. While she aspired to be in films, it would be in book publishing that Thompson would ultimately find immortality, and in the process, turn the dowager Plaza into "a favorite hangout of the pre-teen-age set," transforming the stomping ground of F. Scott Fitzgerald into a kiddie emporium.[2]

After arriving in Los Angeles from the Midwest, Thompson got a job working at Metro-Goldwyn-Mayer. It was not, as she had hoped, a position in front of the cameras. Rather, Thompson became the studio's head vocal coach and musical arranger for its roster of stars. She was one of the few women in an all-boys club, helping the likes of Lena Horne and Judy Garland reach their potential. Thompson ensconced herself among a retinue of famous friends, even becoming the godmother to Garland's daughter Liza Minnelli.

The stars welcomed Thompson's talents. "Professionally she developed me as a singer completely," Horne once said. "She is the best vocal coach in the world."[3] She was "the forty-carat referee at MGM who put the kicker in those champagne Technicolor musicals with her stylish vocal arrangements," wrote Thompson's friend Rex Reed in his book *People Are Crazy Here*. Thompson did manage to land the occasional television and movie spot. Her starring role, however, wouldn't come until after Eloise was born, when Thompson played the character of a fashion editor, based on the legendary Diana Vreeland, opposite Audrey Hepburn and Fred Astaire in 1957's *Funny Face*.

But years before she would appear in *Funny Face*, when she was still working mostly behind the scenes in Hollywood, Thompson decided she'd had her fill. "I learned that in a big studio you are so categorized that you have to become what people think you are or get out," she told the magazine *McCall's*, "so I got out."[4] In 1947, she embarked on a new project that she called the "saloon beat," which wasn't a reference to a drunken binge, but instead, a nightclub act where her abilities would be impossible to ignore.

Her new beat featured Thompson performing cabaret songs accompanied by the Williams Brothers, a group of four male singers. Thompson always wore slacks, which became her trademark at a time when wearing pants was still risqué for a woman. (She designed them herself and later manufactured "Kay Thompson's Fancy Pants" for Saks Fifth Avenue.) Thompson, as the act's star, sang and danced while the Williams Brothers, in dark matching suits, moved in choreographed unison behind her. It was a novel approach during a period when most stages were occupied by acts like Hildegarde, the seductive chanteuse who stood in place and sang.

The Williams Brothers often played straitlaced to Thompson's comical, and their songs were sly and humorous, with many poking fun or highlighting the hypocrisies of show business. The act regularly performed at the Plaza's Persian Room, and Thompson lived at the hotel during the season. "Miss Thompson is an atomic bomb of rhythm songapation with her equally supercharged vocal vitamins, the four Williams Brothers," wrote *Variety* in a review of the Persian Room act. *Billboard* called her "one of the most imaginative performers in the trade."[5]

As the popularity of her nightclub act grew, Thompson became as famed for her slim physique as for her talents as a performer. She was, noted *Harper's Bazaar*, "a silver sliver of a woman with a twenty-three-inch waistline,"[6] which she maintained with a restrictive diet almost entirely dependent on the consumption of Fig Newtons. Thompson supplemented her regimen with regular injections of "vitamin cocktails." This was a potent mix of mostly metham-phetamines, administered by Dr. Max Jacobson, the original "Dr. Feelgood," according to Sam Irvin in his biography *Kay Thompson: From Funny Face to Eloise*. Dr. Jacobson's other patients included such luminaries as John F. Kennedy and Truman Capote.

"The facts about her are," observed the photographer Cecil Bea-ton, "that she is skeletal, hatchet-faced, blonde and American; that she wears tight, tapering slacks, and moves like a mountain goat." Beaton, who shot Thompson for a feature in British *Vogue*, had dif-ficulty capturing his subject's true essence: "The proper language in which to review her is not English at all but Esperanto. Or possibly Morse code."[7]

It was during this period, as Thompson toured as a cabaret singer, that a character she had long toyed with, both on and off the stage, finally came together. There are a multitude of Eloise origin stories, but most claim that for years, Thompson would roll out the character of a stubborn little girl to amuse her friends. While performing with the Williams Brothers, her alter ego took on a life of its own. "I invented her years and years ago during rehearsal," Thompson told the *Los Angeles Times* in 1956. "There'd be some-thing I just couldn't do and I'd start this Eloise-talk: 'I can't can't can't do it. Can't. Me, I can't do it.' In this little-girl voice."[8] The Williams Brothers got a kick out of it and created their own childish characters. Andy Williams, who would become a breakout star in his own right, adopted two personas: Melvin, "who was three and helped his mother shell peas, and Jr., who was nine and wanted to go under the house all the time."[9]

Throughout her life, Thompson was stubbornly mercurial about whether the inspiration for her prepubescent persona was autobio-graphical. Eloise, a derivation of Thompson's middle name, Lou-ise, "is *me*. All me!" she insisted at one point.[10] She told another interviewer, "Understand me, she's completely imaginary. I never knew any little girl like Eloise. I didn't live in hotels as a little girl. I invented her."[11] The actuality probably lay somewhere in the middle. Irvin, Thompson's biographer, surmised it was a compilation of various personalities that Thompson had encountered, from Plaza widow Clara Bell Walsh to scions of Thompson's famous friends. There was Minnelli, her goddaughter, and also Sigourney Weaver, whose father was the president of NBC, and Princess Yasmin Khan, whose mother was Rita Hayworth. Even young boys may have influenced her, like David Carradine, son of the actor John Carradine, and Stephen Bogart, son of Humphrey Bogart.

Once Thompson's Eloise was let loose, her friends embraced the youngster. "Bless them! They kept her alive; I didn't. They just wouldn't let loose of her," Thompson told *McCall's*. "'They'd call and say, 'Hello, Kay, I don't want to talk to you. I want to talk to Eloise.' Then I would go into the bit, and pretty soon it all became habit." One such friend was D. D. Ryan, a woman who was a junior fashion editor at *Harper's Bazaar*. Ryan had long urged Thompson to turn Eloise into a book. Thompson was game to write a book, but not about Eloise. "I wanted to write about the people who live in hotels… I was going to call the book: 'Beds That I Have Slept In,'" she told the *Los Angeles Times*. But Ryan persisted. She finally convinced Thompson to pursue Eloise by making an important introduction.

One Sunday in the winter of 1954, Kay was staying at the Plaza while performing at the Persian Room when she got a call from Ryan. As was her habit, Ryan asked her to speak like Eloise, but then she followed up the joking with serious talk. "Look, Kay, Eloise is a book—and I've got just the person to illustrate it," Ryan said. Hilary Knight was a young artist who was just forging a career as an illustrator. He lived across the hall from Ryan in a walk-up brownstone in Midtown, and would often slip his drawings under Ryan's door. She was convinced he was a perfect foil to bring her friend's fictional creation to the page.[12]

Ryan asked Thompson to come over, so "I went over," Thompson said, "carrying my own ashtray. This girl doesn't smoke and hates dirt. When I arrived, my friend said, 'I'll call Hilary from across the hall.' A Princetonian young man, shy, gentle and soft spoken, came in." Thompson later said of her first impression, "Of course, Hilary's perfectly marvelous. He's so young. He's only 29. The first time we met, I terrified him." In another interview Thompson quipped, "He seemed terribly impressed with me, which naturally impressed me terribly with him."[13] Hilary, who called Thompson "an extremely funny, inventive woman," and "a mad nut job that I adored,"[14] had a different recollection of that first meeting. He remembered it taking place after he accompanied Ryan to see Thompson's act at the Persian Room one night, the two meeting after the show.[15]

Either way, both agree that at the initial meeting, Thompson gave Knight several lines of text written in the voice of Eloise, including banter like, "An egg cup makes a very good hat," and "I put a cabbage leaf on my head when I have a headache." Several weeks later, Knight sent Thompson a holiday card illustrated with Santa Claus "streaking through the sky on a Christmas tree. On the end of the tree, grinning a lovely grin, her wild hair standing on end, was Eloise. It was immediate recognition on my part," Thompson said.[16]

Knight, who grew up in Long Island before moving with his artist parents to Manhattan, had drawn inspiration for the character from the personal, including a painting by his mother of a girl in a Victorian-style dress. Other sources were whimsical, such as illustrations in *Winnie-the-Pooh* and *The Wind in the Willows*, and also obscure, like an 1887 book of manners by Maurice Boutet de Monvel. There was even a real-life inspiration, Eloise Davis, a food writer and one of Knight's relatives, "a roly-poly little woman with this very bizarre hair that went straight out in various uncontrolled angles," Knight said. As for the color scheme, his parents had collaborated on a *New Yorker* cover in 1926 that featured a flapper in pink, black, and white, and Knight resurrected it for *Eloise*.[17]

With the partnership between Thompson and Knight secured, "I holed in at the Plaza and we went to work," Thompson remembered. "I just knew I had to get this done. Eloise was trying to get out. I've never known such stimulation. This girl had complete control of me...We wrote, edited, laughed, outlined, cut, pasted, laughed again, read out loud, laughed and suddenly we had a book."[18]

The portly child with wiry hair lived on the top floor of the Plaza with a pet turtle named Skipperdee ("he eats raisins and wears sneakers"); a dog named Weenie (who "likes to have his back scratched with a wire hanger"); and a nanny named Nanny (who "always says everything 3 times, like Eloise you cawn't cawn't cawn't"). Eloise rode the Plaza elevators like they were local stops on the subway, lost her skate key in a crowd of guests and luggage, and regularly called room service for "one roast-beef bone, one raisin and seven spoons."[19] Discarded bons mots that didn't make the grade included "Nanny eats a cucumber like an apple," and "When I go to sleep, hallways have to wear don't disturb signs."[20]

There were several references to real-life figures in the book, including the Palm Court waiter Thomas, who was "rawther fond of talking" and owned a Corvette. The Persian Room busboy Bill was also in the book: "Here's where he's been Madrid. Here's where I've been Boiler Room." Alphonse Salomone, the hotel's suave, well-mannered manager, wore a suit and bent deeply at the waist in greeting. "I am a nuisance in the lobby Mr. Salomone said so," Eloise says in the book. "I always say 'Good morning, Mr. Salomone' and he always says 'Good morning, Eloise.'"

The book was endearing, with its run-on sentences, playful wording, and wicked humor. There was no plot to speak of, beyond the freewheeling Eloise and her impish antics. The setting of the Plaza lent the story a sense of extravagance, while Eloise's absentee mother and not-so-present Nanny provided a tinge of loneliness. Even a half-century later, the character remains indelible. In 2015, the *New Yorker* called Eloise "a prefeminist hero" who evokes a "freewheeling urbanity, a happy rebelliousness within a realm of sophistication." It was for a review of a film documenting Knight's life, produced by the young writer, actress, and Eloise fan Lena Dunham.[21]

After seeing Thompson's and Knight's work, the editors at Simon & Schuster paid them a $1,000 advance, and in November 1955, the publishing company printed seventy-five hundred copies of *Kay Thompson's Eloise: A Book for Precocious Grown Ups*. It was an immediate hit. "Eloise is likely to be the most controversial literary heroine of the year. She charms and terrifies like a snake," wrote *Life* magazine in a multipage spread introducing its readers to the character.[22] Eloise was "the *Alice in Wonderland* of the Atomic Age," raved the *Los Angeles Times*.[23] Groucho Marx quipped, "I admire Eloise enormously—and I am very happy that I am not her father." Thompson roped in famous pals to bless her endeavor and several offered glowing testimonials, including Lauren Bacall, Douglas Fairbanks, and Cole Porter.

Thompson had longed for fame, and now she embarked on a massive publicity blitz to market the book. She appeared on programs like *Tonight Starring Steve Allen* and held court with journalists at the Plaza. While she was meeting one reporter for tea at the Palm Court, a fellow patron came over to the table and asked if Thompson might "talk Eloise." She "obliged in a voice that penetrated to the four corners of the room and startled customers into unaccustomed silence," wrote the journalist. "I am all over the hotel...half the time I am lost...but mostly I am on the first floor because that's where catering is," Thompson cried through the hushed quiet.[24]

As demand for the book surged, Thompson's publisher rushed more copies of *Eloise* off the printing presses. But still, it wasn't enough. As Christmas approached, with just seventeen thousand copies in print, "frantic buyers rushed from bookstore to bookstore in a futile attempt to locate any remaining copies," wrote Irvin.[25] It was soon obvious that how went Eloise, so went the Plaza.

"It's reported in New York that the small fry set is dropping in on The Plaza in hordes to ask to see Eloise in person," wrote the *Los Angeles Times*. Hotel staff grew accustomed to having young people loiter in the lobby in the hopes of catching a glimpse of her, and soon got in on the act. If a child got up the courage to ask the front desk to ring Eloise's room, the clerk would reach down and pull out a pair of Mary Janes. "Oh, I'm sorry, you just missed her. But if you run into Eloise, please tell her we found her missing shoes," the clerk would remark, the youngsters staring, mouths agape.[26]

Children who lived too far to come in person began clogging the Plaza phone lines asking to speak with their heroine. Operators would apologize that they couldn't call Eloise because she was too busy on the thirteenth floor helping with the air-conditioning, or "swonking" pigeons on the roof. On occasion, calls were put through to Thompson, who would oblige a lucky fan with a few sentences in character. The Plaza even hung a painting of Eloise, made by Knight, in the lobby. It immediately became a mandatory tourist stop, until it disappeared, under mysterious circumstances. The painting's "kidnapping" was announced by Walter Cronkite during the *CBS Evening News*, but despite the attention, the perpetrators were never caught. A few years later, a replacement was hung.

The Plaza sold the *Eloise* book in their shop, as did many other hotels, and they began giving away postcards featuring Knight's rendering of Eloise saluting a Plaza doorman. Soon, demand for the Eloise postcards outstripped those for traditional Plaza postcards. "All the children who come here want my autograph," the Plaza's manager, Alphonse Salomone, told the *New Yorker*.[27] "They also want me to bow to the waist, as I do in the book. I oblige on both accounts." Hilton, in awe of the immense amount of positive publicity the book was generating for the hotel, sent Salomone a telegram, marveling, "How much did you pay her?"[28]

To leverage Eloise's popularity, the Plaza commandeered a vacant area on the Fifty-Eighth Street side of the building. The hotel painted it in red-and-white candy stripes, and christened it a tricycle garage, offering free rentals for Plaza guests.[29] The *New Yorker* sent an intrepid reporter to investigate. "We're not one to be caught napping, or even strolling in the Park, when a big story breaks," it reported, going on to describe the space as "resplendent with a dozen or so glistening tricycles, parked in tiers; a repair shop; and a bright-red mural of Central Park, on which were indicated tricycle routes leading to the Zoo, the carousel, the skating rink and other surefire points of interest."[30]

The Plaza's tricycle garage spurred a toddler craze. "Boom Time for Tricycles," read an article in the *New York Herald Tribune*, which extolled the trend and divulged critical details such as the "most flattering look for a lady tricyclist is a bloomer-legged playsuit under a tie-on apron skirt."[31] Humbert Gatti, the Plaza's executive chef, also participated in catering to the younger demographic, creating the hotel's first-ever children's menu. It featured such Thompson-approved delicacies as the "Kiddie Kar Kocktail," "Teeny Weenies," and "Mary-Had-a-Little-Lamb Chop." For dessert, a "Tricycle Treat" was on hand, replete with a miniature bicycle rider made from vanilla ice cream, riding on sponge cake with whipped cream and raspberry sauce.[32] "Kids, they like something messy," said Gatti. "The whipped cream is for messy."

Despite the tricycle garage and the children's menu, Thompson actually hadn't intended *Eloise* for children—at all. She had insisted that on its cover, the title specify it was "a book for precocious grown-ups." And Thompson was known to charge into bookstores, remove *Eloise* displays from the children's section, and relocate them to the adult fiction area. A close reading of the book, in fact, shows several bawdy, even subversive, references. There is a bottle of gin in Eloise's bedroom, on the shelf next to a handsaw, and the title of a book on her messy floor is *The Little Beaver*. Originally, a passage explaining the difference between Eloise and her mother's lawyer read: "Here's what he likes: Martinis. Here's what I like: Grass." In later editions, the publisher replaced "grass" with "dandelions."

Just as the Plaza had leveraged the success of *Eloise*, so Thompson, too, turned it to her advantage. "Once the inherent value of Eloise was clear, Kay demanded and got free accommodations at the hotel," wrote Irvin.[33] The Plaza gave her suite 937 indefinitely, which she redecorated with white chaise lounges and French theatrical posters. Whether it came to furniture or keepsakes from her career, she was never one for permanency. As she told Rex Reed, "No point in saving memorabilia—somebody always steals it. I own an orange tree here, a rattan chair there, and the rest is in storage in Rome."

While Thompson didn't like permanency, she was certainly a constant at the Plaza. She was "as much a part of the hotel as the palm trees," a Plaza publicity director told Reed. "She moved in two years ago to do some publicity for the Eloise books and we've just never asked her when she plans to leave." Like her furnishings, Thompson collected a series of lovers over the years, including two husbands, but none ever stuck. "I love love and I believe in divorce. Two great things," she said, adding, "I've lived with quite a few men and alone is better."[34]

Down the hall from Thompson's Plaza suite, in room 931, the hotel created a replica of Eloise's room in the book. It was open to the public by appointment only, and children could meet "Nanny" and get a phone call from Eloise, who would make pronouncements like, "Getting bored is not allowed," and "Sometimes I comb my hair with a fork." It was a huge hit. "In 1957, I insisted my mother bring me to the Plaza so I could go to the Eloise room and pick up the telephone," recalled the *Vanity Fair* writer at large Marie Brenner. "And Kay Thompson, herself, still was on that telephone in 1957. And the thrill, at age seven, to hear Kay Thompson's voice saying, 'It's me, Eloise,' I just never—I *still* haven't gotten over it."[35]

Thompson also commandeered a free office on the Plaza's first floor to serve as home base for Eloise Limited, her merchandising arm. One of the first-ever such publishing-inspired marketing endeavors, it churned out novelty items like Eloise life-size dolls and matching Eloise fashions for little girls.[36] An Eloise Emergency Hotel Kit included a ten-inch hat box featuring such necessities as a "Sleep With Me Eloise" pillow and a wooden resting block "for exhausted chewing gum." There were also Eloise records, Eloise sheet music, Eloise stockings, and Eloise "bawth" towels.[37]

In November 1957, Thompson and Knight published *Eloise in Paris*, in which the Lilliputian troublemaker is summoned to Paris by her absentee mother via cablegram. The book is filled with scenes at the Arc de Triomphe and Parisian cafés, with text that is a tongue twister of French references and puns. Within three weeks, the number of copies printed had reached one hundred thousand; it had taken five months for her first book to reach that benchmark.

Eloise at Christmastime followed, with Eloise singing carols and writing holiday greetings on the hotel walls. It received decidedly more mixed reviews, although it was still the sixth-bestselling fiction book of 1958. Then, in 1959, Thompson and Knight published *Eloise in Moscow*. The book was heralded with a big marketing push, replete with a press conference at the Plaza, where Thompson donned a giant Bolshevik winter coat. But the book faced stiff competition from new releases by Dr. Seuss, as well as a new breakthrough toy, Barbie. There was also the tricky matter of the Cold War. *Eloise in Moscow* failed to capture the excitement of the original. "Eloise amid the Soviets isn't the sprightly brat you either wanted to kill or take home," the *New York Times* wrote in a review. "She has become just a dull little girl in a travelogue pretentiously presented."[38]

As the success of the Eloise brand faltered, tension that had been brewing between Thompson and Knight grew more pronounced. Thompson had always been possessive of her creation and had often relegated Knight and his illustrations to bottom billing. She insisted the first book be titled *Kay Thompson's Eloise*, with "Drawings by Hilary Knight" at the bottom of the dust jackets. Originally Knight's name was in a smaller font, although the publisher later increased its size.

Thompson, ever a control freak, was a stickler that her name be prominently placed. She even called one New York City bookstore manager late one night to inquire, "What is the title of the book in the window?" He responded "'Well, it's *Eloise*.' And she shouted, 'That is incorrect! The title of the book is *Kay Thompson's Eloise*.'"[39] The financial agreement between Thompson and Knight was also arguably imbalanced, with Thompson receiving 70 percent of the proceeds to Knight's 30 percent. Thompson also owned the copyright to Knight's illustrations. "I totally trusted her," Knight told *Vanity Fair*'s Marie Brenner. "I totally signed my rights away."

At the same time that her partnership with Knight was fraying, Thompson was becoming increasingly disenchanted with her alter ego. "I just can't seem to keep up with Eloise," she told an interviewer from the Associated Press. "Since then my life hasn't been my own." Thompson wondered, "I don't know how Eloise managed to grow so big, so fast...I'd hate to call her a Frankenstein, but she scares me just the same."[40]

By 1963, more than a million copies of *Eloise* and its sequels had sold, but Thompson had stopped production of Eloise Limited and no new *Eloise* books were forthcoming. "The world is coming apart," Thompson had told her editor, who suggested that she move to Rome to take a break. She immediately did so, bringing along "only a toothbrush."[41] In Rome, Thompson lived in an apartment with zebra carpeting, a piano with its legs sawed off, and windows with dazzling views of the Spanish Steps. She went everywhere with her tiny pet pug, Fenice, whom she spoon-fed Chuckles jelly candy and called "darling baby boy."

After she spent several years abroad, in 1969, there was a large reissue of *Eloise*, and Thompson was ready to return stateside to publicize her creation. She used the buzz to take up residence once more at the Plaza, redecorating her suite to her unusual specifications. "Using pins and scotch tape, she covered chairs, tables, and lamp shades with zebra-striped Porthault sheets," wrote Irvin. "Then she manufactured a fake fireplace out of leftover cardboard boxes." To "further justify squatter's rights," she gave permission to the hotel to reopen the Eloise suite that had closed and created a new Eloise Ice Cream Corner in the lobby.

Thompson even met with Knight, to try to revive some discarded book ideas. But it was soon clear to the artist that their partnership was irreparably broken. As they began brainstorming, Knight took out his pencil to sketch. Thompson reached out and "guided my hand, pushing the pencil across the paper, trying to take control and make the drawing her own," Knight recounted to Irvin. "That was it. I knew right then and there that it was never going to work."

In the winter of 1972, it was clear that Thompson would never write another *Eloise* book. New York City was facing a fiscal crisis, and the Plaza itself was barely staying afloat. The hotel began to look for ways to cut costs. Thompson, who had been living for free at the hotel off and on for years, was asked to start paying her way. "She was so angry, she threatened to move Eloise to another hotel," Thompson's friend Kitty D'Alessio told Irvin. "She was going to paint Eloise's little footprints on the sidewalk leading from The Plaza all the way over to the St. Regis." The Plaza wasn't too bothered; that night, an eviction notice was slipped under Thompson's door. "Kay Thompson, who handed the Plaza Hotel its biggest publicity (via her 'Eloise' books), was given 24 hours to move out by the new management," reported one paper, aghast.[42]

Thompson told the Plaza, " 'Okay, you can't have anything. The Eloise portrait has to come down. The postcards must stop,'" recounted Knight, "and everything to do with Eloise just vanished." The Eloise painting that had replaced the one that was stolen was briefly removed, although, "somehow, it got put back up," Knight reported. "Kay said, 'You can't identify it as Eloise,' so they removed the little gold plaque that was on the frame at the bottom that said it was Eloise. Of course, it didn't matter because everybody knew who she was."[43]

Thompson turned her back on the Plaza for good, finding refuge with her goddaughter Liza Minnelli, living in her apartment on East Sixty-Ninth Street just a few blocks north of the hotel. Over subsequent years, Thompson became increasingly reclusive, seeing no one and returning the calls of only a few friends, and even then, sporadically. Yet she didn't lose her flair. Confined to a wheelchair, Thompson wore her "favorite red Halston sweater and dancing shoes; her feet tapping frequently to a beat that only she can hear," wrote Brenner. In 1988, at the age of eighty-eight, thirty-three years after penning *Kay Thompson's Eloise: A Book for Precocious Grown Ups*, she passed away.

Eloise inspired millions of children, catapulting the hotel into the national conversation. It defined the Plaza for a new generation and rendered the hotel once again a cultural touchpoint. If originally, the Plaza was the purview of Alfred Gwynne Vanderbilt and his ilk, and later became a symbol of wealth and striving in Fitzgerald's Jazz Age, it was now rich in young imaginations, thriving as a beacon of youthful adventure and mischief.

But it would end up that, outside of Eloise's shadows, there were other inventions brewing at the hotel that would prove the book's equal in capturing the essence of the times. In this postwar era, a new wealth-driven consumerism had gripped the country. America's gross natural product had more than doubled, with once-luxury goods such as televisions, dishwashers, and air travel widely accessible.[44] The Eloise fad epitomized this trend, with families so prosperous that even demand from young children could create a lucrative marketing blitz.

This insatiable appetite for consumer goods was also apparent in the new American diet. During World War II, food manufacturers had invented methods for mass-producing, packaging, and preserving foods to send to hungry troops fighting in Europe. After the war was won, these companies refocused their attentions on the nation's grocery store aisles. Frozen entrées, milk in cartons, and electric mixers were suddenly ubiquitous. Jell-O became all the rage, and books such as *The Can-Opener Cookbook* became best sellers.[45] In July 1950, the Plaza's employee newsletter featured the work of Thomas Loutris, a hotel waiter who patented something called "Batter-Rich," a homogenized, emulsified liquid pancake mix. His slogan was, "No fuss, no muss, no dishes to wash."[46]

The Plaza's three Boiardi brothers were even more famous than Loutris. When he was a young man, Richard Paul Boiardi worked in his native Italy as a waiter, where he served the famous tenor Enrico Caruso. Caruso was so impressed with Boiardi's service that he gave the young man his card, telling him to look him up if he should come to America. Boiardi did, and with Caruso's assistance, he landed a job as a waiter, first at the Knickerbocker Hotel, then at the Plaza.[47] When the Plaza opened the Persian Room following the repeal of Prohibition, it appointed Boiardi as its maître d'hôtel.[48] By then, Richard's two brothers, Mario and Hector, had followed him to America and also worked at the Plaza. But Hector, a talented chef, soon left for Cleveland, where he opened a popular Italian restaurant. Mario later joined him, while Richard remained behind at the Persian Room.

One of Richard's loyal customers at the Persian Room was John A. Hartford, president of the Great Atlantic and Pacific Tea Company, the precursor to the A&P grocery chain. One evening, Hartford asked Richard to serve him spaghetti. "I'll make you some from my brother's recipe," he replied. After tasting the dish, Hartford was so impressed that he offered to produce and distribute the pasta in his stores.[49] Packaging the Italian food in a decidedly American wrapping—including anglicizing the name—it was introduced as Chef Boy-Ar-Dee, where it became a mainstay of the 1950s kitchen.

In 1907, on the night before the Plaza was set to open, the hotel served an exclusive dinner to a select group of VIPs. There were magnums of Perrier-Jouet and a sixteen-course menu including terrapin Maryland and lobster aspic. But just as Eloise was a far cry from the likes of Vanderbilt and "Bet-a-Million" Gates, so, too, was Chef Boy-Ar-Dee a world away from this first Plaza meal. The country no longer wanted illustrious fare. Guests clamored for Tricycle Treats and canned spaghetti, and the Plaza had no choice but to appease their appetite.

Chapter 9

PARTY OF THE CENTURY

"New York is a diamond iceberg floating in river water."
—*Truman Capote*

As her family gathered for dinner in the Plaza penthouse where Harry Black had once lived, Lourdes Salomone grew increasingly hysterical. "You can't do this, Daddy!" she screamed. "I'll never speak to you again!" The twelve-year-old began to sob, her narrow shoulders convulsing with each jagged breath. As her mother removed the tops from the silver room-service platters and matter-of-factly set out the dishes, her father looked on in surprise.[1]

Alphonse Salomone, the Plaza manager who was famous for bending deeply at the waist when greeting Eloise, had just finished recounting his day. That afternoon, he told his family, he had made the unusual decision of turning away a reservation. As they sat in the sprawling dining room, just off the marble foyer with its Tiffany glass ceiling, Salomone explained that four famous musicians from England had booked rooms there. But weighing the Plaza's respectability with its need for profit, Salomone had decided that they would have been too disruptive, and the hotel couldn't honor the booking. It was then that his daughter's tears began flowing.

Several months earlier, representatives for the Beatles had called the Plaza's reservation line in London, requesting rooms for four "businessmen" with the seemingly innocuous names of Starr, Harrison, Lennon, and McCartney. This was before the band's first single, "I Want to Hold Your Hand," topped the *Billboard* music charts and hysteria and fainting spells had broken out worldwide among a rash of teenage girls. The oblivious reservationist blocked off five suites and four additional rooms on the Plaza's twelfth floor without pause or comment. It was only in the weeks before the teen idols were scheduled to arrive that the London office cabled Salomone. "Did you know you had booked the Beatles?" the communiqué inquired. It was the first the Plaza manager had heard of it.

The following morning, with his daughter's histrionics fresh in his mind, Salomone began reconsidering his rejection of the Beatles' reservation. Slowly, as so many fathers do, Salomone began to soften and vacillate; finally, he acquiesced. "I stuck by my decision, not hinting for a moment my daughter's tears caused my change of heart," Salomone recalled in his partially completed, unpublished memoir. The Beatles were taking England by storm with their catchy pop songs and were fast becoming equal to Elvis Presley in the minds and hearts of teenagers everywhere. How could he deprive his daughter of such an opportunity? Why else would you be the manager of the Plaza, if not to enjoy such perks? Steeling himself to the bedlam that he was sure would envelop the hotel, Salomone directed his staff to honor the reservations after all.

Salomone was right. Even before the Beatles touched down on US soil for their first-ever stateside visit, there was pandemonium. "By 6:30 a.m. Friday half the kids in the Metropolitan area were already up with their transistors plugged in their skulls," wrote the journalist Tom Wolfe. The British Invasion had taken hold. "It's 9:10 a.m. on B-Day! Which means the Beatles are three hours and 10 minutes out over the Atlantic Ocean—heading for New York!" a disc jockey excitedly announced.[2] When the plane finally landed, nearly four thousand screaming teenyboppers were there to greet it. "Put my name in the papers—I want to get expelled from school for the Beatles!" one teenager screamed.[3] "There were girls, girls and more girls," marveled the *New York Times*. "Whistling girls. Screaming girls. Singing girls."[4] One airport official shook his head and remarked, "We've never seen anything like this here before. Never. Not even for kings and queens."[5]

The band, which was scheduled to perform on the *Ed Sullivan Show*, the very same Ed Sullivan who used to visit Clara Bell Walsh, gave a short press conference, charming the crowd. Then the Fab Four climbed into individual Cadillac limousines, which whisked them into Manhattan, where the Plaza was bracing for their arrival.

For weeks, the hotel staff had been making preparations, but it was still a shock to see thousands of fans gathering in the Grand Army Plaza outside. All hands were on deck, with no Plaza employee allowed a day off for the duration of the Beatles' stay. "In the Fifth Avenue lobby, and especially the Palm Court, there was an air of electricity," Salomone wrote. "I could not help but notice every table was taken." The crowd, mostly female, ranged in age from toddlers to grandmothers. When the Beatles finally arrived, the band members were shielded by security as they were guided up to their rooms. The lucky few who watched them pass politely applauded, while the young girls squealed in delight. In a matter of moments, it was over.

Upstairs, the four fresh-faced boys relaxed in their rooms, disturbing the Plaza staff only to call room service repeatedly for more servings of tea. There was no throwing of television sets or mountains of emptied beer bottles; the boys' most animated behavior was jumping up and down on the plush Plaza beds. "The Beatles were exceptionally well behaved. No noise... No nothing," recounted Salomone. When they finally left there wasn't so much as a coffee stain on a side table.

As calm as it was up in the band's suites, downstairs, chaos reigned. "The police were eight deep. Detectives were swarming around shooing teenage girls, with nests of hair, out of the lobby," reported Gertrude Wilson in the *New York Amsterdam News*. She sat down on one of the lobby sofas next to several confused Plaza widows and a news photographer who had been stationed at the hotel for hours. The photographer began telling the group how, the night before, he had watched as four teenage girls came in carrying two oversized boxes. The teenagers told the front desk clerk that the packages were for the Beatles, but "the manager didn't buy that, and sent them on their way," the photographer said. As the girls staggered out of the hotel holding their unwieldy cartons, the tops were thrust open and two more girls in crumpled outfits jumped out.

Other groupies were even more aggressive in their attempts to meet the band. As Wilson, the widows, and the photographer took in the lawless scene, "three 'little' girls, done up in pastel stretch pants, huge fuzzy sweaters in orange, green, and orchid, enormous hair arrangements topped with fantastic fur helmets," approached. " 'You see them?' said the photographer. 'How could I miss them?'" Wilson answered. " 'Well,' said the photographer, 'They have just finished negotiating the twelve flights of stairs to the Beatle nest three times, only to be carried out bodily each time." The widows sat listening "in common bewilderment. 'Where are their parents?' they sighed."[6]

For her part, Lourdes Salomone was exceedingly satisfied. "I was like the queen of Marymount," she said, referring to her school. "Everyone wanted to be my best friend." Lourdes's older brother Bobby, who was sixteen, turned the Beatles' presence into a small business enterprise. He charged his schoolmates a dollar for the privilege of coming over, and he "would sell things from the rooms, saying they had been used by the Beatles themselves," said Lourdes.

He even sold the band's supposed bedsheets—although Lourdes kept McCartney's pillowcase for herself.[7]

The youngest of the Salomone children, six-year-old Gregg, wasn't nearly as impressed with the occasion as his siblings. The morning after the Beatles' arrival, with crowds of screaming girls congregated outside his windows, Gregg was up in his room, watching *Magilla Gorilla*. His father came in and interrupted his idyll, requiring that Gregg come downstairs and meet the rock stars. But Saturday morning cartoons were stiff competition. "My dad came in and said, 'Come on, it's a once-in-a-lifetime chance to meet them,'" Gregg said. Reluctantly, he pulled himself away from the television, swapped his pajamas for a pair of corduroy pants and a collared shirt, and made his way down to the Beatles' suites.

There, Gregg found George Harrison, Ringo Starr, and Paul McCartney. (John Lennon had gone outside earlier that morning to wander, incognito in a ski mask, past the screaming masses in Grand Army Plaza.) As Gregg stood nervously next to his sister and her friend, posing with the three British stars for a photo, McCartney suddenly asked the photographer to pause. "Wait, mate," McCartney called out. "Your fly's unzipped." The legendary musician then bent down and zipped up Gregg's pants before the photographer snapped away. In the photo, which Gregg keeps framed at his house, his left hand is hovering self-consciously over his crotch, the embarrassing exchange captured for posterity. "No one believes me when I tell them that story," he said.

That Salomone and his family found themselves at the center of such an historical event is something that no one could have predicted, least of all Salomone himself. He was born in Winnipeg, Canada, to an Italian father and a Belgian mother, and the family moved to Knoxville, Tennessee, when Alphonse was three for his father's job running a marble quarry.[8] Salomone attended the University of

Tennessee, but in his junior year, he was drafted, eventually becoming a major and fighting in the battle at Normandy.

Following the war, Salomone returned to the South, working as an elevator operator at the Andrew Jackson Hotel in New Orleans. "He wore a pill cap and would bring guests upstairs," said Gregg. "My father always had the gift of gab, and one day, he was talking with a gentleman as he brought him up to his room, who said, 'I really enjoyed meeting you. Take my business card, I would love to have you come work for me.'" The man was Conrad Hilton.⁹ So, in 1947, the year that Kay Thompson embarked on her "saloon beat," Salomone took Hilton up on his offer. He moved to New York and began work as an assistant manager at the Hilton-owned Plaza. And like the widows who lived there, Salomone immediately felt at home. "He *looks* like the Plaza," said Paul Sonnabend, whose father would eventually buy the hotel from Hilton. "He is well dressed always. He is soft-spoken, handsome."¹⁰

Salomone arrived for his first day at the Plaza on a warm summer afternoon, dressed in a crisp white suit and two-tone shoes. His shift began at three, and by five o'clock, every Plaza executive had gone home, leaving Salomone on his own. Soon, there was a call that a woman had been found dead in one of the rooms. It would turn out to be the secretary of Ferenc Molnar, the Hungarian playwright who lived at the Plaza. She was also Molnar's rumored paramour, and Salomone did his best to comfort the despondent writer. But his day was only just beginning.

Salomone's next task was to calm some fifty would-be Plaza guests who were crowded into the lobby, screaming at a cowering reservationist. It seemed that there had been a strike at the New York docks, which meant passenger ships were not departing on schedule. In turn, guests who were supposed to be checking out were now delaying, so new guests who were arriving found there were no Plaza rooms available. "I had been a Major in Patton's Third Army," Salomone wrote hyperbolically, and "in many ways, it was worse than war."

Even as Salomone contended with a dead woman and furious guests, his first day on the job was about to get worse. Olma Levy, a Plaza widow, marched up to the new manager as he stood in the lobby and began loudly complaining that she was the victim of a plot. A housekeeper was purposefully cutting up the lining of her coat, she claimed. Salomone inspected the offending article but saw no evidence of foul play, only typical wear and tear. As Salomone struggled to appease the widow and calm the frustrated crowd, Dominick, a veteran bellman, took pity on his new boss. He scurried over to say that Salomone was urgently needed on the telephone.

From that moment on, the Plaza staff devised a signal, to be used should any one of their team need saving, of tugging on an earlobe. Salomone would soon come up with other methods of widow avoidance. "The old ladies along the corridor," as he called them, would spend their days on the sofas that lined the Plaza's first floor, where the hotel offices were located. From their perches, they would harass Salomone with barrages of complaints as he walked from one office to another. His solution was simple: Instead of walking through the building, he went "outside the hotel, on the street, even in bad weather, to get from one end of the corridor to the other."[11]

By 1964, Salamone had been promoted from an assistant manager at the Plaza to being in charge of the entire hotel. There had been a hiatus between the two positions, where he had been relocated by Hilton to Puerto Rico, to run the company's newest property, the Caribe Hilton. When the Salomones returned to the Plaza from San Juan, they moved into a large suite on the hotel's seventh floor.

At the time, the Plaza penthouse was being rented by *Gourmet* for use as its magazine headquarters. One day, however, Salomone notified *Gourmet* that it would be replacing the notoriously ornery elevator that was used to access the penthouse floor. The magazine responded with a letter canceling its lease. The hotel was now confronted with a duplex penthouse that—while boasting such ornate features as a walk-in wine cellar and wall murals featuring "goat-footed bacchants on the loose"[12]—had not been renovated for years. It would be costly to make fixes, and besides, it wasn't clear how many guests would want to pay the high price to rent so many rooms.

The enormous apartment was also remote, located on the Plaza's uppermost floors, which were originally intended, back in 1907, as maids' quarters. Aside from the penthouse unit, the rooms on these floors were filled with broken furniture awaiting repair, and towering piles of mattresses used to soak up water that dripped down through the aging roof. Salomone proposed that his family vacate the more rentable seventh-floor suite and, instead, relocate to the penthouse. The hotel readily agreed.

While Plaza guests may not have wanted to stay in the once-elegant but now-dilapidated penthouse, for the Salomones, it was bliss. "One time I wanted a pet lobster," recalled Gregg. "So one of the sous chefs took me downstairs to the kitchens and I picked out my own lobster." It turned out to be a less-than-exhilarating pet. "I put it down on the marble floor up in the penthouse and I remember looking at this thing, and I just got so bored staring at this lobster that wouldn't move." While he found the lobster boring, the apartment's marble floors were perfect for roller skating, and Gregg and his siblings frequently laced up their skates and sped through the oversized rooms. There was also the outside roof area, which, with its paint shed and ungainly hotel utilities, wasn't appropriate for hotel guests but was ideal for the Salomones. The hotel installed an aboveground pool for their use, even building cabanas to provide shade from the hot sun. "It was magical," Gregg said. "But it was also just our home. We didn't really realize how unique it was."

Years later, after Salomone had died, his widow, Bernadette, returned to the Plaza for a visit. She wasn't impressed by the changes to her old home. By then, the Plaza was under Trump's ownership. "Donald and his wife were away, so the manager said, 'Mrs. Salomone, would you like to see your old suite?' I said I would love to, so we went up there and it was like a gold whorehouse. I don't see how you could have lived there without sunglasses it was so bright. That was the '80s, of course."

By the time the Beatles checked into the Plaza, the hotel was no longer under Hilton's purview. He had paid $7.4 million for the Plaza in 1947, and in 1953 he had sold it for $15 million, nearly doubling his money.[13] The buyer was the industrialist A. M. "Sonny" Sonnabend, a conservative businessman who didn't fit the mold of his flashy predecessors. Unlike Harry Black, Sonnabend didn't live in a hotel penthouse, and in contrast to Hilton, he certainly wasn't married to a movie star. Rather, Sonnabend resided in a redbrick Georgian Colonial in Brookline, Massachusetts, with his college sweetheart, Esther, and their three sons, all of whom followed their father into the family business. Sonnabend's parents had been Austrian Jewish immigrants, and he attended Harvard on a scholarship. A workaholic who read a book a day, Sonnabend had been a US Navy aviator during World War I and was a national veterans squash champion.

Sonnabend was best known for pioneering a complex investment strategy that involved combining profitable businesses with those that were not, thereby reaping lucrative tax savings. "It was said of Mr. Sonnabend that he had a rare knack of mixing red and black ink on corporation ledgers and producing pure black," wrote the *New York Times*.[14] He began his career with a $5,000 loan from his father and eventually converted that initial seed money into a sprawling empire, with companies that produced everything from canned clams to prune juice, from shoe polish to lint-cleaning machinery.[15]

When Sonnabend bought the Plaza, America was in the midst of the postwar boom and celebrating almost unprecedented prosperity. But the hotel industry, particularly large and historic properties like the Plaza, was having trouble capturing its share of the affluence. "The place was going to seed and we had a reputation as an old ladies' home," said Paul Sonnabend, one of his sons.[16] The Plaza was "the last stronghold of elegance in New York," added Sonnabend, although he acknowledged, "some of the bathtubs need replacing."[17]

The Plaza's troubles weren't limited to its old-fashioned plunger elevators or the ancient widows milling about the lobby. There were several financial considerations at play. Hotel wages had been increasing for decades, but there had been no commensurate rise in room rates.[18] At the same time, competition was stiff from new hotels that featured such modern technologies as direct-dialing phones and self-operating elevators. Car-obsessed Americans had become infatuated with trendy motels like Howard Johnson's, while the advent of affordable air travel meant that the businessmen who made up the bulk of transient guests at the Plaza could fly into and out of New York in a single day, no longer having to stay the night.

The Plaza wasn't alone in its difficulties. A growing number of large hotels were closing or being converted into more lucrative uses. In just two years, from 1965 to 1967, twenty-one hotels were torn down or revamped into apartments, twice the number of the previous nineteen years.[19] The Savoy-Plaza, for instance, built by Harry Black at the height of the 1920s, was one such casualty. The hotel had been bleeding money for years, and the land that it sat on, located across from the Plaza, was far more valuable than the hotel itself. New owners took over and tore down the building, erecting in its stead a modernist skyscraper. The General Motors Building, as it became known, was named for the car company that was head-quartered there.

The economics of the hotel industry, and especially the destruction of the Savoy-Plaza, raised the possibility that the Plaza, too, could be demolished. No one was more of a proponent of this eventuality than Hilton himself. While he had sold the Plaza to Sonnabend back in 1953, he hadn't completely washed his hands of the property. Hilton continued managing the hotel until March 1960, and he also held an option to buy half of the land beneath the building. In addition, Hilton was the second-largest shareholder in Sonnabend's company.[20]

"The Plaza Hotel is not going to last forever," Hilton wrote in a letter to Sonnabend in 1963, the year before the Beatles arrived. "In fact it is of such an old vintage that the continued cost to keep it up in time make[s] it undesirable to keep as a hotel." In 1964, Hilton was even more direct: "Have you any thoughts about tearing down The Plaza and have a great office building built on this magnificent site?"[21] Sonnabend's son Roger responded: "I can assure you," he wrote, that the family "fully intends to continue to operate The Plaza. We feel that the hotel will benefit significantly in future years from development around it in New York City. It increasingly stands alone as a great traditional hotel."

Sonnabend wasn't the only person committed to keeping the Plaza operating as a hotel. Preservationists had grown increasingly perturbed by the demolition of historic properties. When the Savoy-Plaza was torn down in 1965, protesters held a "funeral march,"[22] and several socially prominent New York women, including Fannie Hurst, the novelist; and Emily Smith, daughter of New York governor Alfred E. Smith, threatened to start a boycott of General Motors.[23]

The destruction of the Savoy-Plaza followed on the heels of the demolition of several other much-loved buildings, most notably

the McKim, Mead & White–designed Pennsylvania Station, torn
down in 1963. Political will was galvanized, and in 1965, New
York City passed a law to landmark and protect historic structures.
The neighborhood surrounding Grand Army Plaza, where numerous hotels hugged the southeast corner of Central Park, including
the Sherry-Netherland, the Pierre, and, of course, the Plaza, was
rezoned. In 1969, the Plaza was given additional protection by being
declared a New York City landmark, thereby preventing its facade
from being altered without city approval. More protections would
follow, including the Plaza's 1986 designation as a National Historic
Landmark.

Around the time that the city passed its landmark protections, the
Plaza's fortunes began to improve. In 1964, the Plaza's occupancy
rate, buoyed by that year's World's Fair and, perhaps, the visit by the
Beatles, soared to 81 percent. This was compared with an occupancy
of only 60 percent in 1961. The Plaza also began a nearly $2 million
renovation, a figure that would eventually balloon to $9 million.[24]
Among Sonnabend's changes was swapping the original 1907 furnishings with mod 1960s-era decor and replacing several hydraulic elevators with high-speed electric lifts able to travel at nearly double the
speed. The restaurant at the corner of Fifth Avenue and Fifty-Ninth
Street was christened the Edwardian Room, and air-conditioning and
television sets were installed in every guest room.[25]

One of the biggest changes occurred in the Plaza basement. The
Plaza barbershop, one of the hotel's last remaining original throw-
backs, where Clara Bell Walsh (and Eloise) once had her hair styled,
was closed.[26] In its stead, the hotel opened a tiki bar that was previously located in the now-shuttered Savoy-Plaza. Trader Vic's was
famous for its colorful Polynesian decor and pupu platters, and
it soon became, as Fitzgerald's Grill Room once was, the favored
hangout for the well-heeled college set. With decor that included an
oversized outrigger canoe and a ceiling covered with paper lanterns,

Trader Vic's served up "Samoan Fog Cutters" and "Suffering Bastards" to crowds of tipsy youngsters and couples on first dates. As Plaza traditionalists tittered, opposed to any new additions, Salomone tried to be reassuring. "'We're the last ones in the world who want anything to happen to the hotel,'" Salomone told reporters at the restaurant's grand opening, as he sipped a tropical drink from a carved-out coconut.[27]

For all these changes, the Plaza retained its character. "It is true that the Plaza's plumbing is prehistoric, its wiring not much better than in Caruso's day, its heating system fickle (ancient thermostats in some of the rooms are apparently only decorative)," admitted the *Wall Street Journal* in a front-page article in 1965. But what other hotel would spend $7,000 a year on chocolate mints, or serve 100,000 eggs and 300 pounds of caviar in a single year? It was undoubtedly a costly endeavor, noted the paper, detailing a staff that included two men tasked with polishing the hotel's 1,650 crystal chandeliers, and "a chicken boner, two furniture cleaners and three ice sculptors who whip up glittering, if temporary, works of art for parties."[28] While ice sculptures and chocolate mints certainly helped bolster the aging hotel's reputation, its position would be cemented in these years by a social event that no one at the Plaza could have predicted.

In 1966, the writer Truman Capote was basking in worldwide fame. His true-life crime book *In Cold Blood*, about the massacre of the Clutter family in Holcomb, Kansas, had been published to widespread acclaim. The fair-haired, urbane Capote graced the covers of *Newsweek* and the *New York Times Book Review*, while paperback rights, movie rights, and foreign rights to the book were generating plenty of cash. A social arbiter with an extensive circle of friends, the Southern-born Capote, whose other career highlights included *Breakfast at Tiffany's*, was firmly ensconced as America's most sought-after dinner guest.

Capote, who was raised in Depression-era Alabama by a mother who was largely absent, never wanted the glow of attention to wane. As he told his friend, the socialite Kay Meehan, "I'm a better publicist than a writer."[29] To keep the spotlight centered on himself, Capote, in a move that harkened back to Clara Bell Walsh's kindergarten-themed cocktail party, devised an event that would etch his celebrity permanently into the social firmament.

Right away, there were a few things Capote was sure of: He would host a party, a *bal masqué*, gathering together his disparate friends, from Princess Luciana Pignatelli to his longtime boyfriend's relatives. The party would be held at New York's most glamorous, luxurious space—the ballroom at the Plaza. It was, after all, "the only really beautiful ballroom left in the United States," Capote would later say.[30] Beyond the room's beauty, there was a significance to having it there. "Just as F. Scott Fitzgerald used the Plaza to signify status in novels such as *The Great Gatsby*, Truman's choice of the Plaza would mean that he had arrived," wrote Deborah Davis in *Party of the Century: The Fabulous Story of Truman Capote and His Black and White Ball*.[31]

Capote's ball would be held on the Monday after Thanksgiving and would require attendees to adhere to a strict black-and-white color scheme. The dress code also required masks and, for the ladies, fans, adding to the air of mystery and fantasy. Capote's color choice was inspired by the Ascot sequence in the 1964 movie *My Fair Lady*, where the cast, in graphic outfits designed by his friend Cecil Beaton, posed and peacocked. It's unsurprising that Capote looked to Beaton for stimulus, as the men had much in common, not least their affection for the Plaza, and for glamorous women. "He is a superb raconteur with a flair for mimicry and gossip," *Good Housekeeping* wrote of Beaton, although the same could have easily been said of Capote.[32]

Realizing a ball held in his honor might seem crass, Capote chose an intriguing honoree who would help drum up additional excitement. Katharine Graham had taken over as publisher of the *Washington Post* three years before, following her husband's suicide. Shy and mostly unknown among the international social set, Graham was a curiosity. As the party's guest of honor, she would prove an irresistible draw. "He had the idea of the party first—I think he had always wanted to give a party at the Plaza," said Graham. "Then afterwards he was looking for a reason, and I guess I was it."[33]

While confident in the theme, the venue, and the honoree, Capote was less sure of the guest list. He waffled and agonized over the names, writing them in a cheap composition book before crossing them out and then writing them again. He asked friends for advice and reassured some they would make the cut, while leaving others to wonder. With an intensity typically devoted to writing, Capote approached the guest list much as he did authoring a book: It was a set of characters to be inserted into the narrative or removed, in whichever way produced the most compelling story line.

In the end, Capote settled on 540 guests, a mix of highbrow and lowbrow, of famous and obscure. "What gave the Black and White brew its intoxicating piquancy was the fact that he had flung together, in a gilt-edged melting pot, the most alluring power brokers in the worlds of high society, politics, the arts, and Hollywood—disconnected universes that collided, if not for the first time that evening, then at least with unprecedented force," wrote Amy Fine Collins in *Vanity Fair*. Eleven Kansans whom Capote had met while writing *In Cold Blood* made the cut, including a farmer named Odd Williams and the local detective Alvin Dewey. But Capote could be capricious and fickle, inviting, for instance, Lynda Bird Johnson, the president's daughter, but excluding her boyfriend, the actor George Hamilton.

Capote leaked news of the impending party in tantalizing dribs and drabs, and anticipation among the society set reached fevered pitch. "The old social routine can be fairly grim with the same round of cocktails, dinners, and benefits repeating year after year," wrote the *Los Angeles Times*. "Leave it to Truman Capote to kindle a romantic fire in the ashes."[34] The party invitation, printed on a white card with a yellow-and-orange border, was simple, reading "Mr. Truman Capote requests the pleasure of your company at a Black and White Dance." Guests were told to arrive at 10 p.m. at the "Grand Ballroom, The Plaza." There was no need to specify the Plaza *Hotel* or to give an address. Invitees would know perfectly well where to go.

Some in Capote's circle were secure in the knowledge that they would receive a coveted invitation. The "swans," as he called his clique of rich, socially prominent female companions, including Gloria Guinness and Babe Paley, were confident. They spent the weeks leading up to the event deciding which designer would create their couture gown, not fretting about whether they would be on the list. But many others found themselves among "the Uninvited," as the press dubbed them. These rejected masses "maintained a flow of 20 letters a day to Capote, some of them poignant, some downright nasty, seeking to get their hands on that coveted invitation," the *Washington Post* salaciously reported. One person offered the equivalent of $11,000 to secure an invite (it didn't work), while another threatened to jump out the window (the effort also failed). Capote loved the desperation. "People are practically committing *suicide* because they didn't get invitations," he marveled. "I suppose there are 100 or 150 more I should have asked, but if I invited everybody, I would have to hire Shea Stadium."[35]

Finally, the appointed day arrived. "It was not a day like any other day; the rain came down and the women poured out—from penthouses, town houses, duplexes and hotels," wrote the *Globe and Mail*. At the entrance to the Plaza, an endless line of limousines waited to discharge their well-heeled passengers. Like the parade of millionaires that marked the Plaza's opening day almost six decades earlier, a march of movie stars, artists, and society royalty commenced. Grande dames like Rose Kennedy and Tallulah Bankhead were followed by the actress Joan Fontaine and Gloria Vanderbilt. There was Princess Lee Radziwill and most of the Kennedy clan, as well as William Buckley and Norman Mailer, who wore "a dirty trench coat thrown over his dinner jacket."[36]

Capote, ever a publicity hound, must have realized that the Plaza was the perfect parade ground to show off his stars. Outside, crowds of onlookers braved the rain for a glimpse of their favorite celebrities, penned in behind police sawhorses. Inside, paparazzi and cameramen lined the lobby and the halls. The path to the ballroom was long, with guests entering through the hotel's revolving doors, then passing the Palm Court, walking up several stairs to the mezzanine, and, finally, ascending an even grander staircase to the ballroom. It provided plenty of opportunities for television anchors to shout their questions and photographers to snap guests blowing air kisses. The fete "closed an era of elegant exclusiveness and ushered in another of media madness—the one in which we still live," noted Peter Duchin, the bandleader who performed at the ball.[37]

As the opulent finery and outrageous fashions paraded by, some of Capote's lucky attendees may have noticed two small girls in their nightgowns watching the procession. A friendly Plaza security guard had allowed the two tiny interlopers, Lourdes Salomone and her best friend, Francesca, to sit unnoticed on one of the steps. "We sat there with our chins in our hands looking and seeing all of these amazing people going up and down the stairs," Lourdes recalled. "It was so glamorous."

When guests finally made it to the ballroom, they were greeted by secretaries who checked their names off a master list, several husky security men standing guard behind them. Once guests were allowed entry, they were formally announced, then waited in a receiving line to greet Graham and Capote, the publisher towering eight inches above her date. The ballroom itself was barely altered. Capote skimped on decorations, having paid for the entire event himself at a cost of $16,000.[38] Tables were covered in a simple red cloth (the hotel didn't charge extra for this color),[39] and golden candelabras were placed around the gold-and-white room, topped with white tapers and intertwined tropical vines. The only other addition was a gathering of iridescent balloons that clung to the ceiling. In addition to the Peter Duchin Orchestra, the rock 'n' roll band the Soul Brothers provided musical accompaniment.

As guests relaxed into the party, they marveled at the fashions, including a whimsical mask of two intertwined swans, one black and one white, worn by journalist and socialite Isabel Eberstadt. The mask was designed by Bill Cunningham, who would soon land at the *New York Times* and become famous in his own right for riding his bike around town in his ubiquitous blue painter's jacket, taking photos of street-style fashions. Amanda Burden, the elegant daughter of Babe Paley, rented one of Beaton's original costumes from *My Fair Lady*. Sixteen-year-old ingénue Penelope Tree, her hair long, with blunt-edged bangs, wowed in a racy black tunic with slits up to her ribs by as-yet-unknown designer Betsey Johnson.[40] Guests mingled, with one famous actress dancing through the night with a handsome, tuxedoed bachelor, never realizing for a moment that he was the doorman from Capote's apartment building. Lauren Bacall waltzed with the choreographer Jerome Robbins. The economist John Kenneth Galbraith, "a sensation" on the dance floor thanks in part to his six-foot-eight-inch frame, and *Paris Review* founder George Plimpton engaged in a strange version of musical football, the pair tossing back and forth napkins and even candelabra.

Finally, at midnight, guests were told to remove their masks—although many already had or, like Andy Warhol, showed up without one. To finish off the evening, a wide-ranging buffet of chicken hash, scrambled eggs, and spaghetti and meatballs was served. Duchin's orchestra played until 3:30 a.m. When the party began winding down, some continued the night at Elaine's, the famous Upper East Side celebrity hangout, while others, like Frank Sinatra, went to a nearby hole-in-the-wall joint. As for Capote, he followed his Kansan friends up to their rooms at the Plaza, where he kept them up for hours dissecting the evening's events.

Capote had set out to achieve the party of the century, a legendary night that would take on cult status. He had succeeded. "It was the Last Great American Party," declared D. D. Ryan, the woman who had introduced Kay Thompson to Hilary Knight and helped birth the creation of *Eloise*. Ryan had been there, wearing a white Kabuki mask by the young designer Halston. "The ball was a carryover from the 50s—the last time when people felt no guilt about expenditures, and were not bothered by any serious social questions," recalled Eberstadt.[41] The war in Vietnam and the social unrest that would come to define the late 1960s had yet to break through. "In 1966—before Vietnam escalated disastrously, before R.F.K.'s and Martin Luther King Jr.'s assassinations, before disillusionment took hold—Capote and the country both felt invincible," wrote Collins in *Vanity Fair*. But it wasn't long before the mood soured.

In short order, the pomp and fantasy evinced at the Black and White Ball appeared in bad taste. The day after the ball, the *New York Times* headline read "Capote's Black and White Ball: 'The Most Exquisite of Spectator Sports.'" But the *New York Post* columnist Pete Hamill took a different tack. In a piece expressing outrage, he juxtaposed imagined frivolous conversations from the party with descriptions from the front lines in Vietnam. "And Truman was just marvelous! He was the first to arrive, along with Mrs. Kay Graham," reads one contrived conversation. "She looked just gorgeous in a white Balmain gown..." This was followed by "The helicopter landed in a scrubby open field six miles north of Bong Son…You could hear the phwup-phwup of a mortar and the snapping of small arms fire…"

As the decade continued, calls for racial equality grew louder, the Vietnam War ratcheted up in intensity, and teenage baby boomers who had embraced Beatlemania in 1964 confronted the draft. In 1967, a year after the ball, *Esquire* magazine published a cover that featured celebrities, including Lynn Redgrave, Ed Sullivan, and Tony Curtis, staring angrily at the camera. The headline above them read, "We wouldn't have come even if you *had* invited us, Truman Capote!" As attitudes shifted, and Capote's ball looked to be in increasingly bad taste, the author himself slipped from his high. In the years that followed, Capote would collapse into alcoholism and drug use, his writing would fall off, and he would alienate many of the celebrity friends who had once clamored for an invitation to his party.

The Plaza, as it had throughout its history, became a place where these changing sentiments played out. In the first half of the 1960s, it hosted the Beatles and Capote's ball, and now, at the close of the era, it became the setting for another type of cultural flashpoint. The Plaza's Oak Room was one of New York's few remaining all-male restaurants, a dark-wooded bastion of masculinity where Wall Street bankers found refuge during their weekday lunches, free from female distraction. It would soon land in the crosshairs of Betty Friedan, feminist and author of the best seller *The Feminine Mystique*, who targeted the fabled restaurant in her stand for equality.

On a winter day in February 1969, as a blizzard began to gather, Friedan and several fellow activists marched in the frigid cold outside the Plaza. They carried signs with slogans including "We have been using knives and forks for years, fellas," and "Don't worry, we'll pay our way." Many of the protesters were dressed in fur coats, to send the message that these "women were the equals of the men inside, not bra burners; there was no reason to exclude them."[42]

Earlier that day, Friedan had called and made a reservation for lunch at the Oak Room, not specifying that it was for several women guests. At the appointed time, the protesters marched inside and asked for their reservation. The Oak Room's flustered maître d' seated the women, but things soon went awry.

"We were sitting at a round table in the center of the room," recounted activist Diana Gartner. "Four waiters came and lifted the table and walked away with it. We were wearing dresses—we were sitting there with our legs, and the men were looking at us. One of them offered us bread sticks." The women sat there, table-less, deciding what to do next. "It looks like we are not going to be served; we'd better leave," Friedan said, finally relenting.[43] While Friedan and her friends weren't successfully served that day, a few months later, the hotel announced that the Oak Room would be opening to female diners. It was a turning point, the first of a string of well-intentioned, if sometimes contentious, changes to bring the Plaza in line with the shifting times.

Chapter 10

PROSTITUTES' PROMENADE

"You might say we lost our shirts in 1971 and our
underwear in 1972."
—*James Lavenson, Plaza manager*

It was just after noon on a Friday in September 1973 when the
manager of the Plaza walked nervously through the plush lobby
of the Waldorf-Astoria. James Lavenson wasn't on a reconnaissance
mission to gather dirt on his biggest competitor, or to have a meeting with one of his hotel colleagues. The situation was far more
nefarious.

During the summer, Lavenson had arrived at work one morning to discover a sliver of paper on his desk. It was a note, threatening to blow up the Plaza unless a $50,000 ransom was paid. The
message was signed "Black September," the name of a Palestinian terrorist group. Lavenson brushed it off as a hoax. But when
he received a second, similar letter just after Labor Day, he grew
increasingly concerned. He called the Federal Bureau of Investigation, who directed Lavenson to respond and set up a drop for the
money. The appointed place was to be Grand Central Terminal, but
Lavenson stood anxiously among the bustle of commuters in vain,
for the terrorist never materialized. A new drop was scheduled, this

time at a phone booth on Fifth Avenue. Again, the terrorist was a no-show.

Now, Lavenson was making his third attempt to deliver the ransom money, walking on shaky legs down the Waldorf's long lobby, gripping in his sweaty palms a brown paper bag stuffed with cash. He finally reached a telephone booth on the Fiftieth Street side of the hotel. Picking up the receiver, Lavenson listened silently as a man on the other end relayed instructions. He then headed to a nearby elevator bank, pressing the button for the fourth floor. Lavenson stepped out of the elevator and into the foyer. Scanning the area, he located a standing ashtray, lifting the top to discover a note hidden underneath. It directed him to leave the money, so Lavenson dropped the bag inside the receptacle and, with relief, returned to the safety of the elevator cab and the lobby below.

As Lavenson retreated, an FBI agent got out of a second elevator and stood nonchalantly, observing. He soon saw a young man repeatedly pass by Lavenson's brown paper bag. On his third pass, the young man finally picked up the package, and when he did, the agent arrested him. The perpetrator turned out to be a twenty-three-year-old housepainter. Pangiotis Vlachos had emigrated from Greece three years earlier and hoped to use the money to open a restaurant. He broke down in tears at the police station, where he was charged with grand larceny, extortion, and burglary. No association with the Black September terrorist group was ever discovered.[1]

The unrest of the 1960s took a decidedly darker turn in the 1970s, with desperate crimes like the bomb threat against the Plaza a disturbingly common phenomenon. Nationally, it was the most financially precarious decade since the Great Depression, marked by oil embargoes and stagflation. The country's social fabric was being torn apart, with divorce rates spiking, the proliferation of illegal drug use, and Watergate. New York City suffered a citywide blackout, as well as acts of particular brutality in the Son of Sam murders and the disappearance of young Etan Patz while he walked to a school bus stop in SoHo. But the event that overshadowed all others was New York City's deepening fiscal crisis. The issue reached a tipping point in the fall of 1975, when Mayor Abe Beame prepared to declare the city bankrupt, only to be saved at the eleventh hour by a loan from the teachers union. The city's utter disrepair stirred a tough rebuke from an unforgiving President Gerald Ford, prompting the *New York Daily News* to run its most famous headline, "FORD TO CITY: DROP DEAD."

In this bleak environment, strikes were common and often interrupted basic city services. A multiday sanitation strike, for instance, left a heap of rotting food, soiled sheets, and broken furniture on the Fifty-Eighth Street side of the Plaza. At one point, the towering garbage pile rose seven feet high and stretched more than five feet wide, according to measurements taken by an exacting reporter, who must have come armed with a tape measure, if not also nose plugs.[2] Photos of the garbage mountain ran in newspapers across the country, a pointed illustration of how the city's disrepair had reached the point where even the fanciest New York institutions were covered in trash.

It was during the 1970s that the *New York Times* uncovered extensive corruption in the ranks of the New York City Police Department, thanks in part to whistle-blower Frank Serpico.[3] The front-page article detailing the graft ran next to another story that reported a failed assassination attempt against the son of Chinese nationalist leader Chiang Kai-shek. The attack took place at the Plaza, as Chiang Ching-kuo was about to enter the hotel's revolving doors on his way to deliver a luncheon keynote address. A would-be assassin shot off his gun, but Chiang Ching-kuo dodged the bullet and proceeded into the hotel. He then gave his speech—never once mentioning his near-death experience just moments before.[4]

Crime also abounded inside the hotel's doors, including a hostage situation. At 4 a.m. one July morning in 1972, the bellman Edner Smith noticed a heavyset man with a mustache and dressed in a suit making his way toward him through the mostly deserted lobby. "Are you looking for a room?" he asked. "No," the man replied quietly. "This is a holdup." As Smith stared at him, the man patted his pocket, inviting Smith to touch what was there. Smith reached out and felt the distinct bulk of a gun beneath the man's well-cut coat.

Ernest Levy, the night manager, was standing near Smith at the front desk, his head bowed as he looked through some paperwork. He didn't notice a second gentleman approach until he paused from his work and raised his head to find the barrel of a gun pointed directly at him. William Leins, a taxi driver, was standing aimlessly outside the Plaza, next to his cab, and shouldn't have been there at all. He was waiting for a fare when he noticed a bottle of Scotch whiskey lying on a seat in the tan Rambler sedan that had pulled up next to him. He had just watched five well-dressed men exit the car and make their way into the Plaza, so he hurried inside to inform them that they had forgotten their bottle. But before he could do more than step inside the vestibule, he had a .45-caliber automatic pistol shoved into the small of his back.

Smith, Levy, Leins, and more than a dozen other Plaza staff who were unlucky enough to be in the lobby in the wee hours that summer morning were marched across the mosaic flooring and crowded into a tiny ten-by-eleven-foot office. The gunmen "were real nice about it," Jimmy Conway, who spent forty-four years manning the old-fashioned Plaza elevators, later told detectives. "They saw my gray hair and told me to sit down. They didn't even handcuff me." Calling their twenty-one captives "sir" and "madam," "they were the politest people I've ever seen—for crooks," said Camille Parr, another Plaza staffer. With their captives secured, the bandits went to work in the hotel's safe room, a red-carpeted chamber with a large crystal chandelier hanging overhead. They broke the locks on forty steel safe-deposit boxes, making off with the equivalent of $265,000 in loot, including an emerald tiara.[5]

Other notable felonies that took place at the hotel during those years included the case of a physician from Connecticut, who was attacked by a knife-wielding assailant when he answered the door to his Plaza suite,[6] and two couples who were robbed at gunpoint after leaving a charity event in the Plaza's ballroom.[7] A German politician, who said he was merely standing outside the Plaza's entrance late one night getting some air, was mugged by two prostitutes. The attack led to a police crackdown on Central Park South, which, by then, had taken on the decidedly less elegant name of Prostitutes' Promenade.[8]

On Sundays, Plaza guests were treated to an impromptu bazaar that had popped up around the Pulitzer Fountain, with vendors hawking everything from illicit drugs like amyl nitrite (or "poppers") to cheap tchotchkes such as inflatable frogs featuring the words "Kiss Me." There was a harpist and also a young man selling India-print skirts "who modeled his wares himself as he smoked a large cigar," the *New York Times* reported. In front of the hotel, a Mister Softee truck belched its mechanical song while a hot-dog cart was squeezed in between a vendor selling rabbit's-foot key chains and another offering watermelon slices.[9]

New York City had become a national punch line, with late-night comics mining its seediness for jokes, while tourists and businessmen mostly chose to stay away. It was no surprise that the Plaza suffered as a result. Whereas in 1969, the Plaza posted a gain of $2.6 million, by 1970, that had diminished to just $915,000, a drop of 65 percent. By 1971, the Plaza was in the red, posting a loss of $1.4 million.[10]

During this time, the unfortunate owner forced to deal with the money-losing Plaza was Roger Sonnabend, the eldest son of A. M. Sonnabend, the industrialist. The senior Sonnabend had died in 1964, leaving Roger to take the helm of the family's businesses. Widely seen as brilliant by friends and business associates, Roger attended the Massachusetts Institute of Technology and Harvard Business School. At first, Roger adhered to the model and strictures set out by his conservative, staid father.

But as the 1960s got underway, Roger grew in confidence and began unshackling himself from his father's narrow perspective, embracing the more liberal ethos of the time. Roger "went through this mid-life crisis and realized that he was living in the image of who his father wanted him to be, not necessarily who he wanted to be," said Stephanie Sonnabend, Roger's daughter.[11] This new Roger began wearing red beads and Nehru jackets, grew facial hair, threw away his glasses, and dropped twenty-five pounds. A profile of Roger that ran in the *Boston Sunday Globe* was illustrated with startling side-by-side photos. In the first, taken in 1966, his face is clean-cut, a slightly pudgy if typical businessman in a suit. In the second, taken for the magazine in 1969, Roger is noticeably thinner, his glasses are gone, and he sports a fashionable, well-trimmed goatee, a wide-lapelled blazer, and a patterned, broad tie.[12]

It was during this period that Roger left his first wife and the mother of his four children, remarrying a fashionable Boston-based art dealer. The wedding was a small affair, held at the Plaza with just a dozen attendees. Afterward, the group went to the Persian Room to hear the 1940s chanteuse Hildegarde perform.[13] Roger brought his newfound aesthetics to the Plaza as well. Whereas his father once boasted that the hotel was "the last stronghold of elegance in New York," his son looked to draw in a new, younger crowd, instituting changes that would result in mixed reviews.

As the 1970s unfolded, the Plaza's management searched for ways to cut costs, leading, for example, to the decision to evict *Eloise* author Kay Thompson from her rooms. There was talk of curtailing such niceties as placing chocolate on beds during the evening turndown service, but managers worried it would hurt the Plaza's standing as a luxury hotel. The hotel did cancel the traditional Thanksgiving turkey giveaway for employees, as well as the employee Christmas party. On the day the holiday party was to have taken place, the hotel's manager exchanged his regular name tag for one that read simply "Scrooge."

But these steps weren't sufficiently drastic. To survive, the Plaza needed to shrug off its reputation as a home for widows and appeal to a new clientele. Just as Roger had shaken off the shackles of his straitlaced father, so, too, the Plaza revamped itself in a new groovy style. The hotel hired a "den mother," the actress Betsy Palmer, whose claim to fame would eventually be her role as the mother of Jason Voorhees in the slasher film *Friday the 13th*. Palmer was brought on to create "a modern exciting atmosphere," although her responsibilities were ill-defined. The hotel also revamped the Persian Room, which was losing the equivalent of nearly $800,000 a year, swapping old-fashioned acts like Hildegarde for pop singers including Robert Goulet and Dusty Springfield.[14] It didn't work, and in 1978, the Persian Room was permanently closed, replaced with a women's clothing boutique.[15]

Undoubtedly, the most controversial alteration was the complete reimagining of the somber, romantic Edwardian Room. A stalwart of old-world elegance, with large windows facing Central Park, the room had always been one of the hotel's most famous dining spots. There, the maître d' oversaw a "hierarchy of seating," whereby "the rich and respected who were above publicity were conducted to wall banquettes and settled in capacious armchairs, where they were ministered to by the best waiters, since they had actually come to eat and drink," wrote *Good Housekeeping*. The round tables in the middle of the room were reserved for politicians, diplomats, and "the visiting tycoons from Texas and Los Angeles," while window

seats were set aside for "the prettiest actresses and the most glamorous models," as well as "Marlene Dietrich or whoever happened to
be wearing a blazing diamond necklace—the window dressing of
any well-run café."[16]

Now, this would all be done away with. The Edwardian Room
was to be modernized and renamed the Green Tulip. The original
dark wood paneling was slathered in white paint, the heavy wood
and leather chairs replaced with pink and green upholstery, and the
red damask drapery exchanged for pastel curtains featuring oversized butterflies. The hotel installed a gazebo made with fake Tiffany glass and a raised platform to allow more diners to glimpse
Central Park. The traditional menu, heavy on steak and chicken,
was replaced with one offering fondue and organic salads, while
formal waiters in tuxedos were replaced by "pretty, perky waitresses"
pushing cocktail carts bedecked with flowers. Instead of classical
concertos, the Muzak of *Jesus Christ Superstar* provided the background sound track.

To announce its new look, the Plaza published a multiple-page
advertising insert that was included in the Sunday *New York Times*.
With a psychedelic, swirling text surrounded by paisley designs,
the advertorial featured a montage of smiling, bellbottom-wearing
staffers. Palmer, the hotel's den mother, was featured in several photos, dressed up in various hotel uniforms. Here she was as a bellman, albeit with hot pants for bottoms, or a waitress, inexplicably
donning a leotard. A flood of flowery language was used to talk up
the new Green Tulip, including "sun-drenched indoor garden," and
"an Eden of cool forest greens" featuring "pastels of rain-washed
blossoms." In contradictory language, the ad claimed the revamped
Plaza would "project the popular hostelry into the world of today
and tomorrow," yet would be so great as to "not let you forget the
fun and excitement of the very current yesterday."

Many Plaza lovers were aghast, and none more so than the *New*

York Times' famed architecture critic Ada Louise Huxtable. "There is now a restaurant called the Green Tulip that the management points out, with awful appropriateness, is 'on the site of the traditional Edwardian Room,'" she wrote, in one of a series of sharply worded columns.[17] The hotel, she bemoaned, had been "cheapened with tricksy restaurants full of familiar and rather loathsome design gimmicks and arch menus and publicity to match."

Huxtable had grown up in the city, with the Plaza as a constant. "From a very early age, my appreciation of the past and even my feeling for New York [was] undoubtedly conditioned by associations with that solid structure... I thought it had been there forever, and was something absolute." These alterations were an anathema, "a kind of creeping, crawling bad taste in which even the authentic is being made to look fake."[18] Of particular ire, the Green Tulip was "a successful attempt to reduce period grandeur to comfortable, gimmicky ordinariness... What is real, now looks fake. Class is out. Confusion is in."[19]

The Plaza went on the defensive, trying to justify the much-maligned changes. "We Are Not 'Raping' the Plaza," was the headline for a letter to the editor published in the *New York Times.* The hotel was only trying to "convey an atmosphere of friendliness, fun and excitement in order to stem a tide of opinion that New York is an unpleasant place to visit," the letter insisted, adding, "We sought to appeal to a wider age group than we had in the past."[20] But despite the protestations, in 1974, the hotel relented to critics. It closed the Green Tulip, scrubbing the paint off the wood and returning the original, dark furnishings. The Edwardian Room 2.0 was meant "to look not 1974-new but 1907-new," the Plaza's manager said. At first, it was called the Plaza Restaurant, but by 1975, the Edwardian Room name was quietly put back into circulation.[21]

By then, the hotel's longtime manager, Alphonse Salomone, had left the Plaza, and James Lavenson, the manager who had been targeted by the bomb scare, was in charge. Lavenson had come from advertising, where he was a successful executive. The Plaza had been one of his clients, and he became friendly with Roger Sonnabend, the hotel's owner. In 1972, Roger convinced his adman to come and run the hotel for him. But before he ever became the Plaza's manager, Lavenson engineered a number of its most popular advertising campaigns.

Perhaps Lavenson's most famous advertisement centered on a fictitious Irish Plaza chambermaid.[22] The salt-of-the-earth Mary O'Sullivan wrote personalized letters that were mailed directly to businessmen across the country. "I'm the chambermaid. I have my own stationery. I take care of the rooms at the Plaza," the letter said. The Plaza's room rates are "reasonable," O'Sullivan concluded, so "won't you come see for yourself?" The letters produced an impressive number of new guests for the hotel, even "if they also raised a few eyebrows from wives who regularly monitor their husband's mail," noted the *New York Times*.[23]

After becoming the Plaza's manager, Lavenson kept in touch with his advertising roots. He even co-opted his teenage son Gary, who spent the summers working as an elevator operator at the hotel, to help him attract business. Lavenson was trying to appeal to New York City cabdrivers, who, he thought, if properly motivated, might suggest that their tourist passengers try out the Plaza. So he dispatched Gary to serve coffee to the long line of notoriously crabby cabbies as they waited outside the hotel for fares. Carrying hot demitasses made of delicate Plaza china, Gary tottered down the line, trying not to spill. "I wasn't too successful," he said.[24]

Lavenson also changed the way employees were managed. The more than one thousand Plaza staff had always worked in isolated silos, rarely venturing outside their narrow job duties. Peter Sonnabend, A.M.'s grandson, recalled one story of a housekeeper who was retiring after fifty years spent cleaning rooms at the Plaza. The hotel wanted to throw a party in her honor and asked her what she would like for a present. She inquired if she might not visit the lobby. "Employees would enter through an employee entrance, and it turns out, the woman was so intimidated that despite working there for half a century, she had never been in the Plaza's lobby," Peter Sonnabend marveled.[25]

Lavenson recognized that such employee isolation had broad consequences for the hotel. How could reservationists, for example, urge guests to book a $125 suite rather than an $85 suite, if they hadn't seen the suites themselves? Or a bellman tout a performer at the Persian Room if he hadn't ever seen the show? Lavenson began requiring that room clerks spend a night in the hotel and that musicians who were playing at the Persian Room first perform for the employees. He also insisted that everyone, from the dishwashers to the general manager, wear a name tag to promote friendliness between staff and make service more personable for guests.

It was all part of Lavenson's larger theory, which he called "Think Strawberries." Plaza waiters would often suggest that diners order a dessert course, but many patrons were diet-conscious and declined. This was unfortunate, Lavenson maintained, since more dessert orders meant the hotel would make more money and the waiters would receive a larger tip. So Lavenson urged them to "think strawberries," or suggest to reluctant diners that they order a bowl of delicious, ripe, diet-friendly fruit. "We widened the aisles between the tables and had the waiters wheel the cart up to each and every table at dessert time," Lavenson said, in a speech on the topic. "The waiter then went into raptures about the bowl of fresh strawberries. There was even a bowl of whipped cream for the slightly wicked."[26]

Lavenson and Roger Sonnabend had much in common, not least of which was the fact that both men were complete departures from their predecessors. Plaza managers like Alphonse Salomone and Frederick Sterry were hotel men who had been promoted through the ranks. Lavenson, on the other hand, was an outsider and career changer who hailed from advertising. Similarly, previous owners like Harry Black and Conrad Hilton reveled in the status that the Plaza brought them, while Roger was circumspect of the trappings of privilege and power.

In fact, once Roger emerged from under his father's shadow, he grew increasingly politically minded. "I was told from when I was very young I had to be like the WASPs if I really wanted to succeed in business and that was the way it was," he told the *Boston Sunday Globe*. Roger rejected this and began eschewing club memberships, quitting Boston's Algonquin Club, which he called "a white racist Christian club of the worst sort," and refusing to attend events at New York's elite Union League Club.

Roger also grew more involved in civil rights and the antiwar movements. His antiwar protests landed him on President Richard Nixon's so-called "enemies list,"[27] and he declared a companywide goal of hiring 150 black executives, to represent as much as 15 percent of the company's top brass. "The company's black hiring policies have brought about many internal confrontations," Sonnabend admitted, but "the company is not permitting the sacrifice of minority workers where executives prove inflexible." Roger also held a three-day seminar in a house in Roxbury, "the heart of the Boston ghetto," for top hotel managers to discuss hiring more unemployed workers, reported the *Jewish Advocate*.[28] Other efforts included partnering with African American developers to build a 230-room motel in Harlem,[29] the news of which was reported in a front-page article in the *New York Times*.[30] Lavenson shared Roger's perspective, working with him on the Harlem motel project and penning a column in the *New York Amsterdam News*, an African American paper.[31]

While Roger was battling for racial equality and against the Vietnam War, he was also fighting for his business. When Roger's father, A. M. Sonnabend, died, he left behind a trail of troubles, including a number of complex, unresolved tax issues. The family's hotel business, called Sonesta, a mash-up of their father's nickname, Sonny, and their mother's name, Esther, was bleeding money and hadn't turned a profit in several quarters. In addition, it was facing an $11 million mortgage on the Plaza. "Today, $11 million doesn't sound like much, but back then, with the city on the verge of bankruptcy, it was a real challenge," said A.M.'s grandson, Peter Sonnabend.

Even worse was a battle that had been brewing for some time over the Plaza's ownership. At issue was a conflict between Sonesta and two of New York City's largest landlords, Sol Goldman and Alex DiLorenzo. Goldman DiLorenzo, as their firm was known, owned the Chrysler Building, as well as dozens of properties near the Plaza, and was notorious for its tough and controversial negotiation tactics. In later years, the firm would be brought to task for running buildings with countless infractions, and for renting to illicit businesses like massage parlors and peep shows.[32] The Brooklyn-bred partners, who were lifelong friends, never had a contract between them.[33] When Goldman DiLorenzo was dissolved years later, they divided their properties with a series of coin tosses, the winner picking one of two envelopes containing addresses, and the loser getting the other one.[34]

In 1965, Goldman DiLorenzo had purchased Hilton's option for half of the land beneath the Plaza.[35] Typically, the sale of a building includes the land beneath the property, but sometimes the land and the building can be separated into different legal entities. As a result of this structure, Sonesta owed Goldman DiLorenzo rent, and disagreement quickly arose over the amount to be paid. They took each other to court, and even as their suit progressed, Goldman DiLorenzo made a number of unsolicited offers to buy the remainder of the land beneath the Plaza and the hotel itself. Sonesta rebuffed all offers to sell.

At one point, Goldman DiLorenzo attempted to take the Plaza by force, initiating a hostile takeover of Sonesta, a public company, by issuing a tender offer for all of its outstanding shares.[36] At the height of his battle with Goldman DiLorenzo, Roger received an anonymous call, the man on the other end of the phone line threatening, "You better watch yourself," before hanging up. "Roger was the type of guy who laughed that off, but others might not have been as cavalier," said Peter Sonnabend. In the end, a judge ruled that unless Goldman DiLorenzo was more transparent with its intentions, it could not pursue the hostile takeover of Sonesta. The landlord duo decided to withdraw.[37]

Even with its win over Goldman Di Lorenzo, Sonesta had a tough several years. "We weren't a big hotel company," George Abrams, a lawyer who was close to Roger and sat on the Sonesta board, said. "The 1970s hit and there was a downturn in the economy and properties were being foreclosed all around us. We decided it was too much and we started looking around for a buyer." Sonesta fielded several offers for the Plaza, including a deal for $18.5 million from Harry Helmsley, a New York City property tycoon and the husband of Leona, dubbed the "Queen of Mean" by New York City tabloids. The deal collapsed, however. Other buyers also came forward, including, once again, the persistent Goldman DiLorenzo, which the *Wall Street Journal* reported had "a verbal agreement" to finally acquire the hotel it had long sought.[38] That, too, fell through. Finally, a white knight arrived in the form of Harry Mullikin, the president of the Seattle, Washington–based Westin Hotels chain.

"We made a couple of passes at The Plaza over the years, but nothing ever came of it," Mullikin told the *Seattle Times*. Then, in November 1974, Mullikin got wind that the Sonnabends were serious about unloading the property. Mullikin had been flying to Europe on a business trip and Paul Sonnabend, Roger's brother, was in Amsterdam at the time. The two men met overseas and began negotiations. The talks continued and by January 1975, a deal was finalized.[39] Westin agreed to pay $25 million in cash, or the equivalent of $114 million today, including the satisfaction of the $11 million mortgage. It was an astounding windfall for Sonesta, which had bought the hotel from Hilton in 1953 for $15 million. At a time when the country's economy was in disarray and investment in New York City was at a low point, it was more than the owners had anticipated and far higher than any other offer they had received.

Roger, however, did leave out one Plaza asset from the deal: "We decided to make an exclusionary clause," said Abrams, the lawyer and Sonesta board member. "We said, 'We're not selling the Everett Shinn paintings.'" Hilton had commissioned the three celebrated murals in the Oak Bar years earlier, and Roger's wife, an art dealer, knew their value. Westin, on the other hand, "didn't pay much attention and didn't care," Abrams said. But the art-minded public did care, and when it became known that the Shinn murals weren't coming with the hotel, controversy erupted.[40] Westin eventually realized that it had no choice but to pony up additional money for the paintings. "A year later, they came back to us and said, 'We didn't realize that the Shinn paintings are so fundamental to the Oak Room and we need to keep them,'" said Abrams. Westin would eventually shell out another $1 million for the artworks.

Plaza observers rejoiced over the new owners. "When the Plaza, after suffering many changes and some frightful indignities of attempted so-called modernization and economic resuscitation," was sold to Westin, there was "a citywide sigh of relief," wrote the *Washington Post*.[41] Unlike Sonesta, which was a midsize hotel company, Westin was a national chain. Its owner, UAL Corporation, which also owned United Airlines, had deep pockets and there was renewed hope that the Plaza could once again be elevated to its previous, high standard.

Like its predecessors, Westin promised to "spend whatever is necessary" to restore the hotel to its former glory. It would turn out to be the equivalent of $32 million, and included steam-washing the hotel's grungy facade and removing sixteen coats of paint, uncovering the hotel's original copper window frames. An art house–style movie theater was opened in the basement, and the Plaza's few remaining hydraulic elevators, among the last of their kind in New York City, were replaced. The old-fashioned "plungers," which carried Princess Parlaghy to her sprawling suite after she offended the Duchess of Manchester, and whisked Eloise to the roof to swonk pigeons, were removed, and their enormous cylinders, buried deep into the bedrock of Manhattan, were drowned in a layer of concrete.

The company also attempted to lease out Harry Black's old penthouse. After the Salomone family had left, it was rented to "various show business personalities for brief periods." The television show *Kojak* used it to shoot several scenes, although never with its bald-headed star, Telly Savalas. Now, according to advertisements, for $150,000 a year, guests could enjoy "a wood-paneled game room, complete with billiard table, a wet bar, and a working fireplace," as well as a bedroom featuring a whirlpool and a sauna.[42]

By the late 1970s, the Plaza's fortunes were turning up again, with net earnings in 1979 of $3.2 million—a 113 percent increase over the previous year.[43] The Plaza seemed poised to enter the 1980s in a strong position. But what would the future bring? In 1965, the hotel ran an unusual, full-page advertisement in the *New Yorker*. Created when Lavenson was still the Plaza's adman, before he took over as manager, the ad copy featured a shot of the city's skyline fading into gray, above the headline, "The day New York almost vanished." The rest of the page was almost entirely covered in text, and told an apocalyptic tale set sometime in the near future. The science-fiction allegory envisioned a world dominated by sleek architecture, where cold, icy glass dominated the landscape and Edwardian opulence and grandeur was rendered extinct. Yet, even in such a bleak universe, the Plaza's permanency persisted:

It didn't happen all at once. They did it very gradually...

They removed a little house here and a great hotel there. And then a few limestone banks and all the cast-iron store-fronts they could find...

A few people grumbled. Some found temporary shelter at The Dakota when Park Avenue disappeared. Others moved to Westchester...

But most people were complacent. Until the day they discovered that their city had been entirely replaced with glass.

Then they complained. But it was too late. So the faces of the city grew grimmer than they had ever been before. Clocks stopped. And the glass began to crack.

Soon after this on one ghastly glittering morning, an observant executive walking to work paused on Fifth Avenue at Fifty-Ninth Street to clean his heavy dark goggles. Squinting, he looked around. And gasped!

There was The Plaza where he had always remembered it. "It can't be!" he said and rubbed his eyes. He looked again. "It is there!" he said...

He called his wife. "We'll go there tonight, before it's too late. Don't tell anyone!" he hissed. So she only told her very best friend. Soon everyone knew.

Crowds gathered. They wandered in the lobbies. They caressed the marble, admired the gilded cherubs. And the caryatids in the Palm Court where palms still swayed...[44]

In the advertisement, aesthetically deprived New Yorkers feasted on rich food and soulful music, and that evening, "the lucky ones who had made reservations" retired upstairs where manicurists and valets awaited them. "The Plaza had thought of everything. It always does. It always will," the advertisement concluded. It was an optimistic sentiment, but one that would prove hopelessly naive.

PART THREE

Chapter 11

TRUMP'S MONA LISA

"This is the perfect end-of-the-'80s story of the mighty falling."

—*Liz Smith, gossip columnist*

Donald Trump was obsessed with the Plaza Hotel. "You know, I'm going to buy this hotel?" he bragged back in 1976, when he was a young, brash would-be real estate tycoon. "How much would you pay for it?" asked J. Philip Hughes, the Plaza's manager. "Twenty-five million," Trump casually responded. That was exactly what Hughes's bosses at Westin had paid just a year earlier, and he dismissed Trump's offer out of hand. So Trump doubled the number. "I called the chief legal guy for Westin in Seattle," Hughes recalled, "and told him Donald Trump was offering $50 million for The Plaza. He said, 'No. And who's Donald Trump?'"[1]

A dozen years later, of course, Westin executives knew full well who Donald Trump was. By then, the tables were turned. Westin was in financial straits while Trump was comfortably ensconced in his position as New York City's best-known and flashiest real estate personality. But one thing remained the same: The man who would eventually become the forty-fifth president of the United States could not shake his desire for the elusive Plaza.

"I would say that the first time I went to the Plaza, I was about seven years old," Trump told an interviewer. "I just remember the feeling of opulence. There's something very haunting and magical about the Plaza."[2] When Trump built his eponymous tower on Fifth Avenue, it was two blocks south of the hotel. His offices on Trump Tower's twenty-sixth floor boasted expansive cityscape views, with the Plaza squarely within its frame. Trump would often swivel around in his desk chair and stare out at the hotel as he contemplated his next big move.

Like many of Trump's favorite things, the Plaza played hard to get, forcing the developer to charm and cajole his way into the hotel. "I was in love with it," Trump said. "I tore myself up to get the Plaza."[3] It also cost him. Trump would spend more than $400 million, or a record-shattering $495,000 per hotel room, to clinch the deal. With its prodigious price and Trump's braggadocio, the transaction epitomized the hubris of the go-go '80s, when greed was good and big shoulder pads and even bigger hair was the rage. "For the first time in my life, I have knowingly made a deal that was not economic," Trump declared in a full-page advertisement touting his acquisition in *New York* magazine. The transaction, however, did satisfy Trump's vanity. "I haven't purchased a building, I have purchased a masterpiece—the Mona Lisa," he boasted.[4]

Eric Trump, the future president's second-oldest son, echoed his father's sentiment. The Plaza was, he told me, his father's "first masterpiece," and it was omnipresent growing up. At Eric's childhood home in the family's Trump Tower triplex, the windows overlooked Fifth Avenue and the Plaza, and as an adult, Eric still lives and works nearby. "I've passed the Plaza at least ten thousand times. In fact, I can see it from my office right now. It's so close, I can literally hit it with a golf ball."

The Westin chain originally dismissed Trump's offer to purchase the Plaza. But by 1987, Westin's parent company was in the midst of a massive corporate restructuring. The conglomerate, which also owned Hilton International and Hertz Corp., was spinning off subsidiaries at a dizzying pace.[5] One of the companies that it was putting up for sale was Westin, owner of the Plaza. It hired bankers to hold an auction, and hundreds of offers came flooding in for the sixty-one-hotel chain. Roughly thirty serious bidders emerged, among them Robert M. Bass, a member of the Bass oil dynasty in Texas, who partnered with the Japanese firm Aoki Corp. to offer $1.4 billion. Trump was also in the running, with a $1.3 billion bid.

The thirty potential buyers were whittled down to twelve finalists, as the lower offers were thrown out. These twelve were then invited to make a second bid, and were put up in suites at the Plaza, each one outfitted with 120 blue binders filled with financial reports, room rates, and other materials. The teams were given several days to read through the binders. To prevent the teams from running into one another, the suites were located on different floors with their own separate elevator banks.[6]

The Bass and Aoki partnership valued the Plaza at $350 million, and they agreed that should they win the auction, Bass would ante up $250 million to acquire a 71 percent stake in the hotel, Aoki getting the remainder. Bass would also have the right to sell the hotel. As the bidders conducted due diligence, Bass decided to identify possible investors interested in buying the Plaza, should his team win the auction. The man he dispatched to locate buyers was an ambitious up-and-coming lawyer and real estate investor, Thomas Barrack. Hungry to impress Bass and earn a hefty commission, Barrack met with several potentially interested parties, including Trump, with whom he had previously worked on deals. "By all accounts, it was a classic meeting between two sophisticated negotiators," said the *New York Times* of the tête-à-tête between Trump and Barrack, the paper comparing the men to chess grand masters. But as the negotiations were progressing, a calamitous event struck, sending the Plaza auction into disarray.

On a Monday in October 1987, as the final bidders were preparing to make offers, the stock market crashed. In what became known as Black Monday, the Dow Jones industrial average plummeted more than 500 points in a single day. The teams were jittery, and several parties tried circumventing the Westin auction by offering preemptive bids. Bass and Aoki also took advantage of the market turmoil, submitting a proposal to buy Westin for $1.3 billion. It was the highest offer the bankers had received that round, and, anxious to close the deal, they engaged in some last-minute haggling before finalizing the price at $1.35 billion in cash and $180 million in Westin debt.

Meanwhile, Trump and Barrack continued their talks, each one trying to outmaneuver the other. At a breakfast at the St. Regis Hotel, just after Bass and Aoki clinched the Westin deal, Trump asked if Bass might now sell him the Plaza. "Barrack told him that Bass wanted to hold onto the hotel, but Trump sensed that Barrack was trolling for an offer Bass couldn't refuse," reported the New York Times.[7] The brinkmanship between the two men dragged on, with Barrack insisting that Bass would not take less than $450 million for the hotel, while Trump said he wouldn't go above $350 million.

Word soon spread among New York's tight-knit real estate universe that Bass was considering flipping the trophy hotel he had just acquired. As talks with Trump ebbed and flowed, other suitors emerged. In February 1988, an article appeared in the New York Times reporting that Bass was close to selling the Plaza to a pair of Manhattan developers who were offering as much as $500 million, with plans to convert much of the hotel into apartments.[8] That same day, Trump called Barrack, this time serious about making a deal. "Tom [Barrack] played Donald like a Stradivarius," the New

York Times reported later, quoting an unnamed real estate executive.[9] For his part, Trump insisted that news of the competing bid had "no effect" on his decision to return to the negotiating table.

With the talks back on, Trump and Barrack met on the twenty-sixth floor of Trump Tower to hammer out terms. Suddenly, "Trump broke off the discussion and spun about in his chair. Through the window, he could see the copper green mansard roof of the Plaza Hotel just two blocks up Fifth Avenue. Finally, Trump turned back and said he would sign."[10] The final deal stipulated that Trump would shell out $407.5 million, or more than twenty-five times the hotel's expected earnings, a lofty multiple for the landmark property.[11] To pay for it, Trump would borrow the entire sum, including additional funding to cover the closing costs and renovations.

It was a stunning coup for Trump, who, a decade earlier, couldn't even get a loan without a guarantor. Back then, in the early 1970s, Trump was an upstart, ambitious young son of a politically connected developer. Fred Trump was a strict father, who evinced the theory that life was a zero-sum game, made up of winners and losers. Fred had made a fortune building middle-class housing in the outer boroughs of the city, and Trump grew up in a fairly large home in an exclusive neighborhood in Queens. A headstrong teen, Trump was sent away to military school for his education.

Trump, who regularly wore a jacket and tie, attended the Wharton School of Business after military school, then, after graduating, began working for his father. He supervised Fred's buildings and collected rents, toiling out of his father's nondescript offices in Brooklyn. While Fred wasn't overtly showy, Trump displayed an early propensity for flamboyance. He traveled from his bachelor pad on the Upper East Side to work each day in a silver Cadillac equipped with an early car phone and a license plate that read "DJT,"[12] and was driven by a chauffeur who had once been a city cop. While Trump's days were spent on housing projects in the outer boroughs, his nights were always in the Manhattan fast lane. Surrounded by leggy models and Wall Street bankers, the young Trump was a regular at posh singles bars and power broker hangouts like Le Club and Maxwell's Plum.

It was while out at Maxwell's Plum, a bar famed for its stained-glass ceiling, crystal chandeliers, and a crowd packed with fashionistas, airline stewardesses, and aspiring actresses, that Trump met Ivana Zelnickova. Wearing a red minidress and high heels, Ivana was standing outside in the hot summer night with a gaggle of friends, hoping to get in. Trump eyed the slim, five-foot-seven model with dyed-blond locks and sauntered over, telling her group that he knew the manager, and asking if the women would like a table. They readily agreed, and at the end of the evening, Trump drove Ivana back to her hotel. The following morning, he sent her dozens of red roses and a note that read, "To Ivana, with affection."[13]

Ivana, who was in town promoting the 1976 Summer Olympics in Montreal, where she was then living, was a Czech native. A former professional skier, she had a throaty voice, a degree in physical education, and fluency in multiple languages. Ivana was more sophisticated than most of the women Trump met, and he pursued her with the same doggedness he used in his real estate deals. When Ivana returned to Canada, Trump called her repeatedly, even flying to Montreal to surprise her at a fashion show, showing up just long enough to say hello. A whirlwind courtship followed, and barely two months later, Trump invited her to move to New York and live with him. "Have you ever seen anybody more beautiful?" he told friends. "Really, is she the most beautiful? Have you ever seen anybody so smart?"[14]

Around the same time, Trump had grown fed up with collecting rents and managing his father's properties. In 1977, he decided to cross the river and make a move into big-league Manhattan development. Leveraging his father's deep political connections, particularly his relationship with New York mayor Abe Beame, Trump negotiated a lucrative arrangement with the city to redevelop the dilapidated Commodore Hotel. Even as New York was gripped by its most severe fiscal crisis ever, it agreed to lease the site to Trump in exchange for a modest rent. The city also awarded Trump an unprecedented forty-year tax abatement that would eventually net more than $350 million in savings.[15] But even armed with these valuable rights, Trump couldn't hide the fact that he had no track record. Banks were wary of taking a chance on him, and in the end, Fred had to act as his guarantor. The Hyatt hotel chain also came into the deal, taking a 50 percent stake in exchange for guaranteeing the $100 million that it took to transform the Commodore into the glossy Grand Hyatt New York.[16]

By the late 1980s, New York's near bankruptcy and Trump's early struggles had disappeared in the rearview mirror. Trump had spent a decade amassing properties, and now, not only did he own a piece of the Grand Hyatt New York, but his portfolio also included the St. Moritz Hotel, the Trump Parc condominium tower, and Trump Tower. There were two casinos in Atlantic City and a battle to take over a third, as well as Trump's plan to build the world's tallest tower on a one-hundred-acre stretch abutting the Hudson River.[17] Trump no longer needed to justify the economics of his deals, let alone get guarantors. "You cannot believe the money the banks were throwing at us," a former unnamed Trump associate told *Vanity Fair*. "For every deal we did, we would have six or eight banks who were willing to give us hundreds of millions of dollars."[18]

In 1988, when he negotiated to buy the Plaza, banks were salivating at the prospect of being Trump's lender. Citibank led the charge, offering Trump a $300 million long-term loan for the Plaza as well as an additional $125 million, which Trump personally guaranteed, to fund the renovations, bringing the total loan to a whopping $425 million. The bank then syndicated all but $100 million of the debt, dividing it into tranches and selling it in pieces to other banks, which were equally anxious to gain access to the '80s golden boy. Citibank earned enormous fees from syndicating its loans, while simultaneously reducing its risks.[19] "Even Donald complained about how 'easy' it had become. Bankers whose coolness to the Hyatt proposition a decade earlier had almost forced him to abandon it were now wooing him," wrote investigative journalist Wayne Barrett, in his book *Trump: The Greatest Show on Earth.* "That's what it meant, Donald marveled, to be on top."[20]

While Trump was forging ahead with his real estate deals, Ivana, who he had since married, insinuated herself in all manner of the business. It had been that way from the earliest stages of their union. Ivana checked in almost daily at the Grand Hyatt, walking the wooden planks of the construction site in her teetering heels, a hard hat over her coiffed hairdo. When Trump acquired the Plaza, Ivana was running one of her husband's Atlantic City casinos. He moved her from New Jersey to become president of the Plaza, the first woman in the hotel's long history to hold such a senior title. Trump, however, soon undercut the accomplishment. At a press conference to announce his wife's new position, Trump famously quipped, "My wife, Ivana, is a brilliant manager. I will pay her one dollar a year and all the dresses she can buy!"

Trump's comment on his wife's compensation provoked outrage, including an editorial in the *New York Times* decrying paternalism. The columnist Marilyn Goldstein wrote in *Newsday,* "No matter how rich your husband, if you don't have your own money, you're still dependent on his whims."[21] Publicly, Ivana dismissed the controversy. Calling her husband's comments "cute," she told the press, "I think it's really ridiculous to ask my husband for a salary. We are a team. We are working together."[22] She even put a framed check in the amount of $1 signed by Trump on the wall of her Plaza office.[23] But privately, there were signs of distress. "How can Donald humiliate me this way?" she confided in friends.[24]

The public embarrassment that Ivana experienced at the Plaza press conference was just the latest in what were increasing marital tensions. Over time, Ivana and Trump had become less a team of equals, with Ivana relegated to more of a Trump employee than a spouse. "My huge professional wins came at a personal cost," she later wrote in her book *Raising Trump*. "My husband and I became more like business partners than spouses. We'd talk about work all the time, about the bottom line, the high rollers coming in that weekend, what was going on at the Plaza. He loved what I did for his company, but, on the other hand, he was frustrated that I spent so much time working."[25]

When Ivana was in Atlantic City running her husband's casino, for instance, "week after week, their helicopters had passed each other in the early evening as she flew home, and he flew to Atlantic City for the weekend," wrote Barrett. Their staff called it "the Asbury Park marriage," for the town in New Jersey where the two helicopters passed closest to each other while on their separate journeys.[26]

Their marriage, in fact, was one of the reasons Trump had decided to move Ivana to the Plaza. When Trump told her he was relocating her to the hotel, he threatened, "Either you act like my wife and come back to New York and take care of your children or you run the casino in Atlantic City and we get divorced."[27] When Ivana gathered her Atlantic City employees together to say good-bye, she tearfully thanked them for their work. "Look at this," Trump said when he got up to speak afterward. "Now that's why I'm sending her back to New York. I don't need this, some woman crying."[28]

Ivana, who was fiercely competitive and had survived a hard-scrabble childhood behind the Iron Curtain, was determined to fix her marriage. She plunged headlong into her responsibilities at the Plaza, hoping its success would please her husband. Dressed in her daily armor of Chanel suit and Charles Jourdan pumps, Ivana would stand at the window of her Trump Tower triplex in the morning before heading to work. There, she would gaze down at the Plaza, just as her husband often did. But while Trump stared wistfully at an object of desire, Ivana eyed the property critically, a set of binoculars gripped in her manicured fingers, scanning the hotel's entrance and scowling if anything was out of place. "Ivana would look down from her apartment," recounted the widow of a longtime Plaza doorman, and if something was amiss, pick up the phone and bark, "There's paper on the sidewalk, get it cleaned up!"[29]

Ivana moved into large offices on the Plaza's second floor, flanked by her manager and two secretaries. There she focused on the smallest minutiae. She ordered that lemon wedges at the Palm Court be sliced a certain way,[30] and directed an employee to wander the corridors stamping the sand of every ashtray throughout the day with the double-P Plaza insignia. "After issuing specific instructions to the housekeeping staff advising that every towel should be folded exactly the same way in all 814 rooms of the hotel, she pulled up the hem of her designer skirt and got down on her hands and knees to demonstrate how the bathroom floors should be scrubbed," recounted Harry Hurt III in his biography of the Trumps, *Lost Tycoon: The Many Lives of Donald J. Trump.*[31]

Employees would often receive diktats such as, "Mrs. Trump would like to walk the Seventh Floor." The staff would then have to scramble to make it immaculate, beyond her reproach. "When Mrs. Trump steps off the elevator, armed with tape recorder and a pair of flat shoes, she unleashes a bright smile and a 'Good morning, kids,'" reported the employee newsletter, *Plaza Pulse*, "as she bee-lines for the first room at the end of the corridor. We all have to pick up our steps in order to keep up with her."[32]

Under Westin's leadership, the hotel had been subsumed into a chain mentality. At one point, the owners had even altered the name of the Plaza to the Westin Plaza, a first in the hotel's history. Ivana set about reversing many of these changes. "Bold is back. And gold is better," noted *Newsday*, who called her designs "Haute Excess."[33] She ripped out ungainly green carpeting and replaced it with plush rugs in deep-wine reds and golds; she decorated the walls with reproductions of antique tapestries; and she scrubbed off the cheap gold paint that covered many of the hotel's ornate details, hiring sixteen artisans who spent a year repainting nearly every surface with real gold leaf.[34]

Enormous floral bouquets with roses in a shade dubbed "Ivana pink" decorated the lobby, while guest rooms were outfitted with Frette linens and Chanel toiletries. She also renovated several existing rooms. There was a $4,000-a-night Vanderbilt Suite, outfitted with a custom whirlpool-for-two,[35] and the Astor Suite, an unfortunate misnomer, since the Astors likely never stayed at the Plaza, preferring their own hotels like the Waldorf-Astoria instead. Ivana even instituted a new dress code—not just for staff, but for every visitor—prohibiting shorts, jeans, or other casual wear in the common areas of the hotel. When a reporter tried to visit dressed in jeans, he barely made it fifteen feet before a security guard, in a tie and jacket, stopped him.

"I remember the way people there dressed; their uniforms were immaculate," Eric Trump told me. "My mom understands quality and luxury. She was a perfect match for the Plaza because she grew up in Europe, traveled the world, and could bring that old-world sensibility to the New World." Like the Salomone children in the 1960s, Eric and his siblings would often skate through the lobby, and spent their Sundays dressed up to attend the lavish brunch at the Palm Court. "There was a massive buffet—you wouldn't even know where to start—and someone playing piano and a harp. It was the place to be," Eric recalled.

Under the Trumps, the Plaza regained its stature within the

world of fashion and celebrity, after having faded during the Westin phase. It was no surprise, as the Trumps occupied a spot in the celebrity stratosphere, a favorite of gossip columnists and regulars on the cover of New York's tabloids. Ivana leveraged her friendships with designers to double the number of fashion shows held there, while their bold-faced friends flocked to parties at the Grand Ballroom. "Everyone wanted to come to the Plaza, from Kim Basinger to the Prince of Wales to Mike Tyson," Didier Le Calvez, the hotel manager at the time, told me.

When *Home Alone 2* was filming at the hotel, Trump snagged a cameo, well before his reality TV days on *The Apprentice*. The hotel's actual reservation number was featured in the movie. It seemed like a smart marketing ploy—until the film came out in video and viewers at home could rewind and replay, resulting in teenage fans inundating the switchboard with prank requests for "Kevin." There was also some disappointment when fans of the movie realized how few similarities the real Plaza shared with its movie alter ego. Where Kevin's room, for instance, was full of dark wood, sedate brown furnishings, and oil paintings of horses, the actual Plaza was "crazily ornate, as if Louis XV were holding a yard sale," with a panoply of gold trim and faucets shaped like swans, wrote a critic in the *New York Times*.[36] Once, a Plaza employee got in the elevator with a family decked out in bathing suits and swim goggles. She informed the unhappy tourists that unlike in the movie, the real Plaza had no pool.

There were also other challenges. For every Michael Jackson, who rented out the pricey Astor Suite and bothered the staff only with daily orders of candy, there was a Mickey Rourke, who trashed his room to the tune of $20,000 in damages.[37] There were also grittier stories, of drug- and sex-fueled parties in the Plaza's luxury corner suites, where young girls and wealthy older men gathered.

According to best-selling author Michael Gross, Trump often flitted in and out of these soirees. The future president was accompanied by "a lot of girls," Andy Lucchesi, a male model and party attendee, told Gross. Drugs like cocaine were rampant, but cigarette smoking, which Trump abhorred, was prohibited.[38]

If Ivana knew about the parties, she never acknowledged it. Under the glare of the press, she kept her gaze focused on making the hotel a success. But her hopes that a profitable Plaza might revive her faltering marriage were not realized. Tensions between the couple continued to intensify, with Ivana's return to New York only exacerbating matters. Trump's "feelings about her were a mass of contradictions," wrote Barrett. "He confessed to others 'the guilt' he felt over having made her 'totally subservient.'" Trump would later say of the breakdown in the marriage, "She wasn't challenging," and "I left essentially because I was bored."[39]

The Trumps had made four nuptial agreements in their fourteen years together. The first was signed just before their wedding ceremony, and their fourth and final contract was completed in 1987. Under the last deal, should the couple divorce, Ivana would receive $10 million in cash, up from $2.5 million in the agreement signed three years earlier. She would also get the house in Greenwich, the use of Trump's Palm Beach estate Mar-a-Lago for one month, and residence at the Trump Tower triplex until it was sold, after which she would get another $4 million. Days after the agreement was finalized, Trump slept for the first time with Marla Maples.[40]

Trump had pursued Marla, a sometime actress and model, wooing her not with dozens of red roses, as he had Ivana, but with reviews and press clippings of his new best seller, *The Art of the Deal*.[41] Before long, Trump installed his mistress in a fourth-floor room at the St. Moritz Hotel, a property he owned on Central Park South. It was a three-minute walk from the Plaza, where Trump's wife was busily running the hotel, and just three blocks from their Trump Tower home. Neil Johnson, a doorman who worked at the St. Moritz at the time, and later became a doorman at the Plaza, frequently saw Marla coming and going. "We were told that she was Donald Trump's niece," he told me. "Then Donald starts coming in, at 11, 11:30 at night...And then he'd leave at 7 a.m. in the morning. It was a big joke."

As the affair continued, a confrontation was inevitable. It finally occurred in the exclusive winter wonderland of Aspen, Colorado. The Trumps were skiing over Christmas break, as was their tradition, and Trump brazenly brought Marla along, hiding her in a nearby condominium. In a scene straight out of a 1980s B movie, the two female rivals faced off against each other at a fashionable slope-side cafeteria. Ivana, in her designer pink snowsuit, stomped over to the black-clad Marla as the paparazzi gleefully snapped away. "Why don't you leave my husband alone?" she demanded.[42]

The Colorado showdown marked the start of the Trumps' split. The divorce quickly grew ugly, but Ivana clung to her job at the Plaza even as the most regular contact she was having with her estranged spouse was his picture hanging in the hotel's gift shop.[43] At one point, Trump tried to fire his wife, stationing two burly security guards at her office door on the Plaza's second floor, barring her from entry. This was in retaliation for her changing the locks on their triplex penthouse in Trump Tower. The stunt didn't last long, however, and by that afternoon, Ivana was back at her station.

All this drama wasn't easy on the Plaza's employees. "One day I saw Ivana sitting by the window at a table at the Edwardian Room," Alain Sailhac, former chef of the famed eatery Le Cirque, who was hired by Ivana as the Plaza's head chef, told me. "I couldn't avoid her, so I walked over and said, 'Hi, Ivana,' and she was crying and then bangs her hand on the table and says, 'That son of a bitch wants to divorce me!'" Sailhac struggled not just with Ivana's emotional state, but also with the fact that he had to answer to two warring bosses. "I always liked Donald and I always liked Ivana. They were very, very generous with me. But it became very uncomfortable," he said. "Ivana was the boss, but Donald was also the boss." Eventually, Sailhac quit.

Trump's troubles weren't isolated to just his failing marriage; there were also his crumbling businesses. In the fog of 1980s excess, Trump had built up his sprawling, debt-laden empire. As the dawn of the 1990s broke, however, the haze cleared, and the economic realities came into view. There was a recession, the real estate market had collapsed, and Wall Street was reeling from the savings and loan crisis.[44] Trump had overpaid and overborrowed in the expectation that his assets would continue appreciating and he could easily cover his debts. But that didn't happen.

Trump owed his lenders several billion dollars, nearly $1 billion of which he had personally guaranteed. This meant that his personal assets, and not just his business assets, could be seized by creditors. One day, Trump was strolling down Fifth Avenue with Marla when he passed by a homeless person. "You see that man?" he asked her. "Right now he's worth $900 million more than me... Right now I'm worth minus $900 million."[45]

Trump's situation became increasingly dire. In 1991, his Taj Mahal casino in Atlantic City, billed as the "Eighth Wonder of the World," was nearly $3 billion in debt and filed for bankruptcy protection. It would be the first of what would eventually amount to six corporate bankruptcies. As he watched his empire and his marriage collapse, Trump retreated to his own apartment in Trump Tower, taking refuge in food, ordering in hamburgers and French fries from the deli downstairs. When a friend commented that he was acting like the reclusive Howard Hughes, he replied, "Thanks, I admire him."[46] In the end, Trump would lose his 282-foot yacht; his private jet; his Trump Shuttle airline; his stake in the Grand Hyatt New York; and his Mona Lisa, the Plaza.

In the first few years that Trump owned the Plaza, the hotel benefited from rising room prices and occupancy rates, as well as a booming banquet business, thanks in part to the Trumps' high-profile celebrity friends.[47] But despite its performance, the underlying financials were shaky. Trump had acquired the Plaza at a market peak, using borrowed funds. He had then saddled the hotel with even more loans, leveraging it to buy an airline and fund construction of his Taj Mahal casino.[48] No matter how much the Plaza made, how many weddings, debutante balls, or bar mitzvahs it hosted, it would never be sufficient to service the debt.

In 1990, the hotel's total accrued debt service was about $41 million, while the hotel's cash flow was just $21 million—a major shortfall. In 1991, it was even worse, with a $42 million debt service and cash flow of $17.6 million.[49] At the same time, Ivana was a profligate spender and blew way past her budget on her many hotel improvements. In fact, as a result of her costly renovations, in one year the Plaza spent a staggering $74 million more than it earned.[50] In the summer of 1990, Trump's lenders agreed to let him defer his interest payments and extend the maturity dates on his loans. But by late 1991, it became obvious that no matter what allowances the bank gave him, Trump could never cover his Plaza debts.

Trump, concerned he would lose the hotel, threw out a possible lifeline. When he had first bought the Plaza, he intended to carve out the building's upper floors into more than a dozen exclusive penthouse apartments, even going so far as to get city approvals for his plan. But not long after Trump closed on the hotel, he grew distracted with his personal life, his Atlantic City casinos, and other Trump-branded ventures. The penthouse plans were put aside. Now, he tried reviving them.

The Plaza's upper floors didn't look like penthouse material.

They had once been the former maids' quarters and were now a warren of small offices and storage rooms. "The seventeenth floor was kind of half empty," Lee Harris Pomeroy, an architect whose offices were there, told me. Pomeroy's conference room, for example, had bathroom tiles along one wall, a throwback from when it had been the maids' shower. These floors were also often used as gathering spots for the prostitutes who hung around the hotel. "We had a couple of public bathrooms on my floor, and there were the prostitutes in the community. They would hang out downstairs in the lobby, but they needed to change their clothes or do whatever they do, so they would come up to the top floor," Pomeroy recalled. To try to dissuade the prostitutes from congregating up there, the hotel removed chairs and other lounge furniture from the hallways so there would be no place for them to sit.

Trump was hoping that the penthouse concept, his last-ditch effort to save the hotel from bankruptcy, could generate massive profits. (He was right. Trump's penthouse plan would eventually be realized—years later, without him—generating $1 billion for the Plaza's then-owners.) Trump hired Pomeroy to execute the designs for his penthouses, and the architect began creating plans. The idea was to convert the seventeenth and eighteenth floors into fourteen ultraexpensive apartments. The ungainly rooftop, which was covered with water tanks and paint sheds made of corrugated metal and chicken wire, would also be cleaned up and become a part of the design.[51] But there were several problems standing in Trump's way, and one of the most challenging presented itself in the shape of a diminutive old lady.

Fannie Lowenstein was one of just a handful of the thirty-nine widows of the Plaza who were still alive. Lowenstein had arrived in 1958, as a young divorcée, and she soon met a fellow hotel resident who became her second husband. Not only did Mr. Lowenstein have a seat on the New York Stock Exchange, but even better, he had a rent-controlled Plaza apartment, one of the lucky few whose rent was frozen in the wake of price controls instituted during World War II. When her husband died, Lowenstein continued to live in splendor in their three-room suite. It would have typically rented for more than $1,250 a night, but Lowenstein paid just $800 a month.

In addition to her fortunate apartment setup, the Plaza staff treated Lowenstein, who was infamous for her tantrums, with deference. "Fannie Lowenstein entered the Palm Court of the Plaza Hotel as the orchestra was playing," reported the *Village Voice*. The maître d' ushered her to her favorite table, the waitress took her regular order of asparagus soup and a Hennessy cognac, and then the violinist came over, offering to play "her" song. "As the crystal chandeliers shimmered and the palm leaves rustled," the musician began playing the theme song from the Broadway musical *Fanny*.[52]

Trump was defenseless against Lowenstein, unable to evict her or raise her rent beyond small annual increments. When Trump had first bought the building, Lowenstein told an inquiring *Newsday* reporter, "I get regular service, and I expect that to continue."[53] And at first, the prickly widow seemed content. But the honeymoon was short-lived, and it wasn't long before Trump ran afoul of the demanding doyenne.

Lowenstein soon began complaining of what she said was "indoor air pollution" in her rooms. She claimed it was caused by the new owner, alleging that the dirty air made it difficult for her to breathe, shrank her curtains, and caused her Steinway grand piano to grow mold. She began waging a "guerrilla war" on Trump, calling the city repeatedly to send over "a battalion" of inspectors, and writing repeated missives to management. "Ivana and Marla have been a lot to handle," Trump told the *National Enquirer*, "but my relationships with them have been smooth as silk in comparison to my contacts with Fannie Lowenstein. When she's done with me, I'm soaked in sweat!"[54]

Even if Trump could have evicted Lowenstein and the remaining widows to make way for condominiums, there was another, even more serious problem with his strategy. In 1988, when Trump acquired the Plaza, the real estate market was robust, and selling costly penthouses atop the hotel made financial sense. But now, the recession left few takers for such luxury apartments. In 1991, when Trump returned to his penthouse idea, the median price for a Manhattan condominium was only $280,000.[55] Trump's purported $8 million price tag was a pipe dream.[56]

Unable to execute on his penthouse plan, Trump was out of options. Almost exactly four years after he had purchased his Mona Lisa for a record amount, Trump lost the hotel to his bankers. In a bankruptcy filing that ran almost fifteen hundred pages, reams of unpaid creditors were listed. New York State was asking for more than $800,000 in back sales tax, while Con Edison claimed it was owed nearly $300,000 for electricity. Manhattan Limousine had an outstanding bill of almost $200,000, Projection Video Services was out more than $120,000, and Atlas Floral Decorators, Ivana's favorite, was asking for $85,000. In total, the Plaza's assets were listed as $375 million, but its liabilities ran to nearly $480 million.[57]

The Chapter 11 filing was what is known as a prepackaged bankruptcy. By the time they filed, Trump and his lenders had already hammered out a deal, with Trump agreeing to hand over 49 percent of the Plaza to Citibank and a consortium of other lenders in exchange for easing the terms on his debt. While Trump nominally retained 51 percent of the hotel, it was only on paper, since he had no equity in the deal. "He had no decision-making authority, and, to the best of my knowledge, he received zero dollars from the transaction. It all went to the banks," Alan J. Pomerantz, the former head of the real estate practice at Weil Gotshal & Manges, the law firm that represented Citibank, told me.

For the Plaza, the bankruptcy was the first in its eighty-five years, and it was a demoralizing blow. "It was a pretty painful place to work," Christopher Knable, the director of guest services at the time, told me. "We were laying staff off during the holidays, even though we were full." It was a tricky balancing act. "With bankruptcy, you are trying to satisfy the bankers, but the hotel still has to run," said Knable. "You can strip away the expenses, but the occupancy and the hotel services needs don't change." Belts were tightened, and Ivana, who had held on even as her dramatic split with Trump played out, was replaced with professional moneymen employed to cut costs and increase revenue.

Ivana, having lost her perch as president of the Plaza, also stopped battling Trump over the terms of the divorce. It had become abundantly clear that Trump had little wealth left to fight for, so after all the dirt-slinging, Ivana agreed to the basic outline of their 1987 marriage contract. Trump was so embattled that he was living off an allowance doled out by his bankers. How he managed to procure the $10 million cash payout that was stipulated in his nuptial agreement remains a mystery. Trump had asked his bankers for the money, but they demurred. It was rumored that his father, Fred, who had previously stepped in to provide financial backing for his son, was a possible source.

Despite his drubbing, Trump behaved as he had throughout his business career—and would continue to do so in the decades hence—by spinning the defeat into a win. One March morning, Trump stood triumphantly on the steps of a Manhattan courthouse waving his $10 million check in front of the gathered press. "I'm here with what I am supposed to give her," he blustered. "What more does she want?"[58] Ivana was a no-show that day, her lawyers claiming the case was not yet settled.

Eventually, Trump did hand the check over to his ex. "I don't think you have any other real estate developer in the country that can write a $10 million check today in terms of cash," he bragged.

"I think I'm doing something for Ivana that nobody else would have done for her."[59] Ivana may have felt differently. Especially when, not long after, Trump wed Marla at Ivana's old stomping ground, pledging his love to his former mistress in the Grand Ballroom of the Plaza, surrounded by a forest of white orchids and guests like O. J. Simpson.

Trump bankrupted and eventually lost the Plaza. But still, his mark on the hotel remains indelible. On the floors where Alfred Gwynne Vanderbilt's maid once slept, billionaire homeowners now stare out at the emerald-green carpeting of Central Park, the realization of Trump's penthouse concept. And as hotel guests today admire the ornate molding and gold trim for which the Plaza is famous, they can be assured that some are vestiges of Ivana's vision. "I was there two weeks ago," Eric told me in the fall of 2017. When he looked up, he saw a familiar sparkle. "There it was, the Trump chandeliers were still there, hanging from the ceiling," he recalled, smiling at the memory.

Chapter 12

THE PRINCE AND THE
BILLIONAIRE

"Owning a luxury hotel today is a little like
owning a baseball team. It gives super-affluent guys
an enormous amount of exposure."
—*Daniel Neidich, banker*

A braham Wallach, a Trump executive and a faithful foot soldier, was determined to save his boss's favorite property. The Plaza was now bankrupt, and its creditors were anxious to sell the hotel to recoup at least some of their original investment. It was a race to the finish. If Citibank and the other lenders found a buyer for the Plaza, Trump would lose the property. But if Trump could identify a buyer first, he might convince that person to let him continue managing the hotel or, perhaps, give him the go-ahead to complete his Plaza penthouses. Wallach was resolute that Trump would triumph.

Wallach's most promising lead was Sun Hung Kai & Co., one of China's largest property investment companies. It was run by the three Kwok brothers, who were among the richest families in all of Asia.[1] Walter Kwok, the eldest brother, was sufficiently intrigued at the prospect of purchasing the Plaza to come for a visit. With his wife, Wendy, and their children in tow, the family was put up in the lavish Presidential Suite, the former home of Harry Black, which Ivana had refurbished. Over the course of several days, Wallach and Trump wooed the Kwoks, Wallach accompanying Wendy on shopping sprees while Trump took Walter on golf outings.

One morning, Wallach arrived to pick up the Kwoks for a day of sightseeing. He nodded to the private security guard who had been hired by the family to stand sentry outside the suite's entrance, and then knocked on the door. There was no answer, so the security guard also knocked. When there was still no answer, the guard called on his walkie-talkie to another guard stationed inside the rooms. He radioed back to say that the family was stuck inside—the door had jammed. Wallach and the guard tried pushing and pulling the ancient door free from its sticky hinges. It refused to budge. As panic set in, Wallach called down to hotel security. Several men arrived with hatchets, which they used to break down the jammed door, after which the traumatized family rushed out in relief.

Wallach took the shaken guests downstairs for tea. "We're in the Palm Court, and there's a violinist playing Viennese waltzes and I started to talk to them, apologizing profusely," Wallach told me. "I know what's coming, so I'm listening to the Strauss waltzes and I said, 'I could start to cry right now.'" Wallach held back tears as he watched his dream of selling the Plaza to the Kwoks evaporate. Walter, his arm around his distressed wife, told him that the Plaza was too old, and it would cost too much to renovate. There was simply no way to justify buying the hotel under these circumstances. Wallach nodded in understanding. After he left the Kwoks, Wallach dejectedly walked the few blocks to Trump Tower to relay the bad news.

"[Trump] was very calm at first. 'A door jammed? What do you mean a door jammed?'" recalled Wallach. Then, "it was as if a tsunami and an earthquake had hit at the same time. There were loud shrieks from the 26th floor. 'A door jammed? A door jammed?'"

Trump ran over to the Plaza, "and he started firing people: 'You're fired! You're fired! You're fired!' He even fired people who didn't work at the hotel, who were guests," Wallach recounted. Once Trump finally calmed down and Wallach could regroup, he realized that, with the prospective buyers now gone, he was once again back to square one.[2]

As Wallach and the Plaza's creditors competed to identify a buyer for the hotel, rumors of deals periodically surfaced. The *New York Post*, for instance, claimed that the wealthy Sultan of Brunei was purchasing the hotel. Trump, maintaining the appearance that he, not the creditors, was in control of the hotel, insisted the story was false and that the Plaza wasn't for sale. He threatened to sue the tabloid for $500 million, calling the *Post* reporter who wrote the piece a "total jerk, a loser if you've ever looked at him."[3] Then, before Wallach could line up a new Plaza buyer, Citibank beat him to the finish line. The bank found not just one credible candidate with deep pockets, but two.

In 1994, two years into the Plaza's bankruptcy, Citibank began discussions with Kwek Leng Beng, a billionaire property developer from Singapore (no affiliation with the similar-sounding Kwoks). Kwek had recently bought two hotels in Manhattan, the Millennium Hotel located downtown, and the Hotel Macklowe, in Midtown. "One of my principal bankers at Citibank approached me and asked me to look at the Plaza," Kwek told me. The hotel was well-located and historic, and "had the potential of generating large profits."

As Kwek was conducting due diligence on the Plaza, Citibank called him again. This time, it was to tell him that Prince Alwaleed bin Talal of Saudi Arabia, a fellow billionaire who also happened to be the bank's largest private shareholder, was also interested in purchasing the property. "I [got] a call to say that Prince Alwaleed would like to form a joint venture with me on the Plaza," said Kwek. Soon, the two billionaires were partnered.[4] The joint force of Kwek and Alwaleed was a devastating blow for Wallach. One billionaire was bad enough, but two of the world's richest men, combining their vast resources, would have no need of Trump. Yet, rather than admit defeat, Wallach decided he still had one more move to make: He could use his cunning to scuttle the deal.

Why Wallach would go to such lengths to help his boss had its roots in an improbable story that had unfolded years earlier, when Wallach had criticized Trump in the press. Back in 1989, Wallach was a senior vice president at First Capital Management, a real estate firm. He appeared on the public television show the *MacNeil/Lehrer NewsHour* for a segment named "Trumpty-Dumpty?" highlighting Trump's increasingly troubled real estate empire. "The reality is, if you pay too much for properties, and if your ego is as large as his was—is—and you just buy everything in sight, part of the blame has to squarely rest in your own lap," the curly-haired, bespectacled Wallach said on air. Earlier, Wallach's firm had also bid on the Plaza, he said, but backed out of the negotiations when it heard what Trump was willing to pay. The price that Trump shelled out for the hotel, Wallach told the camera, "made absolutely no sense."[5]

After his appearance on the news show, Wallach claims he was served with a $250 million lawsuit from Trump, alleging slander and defamation of character. Wallach then received a phone call from Trump inviting him to Trump Tower for a meeting. Angry and somewhat fearful, Wallach went. Several more meetings followed, and then, surprisingly, a job offer.

Trump and Wallach's relationship had begun in an adversarial manner, and it continued to be tumultuous, even after Wallach was hired as a Trump Organization executive, and had proved his usefulness. Wallach, who had personal struggles that would later become public, including bouts of kleptomania that led to jail time,[6] flitted between deep loyalty to his boss and feelings of resentment. For instance, Trump had shown up one day at Wallach's home in

Westchester, which was undergoing a renovation, offering to pay for a new master bathroom. "He says, I want to give you a gift. I'll do the whole bathroom in slabs of granite and marble." At first, Wallach declined his boss's generosity, but Trump persisted. So, weeks later, Wallach accepted, and for the next month, Trump employees came to Wallach's home to install expensive granite and gold finishes.

That year, as Christmas neared, Wallach approached Trump about his annual bonus, but the bathroom gift loomed over him. Not only might Trump skip giving him a bonus, Wallach reasoned to himself, but he might actually owe Trump money on account of the renovation work. Wallach decided to go to his boss armed with a check for $50,000, just in case. "I put [the check] in my shirt sleeve pocket, and went into his office and said, 'Donald, can we talk about a bonus?' He was looking down writing something and he said, 'Sure.' Then he looked up and said, 'Wait a minute, that gorgeous bathroom, wasn't that a Christmas bonus?'" Wallach took the check from his pocket and presented it. "'Donald, here's a check for $50,000. If the bathroom cost more, please let me know and I'll write you another check.'" Trump considered it, and then took the check from Wallach's outstretched hand. "Okay," Trump said, "let's talk about a bonus."[7]

In spite of this "constant push and pull," as Wallach put it, he was committed to helping Trump maintain his Plaza stake. "To be honest with you, I don't understand it," Wallach told me of his loyalty. "I can't stand most of what he's about; I hate limos and glitzy environments and people showing off. So how do I end up really liking him? Maybe there is another Donald that I saw, a guy who was caring." Trump called Wallach "Abelah," using a Yiddish diminutive term of endearment, for instance. "My grandmother was the only other person who used to call me that," Wallach recalled. And in several months' time, when Wallach was finally forced to abandon his attempts to save the Plaza for Trump, his boss offered him genuine reassurance. "I literally started to cry. And he said to me, 'Abe, don't worry about it. There will be bigger deals, better deals.' I took my job incredibly seriously. Too seriously. But that kind of [attention] was unusual in a workplace. And it makes you feel close to someone."[8]

But before Wallach agreed to give up on the Plaza, he had a few tricks up his sleeve. His first step was to advise Trump to ingratiate himself with Kwek. "I said to Donald, 'I think it would be beneficial for you to meet him and see if a deal could be crafted where you're his partner,'" said Wallach. "You manage the hotel and your position doesn't really change except you got a partner, but nobody ever listens to who the partner is. All they hear is Trump." Trump agreed, and soon Wallach and his boss were on the Concorde to London, where the Singaporean's hotel chain was based.

"When Mr. Kwek arrived at London's Lanesborough Hotel to meet Mr. Trump, the New Yorker finished signing an autograph for model Elle Macpherson," the *Wall Street Journal* recounted, "and then promptly proposed that Mr. Kwek take him as a partner, rather than the prince." Kwek declined the offer, possibly because Trump's empire was in tatters and he had already bankrupted the Plaza. Trump, undeterred, then asked whether Kwek would allow him to continue managing the hotel. "Sorry, Mr. Kwek responded: that job was going to the prince's hotel company."[9]

When the meeting with Kwek ended in rejection, Wallach turned to other schemes, namely making himself a nuisance. As the talks between Kwek and Alwaleed progressed, executives from both companies converged in New York to discuss the joint venture. "They all come to New York, all the higher-ups on the Saudi side and all the higher-ups on the Kwek side, and where do they decide to stay? In the Plaza Hotel, which is still owned and run by Donald Trump," Wallach told me. It made his job of getting in the way that much easier. "They're so stupid, they're staying in his property and they don't have a clue."

The executives met in the Plaza's Vanderbilt Suite, sitting in the opulent living room on ornate sofas, discussing specific terms of the proposal. But little did the men know, Wallach was there, too, eavesdropping on the interlopers and scribbling everything they said on a notepad. A longtime doorman had told Wallach that the suite had a secret room, accessed by a back stairway and hidden behind a fake wall. For ten days, Wallach concealed himself in the cramped space and caused mischief. When, for example, the executives discussed a $100 million loan they planned to take out to buy the hotel, Wallach called the same bank and requested a second $100 million Plaza loan, confusing the bankers.

In another instance, which Wallach claims was Trump's brainchild, the fire department was called. "You hear FIRE! And then suddenly, all over Fifty-Ninth Street and Fifth Avenue, firemen come running into the building with hatchets and hoses, and everybody's required to vacate the building because [it] is deemed structurally unstable," Wallach told me. A few days of chaos ensued, where the hotel executives were forced to take refuge at another hotel, but eventually the men returned, determined to forge ahead.[10]

Citibank and the other creditors apparently caught wind of the chicanery. "I drove [Citibank] nuts," Trump later told the *Wall Street Journal*. "I did a number on them that you wouldn't believe."[11] The bank threatened to hold Trump's other deals hostage unless Wallach halted his antics and allowed the sale to move forward. So in the end, Trump was forced to call Wallach off. "Donald shows up in my office and says, 'Abe, we have to stop all of this, we have to stop.' I said, 'Why, Donald? We're really going to be able to create a position for ourselves.'" It was then that Wallach became emotional, and Trump, seeing his faithful lieutenant cry, did his best to offer reassurances.

Trump had no choice but to give up the Plaza. He was in the midst of negotiating with Citibank and his other creditors to save what he could of his empire and he couldn't risk it all falling apart on the basis of one hotel. So in April 1995, the deal with Kwek and Alwaleed finally closed. It valued the hotel at $325 million, or $83 million less than what Trump had paid seven years earlier. The transaction was complex, with Kwek and Alwaleed agreeing to reduce the outstanding debt on the hotel to about $25 million from more than $300 million, in exchange for each receiving a stake in the hotel of just under 42 percent. Citibank was also to stay in the deal, with a 16 percent equity stake.[12]

Kwek told the *Wall Street Journal* that he wanted Citibank to remain an equity partner in the deal to ensure that Trump wouldn't cause him any further trouble. Trump had a so-called right of first refusal, which allowed him to match any offer for the Plaza—an improbable scenario considering the state of his finances. While Trump was unlikely to execute that right, Citibank, as Trump's lead lender, had leverage over him. By keeping Citibank in the deal, it provided additional insurance that Trump wouldn't try to interrupt the sale.[13] Several years later, Kwek and Alwaleed would purchase the remainder of the equity from Citibank to become fifty-fifty owners.

Kwek and Alwaleed also agreed to throw Trump a few scraps: If, under their ownership, the top floors of the Plaza were ever converted into penthouses, Trump would get a cut of the profits. He would also see a small fee if the hotel was sold within seven years. "I was a good listener when negotiating with Trump," Kwek told me. "He wanted to continue managing the hotel and be part of the venture. We eventually narrowed down his role."[14]

Trump's penthouses wouldn't be built during Kwek and Alwaleed's tenure as Plaza owners, and the hotel didn't sell within the allotted time frame, so Trump never saw any profit from the deal. Despite coming out a loser, Trump insisted that he was a part of the new ownership. "We'll be running the hotel. This is a joint venture. As a joint venture, everybody has input," Trump told the *New York Times*.[15] "There will be four partners in the deal," insisted Wallach, naming Kwek, Alwaleed, Citibank, and "Mr. Trump."[16]

With Kwek and Alwaleed at the helm, the hotel was under foreign ownership for the first time. Of course, the Plaza had long welcomed foreign guests and was a favorite of visiting dignitaries. But the acquisition of the hotel by the Singaporean billionaire and the Saudi prince (full name Prince Alwaleed bin Talal bin Abdulaziz Al Saud) indicated an increasing globalization of the real estate market. It was a trend that would only accelerate in future years. "The complexity of the sale announced yesterday and the international scope of the transaction, illustrated how the arenas of real estate and finance have grown beyond national boundaries, and how the business world has shrunk, in ways even the most visionary people could have hardly imagined when the Plaza opened in 1907," wrote the *New York Times* about the deal back in 1995.[17]

New York real estate had always been a somewhat insular industry, largely ruled by a handful of family dynasties. These foreign interlopers sent shock waves through the market. The Saudi prince, a grandchild of the country's founder Ibn Saud, was more well-known than his Singaporean partner. Alwaleed had attended Menlo College in California, where many other Saudi royals also went to school, returning to Riyadh in 1979 after graduating.[18] One of hundreds of Saudi princes, Alwaleed began a real estate firm and spent much of the 1980s under the radar, quietly building up his portfolio of properties. Then, in 1988, Alwaleed orchestrated the takeover of a small Saudi bank, an unusual move in the country's clubby world of banking and one that would foretell his ambition.

Several years later, in 1991, Alwaleed, just thirty-five, garnered international attention. That year, he seemingly came from nowhere to invest $590 million in Citicorp shares, becoming the bank's largest single shareholder and shoring up the ailing but storied institution.[19] Alwaleed became an exemplar of the international order that was then taking shape. The *Economist* dubbed him "Warren Albuffett"[20] and the *New York Times* wrote of him, "The Prince projects the image of being thoroughly modern and financially astute, as at home in his private jet as in his 13-room palace in Riyadh."[21]

Alwaleed, who was trim with a thick mustache and had an air of urbane sophistication, claimed to have started out in 1979 with a loan of $30,000 from his father. He also mortgaged a home for some $400,000 and, as a grandson of Ibn Saud, received a monthly stipend of $15,000. Still, "you could barely clothe a Saudi prince for such sums, let alone furnish him with a multi-billion-dollar empire," quipped the *Economist*, in a piece titled "The Mystery of the World's Second-Richest Businessman."[22] Despite questions surrounding the basis for his wealth, Alwaleed was a billionaire by age thirty-one. And by forty, when he purchased the Plaza, he had a reputation as a self-made mogul with a canny knack for investing.

Like Trump, Alwaleed relished his success, embracing a lavish lifestyle that included a 460,000-square-foot home in Riyadh, a fleet of cars that numbered in the hundreds, and a private Boeing 747 outfitted with a gold throne.[23] Ever colorful, to mark his new Plaza partnership, Alwaleed gave Kwek a singular gift—a gold-plated machine gun.[24] As for Alwaleed's relationship with Trump, the two men had a bumpy history. Back in 1991, when Trump was trying desperately to save his empire, Alwaleed, fresh off his flashy Citicorp investment, bought Trump's enormous 280-foot yacht. The loss of the *Trump Princess*, which had once belonged to Saudi arms dealer Adnan Khashoggi and was featured in the James Bond movie *Never Say Never Again*, was a blow for the New York real estate personality. In later years, the relationship would remain tense, with Alwaleed frequently writing derisive tweets about the US president.

As for Kwek, he welcomed the golden machine gun that he received from Alwaleed, prominently displaying it in his office. But despite his affection for the memento, the Singaporean was far less flamboyant than his partner. A billionaire several times over, Kwek was executive chairman of Hong Leong Group Singapore, a global conglomerate with more than 480 subsidiaries in 26 countries. In 1928, Kwek's father arrived in Singapore as a penniless teenager from China, and in 1941, he started the company with three brothers and a few thousand dollars. By the time Kwek was nearing adulthood, the family business was a success, and after attending the University of London and earning a degree in law, he joined the firm.

While one of Singapore's wealthiest men, Kwek kept a low profile and went largely unrecognized—even within his own company. According to one anecdote, Kwek, who made a hobby of collecting fast cars, often parked his Rolls-Royce in a designated spot at one of his hotels in Singapore. One day, he decided to drive his Ferrari instead. The guard at the hotel failed to recognize his boss and refused to allow Kwek to park there, forcing him to turn his Ferrari around and come back in his Rolls.[25]

Both Alwaleed and Kwek were bullish on the hotel industry. This was Kwek's third hotel purchase in Manhattan, while Alwaleed had recently acquired a stake in two prominent chains, Fairmont Hotels and Resorts and the Four Seasons Hotels. It was Alwaleed's Fairmont brand that was chosen to manage the Plaza.

At the time of the Plaza deal, the recession of the early 1990s was giving way to a rising economic tide. The Plaza seemed poised to benefit, and the new owners said they planned to make only minor renovations, setting aside $28 million for improvements. "Never tamper with greatness," Robert I. Small, the president of Fairmont, told the *New York Times* shortly after Alwaleed and Kwek purchased the hotel. "I love it. Why change it?"[26] The formula seemed to work, with profitability steadily increasing. Five years into their tenure, the Plaza saw one of its best years ever, with net operating income reaching nearly $46 million.

This optimism came to a screeching halt on September 11, 2001. On a blue-sky morning, terrorists crashed two planes into the World Trade Center in Lower Manhattan, killing 2,606 people. The city froze, its citizens reeling as army tanks rumbled down Canal Street and businesses shut their doors against the poisonous smoke billowing from the wreckage. Kwek's Millennium Hotel stood just two hundred yards from what quickly became known as Ground Zero. The building suffered catastrophic damage, with many of its windows blown out and repairs that took years to complete.

For Alwaleed, who was at home in Riyadh when the attack unfolded, 9/11 was personal. "I have many friends in New York. Most of the companies I invest in have bases in New York, and I studied in New York," Alwaleed told his biographer, the journalist Riz Khan. "I wanted to show the American people that they had a friend in the Middle East, especially in Saudi Arabia."[27] Alwaleed, by then the sixth-richest man in the world, wished to fly to New York and deliver a $10 million check to assist the victims of 9/11 and their families.[28] It was a risky move, given the charged political atmosphere at the time and the fact that most of the terrorists hailed from Saudi Arabia. Alwaleed reached out to New York mayor Rudolph Giuliani, who ran the request by the White House and the State Department. They approved the visit, giving the appearance that all would go smoothly.

In October 2001, Alwaleed arrived in New York on his private jet. He spent the night at the Plaza, and the following morning, on the one-month anniversary of the attack, he was driven to the site of the World Trade Center. "I really felt just saddened, upset, and concerned about this horrendous attack," Alwaleed said of seeing the devastation up close.[29] Giuliani interpreted his visit in less-favorable terms. "When Prince Alwaleed arrived he was wearing an opulent gold robe and headdress," Giuliani wrote of the encounter in his book *Leadership*. When the Saudi royal handed Giuliani a cashier's check for $10 million, he was somber and expressed his condolences. "But something wasn't quite right. I thought there was a smirk to his face," wrote Giuliani. "He was the only visitor who was unmoved by what he saw."[30]

After the visit to Ground Zero, Alwaleed prepared to fly home. Before leaving, he issued a press release that expressed his "condolences to the people of New York." It went on to add, "However, at times like this one, we must address some of the issues that led to such a criminal attack. I believe the government of the United States of America should re-examine its policies in the Middle East and adopt a more balanced stance to the Palestinian cause."[31]

The blowback was immediate. "I entirely reject that statement," Giuliani responded. "There is no moral equivalent for this act, there is no justification for it." As the criticism mounted, Giuliani announced he would reject Alwaleed's donation. "Mayor Giuliani told a Saudi prince to take his $10 million donation and stuff it," wrote the *New York Daily News*.[32]

Aside from the pressures the Plaza owners were under in the wake of 9/11, the Plaza itself was also reeling. The terrorist attack brought Manhattan tourism to a halt. The hotel, coming off one of its most profitable years, saw its net operating income drop by 40 percent in 2001, to just shy of $27 million. By 2003, the hotel's financials had further worsened, with a pretax loss of $1.8 million. Kwek and Alwaleed initially wanted to spend $28 million on renovating the Plaza, but the bill had ballooned to more than $65 million by the time the work was completed.[33]

Even as the owners spent more and more money, the nearly century-old building continued deteriorating. Leaks were a particularly pesky problem. Plastic tarps were tacked up on the ceiling where water dripped into the lobby, and visitors who peeked behind pillars could find buckets discreetly placed to collect additional runoff. As many as 30 of the more than 800 rooms were unrentable, suffering from water damage and in need of other repairs.[34] Kwek and Alwaleed were at loggerheads over what to do next. For Kwek, the hotel had now become a money-loser and a drain. His London-based hotel arm had spent the past several years struggling, impacted by 9/11, the SARS epidemic, and the uncertainty posed by the Iraq War. The idea of spending more on the Plaza was anathema to him, and in fact, Kwek had announced he was considering selling some hotel assets.[35] Alwaleed, meanwhile, was committed to investing more.

The globe-trotting prince had a closer connection to the Plaza than that of his joint venture partner. Alwaleed often stayed at the Plaza when he was in New York, holding court in the lobby for hours with his team, meeting with investors and business associates and enjoying the ambience. There was also more than just a personal connection. The fact that Alwaleed's Fairmont Hotels brand managed the Plaza was strategically important for the company. The Plaza was a key asset, Fairmont's New York City flagship, and an important company calling card. Investing in the Plaza would benefit not only the hotel, but also Fairmont's reputation. Alwaleed estimated that to bring the hotel up to its potential would cost $200 million, and he knew that Kwek was unlikely to agree to such an expensive undertaking.[36]

It was around then, in 2004, that a compromise would present itself. Miki Naftali, a young Israeli-born developer and the chief executive of El Ad Properties, had just been thwarted in an attempt to create a massive Manhattan real estate project. Naftali had anticipated that the deal would be his first major stamp on New York. But, his hopes dashed, he now turned his sights to the Plaza, betting that the historic structure would provide his ticket to the prime time, as it had done for several Plaza stewards before him.

Naftali was a condominium developer, not a hotelier, and he stood to benefit greatly from the recent direction the real estate industry had taken. At the time, hotels were barely beginning to rebound following the steep downturn in the wake of 9/11. The condominium market, on the other hand, was booming. In 2004, the average price of a Manhattan apartment exceeded $1 million for the first time ever. The city was gripped by a condominium craze, with cranes dotting the skyline and buyers lining up outside new developments for a chance to make a down payment.[37] Real estate executives follow the strategy of converting buildings into whatever type of use will garner the biggest profit. In the early 1960s, that meant tearing down hotels such as the Savoy-Plaza to build office towers like the General Motors Building, and in the early aughts, it meant replacing hotels with luxury housing. Naftali's company, like its competitors, was actively searching out such deals.

El Ad had been founded in 1992 by Isaac Tshuva, an Israeli self-made billionaire with a gruff manner and an expansive portfolio of assets that included energy, insurance, and telecommunications. While an established company in Israel, its US arm had begun modestly, and Naftali was one of its first hires.

Naftali, who had a slight build and sported wire-rimmed glasses and boyish curls, was an unlikely conqueror of the rough-and-tumble world of New York real estate. He had come to America to attend college, graduating from the University of Southern California. He arrived at El Ad not long after, toiling out of a small headquarters in New Jersey, across the George Washington Bridge from the bright lights of Manhattan. Naftali began by renovating handfuls of apartments, but as the market ratcheted higher, El Ad increased the size of its bets. By 2004, El Ad, with Naftali at the helm locally, was undertaking large-scale Manhattan developments and had become a substantial New York City player. That year, Tshuva gave Naftali marching orders to pursue a headline-making project.

At the time, the site that every big real estate developer was chasing was the Mayflower Hotel. The Mayflower was a subpar hotel, but it was situated on a full city block near the southwest corner of Central Park. A developer who could tear down the building and replace it with luxury condominiums would generate monumental profits. The Greek shipping family who had owned the site for decades was finally ready to sell, and Naftali, along with countless others, wined and dined them in a months-long charm offensive.

In the end, El Ad lost out on the Mayflower to Arthur and William Lie Zeckendorf, brothers who belonged to one of New York's oldest and most established real estate families. The Zeckendorfs would tear down the old hotel and erect 15 Central Park West, New York's most expensive apartment building up to that point, and certainly the one with the most buzz.[38] Dubbed "limestone Jesus," the two-towered structure was designed by the famous architect Robert A. M. Stern and loaded with every imaginable amenity, including a private dining room with wine cellars in the basement, a screening room, a seventy-five-foot swimming pool, and even a special waiting room for chauffeurs.[39]

Naftali was devastated by the loss. Tshuva had set aside hundreds of millions of dollars in expectation of buying the Mayflower, and Naftali, now forty-two, had worked for months to make it happen. This had been his moment, and he blew it. Now he had to regroup. One day, Naftali decided to take a walk and ponder his next move. He headed toward the Mayflower site that he had lost, and when he reached it, he turned east down Central Park South.

Naftali soon found himself staring at the gleaming, château-like Plaza. He had first laid eyes on the hotel as a tourist, but now, as he gazed at the white edifice standing sentry at the edge of Central Park, he did so with the discerning eye of a real estate developer. Like the Mayflower, the Plaza was a hotel that had seen better days, but its location, at the corner of Central Park and Fifth Avenue, was unbeatable. Right then, Naftali decided to stake El Ad's—and his own—reputation on buying the Plaza and converting it into apartments. "The Plaza Hotel was the NFL," Naftali told me. "Before that, I was in the club league."

From the get-go, there were problems with Naftali's plan. Namely, the hotel was not up for sale. Even trickier, its owner was a member of the Saudi ruling family, and Naftali was Jewish and an Israeli. "I didn't think the prince would entertain a meeting with me," Naftali told me one day as he recollected the experience. Unsure what to do, he reached out to his real estate broker for advice. Scott Latham, who had represented Naftali in his ultimately failed bid for the Mayflower, agreed that choosing Alwaleed as a point of contact might not make sense.

Latham had done work over the years in Asia, and he suggested to Naftali that they try to reach Kwek. "A buddy of mine gave me Kwek's private line," Latham told me, "so I stayed late one night at the office and I cold-called Kwek. He picked up the phone and we talked for three minutes." Latham told Kwek he had a buyer for the Plaza. Kwek responded, "Oh, they can't afford it and it's not for sale." Latham said, "Give me a week and I'll prove to you that we're for real."

A game of cat and mouse ensued, replete with international intrigue, hidden buyers, and dead ends. A few days after Latham's phone call with Kwek, the Singapore hotelier's number two, Hong Wong Ren, arrived in New York and requested a meeting. Latham and Naftali went to see him at the Plaza, knocking on the door of one of the hotel's large suites. Inside, they found Ren lounging in an armchair, surrounded by an army of assistants. Ren nodded, and the entourage quickly filed out of the room. For some thirty minutes, Ren asked Naftali and Latham questions about themselves. Then, with an abrupt wave of his hand, indicating the real negotiation was about to start, Ren asked them what they thought the suite they were sitting in was worth. It was a tricky question, since the men didn't have much data to go on. Naftali had few insights into the Plaza's financials or the condition of the building. What's more, if Naftali gave a number that was too low, Ren would dismiss them out of hand, and if it was too high, they might lose their negotiating leverage.

Naftali and Latham gazed around the suite, noting the peeling paint on the windowsills and the aging furniture. To buy some time, the men asked if they could tour the room, pacing the worn carpeting and peeking into dark closets. Finally, wandering into the bathroom, the two closed the door a crack and spoke hurriedly in whispers, so Ren wouldn't overhear. "Miki and I were in the restroom and we were like, 'What do you think he wants to hear?'" Latham said. After a few frantic minutes, the pair walked out of the bathroom and Naftali told Ren he thought he could get $2,000 a square foot if he converted the Plaza into apartments. In other words, a five-hundred-square-foot room, if converted into a for-sale condominium, could sell for $1 million. Ren dismissed the figure as too low. Naftali, feeling the potential for a deal slipping away, approached the window and looked out at the view. He then told Ren he might be able to get $2,500 a square foot.

Ren was still dismissive, and Naftali left the meeting disheartened, but still determined. He continued to push for a meeting with Kwek and began analyzing the property to figure out a real purchase price for the hotel. True, the Plaza was in poor shape, but for El Ad, a condominium developer, it didn't much matter. Unlike a traditional hotel buyer, El Ad planned to gut much of the building's interior and refashion it for apartments. The aging pipes and air-conditioning units, the peeling paint and old-fashioned furnishings would all be replaced.

On a Monday in June 2004, Latham sent a fax to Kwek's office with an offer from El Ad to buy the Plaza for $625 million. A week later, Kwek faxed back a response: He would finally meet them. At 11 a.m. that Thursday, July 1—in Singapore. The timing couldn't have been worse. It was the Fourth of July holiday, and Naftali had tickets to fly to Israel on Friday with his family, while Latham was hosting a large barbecue at his home in Rhode Island. Latham faxed back a response, requesting that the meeting be postponed to the following week. On Tuesday, Kwek's office responded: The Singapore hotelier would meet them on Thursday morning at 11 a.m. In other words, there was no rescheduling. Because of the time difference, the men had to get on a flight in a few hours to make the appointment. "I called Miki and I go, 'We're leaving for Singapore tonight,'" Latham recalled.

For Latham, brokering a deal for the Plaza would be a coup. Husky, with the ruddy face of an Irish bruiser, Latham was born in Vermont and raised in Mexico City, where his father owned Coca-Cola bottling plants.[40] Originally intending to be an artist, Latham had graduated from the Rhode Island School of Design and moved to the East Village. There he became a regular in the early 1980s art scene, Dumpster-diving for collage material and hustling from gallery to gallery, his work hanging in group shows with the likes of Jean-Michel Basquiat and Keith Haring. When he turned twenty-three, Latham got married and figured it was time to find salaried employment. He joined a tiny brokerage firm selling properties in Harlem and the Bronx, working his way up to become one of the city's leading brokers. For Latham, to arrange the sale of the Plaza would cement his reputation.

As dawn broke over the Singapore Changi Airport, Naftali also understood that the day would be a turning point. Either he would leave the country as the new owner of the Plaza, or he would depart dejectedly, forced to once more rethink his ambitions. As they exited the plane, Latham and Naftali walked down an endless corridor in the airport's Terminal Two, searching for the showers. After a grueling nineteen-hour flight, they wanted to look presentable to meet the powerful Kwek, who would determine their fate. The pair checked into the airport's business lounge, where they washed and switched their crinkled khakis for dark, tailored suits. Walking out of the airport into the warm early-morning air, they hailed a taxi. As the driver took them through the spotless streets, Naftali sat pensively in the backseat, watching the morning rush hour and contemplating what awaited him.

Just in time for their 11 a.m. appointment, Latham and Naftali disembarked from the taxi and stood in front of Republic Plaza, a soaring sixty-six-story skyscraper that Kwek had constructed in the center of Singapore's downtown. They entered the marble lobby and were greeted by an entourage of Kwek employees, who ushered them to a separate elevator bank that whisked them up to the building's top floor. They exited into a massive office, where Kwek was sitting at a large desk, a backdrop of the Singapore harbor spread behind him. The sixty-five-year-old Kwek stood up to greet them, and the men began talking. Soon, the half-hour meeting had stretched through the morning hours. At lunchtime, Kwek invited the men to his private dining room, where they feasted on a four-course meal. Then the talks resumed.

As it became clear that the sides were engaged in what would be an all-day marathon, Naftali realized he was facing additional competition from buyers back in New York. Even though the Plaza wasn't officially on the market, word had spread that Naftali was in Singapore. Several times, Kwek paused to take phone calls that appeared to be from competitors who were trying to circumvent the deal. "I swear while we were sitting there, Kwek got a phone call and put the receiver down for a minute to tell us that some guy by the name of Lloyd Goldman was on the phone," said Latham, referring to one of New York's most powerful developers.

Despite fielding other offers, Kwek kept talking to the pair. Finally, as the sun began to set over the Singapore harbor, the men came to an agreement. El Ad would pay $675 million for the Plaza, or $838,500 per hotel room, a record price, and more than double the $325 million the sellers had paid for it. Before the deal could be finalized, Naftali called Tshuva for approval, and Kwek called Alwaleed. All parties gave their assent, and Naftali insisted that they sign a one-page memorandum of understanding.

Naftali knew that the real estate sharks were circling, and he didn't want to leave until the deal was ironclad. By then, however, it was the end of the workday, and most of Kwek's legal team had left the building. The one remaining lawyer was a young relative of Kwek's who was toiling on a lower floor in the now-darkened tower. The men took the elevator and walked among the cubicles until they found the junior clerk's desk, clustering around him as they drafted a document.

Finally, at 8 p.m., thirteen hours after arriving in Singapore, they had their agreement. "As he had to leave in a hurry, we ended negotiations and shook hands on the deal," said Kwek. Naftali and Latham walked out of Kwek's offices, basking in their triumph and relishing the moment. The men were driven back to Changi Airport, where Naftali jumped on a flight that took him first to Bangkok, then to Zurich, and finally to Tel Aviv, arriving thirty minutes before the rest of his family. Latham flew home separately, making it to his barbecue gathering in Rhode Island just in time. "The whole way back I was just dying to talk to somebody," Latham later told me. "I felt like I was floating. We just did a deal on the Plaza Hotel!"

When Kwek first bought the Plaza, he told *Fortune*, "We're not short-term investors, but we have to be practical. If somebody in two years offers $700 million to $800 million for the Plaza, we say goodbye. Why be sentimental about it? It's an asset."[41] Now Kwek called El Ad's offer "too good to refuse."[42] He added, "The hotel needs renovation and I don't want to spend any more money on it." Despite his initial misgivings, Alwaleed, too, was ecstatic over the sale, according to Kwek. "He's invited me to Paris, where he wants to give me a big dinner," the Singapore partner beamed.

The deal produced a tidy profit for Kwek and Alwaleed, but it put the Plaza in unprecedented terrain. Over its long history, the hotel had seen owners and guests come and go. It had undergone renovation after renovation. It had experienced heady times, when its rooms were so full that management put cots in the Grand Ballroom, to desperate periods, when its entrance was obscured by a seven-foot pile of rancid trash. But this was different. For the first time ever, the Plaza would not be solely a hotel.

Chapter 13

SAVE THE PLAZA

"It's amazing people think it's one of the best
hotels in the world. It's not."
—*Miki Naftali, owner of the Plaza*

Naftali was in Israel for barely a week. By the time he returned
in the summer of 2004, news that a condominium developer
had purchased the Plaza broke in the press and rumors were swirling over the fate of New York's grandest hotel. El Ad remained
mum throughout the fall, and then, just before Christmas, the company announced it was closing the Oak Room and the basement-
level Oyster Bar and handing nearly two hundred employees their
pink slips.[1]

Anxious doormen and maids gathered in hushed groups in the
Plaza's hallways, while preservationists and Plaza devotees began to
panic. The formal Edwardian Room would be closing, they heard,
to make way for a fancy clothing shop. The Grand Ballroom, where
Truman Capote held his famous ball, was turning into a department store (London-based Harrods was supposedly in the running). An escalator was purportedly being installed in the stately
Terrace Room to ease the feet of weary shoppers, and of course, the
bulk of the hotel rooms were being turned into multimillion-dollar

apartments. "The year is not off to a good start," wrote Plaza historian Curtis Gathje in a *New York Times* op-ed headlined "What Would Eloise Say?"[2]

The rumors weren't entirely wrong. El Ad planned to close the Plaza while it underwent a renovation that would ultimately take over two and a half years and cost $450 million. In 2007, when the grand hotel reopened, it would be reborn as a multiuse department store cum condominium cum boutique hotel, a project that El Ad estimated would generate at least $1 billion in profit. The new Plaza would encompass a small number of hotel guest rooms with windows facing the dark corridor along West Fifty-Eighth Street. The upper stories and those rooms with coveted views of Fifth Avenue and Central Park would become expensive homes for sale, including penthouses loosely based on Donald Trump's designs. And there would be shops everywhere—an enormous indoor mall with clothing racks full of expensive suits and shelves stuffed with silk kerchiefs.

El Ad assumed that as the new owners of the Plaza, the company could largely do as it pleased. It barreled ahead with its plans, giving little thought to public input from civic leaders, landmark officials, or politicians. The new owners sorely underestimated their challenge. Immediately, architectural historians and fans of old New York voiced concern. "Serious alterations" of the historic hotel would not only hurt the Plaza's bottom line, it "would be a public relations disaster," warned Peg Breen, president of the New York City Landmarks Conservancy, a group dedicated to preserving historic buildings.[3] "It just feels stripped of its dignity," Mary Alice Kellogg, a longtime patron of the Oak Room, said of the Plaza's impending changes. "I don't know who the new owners are, but I already don't like them."[4]

While many were apprehensive, opposition to El Ad's plan would find its strongest voice in an unlikely corner of the city. The New

York Hotel and Motel Trades Council was made up of thirty-five thousand members, including bellmen, doormen, banquet waiters, and maids. It had taken the union decades to gain recognition, but it was now a powerhouse organization led by the politically savvy and charming Peter Ward. The union leader was steeped in city politics, and he would use his knowledge and connections to great effect when it came to the Plaza.

Raised in a working-class section of Brooklyn, Ward had joined the union as a clerk, straight from high school, and over the years had held nearly every job there. With a swoosh of blondish hair and a talent for storytelling, Ward married the daughter of the powerful union boss, Vito Pitta. In 1996, when Pitta retired, his son-in-law took over as union president. For Ward, the Plaza had special meaning. Not only was it New York's most famous hotel and one of the union's largest employers, but there was also a personal connection. Pitta, his father-in-law, had once been a Plaza banquet waiter. Ward himself had worked there, in the early 1980s as a business agent, liaising between the union and the Plaza's management. When Ward got married, it was in front of three hundred guests in the Plaza's Grand Ballroom.[5]

With the real estate market booming and the condominium craze sweeping Manhattan, it was a tough time for Ward's union. In 2004, six out of seven hotels that were sold were converted into apartments. This meant that in a twelve-month period, nearly 1,100 hotel rooms were lost, and more than one thousand union positions were eliminated. The prospect of the Plaza closing, taking its nine hundred good-paying jobs with it, was unthinkable.[6] By taking a stand on the Plaza, Ward hoped to set a precedent and safeguard his union's future. It would turn out to be a prescient decision.

El Ad was not focused on Ward or his union. The developer argued that under city ordinances, it was allowed to complete its condominium conversion, as long as it adhered to certain regulations. If its plan resulted in fewer hotel union jobs, so what? Ward had little leverage to stop it. In fact, El Ad argued, it had an ironclad union contract, which laid out the severance packages that union employees would receive in such a scenario. If and when it converted the building, El Ad made clear that it would not veer from its agreement.

Despite El Ad's stance, Ward hoped he might convince the developer to take a different tack. El Ad's plan called for only 150 hotel rooms, from the current 805. Ward wanted the developer to increase that number, as well as sign a new severance agreement that would double the payout, to two weeks' salary for every year an employee worked at the hotel. Ward pushed for a meeting to negotiate these points, but Naftali and Tshuva rebuffed his overtures. Eventually, El Ad sent a junior executive to meet Ward. The El Ad employee had a message for the union boss: "The owners don't think they need your help and they have no interest in doing anything other than paying the severance," Ward told me of their interaction.[7]

Ward, his back up against the wall, considered his options. He was president of a union with tens of thousands of members who could be mobilized into a large voting bloc. He had relationships with numerous local politicians, and what's more, he had enthusiastically supported some of New York City mayor Michael Bloomberg's less popular projects, such as an ultimately failed bid to erect a football stadium on Manhattan's West Side. Maybe now was the time to call in a few favors.

El Ad, meanwhile, was not politically connected. Neither Tshuva, who spent much of his time abroad, nor Naftali had long-standing relationships with the city's top leaders. While Ward was involved in several of the city's charitable groups, the El Ad executives didn't sit on any high-profile New York City cultural or civic boards. And neither were regulars on the charity gala circuit, where so many other developers networked and glad-handed politicians.

Before they bought the Plaza, these connections didn't much matter. "Isaac [Tshuva] wanted to stay below the radar," Suri Kasirer, president of Kasirer, a lobbying firm hired by El Ad, told me. "Every single time I said, 'Why don't you contribute to this, or meet this person,' he would say no. Then one day he bought the Plaza Hotel and he was out there in such a big way, it was just huge. He was unprepared for what came with it."

El Ad underestimated how debilitating its decision not to curry political favor could be, especially when facing off against someone like Ward. And while the developer was allowed to convert the Plaza guest rooms into apartments, it needed a number of city approvals in order to execute all of the sweeping changes it planned to the historic hotel. Most importantly, El Ad could not create its numerous retail shops without getting the assent of city agencies.

Because of a zoning quirk that harkened back to the fact that the Plaza was built nearly a decade before New York implemented its zoning code, an invisible line ran through the Grand Ballroom. On one side, El Ad was allowed to create retail stores, while on the other, it was prohibited. El Ad had little political capital to spend to obtain these approvals. "Nobody felt, 'We can't do that to Isaac, he's a major player, look what he does for New York,'" said Kasirer.

Ward realized his advantage and declared all-out war. To get El Ad to carve out more hotel rooms and increase the severance payments, he would rally support among his political allies. Specifically, if Ward could convince elected officials to withhold approvals for El Ad's desired retail zoning change, he had a chance of success. So in January 2005, Ward set aside $2 million of the union's coffers for a massive campaign. Called "Save the Plaza," the effort included rallies, celebrity endorsements, and television and radio spots. "It was the best $2 million we ever spent," Ward told me.

One of Ward's first moves was to organize noisy, raucous rallies around the Pulitzer Fountain at the Plaza's front door. In the February cold, thousands of workers, politicians, and supporters gathered, shouting slogans and carrying signs. One young girl held up a placard that read "My name is Eloise/I used to live in the Plaza/Now I'm homeless." Neil Johnson, a Plaza doorman, told the crowd, "We don't want to walk into our gorgeous building and see escalators with a sign over them saying, 'Starbucks and Zabars second floor!'"[8] Camera crews from as far afield as Italy, Brazil, and Japan turned up, recording and reporting on the controversy. Actress Sarah Jessica Parker held her birthday party at the Grand Ballroom in solidarity, while the film director Peter Bogdanovich gave a rousing speech expounding on the building's significance. The Reverend Jesse Jackson also made an appearance, leading the crowd in chants of "America is not for sale" and "Save the Plaza! Save the jobs! Save the families!"[9]

When a hearing at the local community board was planned on El Ad's proposed zoning change, Ward lobbied the officials to his cause and enlisted hundreds of union members to show up in protest. The community board, which had only an advisory role, voted overwhelmingly against El Ad's proposal. Ward also backed new city legislation that would have prevented hotels from converting more than 20 percent of their space into apartments. If passed, it would have effectively killed El Ad's Plaza plans. Swayed by Ward's charm, or the power of his voting bloc, or simply the rationale that the city was becoming oversaturated with costly condominiums, 35 of the 51 members of the New York City Council immediately signed on to sponsor the measure.[10]

As the Plaza controversy grabbed worldwide attention, Ward

dispatched union members to London to protest in front of the Harrods department store, which El Ad had continuously referenced as a possible retail tenant. In response, Harrods owner Mohamed Al Fayed wrote a letter to Mayor Bloomberg denying the retailer was in any talks to open at the Plaza. "It angers me that there are unscrupulous brokers and the developer who appear to be touting my name and the Harrods brand name in order to drum up interest in the project," he wrote.[11]

Two Plaza hotel workers also traveled to Israel to pressure Tshuva on his home turf. "You have the King David Hotel here in Israel, right?" Johnson, the Plaza doorman, said on national television, referencing Jerusalem's fanciest hotel. "How would the people of Israel like it if Donald Trump came over here, purchased the King David Hotel, turned it all into condos [and] had a shopping mall on the fourth floor with McDonald's and Burger Kings?" As Israeli TV anchors and newspapers reported on the controversy, El Ad issued a scolding statement that read, in part, "We think it would be better for the union to invest its funds in the welfare of the workers and not in globe-trotting."[12]

Ward was also helped along in his efforts by preservationists. While the Plaza's facade had been designated a landmark in 1969, its interior rooms, several of which still featured original details of Henry Janeway Hardenbergh's designs, were not protected, and were at risk of being destroyed.

The New York Landmarks Conservancy took out a full-page advertisement in the *New York Times* urging supporters to rally to the cause and call their representatives.[13] Ronald S. Lauder, a Landmarks Conservancy board member and billionaire scion of makeup company founder Estée Lauder, flew to Israel to meet with Tshuva personally and urge him to protect the building. "All the New Yorkers who demanded that the Plaza be saved should realize that a

speculative mall places it in danger," Lauder wrote in a letter to the
New York Post. He called it "lunacy" to fail "to protect this iconic
hotel for generations to come,"[14] and vowed to prevent the hotel
"from being transformed into another gaudy bazaar."[15]

As the Plaza conflict swirled, it began to take on greater sym-
bolism. In a city where apartment prices were soaring, and the
cost of living was becoming prohibitive to many, the Plaza became
emblematic of the widening gap between the ultrawealthy and
everyone else. An unfeeling developer was pursuing $1 billion in
profit by cutting hundreds of middle-class jobs, laying off Plaza
employees who in some cases had worked there for half a century.
Adding insult to injury, the Plaza, while a capital of consumerism
and a paean to wealth, had always been open to the public. Countless New Yorkers knew it was the most elegant place for a bathroom
break in all of Midtown, and natives and tourists alike regularly
sat in the plush lobby for a momentary pause from the hubbub
outside. Now a building that was central to the fabric of city life
would become a private home, a place where only billionaires were
allowed to tread.

Despite the immense pressure El Ad was under, the developer
stubbornly dug in its heels. "It was pretty ugly," recalled Kasirer of
the battles her client faced. "We were spending lots of money on
legal fees [and] we felt like we were getting killed in the media." El
Ad was spending hundreds of thousands of dollars to fight Ward,
including shelling out nearly $216,000 to Kasirer, helping to make
her New York's highest-paid lobbyist in 2005.[16]

The company also didn't do itself any favors to generate sym-
pathy. Even as workers were marching in front of the hotel, El Ad
circulated an aggressively worded letter that was leaked to the press.
"The Plaza will close its doors on schedule," it told its employees.
"Nothing that the union's destructive political and public relations
campaign against us can do will change this reality...If anybody

tries to convince you that these efforts stand the slightest chance of keeping the Plaza the way it currently is—or of increasing the number of hotel jobs after the renovation is complete—they are wrong, and you shouldn't be deceived."[17]

But Ward and his ilk were undeterred. This was a fight to the death, and, as Ward saw it, the union had little to lose. In early April, more than six thousand union members crowded into Radio City Music Hall, with another two thousand members spilling onto the sidewalks outside. Mayor Bloomberg gave the keynote speech, telling the gathered bellmen and maids that he had made his "office and staff members available to both parties in an attempt to reach a compromise." He added, "I am very confident that if the union and the owners continue to meet there will be a settlement that pleases both parties."[18]

In fact, Bloomberg had been working for weeks behind the scenes to foster a compromise. The billionaire businessman turned politician had long prided himself on his independence, often saying, "I'm not going to spend my life pandering to anybody." But the mayor was facing a tough reelection campaign in November, and support from the union would prove pivotal. As the *New York Observer* noted, Bloomberg "took an uncharacteristic stance against the free market, and on the side of nostalgia and Big Labor in the Plaza Hotel fight."[19]

In addition to the looming election, Bloomberg was also actively pursuing the 2012 Summer Olympics, hoping that New York would be picked as the host city. It just so happened that the Olympic delegation was coming to New York—and staying at the Plaza. The visit coincided with the Save the Plaza campaign, with crowds rallying at the Pulitzer Fountain, and the hotel staffed by disgruntled workers about to lose their jobs. Even worse, the Plaza was closing to undergo its years-long renovation just one month after the Olympic committee's arrival.

The delegates would not be treated to the classic Plaza experience.

"Unfortunately, the storied hotel, where guests pay up to $1,100 a
night for a luxury suite, is starting to resemble a Motel 6," reported
the *New York Daily News*. "They should replace the concierge desk
with a complaints bureau," it quoted a disgruntled employee as saying, adding, "They're cannibalizing the place and not buying any
equipment or resources."

The most egregious complaint was not that the minibars in rooms
were empty, or even that the Palm Court was serving food on mis-
matched plates. The most flagrant display of the hotel's downfall
had to be the fact that "when guests check out, the unused portions
of their complimentary bottles of lotion and shampoo are taken
downstairs, emptied and blended into other bottles," the employee
revealed.[20] In the end, London was chosen to host the 2012 Olympic
Summer Games. It was never known whether the delegates' stay at
the Plaza played any role in the decision.

One morning in February 2005, a month into Ward's Save
the Plaza campaign, Joshua Sirefman, the chief of staff for one of
Bloomberg's deputy mayors, was at work. "I was just sitting at my
desk; I think it was probably early morning, because for a long
time [Bloomberg] and I were the two earliest arrivals," Sirefman
told me, "and he was just like, 'Come with me to this meeting.'"
Sirefman followed the mayor into a conference room, and there
they were greeted by Ward. The union boss had come to discuss
the Plaza controversy, and as the meeting concluded, Bloomberg,
without much preamble or notice, gestured to Sirefman and told the
younger man to solve the problem.

Sirefman was thrown headfirst into the contentious issue, and
he began by inviting Naftali and Ward to the mayor's official residence, Gracie Mansion, for talks. "I remember in the car on the
way to Gracie Mansion I called my dad, who is an arbitrator,"
said Sirefman. "I was like, 'What do I do?'" His father gave him

some useful pointers and the meeting turned out to be the first in a series of discussions. As negotiations between El Ad and the union dragged on, pressure from the Save the Plaza rallies, television ads, and newspaper stories began to mount. Meanwhile, El Ad had set itself an April 30 deadline for closing and overhauling the hotel, further intensifying the sense of urgency.

A couple of weeks after Mayor Bloomberg spoke to the crowd of six thousand hotel union members at Radio City Music Hall, Naftali and Ward and their teams of lawyers descended on City Hall. The plan was to remain there until they had struck a deal. Inside the Lower Manhattan building, the country's oldest city hall still used for its original function, Sirefman traveled back and forth between conference rooms, relaying messages and urging a consensus. "There was a whole stretch of proverbial shuttle diplomacy," he said. "Many pizzas were delivered," added Kasirer, who was also there. "Josh and I spent hours and hours together."

The El Ad executives felt "total outrage that they were, you know, being held hostage to these talks," said Sirefman. Naftali agreed that it was tough going, even getting agitated as he related the story years later. "I spent five days and nights in City Hall, okay?" Naftali told me. "I mean, it was very intense." Naftali resented the political pressure he was being forced to endure. "I don't have to do this," he said, describing his feelings at the time. "It's a private building, private funding. I'm sorry, but I don't owe you anything. I don't owe the mayor anything."

El Ad's team, which included Naftali, a handful of lawyers, and Kasirer, were "masterful, consummate negotiators," said Ward. He recalled how, at one point, the sides had been negotiating all night and he was under the impression they had finally come to an agreement. Exhausted but satisfied, Ward arrived the following morning expecting to sign a deal. Instead, Sirefman sheepishly appeared with bad news—El Ad had changed its mind.

"I was like, 'No way!'" Ward told me, adding a colorful expletive. When one of El Ad's lawyers entered the room, Ward turned on him in fury. "I'm screaming like, 'You did not just wait all those hours and now change your mind?! You wasted my time!'" El Ad's lawyer was nonplussed at Ward's outburst. "What?" he responded, in his thick Eastern European Jewish accent, shrugging his shoulders. "I can't change my mind? A man can't change his mind? That's so terrible?" Then the lawyer threw down a set of keys on the table with a dramatic flourish. " 'Fine. If that's how you feel, then you run the Plaza.' And he walked out," Ward recounted. "They think that they're going to outlast us and they're just going to be stubborn, but they don't know how stubborn the Irish are," he remembered thinking at the time. "There was," added Sirefman, "no shortage of tense and dramatic moments."[21]

Eventually, after more than sixty hours of constant negotiating, both sides were worn down. And at 5:30 a.m. on Thursday, April 14, 2005, the parties finally agreed to terms.[22] The Plaza would continue to operate as a hotel, with 282 rooms, an increase over the 150 that El Ad had originally wanted. Common spaces, including the Grand Ballroom, the Oak Room, and the Palm Court, would be renovated and preserved. Of the 900 Plaza union employees, 350 would be allowed to keep their jobs.[23] Those who were let go would get more generous severance packages, with two weeks' pay for every year worked. The plan was so specific that Naftali and Ward took out the hotel's blueprints and detailed the plans for each room, sealing the agreement with their initials so there could be no confusion.

Several hours later, at 3 p.m., a well-rested mayor, followed by the exhausted but jubilant Ward, an equally tired Naftali, Tshuva, and a staff that included Kasirer and Sirefman, filed into the Plaza's Grand Ballroom. "This is another great day for New York," Bloomberg triumphantly declared as the crowd of hotel workers cheered wildly.[24] As he detailed the hundreds of jobs that would be saved, the ornate room filled with a pulsing chant of "Four more years! Four more years!"[25] Sirefman described the mood in the room as "madness," with celebrating workers crying and embracing one another in relief. "It was a very immediate and visceral experience," he told me. "To have seen the benefit for people with real lives, real jobs, it was so concrete. It was a real high."

The Save the Plaza campaign ended in triumph for the mayor, and it also proved a huge win for the union, even though there was the inescapable fact that several hundred people would still be losing their jobs. More Plaza employees would be returning to work than originally planned, and those who would be out of work would receive increased severance pay. The deal also set an important precedent. Hotel conversions that followed the Plaza controversy were tidy affairs that often resulted in large payouts to union members. "People who want to reposition a hotel now come in and say, 'Okay, we get it. So we got to pay, we're going to take care of your guys,'" said Ward. "Management now understands rather than have a fight, why don't we just come in and sit down and talk." In 2015, for instance, when the Waldorf-Astoria began undergoing a similar condominium conversion, there was little blowback. The hotel's owners met early in the process with Ward, and in the end agreed to a record severance package for union employees of nearly $149 million.[26]

As the April 30 deadline for closing the hotel loomed, Plaza employees said their good-byes. One regaled a reporter with the memory of movie star Eddie Murphy handing out hundred-dollar bills after his elaborate marriage ceremony in the Grand Ballroom. Another doorman recalled how he had once opened a limousine door for a woman in short shorts, a halter top, and thigh-high boots. As he lugged her suitcase from the trunk, the zipper came undone, revealing the top of a man's head. The doorman dropped the luggage in horror, and out rolled a (living) man in high heels, a dog collar, and makeup.

Other employees' good-byes were bittersweet. Salvatore Lercara, who came from a long line of Plaza workers, including both grandfathers, his father, and an uncle, was ambivalent about the end; while Freddy Davila called it "a very sad chapter in my life right now." Since many of the Plaza workers wouldn't be returning, the employees created a phonebook with all of their contacts. "We have developed a special bond unlike any we can think of encountering at any other place of employment," read the introduction. "The fat lady has sung, the curtain will drop, standing ovations are given. Farewell to all players on every level."[27]

On the last Thursday in April 2005, hundreds of Plaza employees and their families gathered in the Grand Ballroom again, this time for a blowout party. And on the final Saturday, the last guest checked out of the hotel before construction work began. It was exactly one hundred years earlier that the first Plaza had closed to make way for the current building. And just as it had been in 1905, when guests vied to be the last one to leave, there was a contest.

"It came down to a test of wills: who'd flinch in his bid to be the last guest out of The Plaza before it closed forever as an 805-room hotel," reported the *New York Post*. "For days, Joe McGinnis, a regular for half a century at the world's most celebrated inn, had been vowing to claim the title... What he hadn't counted on was the steely determination of John Finan." In the end, Finan, a thirty-eight-year-old real estate investor from Long Island, bested the fifty-two-year-old publisher from St. Pete Beach, Florida, to claim the title. On that final afternoon, Finan emerged last, clutching his Bernese mountain dog and his hotel bill, striding through the Plaza's revolving doors for the last time, before driving off in his Jaguar.[28]

With employees and guests finally departed, El Ad began cleaning out the building, ridding the hotel of ninety-eight years' worth of bric-a-brac. It advertised a tag sale that drew hundreds of fans, who stood for hours in the drizzling rain in a line that started at the Fifth Avenue entrance and wrapped around Central Park South. For an entry fee of $10 apiece, gawkers could enter the hotel to stroll past piles of doorknobs, bedsheets, and cutlery, shelling out as little as $1 for a water glass. National Content Liquidators ran the free-for-all, and it was chaotic from the start.

"Buyer grumbling began almost immediately," reported the *New York Times*. "Shoppers wandered a half-dozen hotel floors, poking through rooms and scooping up lamps, chairs and small paintings. But most didn't know what was for sale or how to carry it away." At the end of the day, when the Plaza closed its doors to the lines of shoppers— an hour earlier than scheduled—there was near pandemonium. Many had waited for hours but still hadn't made it to the front of the line, and tempers flared. Inside, disappointed shoppers abounded. "We wuz robbed. I want my $10 back," one man shouted to his friend.[29]

A year later, the Plaza held another yard sale, but this time, it was conducted by Christie's, and instead of $1 water glasses, there was a $10,000 Steinway baby grand piano on offer. The night before the auction, Christie's hosted a party meant to mimic Capote's Black and White Ball. In a room at the auction house filled with Plaza furnishings, albeit each one with a price sticker, Peter Duchin, the bandleader for the original soiree, and Kitty Carlisle Hart, an original guest, sipped champagne and reminisced. "Nostalgia can make people do crazy things, like trying to reenact a forty-year-old social event," reported National Public Radio. Despite Christie's best efforts, the party was a far cry from Truman's ball. Rather than hundreds of elegant guests, a crowd of fans, and dozens of paparazzi, there were only a handful of photographers in attendance. Most were there to capture images of the rock star David Bowie and his model wife, Iman, but neither bothered to show.[30]

The auction that was held the next morning was better attended, with 400 bidders vying for 346 lots. Items ranged from a pair of

mahogany and etched glass doors from the Oyster Bar, estimated
to go for $1,200; to a piece of the oak parquet dance floor from the
Grand Ballroom, estimated at $3,000. Most items were modern,
but one of the few older pieces was a silver-plated carte de boeuf,
circa 1920, with "the hinged roll top above a molded base with
handles," estimated at $10,000.[31] In the end, the auction drew $1.76
million in sales, far outpacing the $750,000 that Christie's had
anticipated. The 1920 serving cart, for instance, sold for $50,400,
more than five times the estimate, while the Steinway baby grand
sold for $42,000.[32]

As El Ad began emptying the building in preparation for the
hotel's rebirth as a condominium, it still had one more hurdle to
clear. While the fight with Ward and the union had been settled,
the developer was still locked in ongoing negotiations with preservationists. El Ad had surprised some by supporting the preservationists' efforts to landmark the interior rooms, perhaps reasoning that
retaining some of the Plaza's original details would bolster condominium sales. But more likely, El Ad hoped that if it backed efforts
to landmark the interior of the Plaza, the city might finally approve
its desired retail zoning changes. In July 2005, three months after
El Ad struck its compromise with the hotel union, the city declared
that eight Plaza rooms were now under landmark protection,
including the Terrace Room, the Oak Room and Oak Bar, and the
Palm Court. Officials also permitted El Ad to carve out its desired
thirty-nine thousand square feet of retail space.

While these interior rooms were now under landmark protection, it didn't mean they would continue to serve the same functions
as before. When it reopened in 2007, the Plaza's Grand Ballroom
would still serve brides and bar mitzvahs as it always had. So, too,
would the Terrace Room, the Oak Room, and the Palm Court.
But the Edwardian Room, where countless couples on dates dined
beside windows facing Central Park, and where once the Green

Tulip drew ire, would now become a retail store. And the lower level, where the widow Clara Bell Walsh and the fictional Eloise went to get their hair cut at the Plaza barber, and where Trader Vic's once served colorful Polynesian drinks, would also be converted into a retail space.

In addition, the Central Park South doorway—the original hotel entrance as imagined by Hardenbergh—would be closed to hotel guests for the first time ever. From now on, only owners of the expensive Plaza condominiums and their guests would be allowed access. Upstairs, where once New York's wealthiest elite, tired businessmen, and excited tourists had gazed from oversized windows across at Central Park, there would be 181 apartments (the final figure was closer to 167 because of combinations), with price tags that reached as high as $50 million.

As for the hotel guests, they would be relegated to the Fifth Avenue entrance, where they would be directed to the left. There, in the space where the Persian Room once stood, would be the hotel lobby, renamed the Champagne Bar in honor of a collection of champagne bottles that decorated one wall. The revamped Plaza would be made up of 130 traditional guest rooms on the lower floors, with views of the backs of buildings along West Fifty-Eighth Street or the hotel's interior courtyard. There would also be 152 hotel condominiums on the upper floors, which looked just like the hotel rooms, although with better views and more space. These hybrids would be sold like condominiums, but buyers would be permitted to stay there only up to 120 days a year. The remainder of the time, the hotel condominium units could revert back to the hotel or remain vacant.

Now that the plans were finalized, there was the issue of who would design the spaces. El Ad did not go far to find someone. The developer hired thirty-five-year-old Gal Nauer, who had never worked on such a large project and was less than a decade out of school. Nauer also happened to be Tshuva's daughter. "For the interiors,

Tshuva might have chosen someone like I. M. Pei, who designed the Four Seasons Hotel in Manhattan," wrote *Vanity Fair* in a piece reviewing the project. "Instead, he picked his own daughter."[33] The Israeli Ranni Ziss was hired as the concept design architect; and Costas Kondylis, a prolific architect who designed many buildings for Donald Trump, including the stretch of towers along the West Side Highway known as Riverside South, was the architect of record.

The eight rooms that were now landmarks would be under the purview of landmark architects who specialized in the painstaking work. Construction commenced, and the Plaza's once-glamorous interiors were rendered a construction zone. Walls were knocked out to expose steel beams, tarps were spread across the floors, and there was a relentless orchestra of bangs and whining power tools. The costs of renovation, which would take longer than it took to erect the entire Plaza in 1907, eventually ballooned to $450 million. El Ad spent $30 million to repair the roof, for instance, and $15 million for the Palm Court. "This was a very careful restoration, and it was significant, an amazing amount of work," Walter B. Melvin, whose namesake firm oversaw much of the restoration of the landmark spaces, told me.

Among the complexities of the project was dividing the building between hotel guests and condominium owners. To separate the condominium lobby from the hotel, an enormous new glass wall was installed next to the Palm Court, measuring twelve feet wide by thirty feet high. Guests at the hotel and diners at the Palm Court could see through the glass into the condominium lobby, but they were prohibited from entering. Most of the Plaza's historical features were still there, buried beneath layers of paint and dirt, but the architects also re-created some details whole-cloth. The most dramatic was the re-creation of the Palm Court's original ceiling.[34]

Originally, the Plaza had a skylight, beneath which Hardenbergh had built his domed glass ceiling known as a laylight. The skylight let in sun and gave the Palm Court a garden-like ambience. But when Harry Black built the Plaza extension in 1921, the skylight was covered to make way for the ballroom. The laylight remained until 1944, when Hilton finally removed it, lowering the ceiling to install air-conditioning units and fluorescent lighting.

Melvin and his team of architects could find scant historical information on the original dimensions of the laylight, or even the exact color of the glass. The only things they had to go on were a few black-and-white photographs and a sketch that Hardenbergh had once done. Luckily, Lee Harris Pomeroy, the architect who once had offices on the Plaza's seventeenth floor and who had designed the Plaza penthouses for Trump, had, many years earlier, been given a few shards of the original laylight glass. He now shared them with those working on the project.

"Someone cleaning the attic had found the shards among the beer cans and cigarette butts, so it was a very lucky find," Kevin Daly, a technical director at Walter B. Melvin Architects, who worked on the project, told me. "Only when we were able to see the laylight built and installed were we able to say once and for all that it worked." The total cost for the ceiling was $1 million.[35]

There were other challenges as well. The Terrace Room had a ceiling that featured paintings of classically inspired figures and ancient ruins, but it was covered in decades of grime. "It was so badly coated with smoke and dirt over the years that you couldn't see any of the paintings at all," Melvin said. His team had used blue painter's tape to mark off a twelve-inch square of the ceiling and were applying different cleaners and strippers to try to remove the dirt. They were struggling to find a solution, until one day, someone removed the blue painter's tape and realized that it was, in fact, the most effective way of cleaning it—an accidental, but fortuitous, discovery.[36]

Other efforts included removing a thick layer of insulation from the Oak Room to reveal the room's original polychrome moldings of grapevines, and an extensive face-lift for the Grand Ballroom that included adding kitchen facilities, restoring the room's original painted plaster, and installing a new dance floor. The architects also uncovered the muted cast bronze detailing that had once added an elegant decorative element to the rooms. The cast bronze column capitals in the Palm Court, for instance, were covered in garish gold paint during Trump's ownership, which was now removed.

The restoration architects, who were hired to adhere to the original designs as created by Hardenbergh, and also the taste evinced by El Ad, were sometimes in conflict. El Ad, for instance, wanted an escalator in the middle of the Terrace Room so that shoppers could be connected directly to the retail spaces below. The architects argued that an escalator would destroy the ambience and integrity of the landmark room. "They had a number of big ideas," Daly said of El Ad, "but they were willing to set some aside if we told them they would be difficult or inappropriate."

It was when these renovations were proceeding that Naftali received a surprising call. Prince Alwaleed bin Talal wanted to know if the developer would have lunch with him. Naftali agreed and went to the Four Seasons to meet the Saudi royal, bringing blueprints of the Plaza with him. Unsure of what to expect, Naftali found Alwaleed reclining comfortably in his seat, surrounded by a large entourage. As Naftali approached, the prince graciously waved and indicated he should come and sit next to him. The two men began to talk—about everything but the Plaza. "Very smart guy," Naftali later told me of his first impression, "he was just asking me about politics in Israel…He was very, very, very aware. He knew everything."[37]

After engaging in small talk for some time, the prince finally asked Naftali about the Plaza. The developer explained his strategy, pulling out his drawings to point out the various changes. Toward the end of the conversation, the prince asked Naftali if he might not join in the venture as a partner. Naftali was circumspect at the proposition. The Plaza was sure to generate massive profits, particularly the condominiums and the retail portion, and it wasn't clear what the benefit of splitting the returns would be.

"I said, 'Look, let me think about it okay? I might be able to find an opening to get you involved in some portion of the new plan, but not in everything,'" Naftali recounted. In the end, El Ad agreed to bring on Alwaleed as a fifty-fifty partner in the Plaza's hotel, as well as a 25 percent stakeholder in the hotel condominiums. El Ad also struck a deal with Alwaleed's Fairmont hotel brand to once again manage the Plaza.

El Ad's transformation of the Plaza went beyond the physical changes to the hotel. While the developer moved lobbies and delineated separate areas for the condominium owners, the company also transformed who controlled these various spaces. Wealthy individuals would now own the majority of the hotel's former guest rooms. The public rooms were also parceled out. An Italian clothing store signed a long-term lease for the Edwardian Room, for instance, while a restaurateur agreed to take over operations of the Oak Room. A Viennese bakery was building a large outpost to sell its goods in the basement. Even the Grand Ballroom would essentially be sold, with a third-party event planning company signing a twenty-five-year deal for the rights to book and run all of the events held there.

No longer was the Plaza in charge of its fate. It had been carved up and sold off piecemeal. The strategy generated blockbuster returns for El Ad, which monetized every area of the hotel by selling or leasing it. But it also sealed the Plaza's fate, permanently hamstringing a building that had once operated in concert. El Ad walked away with $1 billion in profit, but the grand old dame was crippled.

Chapter 14

SHELL GAME

"It was the wild west. If you got in under the wire, you were golden. Nobody asked questions."
—*Aaron Shmulewitz, real estate lawyer*

In 1992, Vanuatu, a tiny archipelago nation of just 280,000 people some six hundred miles west of Fiji, was devastated by Cyclone Betsy. The storm brought hurricane-force winds and storm surges, pummeling remote tribal villages and small towns and causing widespread flooding. Foreign aid flowed in from countries like the United States, China, and Australia. But Vanuatu's devastated citizens weren't the only beneficiaries of this money. Some of the aid also went to pad the personal accounts of the country's then–prime minister, Maxime Carlot Korman.[1]

Vanuatu's Office of the Ombudsman investigated the funds, but Korman was never prosecuted and it isn't clear what became of the money. Sixteen years later, however, in 2008, Mascot Holdings Limited, a shell company associated with Korman, and a beneficiary of the storm aid, acquired a multimillion-dollar condominium at the Plaza. Mascot, which was listed in a database of the World Bank and the United Nations Office on Drugs and Crime that tracks money laundering,[2] paid $14.74 million for a three-bedroom unit on the Plaza's sixteenth floor. The all-cash purchase was not previously reported before I uncovered it. "This raises some pretty obvious questions about source of funds," said Dan McGarry, a veteran Vanuatu journalist, reacting to the news. "Fifteen million is a lot of cash to have on hand."[3]

Korman is now seventy-seven and retired, living a quiet life on his homestead on the island of Efate. It isn't clear if he ever visited the Plaza apartment. In 2010, the unit, with its unimpeded views of Central Park and Fifth Avenue, was sold for $12.35 million in cash to Plaza 1609 Limited, another anonymous shell company whose owner is not known. As for Korman, while no longer an elected official, the elder statesman still likes to pontificate on politics. "The problem today is that there are politicians with selfish ambitions," Korman told a Vanuatu newspaper in 2015. "Today, the issue of bribery and corruption appears to be a normal thing to politicians."[4]

In New York, luxury condominiums are chock-full of owners who purchase their units through shell companies, using money obtained through possibly illicit means. But who these buyers are, and how they arrive at the building, isn't a primary concern for developers and brokers. Like other condominium developers, when El Ad began selling the Plaza Private Residences, as the reimagined hotel rooms were called, its chief priority was to generate as large a profit as possible. A team of real estate brokers was hired to accomplish this and their responsibilities included marketing and sales—not investigating their clients.

Alexa Lambert, an agent at the brokerage firm Stribling, was put in charge of marketing the Plaza's splashy new condominiums. "I've never worked so hard in my life," she told me. For Lambert and her three-person team, pitching the Plaza units was challenging, mostly because they didn't yet exist. Unlike the grand celebration in 1907 that greeted Vanderbilt, Gates, and other guests on the Plaza's opening day, in 2005, buyers were introduced to a property that was a complete wreck. Rather than red carpets, claw-foot bathtubs, and arched windows overlooking Central Park, they found a gutted structure filled with dust, loud banging, and a constant crush of construction workers. Potential buyers entering on Fifth Avenue were ushered around mountains of debris and equipment to the corner where Fifth Avenue and Central Park meet. In the space that had once been the Café, the Edwardian Room, and, for a brief time, the Green Tulip, they found a sales office, the room's dark wood paneling and gracious interiors converted into cubicles and oversized video screens.

It would be more than two years before the Plaza condos were complete, so Lambert and her brokerage team showed buyers idealized digital depictions of what El Ad planned to build. This was before the widespread use of virtual reality, and buyers were offered a panoply of video renderings, as well as blown-up photos of the various views, taken from every window of the gutted interior. A Plaza replica in miniature helped them envision their new homes using light-up apartments to illustrate the units and floor plans. The model, while accurate in many details, was inexplicably surrounded by bucolic green hills rather than a bustling cityscape.

Even with the chaos of construction, and the fact that there were no apartments to see, that first day, multiple contracts were sent out to interested buyers and the calendar was already booked with appointments. Colleagues at other brokerage firms who wanted to see the new project complained that their calls weren't being returned fast enough, and many grew frustrated when their high-profile clients were forced to wait days to get inside. Lambert, a pretty brunette with a friendly smile and a no-nonsense persona, did her best to handle the velocity of calls and appointments. Even with two small children at home, she would often arrive at six o'clock in the morning and still be there at eleven o'clock at night. It became so crazy that her harried team started ordering lunch as soon as they arrived in the morning, in the hopes they could find a few minutes to scarf down sandwiches between appointments.

Prospective buyers were willing to spend astronomically on these imagined apartments. Even by the elevated standards of the mid-aughts, when a historic real estate bubble was reaching its peak, the Plaza's prices were high. If an exclusive Fifth Avenue home was selling for $3 million, at the Plaza a similar unit was asking $5 million; if that Plaza unit overlooked Central Park, it was even more. And absolutely everything was extra: The basement storage bins cost more than $40,000 each; the Plaza's fitness center was accessible only by shelling out $10,000 in dues before stepping foot on a treadmill; and maid service, provided by the hotel, cost nearly $500 for a full day's work. "It was hard to understand what a new frontier it was in terms of pricing," Lambert told me. "It was completely new to have a $5 or $6 million one-bedroom... It was just nuts."

The real estate market had just begun rising when El Ad acquired the Plaza, and it was generating new records every day. The average Manhattan apartment broke the $1 million mark in 2004, and by 2005, it had topped $1.3 million.[5] Over the same period, the number of apartments that sold for more than $20 million quintupled. Wall Street was booming, and in 2005, bankers earned a record-breaking $21.5 billion in bonuses. Much of that windfall was put toward buying expensive new homes, and the types of apartments the Wall Street bankers were purchasing at a feverish pace were condominiums.[6]

When people think of an apartment, they typically envision a buyer acquiring a unit outright, just as a homeowner buys a home. But for generations, the majority of the city's apartments, in particular the grand houses lining Park Avenue and Fifth Avenue, were

cooperatives. Like stocks purchased in a public company, in cooperatives, buyers acquired shares in an entire building, not their individual apartment. The larger the apartment, the more shares it had.

Cooperatives were run by powerful resident boards, made up of a
handful of shareholders who decided who could—and more importantly, who could not—buy an apartment. Co-op boards were free
to run their buildings as they wished, and in deciding who should
live there, many required prospective buyers to undergo a rigorous
review. The Park Avenue and Fifth Avenue co-ops were especially
notorious for requiring reams of financial documentation, including bank accounts and personal and professional references. Boards
could then reject or accept an applicant at their whim, with little
need for public justification. Often, the goal of co-op boards was to
keep out undesirables, whether they didn't belong to the right social
clubs or had the wrong color skin, religion, or sexual orientation.

Condominiums, on the other hand, had few of the diktats of
cooperative buildings. For those hoping to buy in posh New York
neighborhoods, but unwilling or unable to pass muster with a co-op
board, condominiums offered the opportunity to evade the gate-
keepers. While nearly all Park Avenue cooperatives required buyers to live at their apartments full-time and restricted them from
renting out their units at will, condominiums didn't care whether
their neighbors ever slept there, or rented their units to a steady
string of tenants. And on Fifth Avenue, most cooperatives wanted
to know how buyers achieved their wealth, and that it came from a
stable, ethical source, but condominiums typically didn't look past
whether their prospective neighbors could afford the purchase price
and monthly common charges.

The first New York City condominium was built in 1965, but
it was really in the 1980s that they first gained popularity. By the
early 2000s, just as the Plaza condominiums were going on sale, a
second condominium wave hit. Driving condominiums' popularity

wasn't just the freedom they offered. For some, they were also a stable investment opportunity. For those coming from countries like Vanuatu, buying a New York condominium was akin to depositing money in the real estate version of a Swiss bank account. Not only did condominiums ask few questions, but the money invested was unlikely to lose its value. One of the most desirable markets in the world, Manhattan is an island and, therefore, supply-constrained. The city was unlikely to ever go bankrupt, the 1970s notwithstanding, and over the long term, real estate prices moved in only one direction—up.

The Plaza wasn't the only building taking advantage of the surging demand for condominiums. Across Manhattan, developers were building new high-rise towers and converting old buildings at a fast clip. So-called starchitects, such as Jean Nouvel and Herzog & De Meuron, were designing iconic structures and pushing up values, one record-breaking quarter after another. In fact, the Plaza was facing stiff competition from two buildings just down the block: Fifteen Central Park West, the former Mayflower Hotel, was equally if not more inundated with eager buyers, while just to the west, at Columbus Circle, the Time Warner Center was also seeing record deals. The units at the Time Warner Center were the first to hit the market, and in 2005, the building boasted the fifth-, sixth-, seventh-, and eighth-highest sales prices.[7]

At the Plaza, the elevated price tags seemed only to stoke more interest. There were high-powered New York lawyers, Wall Street hedge funders, Hollywood executives, and foreign tycoons who put down deposits, some sight-unseen. One buyer was driving down a Los Angeles freeway in his convertible when he called the sales center. As the broker struggled to tell him about the different apartments over the din of the traffic and the strong wind, he brushed her off. Instead, the caller decided on the spot to buy a $12 million pad with Central Park views. In another case, a multimillionaire had promised his wife that should he ever become successful, they would live at the Plaza. He called the sales office and ordered her a penthouse for $20 million, with about as much due diligence as if he were ordering Chinese takeout.

Other buyers who did come to the sales center shocked the staid brokers with their behavior. There was one foreigner who arrived with an armed security detail, the guards standing at attention with their guns in full view while he perused the marketing materials. In other instances, buyers inquired if they might not pay with a suitcase of gold; or bags of cash; or half in euros. The brokers told them that real estate sales must be transacted through a lawyer, and the offers were politely declined. Brokers couldn't accept cash for an apartment, but they could accept buyers without having to check their backgrounds. This proved a problem when a Brazilian woman, for instance, who was in the process of buying several units at the Plaza, was arrested for running a high-priced call girl ring on the Upper West Side; she was sent to prison before the transaction closed.[8]

Buyers who wanted to do more than sit around in the sales office looking at renderings were out of luck. El Ad strictly forbade any prospective buyer from venturing into the building's construction zone. Not only would that have hurt the rarefied image it was trying to project, but El Ad didn't want to take a chance that one of the world's wealthiest people might accidentally injure themselves in a mishap. Some potential buyers, used to getting their way, bristled at the rule. "It's kind of silly," Maria Baibakova, the daughter of Oleg Baibakov, a former Russian metals magnate, told *Bloomberg News*. "If you are buying a $30 million apartment, you are entitled to see the view."[9]

At least one VIP circumvented the prohibition. "I got to know Tshuva," Robert Kraft, owner of the New England Patriots football team, told me, referring to the Israeli developer. "We were playing the Jets and I came in early, before going to MetLife [Stadium], and

I walked the building." Kraft likened the half-built condominium to visiting a bombed-out city, but it didn't deter him from buying. Like many others, Kraft had a nostalgic connection to the Plaza. As a student in the early 1960s at Columbia, he often frequented Trader Vic's with his buddies, and later, during the years when Alphonse Salomone was running the hotel, Kraft spent his wedding night there.

Having led the Patriots to a record-breaking eleven Super Bowls, Kraft used his team to help him decide which unit to buy. "They said I could have any apartment I wanted, so I was thinking I would do the twelfth [floor] because that's Brady," he said, referring to the legendary Patriots quarterback Tom Brady, whose jersey number is 12. But then Kraft decided to expand into two units and combine them, and there was only one option that hadn't already sold, on the eleventh floor. "So I went from Brady to Edelman," Kraft said, referencing Patriots wide receiver Julian Edelman, who wears number 11.

The floors surrounding Kraft would be filled with a who's who of the business world. His neighbor on the eleventh floor was Dave Barger, the former CEO of JetBlue. One floor below was Thomas Mendoza, the vice chairman of NetApp; and one floor above was Amir Elstein, an executive at the pharmaceutical giant Teva. There were several Hollywood executives, including Simon Fuller, the creator of the reality TV singing contest *American Idol*, on the ninth floor; and the COO of Viacom, Thomas Dooley, who moved in down the hall. Doug Morris, the chief executive of Sony Music Entertainment, was upstairs on the sixteenth floor; while Paul Schindler, a powerful entertainment lawyer, was on the seventeenth floor.

Other famous buyers included Tommy Hilfiger, who purchased a penthouse that featured a cupola, the fashion designer hiring the illustrator Hilary Knight to cover its walls with an *Eloise*-inspired mural. The Plaza condominium also drew Guy Wildenstein, an art collector and gallery owner, who snatched up several apartments to create a duplex large enough for his extended family.[10] Several Wall Street figures were also buyers, including the hedge funder Martin D. Sass, who bought a penthouse; Earl McEvoy, an asset manager at mutual fund Vanguard; and Kenneth Moelis, an investment banker who once worked for Donald Trump.[11] The chief executive of Bear Stearns, James Cayne, purchased two apartments for $28 million on the fourteenth floor. He closed on the units just a month before his bank collapsed in the wake of the 2008 financial crisis; despite the turmoil, Cayne didn't sell his new home.

Harking back to when the thirty-nine widows walked the corridors, the Plaza condos also boasted several women owners. Suze Orman, the financial guru, bought on the twelfth floor; while the socialite and philanthropist Mary Q. Pedersen bought on the fifth floor. Patty Farmer, an informal Plaza historian who wrote two books on the hotel, bought on the eighth floor. There was even an Olympian, Ann-Kathrin Linsenhoff, a gold medalist in dressage at the 1988 Seoul Olympic Games, who bought on the fourteenth floor.

Lambert and her team of brokers welcomed countless would-be buyers who arrived wearing Prada and dripping with diamonds. But many failed to look the part. Before appointments, the brokers were often frantically googling names to determine who had sufficient financial backing and who was merely window-shopping. One wealthy couple, for instance, owned a car dealership in Ohio. "If I didn't know better, I would have thought I was being punked by one of my friends," said one of the Plaza brokers. "The guy had a really bad toupee, and a tacky wife with platinum blond hair. I was like, 'for real?'" (The couple didn't end up buying.) After the appointments, the agents handed out marketing materials to potential buyers, enclosing the brochures either in expensive leather pouches embossed with the Plaza logo or in cheaper linen versions. They took to examining visitors' shoes to determine who was worthy of the leather pouch, and who the linen: Those with expensive footwear were given the leather cases.

One buyer who didn't need his footwear scrutinized, being well-known to the brokers, was Harry Macklowe. The real estate developer, who won and lost several fortunes over the years, is known for building the tallest condominium tower in the Western Hemisphere, 432 Park Avenue, a few blocks from the Plaza. Macklowe and his wife acquired the Plaza's largest home, combining seven units on the seventh floor. The fourteen-thousand-square-foot apartment featured New York's largest master bedroom and fifty-four windows. Purchased for $51.5 million, it served mostly as an exhibit space for the couple's massive art collection and would later become a pawn in the acrimonious divorce battle that broke out over their $2 billion fortune.

Many buyers were foreigners, with Russians being the most well-represented; followed by Mexicans; then Spanish, Italian, and Turkish buyers. There were also buyers from as far afield as Kazakhstan and Kuwait. Among the Russians were Vladimir Stolyarenko, a banker with ties to Vladimir Putin; and Boris Belotserkovsky, a casino mogul and one-time Putin foe. The composer Igor Krutoy also bought at the Plaza, paying $48 million for a twelfth-floor unit in 2011, a year after the Putin ally met Donald and Ivanka Trump at Trump Tower to discuss a possible real estate project in Latvia, according to the *Guardian* newspaper. The project never got off the ground, scuttled in part because of an investigation by Latvian authorities.[12]

The buyers from Mexico included Juan Beckmann Vidal, the billionaire owner of the liquor company Jose Cuervo; as well as Rogerio Azcarraga Madero, a Mexican radio magnate. Pedro Zaragoza Fuentes, who started a dairy empire, also owned at the Plaza, buying a ground-floor duplex maisonette. Like several of his Plaza neighbors, Fuentes, who hailed from Ciudad Juárez, was caught up in controversy and in the news for battling his brother over their dairy business. Fuentes was also infamous for a land dispute along the US-Mexico border. His family, who owned property that was slated to become a border crossing, had allegedly engaged in mass evictions, throwing indigent Mexicans off land that they had called home for decades. "Farm animals have been killed. A resident was beaten to death. Two children died in a mysterious fire," wrote the Pulitzer prize–winning journalist Eileen Welsome in a 2007 piece. She called the area a "veritable concentration camp."[13]

There were other buyers who likely used money generated from unsavory or illicit sources to buy Plaza condos. In early 2008, for instance, Bolat Nazarbayev, the brother of the long-ruling dictator of Kazakhstan, bought his wife, Maira, a four-bedroom apartment at the building. Nazarbayev paid $20 million for the eighteenth-floor apartment. Then, unbeknownst to her husband, Maira transferred ownership of the apartment to her twenty-two-year-old son from another marriage. Bolat and Maira's marriage soon hit the skids—supposedly because Bolat was already married to at least two other women—and Maira's Plaza ruse was uncovered.[14]

Throughout the summer of 2013, Bolat and Maira engaged in lengthy postdivorce negotiations, replete with accusations of organized crime, witnesses who feared for their lives, and an investigation by Kazakhstan officials into Maira's businesses. Maira, whose son would go on to marry the Malaysian prime minister's daughter, was accused of spending $75 million of Bolat's fortune at Jacob the Jeweler, a favorite of rap stars like Jay-Z; and, at one point, Interpol arrested her as she traveled in Dubai.[15] Finally, the couple struck a compromise. Maira agreed to return the Plaza apartment she had taken from Bolat in exchange for all charges against her being dropped.

The deal was notable, not just for the family drama. As part of the litigation, Bolat was asked to provide proof that he had used his personal funds to buy the Plaza unit. He was unable, or unwilling, to comply. "Presumably," wrote Maira's lawyer, Bolat "does not remember where the money came from and whose funds were used."[16] This question of the source of funds used to purchase expensive real estate would become, in the years that followed, a pressing concern.

At the time El Ad was selling Plaza condominiums, between 2005 and 2008, economies and the flow of money were becoming increasingly globalized. Foreign investors, particularly ones from unstable countries, saw these types of apartments as a place to safely park their cash. Most importantly, if these buyers purchased the apartments using certain structures, such as shell corporations, their identities could be shielded and the transactions virtually untraceable.

Shell companies, such as limited liability companies or trusts, are entities that lack a physical presence, save for a mailing address. They also have little value aside from the specific purchase for which they are created. There is nothing illegal about shell companies per se, and they are most often used for legitimate tax reasons. At the Plaza, more than half of the buyers were anonymous shell companies, with names like Mirabella, LLC, or the maddeningly bland Plaza Condominium Unit 615 Limited Liability Corporation.

But shell companies are vulnerable to manipulation by criminals. And during those years, before the structures were widely understood and investigated, shell companies were a popular way to launder money. It is relatively simple to create a shell company, use it to purchase an asset like a New York condominium, and thereby anonymously park felonious profits in a seemingly legitimate purchase. When the shell company then sells the unit, it conveniently "launders" the ill-gotten gains, obscuring the criminal act that generated the wealth in the first place.

The brokers selling the Plaza units weren't allowed to accept bags of cash at the sales center, but there were few other restrictions they had to follow. It wasn't necessary for the brokers, El Ad, or anyone else to know who was actually purchasing the units that were being sold, or where the money to purchase them came from. If a lawyer was representing an unidentified buyer, and the name listed on the deed was a generic shell company, that was perfectly fine, as long as they could afford the price.

Further obscuring these buyers' identities was the fact that the majority of the purchases were completed using all cash. All-cash transactions provide an added level of anonymity, since without any mortgage or other financial documentation, the true owner behind a shell company can be hard, if not impossible, to discern. More than half of the Plaza apartments—a whopping 63 percent—were acquired using all-cash payments.

In recent years, the Panama Papers and subsequent leaks of off-shore documents from various tax havens where shell companies originate, have shed light on how they can shield criminal activity. Such leaks have spurred more scrutiny from organizations such as the Financial Crimes Enforcement Network (FinCEN), a bureau of the US Department of the Treasury. Unbelievably, a FinCEN investigation found that from 2016 until mid-2017, in many cities, including New York, about 30 percent of all luxury real estate deals involved an owner who had been flagged for possible money laundering or fraud. "Real estate transactions involving luxury property purchased through shell companies—particularly when conducted with cash and no financing—can be an attractive avenue for criminals to launder illegal proceeds," the bureau wrote in an advisory.[17]

While shell companies are by their very nature difficult to trace, with true owners obscured behind several levels of legal entities, it is possible to identify some owners by searching signatures on deeds or other public documents. At the Plaza, many true owners can be identified, while others remain obscured. For instance,

Jet Confitrade S.A., an offshore entity, acquired three Plaza apartments. It is associated with the Russian Boris Lantsman, who was identified in the Panama Papers. Another shell company, TNC Management Inc., which purchased a one-bedroom on the Plaza's eighteenth floor, was mentioned in the Bahamas Leaks, a cache of internal files from the tax haven's company register. But the owner of TNC Management isn't known. It is important to note that just being included in leaked documents does not mean that the individuals or shell companies engaged in illegal activity.[18]

Shell companies, however, do appear frequently in connection with criminal investigations. In 2007, for example, Gerardo Díaz Ferrán was a powerful executive, the head of Grupo Marsans, a Spanish conglomerate that included tour operators and charter airlines. That year, Ferrán purchased two one-bedroom apartments at the Plaza, on the eighth and the sixteenth floors, through shell companies registered to various family members.[19] The following year, he purchased a two-bedroom on the third floor. In total, Ferrán spent more than $13.5 million on the homes.

In 2010, Ferrán's fate took a turn for the worse. With his company struggling to turn a profit, Ferrán declared personal bankruptcy and his assets were frozen. The following year, pursued by creditors, Ferrán sold two of his Plaza apartments, the proceeds going to pay down his debts. Then, in 2012, Ferrán sold his third Plaza unit, and it isn't known what became of the proceeds. The existence of this third apartment, in fact, had not been previously reported before I uncovered it.

A few months after Ferrán sold his last Plaza condominium, he was arrested by Spanish authorities for crimes that included money laundering. When police entered his home, they found one kilo of gold and 150,000 euros in cash.[20] Among the shell companies listed as part of the criminal investigation were those used to purchase the two Plaza condominiums that were known. Since being told of the existence of the third Plaza apartment, a lawyer who represents several of Ferran's creditors has been investigating the matter. Ferrán was imprisoned and spent several years in jail, although he was released early, in 2018, for good behavior.

While buyers like Ferrán may have never used their Plaza pads, others did. And when, in the summer of 2007, the apartments were finally ready for occupancy, there was a rush of excitement. The celebrations, however, would turn out to be premature. It was like *"Extreme Makeover, Home Edition—*only the total opposite," quipped *Vanity Fair.*[21] The apartments were finished, yet there was a litany of complaints. One couple moved into their $4.75 million two-bedroom to find the doors were missing their doorknobs, while another complained the hallway carpeting on the penthouse floors was cut and pieced together, a cheap method known as "patch-n-match."

There were allegations that El Ad had taken a number of shortcuts, including using low-density marble from China rather than Italian marble, and installing mahogany closets that were really just veneer over industrial particleboard. Lawsuits and countersuits were filed between El Ad and various contractors over unfinished work and unpaid bills. The restaurateur who signed a lease for the Oak Room also ended up in litigation with El Ad, as did other retail tenants. In all fairness, the process of creating luxury apartments in a building that was more than one hundred years old, and protected by landmark status, would be a challenge to any developer. Zoltan Saro, a partner at Costas Kondylis's architecture firm, called the redevelopment project "my two-year nightmare," complaining that every wall they opened, every steel beam they removed, resulted in some unforeseen challenge that led to costly adjustments.

Still, the Plaza buyers were an exacting group, and there was little patience for excuses. Particularly aggrieved was "the Russian in the penthouse," as Andrey Vavilov, a hedge fund billionaire and energy magnate, was known among the residents.[22] Vavilov, a former Russian finance minister, was so rich he reportedly kept large bags of cash in his Moscow home[23] and expressed his love for his wife, the actress Maryana Tsaregradskaya, by posting amorous declarations to her on enormous billboards across the Russian capital.[24] The colorful oligarch was also known for having narrowly escaped death when, in 1997, a bomb blew up his empty Saab while it was parked in front of the Finance Ministry; the perpetrators were never caught.

A decade after his near-death experience, in 2007, Vavilov told the Plaza brokers "in no uncertain terms that he wished to own the largest and most expensive apartment at the Plaza," according to lawsuits that were later filed. He zeroed in on the Plaza's penthouses, but in one of the ironies of the building, these upper floors had been built more than a century earlier to serve as servants' quarters. When Trump acquired the hotel, he submitted and received approvals to carve these upper floors into penthouses, and his permits were still valid. El Ad relied on Trump's designs, but it was still hamstrung in what it could alter because of the building's original layout and its landmark status.

In its offering plan, El Ad noted that the ceiling heights and apartment sizes might vary due to the historic nature of the building and its accompanying restrictions. But Vavilov claimed that the sales pitch he received glossed over such specifics. He readily plunked down $53.5 million to buy a duplex and a triplex on the top floors that he planned to combine. It would have been the highest price at the Plaza, and the second-highest price ever for a Manhattan condominium. (The honor of the priciest unit at the Plaza would instead go to Harry Macklowe and his $51.5 million one-bedroom.)

In June 2008, more than a year after Vavilov gave his deposit, his new penthouse residence was ready. His wife, who had been plotting her entrance into New York society and had hoped the fabulous new home would cement her standing, arrived for a tour.

But when she entered the space, what greeted her was a decided step down from the vision she had conjured up in her imagination. Rather than a spectacular home that would inspire awe and incite jealousy among her rich Russian friends and New York's upper crust, the home was an embarrassment. The narrow windows were small and oddly shaped, beginning partway up the wall and then sloping inward into the apartment, more like skylights than a wall of glass. Outside, enormous drainage grates and large setbacks blocked what was supposed to be unimpeded views of Central Park. Most egregiously, there was an enormous column, which housed air-conditioning units, situated directly in the middle of the living room. Upon seeing her new home, Tsaregradskaya burst into tears.

Promptly, Vavilov went on the attack. He refused to close on his purchase and filed a suit alleging the home was a "glorified attic space." The couple put out a press release titled "Fraud at the Plaza?" calling it "a classic bait-and-switch." "My client was led to believe that it would receive one of the most luxurious apartments in New York history; it got far less than what it bargained for," Vavilov's lawyer, Y. David Scharf, declared.

El Ad was frantic that the bad press might create a run on other apartment buyers who wanted their deposits back. It aggressively punched back, filing a countersuit alleging defamation. Vavilov, El Ad insisted, was just bitter because Macklowe usurped him in the race to purchase the biggest apartment at the Plaza. Vavilov had tried to buy more penthouses, El Ad said, but it was too late, and they were already sold out.

After months of mudslinging, the two sides settled. Vavilov agreed to complete his purchase of the smaller of the two units, buying the duplex for $11.2 million. As soon as Vavilov closed, he relisted the apartment, selling it to Maribel Unanue McVicar, an heiress to the Goya food fortune, for just $8.4 million. The Vavilovs ended up staying in the neighborhood, passing up the Plaza to purchase a full-floor penthouse at the nearby Time Warner Center.

This wasn't the end of El Ad's troubles, however. Another penthouse buyer, the hedge funder Scott Shleifer, was equally dismayed when he finally saw what $31 million had bought him. The 5,600-square-foot duplex penthouse also featured tiny windows, grates that blocked his views, and the oversized, ungainly pillars that awkwardly cut up the apartment's layout. Shleifer hired Vavilov's attorney to represent him, but while El Ad was anxious to settle with Vavilov, the case having become embarrassingly public, this time, El Ad fought on. Eventually, a judge dismissed Shleifer's suit, arguing the only thing he suffered from was buyer's remorse. Rather than closing on his purchase, Shleifer walked away from his more than $6 million deposit.

In 2010, Steve Wynn, who would later be disgraced in the #MeToo era, bought Shleifer's unit for $23.5 million, or $7.5 million less than what Shleifer had agreed to pay. Wynn flipped the apartment four months later, at a slight premium. Meanwhile, it took four years for the triplex that Vavilov had originally agreed to buy to finally sell. The British real estate developer Christian Candy eventually bought it in 2012, for just shy of $26 million; he sold it after a handful of years for $32.7 million.

While several billionaires bought and sold Plaza units like they were playing a game of Monopoly, treating the apartments as mostly investments, inside the building, a handful of owners actually moved in. It was immediately clear that these full-time residents were in the minority. In fact, fully two-thirds of the Plaza condominium owners were either part-time residents or absentee owners.[25] "I keep asking, 'Has anybody else moved in?' and they shake their head. The place has been deserted," Kathy Ruland, one of the early residents, told the *New York Times* in an article titled

"It's Lonely at the Plaza Hotel..."[26] For those who did live in the building full-time, the high number of vacancies would turn out to mean not just deserted hallways and empty elevators. It actually proved a hazard.

In early 2008, Joanna Cutler moved into the Plaza and was one of the few people living on her floor. One evening at around eleven o'clock, Cutler, a real estate broker with long black hair and a tall, lanky gait, was getting ready for bed. Dressed in socks, yoga pants, and a short-sleeved shirt, she ran out into the hall to throw away a bag of trash. But as she entered the garbage room, the door closed behind her—and then jammed. It was the start of what would become a terrifying, overnight ordeal that left Cutler bloodied and covered in dirt.

She tried to free herself from the cramped space that was filled with debris from the still-ongoing construction, squeezing her fingers against particleboard that had stuck in the door. Then Cutler used her feet and her butt to try to push the door open. Eventually, she began screaming and banging as loud as she could, but there was nobody to hear.[27] Unable to sit on the cold floor of the garbage room, Cutler stood, for hours. She told me that she blacked out at one point. It wasn't until 6 a.m. the following morning, when the Plaza's superintendent, who lived on the floor, went out for a run, that Cutler was finally freed. While traumatized and humiliated, in the end, Cutler, who still lives at the building, declined to sue.

Cutler's harrowing night stuck in the garbage room at the Plaza was fodder for the New York tabloids. One publication ran a photo of Cutler with her Fabergé egg, which she had worried might be stolen as the door to her apartment stood ajar while she spent the night imprisoned.[28] Cutler's saga added to the generally poor publicity the Plaza was receiving. And in some respects, the news would only worsen for the condominium buyers.

While Alexa Lambert and her team had begun selling the Plaza units just as real estate prices were peaking to historic levels, by the time most of the apartments were completed and ready for occupancy, the 2008 recession had taken hold. A few buyers couldn't afford to close on their purchases, while others quickly flipped them. In 2009, about thirty units, or 18 percent of the condos, were back on the market.[29]

Many of these resales were being listed at steep discounts to what the first buyers had paid. The biggest Plaza loser turned out to be the art dealer Guy Wildenstein, who earned the dubious distinction of having the single worst real estate sale in New York City in a decade. Wildenstein had purchased a sprawling four-bedroom that had once been the home of architect Frank Lloyd Wright for nearly $22 million. Two years later, he sold it for a paltry $13 million—a 40 percent loss.[30] Wildenstein ended up spending a total of almost $40 million for three apartments at the Plaza, but eventually unloaded them for just $25.5 million.

Wildenstein wasn't the only Plaza buyer to walk away from his purchases a great deal poorer. Of the thirty worst money-losing luxury Manhattan home sales to take place between 2007 and 2017, eight were at the Plaza. "It was a pretty shocking result," Amir Korangy, the publisher of the *Real Deal*, an industry trade publication that analyzed the data, told me. "Here's proof that over the past decade, the Plaza was the single worst condominium investment in New York." Plaza owners collectively lost more on their resales than at any other building in Manhattan, he added. Ironically, the most profitable building was 15 Central Park West, the former Mayflower Hotel site that prompted Naftali to pursue the Plaza in the first place.

Chapter 15

THE INDIAN GREAT GATSBY

"A kind of sword is hanging over his head. He has to pay."
—*Gautam Awasthi, lawyer for Subrata Roy*

In 2011, Subrata Roy was one of India's best-known business tycoons, with more than a million employees and a business empire that encompassed television stations, luxury real estate, and sports franchises. But the self-made billionaire wanted to build an international presence, and there were few ways better to accomplish that than buying an iconic hotel. So, during a trip to New York, Roy asked his friend Sant Singh Chatwal, a prominent restaurateur and hotelier, what he thought about the Four Seasons, where Roy was then staying. "I said, 'What's wrong with you? Don't do a stupid thing like the Four Seasons,'" said Chatwal, who was based in New York. He had a much more impressive hotel to show his friend. "I told him, 'Stop it. If you really want to buy a hotel—the one hotel where, when you walk in, you will fall in love with it—come.'"

Chatwal then led Roy one block north to the Plaza. The two men wandered the building, peering into the Palm Court and peeking in at the Oak Room. Roy was sufficiently impressed. Chatwal had long coveted the hotel himself, ever since he had first stayed there in 1975. But unlike Roy, Chatwal didn't have enough money to buy it. Instead, Chatwal introduced his wealthy friend to El Ad's Tshuva, who was a business acquaintance. Roy and Tshuva began discussing the sale of the Plaza, and in July 2012, after nearly a year of haggling, they had an agreement.

The deal stipulated that Roy would pay $570 million for 70 percent of the Plaza's hotel rooms, hotel condominiums, public rooms, and retail spaces. Chatwal, as compensation for putting the transaction together, was given 5 percent. Meanwhile Alwaleed, who initially opposed selling to Roy, eventually acquiesced and retained a 25 percent ownership stake. Roy, an Indian business magnate, could now claim to be the majority owner of a famous New York hotel, which he had visited just once, and where he had never spent a single night.

For El Ad, the sale of the Plaza to Roy was the culmination of a complicated, years-long investment. By then, the developer had squeezed what value it could from the project. It had raced to sell the condominiums against a worsening recession, managing to offload the apartments, albeit over a longer period and at sometimes-lower prices than it had hoped. In the end, it walked away with an impressive $1.4 billion from the sales. When the cost of its renovations and other expenses were added in, El Ad claimed a net profit from the entire Plaza project of $1 billion.[1]

It wasn't just by selling condominiums that El Ad was able to wring value out of the development. In a playbook that could have come straight from Conrad Hilton, the developer optimized every piece of the Plaza with an eye toward profitability. Each of the hotel's public rooms, which had been losing money for decades, such as the Oak Room and the Edwardian Room, was leased to outside operators who paid the developer hefty rents. Even the basement, its low ceiling covered with defunct ductwork and old pipes, was cleaned out and divided into small kiosks, which El Ad then rented out to food purveyors.

The restaurateurs and retailers who leased these spaces ran their areas independently, without much input or oversight from the Plaza's hotel component. This marked the first time in the building's history that the management of its common spaces was separate from the hotel. And while these rental streams generated a steady income flow for El Ad, the structure would eventually wreak havoc on the ecosystem that had helped sustain the Plaza for more than a century.

El Ad had had other plans to monetize its Plaza investment. It had wanted to use the New York hotel as a basis for creating an international chain, with Plazas stretching from London to Shanghai. But around the time that Roy made his overtures to Tshuva, the developer's concept for a series of Plaza-branded hotels was faltering. El Ad's first new Plaza was supposed to be in Las Vegas, where the developer had acquired an enormous tract of land near the strip and was planning a three-thousand-room Plaza hotel and casino—more than ten times the number of guest rooms it had in New York. But El Ad's timing was off. The recession had hurt values, and the Vegas project had devolved into a billion-dollar morass, making the developer eager to sell its New York hotel.

The difficulties in Vegas also proved a breaking point for Naftali. The executive who had overseen the conversion of the New York Plaza had never been bullish on the Vegas concept, advocating instead to inaugurate the hotel chain in Beverly Hills or Paris. Now that the Vegas project was under water, and the Plaza conversion was mostly complete, Naftali began looking for the exit. In 2011, he finally quit to start his own eponymous real estate development firm. "I used to leave my house at 5:30 or six o'clock in the morning, and I used to come back at 9, 9:30 at night, and I built something," Naftali said of his time with El Ad. "It wasn't easy for me. I worked my ass off, and I built something." After so many years at the helm, it was difficult to extricate himself from the company, and from Tshuva. "Frankly, I felt, you know, I had a very, very close relationship with Isaac for many years, and I didn't want to hurt him."

Roy, meanwhile, may have landed the white whale, but he had little time to rejoice in his newest acquisition. Back at home, the high-flying Indian tycoon was about to be dealt a devastating blow. In one of the world's most populous countries, the size of Roy's empire boggled the mind. His privately held conglomerate, Sahara India Pariwar, with its 1.1 million workers, was second only to the Indian railroad in terms of number of employees.[2] Its subsidiaries ranged from soap opera programming to grocery store chains.[3] And while the private company rarely publicized any of its financial figures, it was valued at an estimated $10 billion.[4]

But Sahara had been in the sights of government regulators for years. There was a cloud of litigation hanging over the company, and in August 2012, just a month after the Plaza deal was announced, India's Supreme Court issued a ruling that threatened to jeopardize Sahara's very existence. At issue was more than $3 billion in bonds that the company had sold to tens of millions of poor Indian investors. The court ruled that Sahara had improperly marketed these financial instruments, and it ordered the company to repay its victims. Even more dire, the court tacked on an eye-popping 15 percent annual interest to the money that Sahara owed.[5]

How Roy arrived at this predicament is a convoluted tale that begins in relative obscurity in Gorakhpur, a city not far from the Nepalese border. Roy was born there, the eldest son of an engineer. An entrepreneurial spirit, Roy began a number of disparate businesses, from an enterprise that loaded packages onto trucks to one that sold electric fans, before he found success. In 1978, when he was thirty, Roy set off with his father's scooter and the equivalent of $30.[6] His plan was to start a chit fund, a type of savings program that is popular in India, where rural villagers are often too poor to open traditional bank accounts.

Three decades later, Roy had transformed his humble chit fund into one of India's most famous companies. As Sahara's leader, Roy was a colorful, almost cult-like figure, often likened to Robin Hood, providing banking services for countrymen who otherwise couldn't afford it. "Pariwar" means family in Hindi, and Roy affectionately referred to his firm as "India's largest family," casting himself as the father. Roy's official title was, alternatingly, Sahara's "chief guardian" or its "managing worker," and his millions of employees called him Saharashri and touched his feet as a sign of respect. Sahara workers themselves had their own special handshake and even a company greeting.[7]

As his profile grew, Roy became known for shows of grandiosity. He orchestrated multiple Guinness world records, including corralling some 122,000 workers to stand in the oppressive heat, with temperatures soaring to 99 degrees, and sing India's national anthem. It broke the record, temporarily, for the greatest number of people singing the national anthem at the same time. Roy also built a 360-acre private development, known as Sahara Shaher, with a cricket stadium, a helipad, an artificial lake, and a twenty-six-foot sculpture of "Mother India," wearing a sari and waving the national flag. Roy built a marble mansion for himself that was modeled after the White House, and erected Swiss chalets for his guests.[8] When his sons were married, some 10,500 guests were at the festivities. It was so widely attended that while the affair was underway, "shooting in Bollywood ground to a halt and politicking in Delhi was put on hold," reported India Today.[9]

While he was often photographed partying with Bollywood actresses and cricket stars, Roy managed to maintain a populist appeal. An admirer of Mother Teresa, he met with her several times and said of their connection, "Whenever she held my hand, a current would pass through me."[10] Every year, Roy hosted a wedding ceremony for 101 poor couples of various religious faiths, showering them with extravagant gifts like refrigerators and television sets.[11] Roy was also a sports enthusiast, with ownership stakes in Formula One racing. And in a cricket-crazed country, he sponsored the national team, splashing the name Sahara, with its ubiquitous white, green, and orange circular logo, across jerseys and stadium banners.

As Roy built up his empire, he continued offering savings plans to poor Indians who lacked access to formal banks. Hundreds of thousands of Sahara agents spread across the Indian countryside, going door to door, collecting deposits of as little as one rupee from impoverished rickshaw drivers, tea stall owners, and farm laborers.[12] By 2008, Sahara India Financial Corp., Roy's flagship subsidiary, boasted forty-two million clients—or more than 3 percent of India's entire populace.[13]

It was that year, 2008, that Sahara's regulatory troubles began. The Reserve Bank of India, the country's central bank, accused Sahara of failing to conform to certain financial requirements and, among other things, of slashing depositors' interest payments when they fell behind on their installments. More than 70 percent of Sahara's customers paid penalties, the bank alleged, noting in a court filing, "Small depositors in the lower strata of society are being exploited."[14] Roy denied the charges, but in the end, Sahara agreed to stop taking new deposits and eventually to wind down the business.[15]

But it was not the end of Roy's difficulties. Two years later, in 2010, financial regulators accused Sahara of improperly marketing more than $3 billion in bonds, selling them to nearly thirty-one million poor and often illiterate investors.[16] It was this case that would eventually lead to the court ruling issued just a month after Roy's Plaza purchase.

Following the 2012 ruling against him, Roy argued that he was being unfairly targeted by the authorities, and he refused to cooperate. When the investigators asked for documents detailing his investors' identities, for example, Roy insisted that he couldn't comply because everyone in his office was away for summer holiday. He later swamped the government with data, directing 127 trucks be driven to the regulators' office, unloading thirty-one thousand aluminum cartons stuffed with files.[17] As regulators made their way through the paper dump, they found that much of it was a jumble of nonsensical information, with investors who had no house numbers or street addresses listed.[18] In one instance, the same investor name appeared nearly six thousand times.[19]

Roy battled the regulators in court and the case wound its way through the Indian judicial system, eventually reaching its Supreme Court. In its almost three-hundred-page ruling, the country's highest court compared Sahara's haphazard record keeping to that of "a street hawker" and, considering billions of dollars were "allegedly collected from the poor rural inhabitants of India," wrote that "the whole affair seems to be doubtful, dubious and questionable."[20] If at least some of the investors were "fictitious," as the court put it, there was a question of where the billions of dollars that Sahara had raised had, in fact, come from. The question of whether Roy was using made-up investor identities to hide the source of the funds for illicit activities, or was merely bad at bookkeeping, persisted. A year later, regulators would try to solve the mystery.

In 2013, a year after Roy had purchased the Plaza, India's Enforcement Directorate, a specialized financial investigation agency, registered a case against Sahara under the country's Prevention of Money Laundering Act.[21] Again, Roy denied wrongdoing. "I challenge the entire system to look into the matter and prove even one single fictitious account or any single paisa of money laundering," Roy told reporters, using the word for a small unit of Indian money.[22] "People cannot accept Sahara's meteoric growth," the company declared in full-page advertisements it took out in Indian newspapers. "Instead of being appreciated, all along we have been at the receiving end of bashing from all authorities again and again."[23] Among the Enforcement Directorate's allegations was that Roy's foreign hotels, including the Plaza, were "proceeds of crime."[24]

It was while the investigation into Roy was heating up that the billionaire had begun his foreign hotel buying spree. For an avowed Indian nationalist, whose company motto was "Nationalism is the supreme religion,"[25] it was an unexpected move. First, in 2010, Roy purchased the luxury Grosvenor House, a historic London hotel built in 1929, for $730 million. Then he went to New York and began negotiating for the Plaza.

After the Plaza purchase, Roy's troubles intensified. Following its initial ruling, the Supreme Court barred him from traveling abroad, including taking any overseas trips to supervise investments like his New York hotel.[26] Then, when Roy failed to appear at a court-mandated hearing, the incensed justices charged him with contempt and issued a warrant for his arrest.[27] In March 2014, Roy was remanded into custody. As the fallen tycoon began his perp walk, a mob of Sahara supporters, protesters, and cameramen crowded and jostled him. Roy waved and flashed an unsteady smile. Suddenly, a protester flung black ink at him, staining Roy's face and splattering his crisp white shirt. As the perpetrator cried out that the Sahara boss was a thief, Roy's bodyguards ushered him inside, a humiliating downfall for a man once so rich and politically connected.

Roy's new home was a far cry from the luxury of the Plaza or his palatial Indian estate. Tihar Jail, located in west Delhi, was a seething repository for twelve thousand of some of the country's most violent criminals. The largest prison complex in South Asia, it housed terrorists and murderers, as well as drug addicts and petty thieves.[28] Some 6 percent of prisoners had HIV; and contagious diseases like tuberculosis, hepatitis, and typhoid were rife, according to reports in the Indian press.[29] As for Roy, his bail was set at $1.6 billion—a record amount. The tycoon immediately scrambled to raise money.

As Roy's predicament became more widely known, several characters came out of the woodwork hoping to snatch up the Plaza, their efforts resulting in varying calamitous outcomes. One of the first to make his approach was a brash young stockbroker living in San Francisco. Saransh Sharma, a thirty-four-year-old of Indian descent, had been raised in Oman and had come to America for school, staying after graduation to work in finance. Sharma had been following Roy's mounting troubles from afar, and he decided to send a nervy email to Sandeep Wadhwa, a Sahara executive. He reached out through the business networking platform LinkedIn, an Internet version of a cold call. It was a shot in the dark, and against all odds, Wadhwa responded.

Sharma and Wadhwa began talking, and, "for the next eight or nine months, I traveled the world four or five times, from San Francisco to Beijing, to India, Dubai, London, New York, and back to San Francisco putting the deal together," Sharma told me. At the end of the grueling process, Sharma claimed to have a group of wealthy investors from the United Kingdom and the United States, none of whom he would name, who were ready to pony over several hundred million dollars for the New York property.

In January 2015, Sharma boarded a flight to New Delhi, then hired a driver to take him to Tihar Jail. He was driven down a narrow, winding road penned in on both sides by soaring thirty-five-foot walls. The car stopped in front of a large metallic door, and when Sharma stepped out, a putrid stench of raw sewage, body odor, and rotting food burned his nostrils. "It was surreal," Sharma told me of the experience. He entered the jail and walked down a corridor to the office of the superintendent. There, in a room with a grungy couch and some wilting food platters, a team of Sahara employees, including Roy, waited to greet him. As Sharma watched a rodent scamper across the floor, he began discussing what the press would later dub the "largest ever deal from a prison."[30]

Over the ensuing weeks, as Sharma and Roy continued negotiating, Roy pleaded with the courts to be moved to better accommodations to facilitate his dealmaking with Sharma. The court finally agreed to remove Roy from the general population. His new, improved jail cell was a cottage, typically reserved for lawyers or judges who had business at the prison. The house was loosely guarded, and featured a Ping-Pong table, an elliptical machine, and the ability to get food delivered from restaurants outside the prison walls. Roy was also given access to a conference room with air-conditioning, video equipment, two laptops, and a mobile phone.[31] "He was not living like someone in jail," Sharma said. The Indian press reported that Roy was enjoying "a luxurious lifestyle" inside Tihar Jail, with two assistants and a superintendent who "makes sure his every need is taken care of."[32]

Months after Sharma had first approached Wadhwa via LinkedIn, the sides agreed to the terms of a deal. Sharma and his syndicate of buyers would invest $2 billion to take over the Plaza, as well as refinance several Sahara loans and provide additional investment in Sahara properties in India.[33] How the refinancing of loans and investing in Sahara properties would help Roy make his bail or pay back his bondholders was unclear. Journalists began inquiring about the deal. They also started to sniff around Sharma himself, looking into his background and trying to identify his mysterious syndicate of buyers.

It soon became clear that Sharma had no track record for transactions of this size—or, in fact, a real estate investment deal of any size. But even as questions began to percolate, Sharma was hungry to speak to the press, providing numerous interviews where he bragged about his chemistry with Roy and his dealmaking prowess.

"I have to be careful when I say these things," he told one reporter in a typical exchange, "but I can be sweet when I talk. Let's just leave it at that. I was a Mr. Nice Guy and I approached [Roy] in a very soft sense."[34]

It all seemed to be working well enough. That is, until Reuters broke a story that revealed more troubling discrepancies. Sharma had provided an email that was purported to have come from Bank of America, confirming that he had $1 billion in an account earmarked for the transaction. But when Reuters reporters called Bank of America to confirm the legitimacy of this email, the bank denied sending it and claimed it was not part of the transaction. What's more, Reuters discovered that Sharma himself had a number of troubling legal issues clouding his reputation, including a sworn deposition in which Sharma had admitted to stealing a client database from a former employer and selling it for $10,000.[35]

Sahara said it was blindsided. "We are astonished and feel cheated in such an adverse environment against us," the company said in a statement.[36] Sharma blamed it on a simple misunderstanding. Roy's company then sued Sharma, who retaliated with a defamation countersuit. There was even a report that the Federal Bureau of Investigation was looking into the matter.[37] In the end, however, the lawsuits and the investigation, like the deal itself, petered out. Sharma returned to America, and Roy was left to stew in jail.

For the next year, Roy remained imprisoned, trying to raise money for bail. Then, in May 2016, four years after he bought the Plaza, Roy won his freedom—sort of. Roy's mother, with whom he was close, had died, and he petitioned the Supreme Court for a temporary reprieve to attend her last rites. The justices acquiesced, and Roy left his cell, never to return. The court allowed Roy to remain free on parole, as long as he appeared in court every few months, where he handed over checks for hundreds of millions of dollars. The money was put in a government account, to be eventually repaid to his bondholders. "Here it is, two and a half billion [dollars] lying there [but] we are still to pay more," Roy complained to me. While no longer in prison, Roy was still confined to India, prohibited from traveling abroad.

While Roy battled the Supreme Court, his Indian business empire was unraveling. His company's coffers were quickly being depleted and employees complained of not being paid. Stories emerged in the Indian press of Sahara workers suffering severe hardship and anguish, including one case of a manager who, having not received a paycheck in four months, jumped off the roof of a Sahara building.[38]

In some cases, Roy's loyal workers willingly gave up their paychecks to contribute to his legal defense. "We thought, 'He's our caretaker. Once he will be out of jail, the company will progress,'" Rishi Kumar Trivedi, who worked as a low-level assistant for Roy for almost two decades, told me. Trivedi went for more than two years without a salary. He eventually grew disillusioned and quit, starting an organization that fights to recoup money owed to Sahara employees.[39]

As for the Plaza back in New York, it continued to operate without much guidance from its embattled owner. The hotel's employees remained out of the loop, forced to rely on news stories in the Indian press to stay up-to-date on their boss's latest travails. They set up Google alerts for "Subrata Roy" and "Sahara India Pariwar," and heard about the suicide of the Sahara employee and of the vast number of Indians who were not being paid. Luckily for them, salaries at the Plaza came from a separate account that was regularly replenished with cash directly generated by the operations of the hotel. "When things started to get frozen, like [Roy's] assets and bank accounts, I kept getting paid, although I was pretty freaked out about job security," said one employee.

The daily operations of the hotel, such as overseeing the maids and bellmen, and caring for guests' needs, was the responsibility of Fairmont Hotels, the management company owned by Plaza minority shareholder Prince Alwaleed. But the business side of the Plaza, including handling the multiple retail and restaurant leases, and ensuring that the hotel turned a profit, was a separate operation. That piece of the business was, for several years, the purview of Chatwal, Roy's friend who had a 5 percent stake in the Plaza and was the only owner based in New York. Chatwal was assisted in his efforts by a skeletal staff, toiling out of offices in the Plaza basement next to the garbage room. They were faced with a herculean task.

When Roy first bought the Plaza in 2012, its net income was $3.67 million. By 2014, as Roy languished in prison, it dropped into the red, posting a loss of more than $1.2 million. By 2016, the Plaza's losses had more than tripled, and in 2017, it bled a whopping $10 million.[40] "You see [in] any hotel, the most important [thing] is very good service," Roy told me in his heavily accented English. "Maintenance, proper maintenance, good food, good service," he continued, trying to explain why the Plaza was such a money-loser. "I'm sorry I haven't gone there for the last four years so I can't tell you exactly what is happening, but I personally feel that probably we're lacking there."

While his New York hotel was losing money, the mortgage that Roy had on the property was an even bigger liability. Roy had taken out an $880 million loan with the Bank of China for his three foreign hotels, including the Plaza; the Dream Downtown, which was another New York City hotel he owned with Chatwal; and London's Grosvenor House. As Roy's legal troubles and the Plaza's losses mounted, the bank increased its oversight of the hotels. It became so involved in the minutiae of running the Plaza, for instance, that at one point, the bank zeroed in on the interest rate being charged on the security deposit for a tiny kiosk in the basement-level food court. "I had a six-week debate with the Bank of China about returning a tenant's security deposit," one employee told me. "We are talking about a 150-square-foot kiosk tenant. The difference was like $17. I finally told them I would take the $20 out of my pocket right now and give it to them, just so we don't have to have another call about this."

There were also bigger issues at play. Every quarter, the Plaza had to present a budget to the Bank of China, and every quarter, "our numbers were full of shit," one employee said. Sahara also had to provide its lender with a revenue target, and "every quarter the Bank of China would take us at face value, and we would miss it by $5 million. Literally. We were just like, 'Oh, did we tell you we would make money? Sorry about that.'"

One major reason the Plaza was struggling financially was the decision that was made by El Ad to lease out the hotel's public rooms to third parties. The Plaza had become a jumble of tangled interests that rarely aligned. For example, a major investment bank had wanted to book a multiday conference at the Plaza, and was looking to rent out a large block of hotel rooms and reserve the Grand Ballroom for events. The hotel was thrilled to take the business, but the event planner that leased the Grand Ballroom had already booked a birthday party for one of those nights. Since the ballroom wasn't available, the investment bank took its business elsewhere.

The one relative bright spot was the Plaza's basement-level food court, made up of some twenty-five small gourmet kiosks. Measuring just a few hundred square feet each, the kiosks ranged from a cupcake vendor to a sushi bar. Anchored by the Todd English Food Hall, a restaurant by the well-known chef, it also included a store that hawked Eloise paraphernalia, including books, slippers, and stationery, and hosted children's birthday parties. On most days, the subterranean space was packed with tourists. Whereas once they might have taken a break from shopping to listen to a harpist at the Palm Court, now they sat on wire chairs beneath the escalator, sipping cappuccinos or munching on take-out salads.

As the Plaza continued bleeding money and Roy remained stuck in India, a bevy of other suitors circled the hotel. There were rumors that a group of buyers including the sports agent David Sugarman and the Grammy-winning member of the Fugees rap group Pras Michel was interested, although that improbable offer vanished as quickly as it was reported.[41] The Sultan of Brunei, a name that was bandied about back when Trump was facing financial ruin, supposedly was a buyer, although the sultan was embroiled in a controversy after passing a draconian law that permitted the stoning of gays and adulterers.[42] It was unclear if his country's new rules, or the reported $680 million offer—deemed too low by Roy—scuttled the deal.[43]

At one point, it seemed as if a sale might actually happen. Shahal Khan, an American entrepreneur, began regularly appearing at the Plaza, as if spending time there increased the likelihood he would one day own it. "It got really intense for like ten days to two weeks," one employee told me. "He showed up rolling through the property like, 'I'm buying this thing.'"

Like Sharma before him, Khan was an American of Indian descent. His parents moved to Great Neck, Long Island, from India, where Khan was born, although his parents sent him back there to live until he was eight. "I grew up with my grandparents on both sides," he told me of his childhood. "When I returned to the US, for me it was a big shock. I went from having servants to having to mow lawns." Khan graduated from Johns Hopkins with a master's degree, and after an initial stint in government, he joined an early Internet start-up. He continued working in tech, finding positions in places as varied as Portugal and Bahrain. At the time he became interested in the Plaza, Khan's investments included a solar power company in India and a mine in Pakistan.

In 2014, Khan was in Dubai for business when a friend introduced him to the Sahara executive Wadhwa. The two went to dinner and began discussing the fate of the hotel. "I said I had all this collateral net worth. Here UBS is, dying to finance my mines in Pakistan, and here Roy is, overleveraged," said Khan. He proposed acquiring the Plaza and providing loans to Roy totaling $1.5 billion, similar to the offer Sharma had once made. The Swiss bank UBS had agreed to underwrite the deal—this time around the money seemed to be real—and Khan also agreed to provide a personal guarantee.

Khan said he had always loved the Plaza. Growing up near the setting for *The Great Gatsby*, he first became passionate about the hotel after reading the novel in English class. "I always felt like I was born in that era," Khan told me. "It was a story that connected to me on many levels: Even though for Gatsby it didn't end up well, there was that ambition of trying to do your best and going up and up and up."

Khan couldn't afford to do the Plaza deal by himself, so he took on a partner. A Hong Kong–based firm that claimed to represent high net worth Chinese investors agreed to supply $850 million toward a joint venture, with Khan supplying $250 million. At the time, the Bank of China was growing increasingly antsy and was considering foreclosing on the Plaza. At one point, "Roy said, 'We have to move, we have to hurry, or I'll lose the hotels,'" said Khan. UBS issued a letter confirming that Khan had sufficient financing for the deal, and Khan signed a term sheet with Sahara. But when it was time for the money to be handed over, Khan alleged that his Hong Kong partners failed to come through with the promised $850 million. Khan decided to push ahead with the deal anyway. The Hong Kong partners filed a suit, alleging breach of contract against Khan, Sahara India Pariwar, and UBS.[44]

The tensions between the sides soon escalated dramatically. In an attempt to smooth over the matter and find a solution, Khan invited Wadhwa and his former Chinese partners—whom he had never met in person—to dinner at the Plaza's Palm Court. But when Khan showed up, he was shocked to find that the supposed Hong Kong–based executives were not Chinese at all, but Australian. They were also "just kids," he told me, in their mid-thirties. Even more disturbing, the men appeared to be intoxicated. "It takes a lot to get me upset. And these guys are sitting there completely drunk. I couldn't believe I was sitting in front of them. They looked like fraternity brothers. I was livid," said Khan.

In a flash, Khan, who is compact and brawny, leapt across the table and grabbed one of the executives in a choke hold. Wadhwa, who happened to have injured his foot and was wearing a support boot, backed away from the fracas. As Khan held his victim, a bartender who had seen the fight break out jumped over the bar and broke the men apart. Khan was bleeding from his mouth, and a security guard escorted his ex-partners from the hotel. The following morning, the men threatened to sue Khan for assault. They didn't, but they did pursue their claim of breach of contract. Two years later, a judge dismissed their case.[45] Despite the deal's failure, Khan never gave up hope of buying the Plaza. Over the subsequent years, he continued making overtures to Roy. "I understood him," Khan said of the embattled Plaza owner, despite the fact that the two men had never met in person. "He is like an Indian Great Gatsby."

Around the time that Khan brawled at the Palm Court, the Bank of China finally threw up its hands. A pair of London-based billionaire brothers, Simon and David Reuben, took over the debt.[46] The Indian Supreme Court, meanwhile, began threatening that unless Roy sold his properties to pay back his bondholders, the government would seize them and auction them off itself. It wasn't clear what jurisdiction the court had over foreign properties like the Plaza, but it did begin making plans to auction Roy's more valuable Indian landholdings.[47]

Then, the most bizarre offer yet surfaced for the Plaza—replete with another prisoner sent to the dreaded Tihar Jail. In the winter of 2016, Prakash Swamy, a sixty-three-year-old veteran reporter who had spent a career covering the United Nations for various Indian media organizations, was attending a cocktail party in Midtown Manhattan. There, he was approached by two financiers who said they represented a Chinese equity firm that was interested in buying the Plaza. The investors hoped to circumvent Roy and make an offer for the hotel directly to the Indian Supreme Court. They wanted Swamy, with his Indian network, to assist them. If a deal materialized, they would pay the journalist a consulting fee, they said.

After some initial hesitation, Swamy agreed to the deal. His main point of contact was the financier Anton Werner, who claimed an unusual background. Werner's career spanned everything from consulting with United Nations agencies to developing an HDTV broadcasting station in New Jersey where the show *Cake Boss* was taped. According to his executive profile, Werner spoke fluent German, Czech, and Russian, and listed his education as, vaguely, "M.B.A. (Finance, Economics, Business Management, Marketing) 1980–1994." His firm reportedly owned more than five hundred aircraft, operating three hundred domestic and international routes, although no specific airlines were named.

In February 2017, two months after the cocktail party in New York, Swamy traveled to Delhi. There, he presented an offer to the Supreme Court to acquire the Plaza for $550 million. The justices were skeptical. After so many rumored buyers had come and gone, the court wanted proof that the Plaza offer was legitimate. It ordered Swamy to return in one month, and bring with him a check for the equivalent of $110 million. If the deal fell through, the justices warned, the money would be forfeited.[48]

Over the ensuing weeks, Werner sent a flurry of emails to Swamy.

They were often frantic in tone, with capital letters and exclamation points for emphasis. Werner struggled to conduct due diligence on the Plaza, and was often forced to rely on published news accounts to gather basic research. It soon dawned on Werner that not only would they have to pony up the $550 million to buy the Plaza, but any purchase would also have to include the repayment of the $880 million mortgage Roy had taken out on his foreign hotels. As the complexity of the deal became clear, Werner and his investors balked.

On the appointed day, Swamy was forced to return to the Delhi courtroom empty-handed. Frustrated with having its time wasted, the court ordered Swamy's passport seized and told the journalist to return in ten days to pay a fine of nearly of $1.5 million. If Swamy did not return with the money, the court warned, he faced imprisonment.[49]

Swamy realized that any chance of earning a consulting fee from Werner had disappeared and that a prison sentence was imminent. In desperation, Swamy filed petitions with the court, pleading for leniency.[50] But the justices were unmoved. "You should have realized the gravity of the case," one justice admonished Swamy when he reappeared in court at the appointed time but without the money. "If we do not punish you then it would send a wrong message," added another justice.[51] "Temptation sometimes leads to confinement." As Swamy "sobbed and pleaded with folded hands for forgiveness,"[52] the justices waved over a marshal who immediately took the journalist into custody.

Directly from the courthouse, Swamy was put into a van and driven to the same prison where Roy had spent two years. But that is where the similarities ended. Unlike Roy, Swamy couldn't game the prison system, leveraging his renown to live in relative comfort. Instead, Swamy was thrown into a bare-bones cell packed with other prisoners. There, he curled up on the filthy floor, using his balled-up trousers for a pillow. "It was very unhygienic, with people pissing all over the area," Swamy told me. "I found it disgusting. I was sleeping on the pavement like a homeless guy."

Swamy's stay at Tihar was made worse by the fact that the journalist had recently undergone bariatric bypass surgery to lose weight and had a restricted diet. As the guards and fellow inmates hurled insults at him, Swamy existed on meager meals of milk and fruit, dropping thirty pounds in two weeks, he told me. To pass the time, Swamy tried to access the library, but was told it would cost him 10,000 rupees, or roughly $150. And when he began writing down his experiences, guards "forcibly took away my notepad," he said, adding that they told him "not to write anything negative about my stay there." After one month, Swamy was released from Tihar Jail. "The experience was mental agony; I am still not over it," Swamy said almost a year later. He is now writing a book on his time in prison, which he has titled *Judicial Terrorism*.

It seemed as if the saga of Roy's troubled ownership, and the parade of unlikely buyers, was to continue. But in the summer of 2018, it came to a rapid, if messy, conclusion. In June, the beleaguered owner was not only contending with pressure from the Indian Supreme Court, but also facing down the looming due date on his Plaza mortgage. As Roy's difficulties mounted, a familiar roster of names bubbled to the surface, offering to take the New York hotel off his hands. There was Shahal Khan, who was reportedly planning to use cryptocurrency this time to purchase the Plaza,[53] and Prince Alwaleed, although the Saudi royal seemed an unlikely choice. Several months earlier, the prince had sold half of his Plaza stake to Ben Ashkenazy, a New York City–based developer,[54] and he was facing political headwinds back at home. A new Saudi crown prince had come to power, and Alwaleed had been caught up in an "anti-corruption" crackdown that had resulted in his extended detainment at a luxury hotel in Riyadh, and a subsequent $6 billion payout to the government.[55]

Soon, Khan and another investor announced they had clinched a deal to pay $600 million for Roy's stake in the Plaza. But Alwaleed's new partner, Ashkenazy, threw a wrench in the proceedings when he claimed his intention to buy the hotel. The sides soon began lobbing recriminations and legal missives at one another, and it looked as though the turmoil would never end. But then, as the battle waged, a stealth bidder emerged.[56]

Over a quiet July 4 weekend, reminiscent of Miki Naftali's trip to Singapore years earlier, a subsidiary of Qatar's wealth fund announced that, in fact, it had purchased the Plaza.[57] Katara Hospitality, the hotel arm of the Qatar Investment Authority, paid $600 million for the entire property, including the guest rooms, unsold hotel condominiums, and retail spaces, buying up Roy's majority share, as well as Ashkenazy's and Alwaleed's stakes. The luxury condominiums, owned by individual buyers, were not part of the deal. As a result of the transaction, Roy, like Trump before him, was unlikely to ever see much, if any, proceeds from the sale.

But while Roy was not fated to get a windfall, for Plaza enthusiasts, the deal with Katara was a welcome resolution. Finally, the hotel was unified once more under a single entity, and more importantly, one that had the seemingly inexhaustible wealth of a gulf nation. While its reputation was somewhat tarnished, the Plaza had shaken off the yoke of Subrata Roy and his troubled tenure. And while it was undeniable that foreign capital was now melded to its DNA, the hotel remained a quintessential New York institution. That was, for many hotel enthusiasts, reason enough to rejoice.

Epilogue

In the summer of 2018, when Katara Hospitality announced its surprise deal, I was three years into my research on the Plaza, and nearly finished with this book. During these many months, I had visited the hotel countless times as an observer, wandering the building's halls, taking notes on its goings-on, and interviewing employees during their shift breaks. But I had not stayed over as a hotel guest since the night before my wedding nearly a decade before.

Back then, the Plaza was, for me, little more than a fancy destination, a symbol of elegance and glamour. Now, of course, I was a walking encyclopedia of Plaza history, the filing cabinets in my office as well as my brain jammed with anecdotes, statistics, and personalities. I wanted to see how, given what I now knew, spending a night at the hotel would color my perspective. It would turn out to be a lot more discombobulating than I had anticipated, with the ghosts of the Plaza looming large, a constant bombardment of the past and present.

On a steamy Monday afternoon in August, when the city's pace had slowed to a summer crawl, I walked past the crowds milling about the Pulitzer Fountain and families waiting for taxis at the Plaza's Fifth Avenue entrance. I entered the hotel's revolving doors and made my way through the air-conditioned lobby with my overnight bag. Turning left, I passed a velvet rope that cordoned off the hotel entrance, a sign posted in a brass frame warning visitors that only paying guests could proceed past this point. I continued on, striding through the marble lobby to the front desk, where a clerk was positioned behind an enormous floral bouquet.

I gave her my name, and as she checked her computer for my reservation, I couldn't help but think of Mary Doyle, the young Irish newsstand girl who, more than a hundred years earlier, had wandered away from her stack of papers to prop herself atop the front desk, just moments before Alfred Gwynne Vanderbilt made his entrance. As I recalled those events, a uniformed bellman passed by, pushing a cart filled with suitcases. I had a sudden urge to grab his lapels and tell him that during World War II, so many men had been drafted into the military that women were hired to his position, and the term "bellwomen" had been bandied about. And when I entered the elevator to go to my room on the sixteenth floor, it was impossible not to envision the hydraulic cabs that had once slid up and down this same shaft, their glass doors revealing the inner workings of the pistons. How much less romantic were today's cabs, I thought, with their mirrored walls and automatic buttons that shot guests upward with smooth efficiency.

The flood of memories—or of lives past and stories retold, if not personal recollections—continued to assail me as I settled into my room. Here was a Victorian sofa, a reproduction that recalled the original Edwardian furnishings that the Plaza's first manager, Frederick Sterry, had chosen with such care. The fanciful gold faucets of the bathroom reminded me of Donald Trump's gilding of the hotel, and the oversized tub couldn't help but evoke thoughts of Harry Black, the hotel's builder, who nearly drowned himself in his Plaza penthouse.

My room featured several portraits of medieval characters, painted in the dark-lit style of Rembrandt, spurring thoughts of Princess Parlaghy, the colorful portrait painter who arrived at the

Plaza with much fanfare and a small zoo. Before she lost her wealth and was forced to abscond from the Plaza without paying her bills, Parlaghy had lived in a sprawling suite outfitted with priceless artworks and tapestries. True, my room wasn't nearly as large, and the paintings on my walls looked to be prints, covered in a faux-marbling effect that was supposed to make them appear aged, but it evoked the past nonetheless.

Later that evening, I wandered down to the lobby and sat in one of the high-backed chairs. There I watched a uniformed bartender mix cocktails against a backdrop of hundreds of champagne bottles and I couldn't help wondering whether the handful of patrons he served knew that, following Prohibition, this corner had once been the swank Persian Room, where Kay Thompson wowed crowds with her clever musical numbers. Or if the small group of young businessmen gathered against one wall, or the women in hijabs sipping tea, knew that the lobby had once been the purview of the thirty-nine widows of the Plaza. Today, few people have the time or wherewithal to spend afternoons lounging in hotel lobbies, unless to stare at their phones or wait for their Uber drivers. Yet the spirit of those eccentric women, who once arranged themselves on their settees to watch the bustle or complain to their favorite Plaza employee, somehow remained.

The following morning, I continued my tour, passing along the hallway where Hilary Knight's portrait of Eloise still hangs. There, two young women were posing and taking photos, the popularity of the literary heroine refusing to wane half a century after her publishing debut. I continued on toward the West Fifty-Eighth Street entrance of the hotel, which had been constructed in 1921 as part of the extension. There I peeked into a children's boutique that was hawking $300 Fendi baby sneakers and toddler-sized Versace T-shirts covered in dollar signs. I wondered what Black, who had lived a life of wealth, traveling in his own personal Pullman car, would have thought of such merchandise.

I continued on, past the bustling escalators that descended into the subterranean Plaza Food Hall, and made my way instead to a white marble staircase that was situated unobtrusively and largely unnoticed, behind the whirring of hair dryers emanating from a ladies' hair salon. I ascended the stairs one flight, to the ornate Terrace Room, with its paneled ceiling and muraled walls of Roman statues and gold-inflected flowers. I stepped across the empty room, wandering unseen into the space where I had been married. A flood of memories came back to me, of waiting outside the door with my father, filled with anticipation and nerves, and of making my way toward the dais, teetering in my heels, my vision obscured by my veil. The room, devoid of furnishings or people, was still breathtakingly beautiful. It was my private moment, but I couldn't help but think of the countless other brides and grooms who had traversed that same path, a shared experience forever connecting us with the hotel.

I walked back up the marble staircase one flight to the Grand Ballroom, the site of Truman Capote's Black and White Ball, where high society converged for one of New York's last great hurrahs. The ballroom was also empty, and I wandered through the white-and-gold space with its columns, curtains, and crystal chandeliers. I climbed a few small stairs to the private boxes that lined the room's circumference, imagining the debutantes and their dates who once gazed out at the waltzing couples dancing on the floor below. As I made my way to the exit, I impulsively executed a jeté leap across the carpeted floor before scurrying out, feeling like a naughty Eloise.

With each room that I entered, I shed more of my journalistic impartiality, and in turn, felt the increasing power of my affection for the Plaza. It was, I realized, this kind of connection, the

memories that the hotel prompted and inspired, that gave the building its character and staying power. After my exploration upstairs,
I headed to breakfast at the Palm Court, where patrons still dine at
tables surrounded by oversized shrubbery, beneath the diffuse light
emanating from the re-created laylight ceiling. I asked the hostess for
a table in the front left corner, where I had last sat with my ninety-
eight-year-old grandmother several months earlier, just before she
suffered a stroke that stole much of her long-term thoughts.

For my grandmother, a trip from her small town in western Pennsylvania to New York meant a stay at the Plaza. It was the base from
which she experienced the excitement of the metropolis, where, as
a musician and music lover, she saw such acts as Eartha Kitt at the
Persian Room, or Frank Sinatra, who once sang happy birthday to
my young uncle, according to family lore. My grandmother's experience wasn't unique. Countless others have enjoyed similar and
meaningful adventures, the Plaza acting as their conduit to culture
and society, their escape from the drudgery of every day.

While my grandmother's stroke damaged her brain's ability to
recall, it's true that even among those who have had no such ill-
nesses, memories can be like a dream, easily slipping into the sub-
conscious or simply forgotten. In researching the hotel, I unearthed
stories where the protagonists had long since died and their tales
had been lost. In other cases, I tried to shed new light on stories that
were already well-known. It is memory, particularly collective memory, I realized, that is the unique essence of the Plaza. These shared
remembrances—of elegant tea service at the Palm Court, of the
childhood joy of discovering Eloise, or the hysteria of the Beatles'
first stateside visit—are what make the hotel indelible, imprinting
it on the New York narrative alongside other iconic locations like
Times Square or the Empire State Building.

Whatever its next chapter may bring, the hotel is much more than
its marble pillars or chandeliers. The Plaza's core is the experiences

of its guests, its owners, and its employees. It is their recollections that have been baked into the walls, giving it a unique patina. Some critics lament the many changes that have been foisted on the Plaza over its long life. But through it all, it has retained its identity in its most basic sense. Its bones are intact, many of its famous rooms are unblemished, and it is still a hotel. It is a true New Yorker, one that has coolly observed from its corner of Central Park the evolution of its surroundings, from the Vanderbilt mansion to Bergdorf Goodman, from hansom cabs to traffic jams. There is no reason to think that the white marble tower envisioned by Henry Janeway Hardenbergh won't keep an eye on the proceedings for yet another century.

Acknowledgments

As a first-time author, writing this book was a daunting, years-long process, and I couldn't have accomplished it without a team of talented editors, valued friends, and supportive family. First and foremost, a big thank-you to Sean Desmond, my editor at Twelve, for being an enthusiastic cheerleader and believing in this book from the outset. I am ever appreciative that you always answered the abundance of questions that I lobbed at you, no matter how small. I also am indebted to the skilled Twelve team, who have worked tirelessly to help me create this book, including Rachel Kambury and the production and design staff.

I was lucky enough to have an accomplished group of women to whom I returned repeatedly throughout this writing process. Thank you, Libby Burton, for shepherding me along during those critical first phases, when I was overwhelmed with tackling and organizing my mountain of material. You fought for my book from the very first, convincing Twelve it should be added to their canon, and even after moving on from the imprint, you continued to make yourself available. I am eternally grateful for your friendship and wisdom.

My gratitude to Rachel Vogel, my agent, who helped me fine-tune the vision for this book, reading endless iterations of my proposal, and patiently calming my anxieties through the various, stressful phases of publishing. You were an ace at handling the business side. And Vanessa Mobley, a brilliant editor whom I am lucky to call a friend, you are ever ready with a warm smile and a kind word of encouragement. From snatched conversations at morning drop-off to kids' birthday parties, you have always been a font of advice and reassurance, and I am so glad that our paths crossed.

There are many others who have been essential in helping me complete this book. To Sameen Gauhar, a fact-checker extraordinaire, while the hours we spent combing through the manuscript in such minutiae were admittedly painful, the finished product was far superior to the original. And to Atiba Pertilla, who helped ensure that the facts surrounding the early history of the Plaza were correct; any mistakes are mine alone.

Aayush Soni helped me navigate my way through the chaos of Delhi, braving the crazy traffic and translating and transcribing as needed. Our nightmare trip to the Indian Supreme Court notwithstanding, I am grateful for your efforts. Another shout-out goes to Kyna Doles, whose research assistance proved critical in deciphering the web of shell companies at the Plaza condominiums. David Ludwig also provided much-needed assistance with transcribing interviews.

Countless sources helped inform this work. Some requested anonymity, but among those who can be named, I couldn't have done it without Miki Naftali, whose willingness to take a chance and share his memories of the transformative time when he owned the Plaza made it possible to write my initial chapter. This set in motion the process that ended up with my finished book, so an enduring thank-you is owed. Other former owners of the hotel were also helpful, including Sant Chatwal, who provided important introductions and was always readily available on WhatsApp.

I am also indebted to the many family members of Plaza owners and managers who are no longer living, including Stephanie Sonnabend, who allowed me to bury myself among boxes of old press clippings and family photos at her New Hampshire home; and also Peter Sonnabend and Gary Lavenson, who spoke with me on several occasions. Their stories and recollections helped fill out a period in the hotel's history that has long been glossed over. Gregg Salomone was a significant source, sharing his father's partially finished memoir and introducing me to his elegant mother, Bernadette. Lourdes Salomone was also generous with her time, even sending me materials from across the pond. I am grateful to all of you for entrusting me with your family histories, and I hope that I have done them justice.

Kudos to John Turchiano at the New York Hotel and Motel Trades Council, whose door was always open, and who gave me unfettered access to the union's extensive archives. I am also grateful to Abe Wallach, who spent hours with me sharing his anecdotes and feelings about Donald Trump. Others who have been helpful in this process include Curtis Gathje, Mason Williams, David Oliver Cohen, Sharat Pradhan, Tamal Bandyopadhyay, Prakash Swamy, and the indomitable and inspiring Stanley Turkel. I'm sure there are those whom I have missed, so apologies to anyone I mistakenly left out. Please know that I am in your debt.

The Allen Room of the New York Public Library was a valuable resource, and the fact that Frederick Lewis Allen, for whom the room was named, guided my research of the 1920s was a joyful coincidence. I want to give a special thanks to Melanie Locay, the research study liaison, who was always ready with a smile and a key card, should I forget mine, and the librarian John Balow, who helped me tackle the Plaza's early finances.

The book took me to various archives around the country, and I am indebted to the librarians and hotel archivists who assisted with my research. To Mark E. Young and Maria Corsi at the Hospitality Industry Archives at the Conrad N. Hilton College of Hotel & Restaurant Management in Houston, being with you on the morning after the 2016 election, when one of the Plaza's former owners was elected president, will remain an indelible memory. Thank you also to Cheryl Gunselman, who helped me dig through the Westin Hotels and Resorts Archive at the Washington State University Libraries in Pullman; and Pat Mueller, who, it being the dead of winter, provided me with a steady stream of Sudafed and Kleenex. I would also like to express gratitude to the staff at the Beinecke Library at Yale.

The lion's share of my gratitude goes to the countless Plaza bellmen, doormen, housekeeping staff, and so many others who, over these many decades, have worked their hardest to keep the historic building running so that all of us may enjoy it. This is your book. Many of you willingly shared your experiences at the Plaza, and while I was unable to name you all, know that I can never again walk into a hotel—the Plaza or any other—without noting how much effort goes on behind the scenes to make things run.

I also want to share a brief note about process. While libraries and archives were wonderful resources, and many books helped inform this work, it was newspapers—the daily account of history—that often proved critical. Researchers can never discover in microfiche what they can accomplish using keyword searches. The continued digitization of newspapers enabled me to locate tens of thousands of articles related to the hotel, resurrecting stories and details that had long disappeared from our collective memory.

While I saved this to the end, my most heartfelt thanks are reserved for my family, who suffered and celebrated with me in equal turns. My parents not only provided emotional support, but also gave of their time freely, babysitting at a moment's notice and reading and rereading my manuscript. My father, in particular, is responsible for fostering my love of books. If he hadn't constantly fed my hunger—handing me everything from *A Raisin in the Sun* to *The Chosen* to *Great Expectations*—I'm not sure I would be writing these acknowledgments today. Thank you also to the rest of my family, including Jed, Michael, Barbara, Max, Jackson, and Dylan, and Beth, Rob, and Cara.

None of this would have been possible without myriad reinforcements at home. Writing this book required many late nights, the occasional weekend, and the longest trip I've ever taken solo since becoming a mother. To our nanny, Penny, who helped keep things running when I was away writing, and whose caring nature and affection have imbued our children with security and love. And to my S's and J's: my husband, Stuart, harsh but brilliant in his editing and steadfast and generous in life; and my children, Sophie and Jonah, I love you, no matter what.

NOTES

Note on Dollar Figures: Historic dollar figures that have been converted into today's values are based on a purchasing power calculator that can be found at http://www .measuringworth.com/uscompare/.

Introduction

1. Neha Thirani, "Indian Conglomerate Buys New York's Plaza Hotel," *New York Times*, August 1, 2012.
2. J. Venkatesan, "SC orders Sahara to refund Rs. 24,400 crore," *Hindu*, August 31, 2012.
3. Paul Goldberger, "A Spot of Paint Won't Hurt This Lily," *New York Times*, January 22, 1989.

Chapter 1: Parade of Millionaires

1. Mary Doyle, *Life Was Like That* (Boston: Houghton Mifflin, 1936), 47–48.
2. Leslie Dorsey and Janice Devine, *Fare Thee Well: A Backward Look at Two Centuries of Historic American Hostelries, Fashionable Spas & Seaside Resorts* (New York: Crown, 1964), 139.
3. "FYI," *New York Times*, August 15, 2004.
4. "Gates Pays $46,000 Rent for His Suite," *Evening World*, April 23, 1907.
5. Lloyd Wendt and Herman Kogan, *Bet a Million! The Story of John W. Gates* (New York: Bobbs-Merrill, 1948), 278.
6. Earnest Poole, "Cowboys of the Sky," *Everybody's Magazine*, November 1908.
7. David Weitzman, *Skywalkers: Mohawk Ironworkers Build the City* (New York: Roaring Brook Press, 2010), 29.
8. "A Few Facts Regarding the Plaza Hotel," *Carpentry and Building*, May 1, 1907.
9. "Housesmiths to Work," *New-York Daily Tribune*, February 11, 1906.
10. *Bridgemen's Magazine*, January 1907, 29.
11. "Ironworkers' Memory Weak," *New York Sun*, July 25, 1906.

12. *Building Trades Employers Association Bulletin* 7, no. 8 (August 1906).

13. "Butler's Death Accident," *New York Sun*, July 27, 1906.

14. "Murder in Mid-Air by Union Workers," *New York Times*, July 12, 1906.

15. "Murder by Iron Workers," *New York Sun*, July 16, 1906.

16. "The Taxi 'Invasion' of 1907," *Cosmopolitan*, October 1947, 186.

17. "Few Hansoms Now; It's All Taxicab," *New York Times*, July 3, 1910.

18. "Motor Cars Lead Horses," *New York Times,* May 19, 1912.

19. Eve Brown, *The Plaza, 1907–1967: Its Life and Times* (New York: Meredith Press, 1967), 117.

20. "High Rentals Paid in New York," *New York Times*, April 28, 1907.

21. "The Lure of Life at a Modern Hotel," *Vogue*, April 16, 1908.

22. "Another Fine Hotel Now on the City's List," *New York Times*, September 29, 1907.

23. "Time Halts for Caruso," *Baltimore Sun*, December 3, 1907.

24. Paul Groth, *Living Downtown: The History of Residential Hotels in the United States* (Berkeley: University of California Press, 1994), 51.

25. "Jewels Outside Your Furs," *New York Times*, February 12, 1908.

26. Groth, *Living Downtown*, 46.

27. "Crush to See Brides Who'll Wear Titles," *New York Times*, January 12, 1908.

28. Groth, *Living Downtown*, 30.

29. "Grille Room for Dogs," *Daily People*, November 23, 1908.

30. "The Plaza," *Life*, November 18, 1946.

31. Thorstein Veblen, *The Theory of the Leisure Class: An Economic Study of Institutions* (New York: Macmillan, 1912), 141–42.

32. "Her Pet Dog Finds $3,000 Diamond Ring After Detectives Fail," *Washington Post*, February 11, 1915.

33. M. Jagendorf, "The Rich Lore of a Rich Hotel: The Plaza," *New York Folklore Quarterly* (Spring 1953): 176–82.

34. "Another Fine Hotel Now on the City's List," *New York Times*, September 29, 1907.

35. "The Lure of Life at a Modern Hotel," *Vogue*, April 16, 1908.

36. *Hotel Monthly* 15, no. 176 (November 1907).

37. "New York Hotel Finest in World," *East Oregonian*, September 19, 1907.

38. "Coming to New York, Waiter Changes Accent," *Washington Times*, August 15, 1907.

39. Doyle, *Life Was Like That*, 49.

40. Robert F. Bruner and Sean D. Carr, *The Panic of 1907: Lessons Learned from the Market's Perfect Storm* (Hoboken, NJ: Wiley, 2007), 7.

41. Ibid., 32, 151.

42. Brown, *Plaza*, 35.

43. "Hotel Santa Claus Ran Out of Cash," *New York Times*, December 26, 1907.

Chapter 2: A Typical French House

1. "Sam Parks Men Now Say a Fall Killed Butler," *World*, July 20, 1906.
2. "Says Fuller Company Brought on Trouble," *New York Times*, July 26, 1906.
3. "No Ironworker Saw Watchman Murdered," *New York Times*, July 25, 1906.
4. "Murder in Mid-Air by Union Workers," *New York Times*, July 12, 1906.
5. "Union Killing Not Murder," *New York Sun*, July 21, 1906.
6. "Murderers 'Exonerated,'" *New York Times*, July 28, 1906.
7. "Murder Hearing Begun," *New-York Daily Tribune*, July 17, 1906.
8. "Another Fine Hotel Now on the City's List," *New York Times*, September 29, 1907.
9. Curtis Gathje, *At The Plaza: An Illustrated History of the World's Most Famous Hotel* (New York: St. Martin's Press, 2000), 2, 4.
10. Robert A. M. Stern, Gregory Gilmartin, and John Montague Massengale, *New York 1900: Metropolitan Architecture and Urbanism, 1890–1915* (New York: Rizzoli, 1983), 529.
11. Moses King, *King's Handbook of New York City: An Outline History and Description of the American Metropolis* (Boston: Moses King, 1892), 208.
12. Moses King, *King's Handbook of New York City* (Boston: Moses King, 1893), 222.
13. "A Great Hotel Finished," *New-York Tribune*, September 30, 1890.
14. Henry S. Mower, *Reminiscences of a Hotel Man: Of Forty Years' Service* (Boston: Worcester, 1912).
15. "Two Miles of Millionaires," *Munsey's Magazine*, June 1898, 345–60; and Stern, Gilmartin, and Massengale, *New York 1900*, 307.
16. "Plaza Hotel Reconstruction," *New York Times*, June 3, 1902.
17. "Lunches and Other Adjuncts," *Cincinnati Enquirer*, May 4, 1907.
18. "Another Fine Hotel Now on the City's List," *New York Times*, September 29, 1907.
19. William S. Beinecke, *Bernhard Beinecke: A Memoir* (New York: Prospect Hill Press, 2005), 14.
20. Eve Brown, *The Plaza, 1907–1967: Its Life and Times* (New York: Meredith Press, 1967), 16.
21. Paul Starrett, *Changing the Skyline: An Autobiography* (New York: McGraw-Hill, 1938), 66.
22. "H.S. Black Ends Life by Bullet in Home; No Motive Revealed," *New York Times*, July 20, 1930; and Alice Sparberg Alexiou, *The Flatiron: The New York Landmark and the Incomparable City That Arose with It* (New York: St. Martin's Press, 2010), 21.
23. Alexiou, *Flatiron*, 21.
24. Gene Coughlin, Heartbreaks of Society (column), *American Weekly*, n.d.
25. Brown, *Plaza*, 20.

26. "Frederick Sterry, Hotel Man, Dead," *New York Times*, July 12, 1933.

27. "Was President of Hotels Plaza and Savoy Plaza in N.Y.C., and National in Havana," *Hotel Monthly*, 1933.

28. "Won't Leave Plaza," *New-York Tribune*, June 13, 1905.

29. "Last Guests Leave the Plaza," *New-York Daily Tribune*, June 11, 1905; and "Four Guests Still Remain—Furniture Auction Begins," *New-York Daily Tribune*, June 13, 1905.

30. Andrew Alpern, *The Dakota: A History of the World's Best-Known Apartment Building* (Hudson, NY: Princeton Architectural Press, 2015), 23, 28.

31. *Architectural Record* 44 (July 1918): 93.

32. "A Conversation with Henry Janeway Hardenbergh," *Architectural Record* 19, no. 5 (May 1906).

33. "The Plaza of New York," *Hotel Monthly*, November 1907.

34. Stern, Gilmartin, and Massengale, *New York 1900*, 262.

35. "Another Fine Hotel Now on the City's List," *New York Times*, September 29, 1907; and "New Plaza Hotel," *Architecture*, November 15, 1907, 179.

36. Mary Doyle, *Life Was Like That* (Boston: Houghton Mifflin, 1936), 53.

37. "The Plaza Hotel Dining-Rooms," *American Architect and Building News*, October 26, 1907.

38. Brown, *Plaza*, 23–25.

39. *The Plaza*, a commemorative book published by Westin Hotels for its seventy-fifth anniversary (Secaucus, NJ: Poplar Books Inc., 1981).

40. "The Plaza of New York," *Hotel Monthly*, November 1907.

41. "New Plaza Hotel," *Architecture*, November 15, 1907.

42. Stephen Graham, *New York Nights* (New York: Doran, 1927), 224.

Chapter 3: A Greek Tragedy

1. "Arrest a Baron in the Plaza Lobby," *New York Times*, March 2, 1911.

2. "Hungarian 'Baron' Held for Larceny," *New-York Tribune*, March 2, 1911.

3. Ibid.

4. "Drops Theft Charge Against Von Arkovy," *New York Times*, March 4, 1911.

5. "New Accusers Face 'Baron' Von Arkovy," *New York Times*, March 3, 1911.

6. "Drops Theft Charge Against Von Arkovy," *New York Times*, March 4, 1911.

7. "Baron Ruined on Wall Street, Attempts to Die," *St. Louis Post-Dispatch*, August 16, 1908.

8. "Broker Kills Self Like Wife Did When Child Wedded Bogus Baron," *World*, July 25, 1913.

9. "His Wife an Heiress," *Washington Post*, March 3, 1911.

10. "Three Suicides in Arkovy Romance," *San Francisco Call*, August 25, 1913.

11. "Three Suicides Now in Arkovy Romance," *New York Times*, July 26, 1913.

12. "New Accusers Face 'Baron' Von Arkovy," *New York Times*, March 3, 1911.

13. "The Plaza Loses 'Baron' Von Arkovy," *New York Times*, March 5, 1911.

14. "Von Arkovy Has Departed," *New York Times*, March 15, 1911.

15. "Third Suicide in Wake of Girl's Elopement," *New-York Tribune*, July 26, 1913.

16. "Ill Luck at Tables," *Bismarck Daily Tribune*, August 18, 1911.

17. "'Baron' Arkovy a Suicide," *New York Sun*, April 19, 1913; "Gambling, Insomnia, and Morphia," *Manchester Guardian*, April 19, 1913.

18. *Town Topics* 69 (January–June 1913).

19. *Town Topics*, March 9, 1905.

20. Alice Sparberg Alexiou, *The Flatiron: The New York Landmark and the Incomparable City That Arose with It* (New York: St. Martin's Press, 2010), 178–83.

21. Lucius M. Beebe, *The Lucius Beebe Reader*, ed. Clarles Clegg and Duncan Emrich (New York: Doubleday, 1967), 119.

22. *Town Topics*, March 9, 1905.

23. *Town Topics* 57 (January–June 1907).

24. *Town Topics* 57, no. 6 (February 7, 1907).

25. "Songs of Winter," *Town Topics* 61, no. 7 (February 18, 1909).

26. "United States Realty: A Pioneer in Realty," *Wall Street Journal*, August 12, 1902.

27. "Waiters Don't Want to Take Your Tips," *New York Times*, October 31, 1911.

28. "Smiles Cost $1 Each," *Washington Post*, May 10, 1912.

29. "Waiters Strike Spreading Fast," *New York Times*, May 31, 1912.

30. "Waiters Quitting Hotel After Hotel," *New-York Tribune*, May 31, 1912.

31. Marcy S. Sacks, *Before Harlem: The Black Experience in New York City Before World War I* (Philadelphia: University of Pennsylvania Press, 2006), 108–9.

32. "Hotel Men Face Grave Situation," *New York Age*, October 19, 1911, 1; and "Colored Waiters Plan National Conference," *New York Age*, April 25, 1912.

33. "Waiters Quitting Hotel After Hotel," *New-York Tribune*, May 31, 1912.

34. "Waiters Strike Spreading Fast," *New York Times*, May 31, 1912.

35. "Negro Waiters in Best Hotels," *New York Age*, June 6, 1912, 1.

36. "Waiters Out in 17 More Places," *New York Times*, June 1, 1912.

37. "Negro Waiters in Best Hotels," *New York Age*, June 6, 1912, 1; and Sacks, *Before Harlem*, 128.

38. "Police Draw Guns on Rioting Waiters," *New-York Tribune*, June 2, 1912.

39. *State of New York Department of Labor Bulletin* 14, nos. 50–53 (1912): 275–77.

40. "Waiters Out in 17 More Places," *New York Times*, June 1, 1912.

41. "Police Draw Guns on Rioting Waiters," *New-York Tribune*, June 2, 1912.

42. "Won't Take Back Waiters Who Struck," *New York Times*, June 27, 1912.

43. "Colored Waiters to Give Up Positions," *New York Age*, June 13, 1912.

Chapter 4: The Wet Age

1. "Dogs Dyed to Match Milady's Gown Even If It's 'Yaller,'" *New-York Tribune*, October 24, 1914.
2. "Women Drivers in Endurance Auto Run," *Farmer*, January 11, 1909.
3. "Costly Wedding," *Courier-Journal*, January 30, 1910.
4. "Loss of Beauty Led to Suicide," *Nashville American*, June 13, 1909.
5. "Crushed: By Neglect of Her Son," *Cincinnati Enquirer*, April 23, 1908.
6. "Bought Secrecy for Ruiz Suicide," *New York Times*, June 12, 1909.
7. Erik Larson, *Dead Wake: The Last Crossing of the Lusitania* (New York: Penguin, 2015).
8. Diana Preston, *Lusitania: An Epic Tragedy* (New York: Bloomsbury, 2002).
9. Eve Brown, *The Plaza, 1907–1967: Its Life and Times* (New York: Meredith Press, 1967), 62.
10. Albert W. Fox, "Paid 'Peace' Millions," *Washington Post*, October 1, 1917.
11. "A Separate Peace with France was the Object of Bolo's Plotting," *New York Times*, October 5, 1917, 1; "Activities of Bolo Pasha as German Agent," *New York Times Current History*, November 1, 1917; "Bolo Letter Named Hearst as 'My Friend,'" *New-York Tribune*, July 31, 1918.
12. Brown, *Plaza*, 62.
13. "Oh, Dear! War Luncheon Is Frugal at $10 a Plate," *Brotherhood of Locomotive Firemen and Enginemen's Magazine*, January 15, 1917.
14. "War-Bread Menu for All Hotels Here," *New York Times*, July 11, 1917.
15. "Penalize Big Hotels for Sugar Hoarding," *New York Times*, August 4, 1918.
16. "Patrons Offer to Help," *New York Times*, November 11, 1918.
17. Brown, *Plaza*, 64.
18. Michael A. Lerner, *Dry Manhattan: Prohibition in New York City* (Cambridge, MA: Harvard University Press, 2008), 42.
19. "The Dry Fashion," *New York Times*, January 16, 1919, 12.
20. Frederick L. Allen, *Only Yesterday: An Informal History of the 1920s* (New York: Wiley, 1997), 213.
21. "In the Hotel Field: National Hotelmen's Exposition," *Bonfort's Circular*, June 15, 1917.
22. "Anti-Saloon League Inquiry Called For," *New York Times*, March 4, 1919.
23. "Hotel Men to Fight to Restore Liquor," *New York Times*, January 24, 1919.
24. Lerner, *Dry Manhattan*, 134.
25. "Near-Dry New York Amends Old Drinking Customs," *New York Times*, July 20, 1919.
26. "At Last Prohibition Clamps the Lid on Tight," *New-York Tribune*, November 2, 1919.

27. "When Hotels Mirrored New York's Life," *New York Times Magazine*, March 6, 1932.

28. "Near-Dry New York Amends Old Drinking Customs," *New York Times*, July 20, 1919.

29. "What Will New York Hotels Do Without Bars?" *New-York Tribune*, April 13, 1919.

30. "The Hotel Under Prohibition," *Saturday Evening Post*, October 14, 1922.

31. W. L. Hamilton, *Promoting New Hotels: When Does It Pay?* (New York: Harper & Brothers, 1930), 136.

32. "What Is Your Room Cost per Day?" *Hotel World*, February 5, 1921.

33. "Near-Dry New York Amends Old Drinking Customs," *New York Times*, July 20, 1919.

34. Lerner, *Dry Manhattan*, 45.

35. Stanley Walker, *The Night Club Era* (New York: Blue Ribbon Books, 1933), 61.

36. "Drought Closes Hotel," *New York Times*, January 25, 1920.

37. "Woolworth Heiress Robbed at the Plaza of $750,000 in Gems," *New York Times*, October 2, 1925.

38. "Donahue Gem Thief Is Sought in London," *New York Times*, November 12, 1925.

39. "'Flask Parties' Will Enhance Joy of New Year's Eve," *New-York Tribune*, December 27, 1919.

40. H. I. Brock, "New York's Cocktail Hour," *New Republic*, January 11, 1922.

41. "At Last Prohibition Clamps the Lid on Tight," *New-York Tribune*, November 2, 1919.

42. "Plaza Waiter Arrested," *New York Times*, June 1, 1921.

43. "33 Got Christmas Rum," *New York Times*, April 8, 1921.

44. "Along Fifth Avenue," *Hartford Courant*, November 11, 1923.

45. Brown, *Plaza*, 66–67.

46. "New York Society," *Chicago Daily Tribune*, January 29, 1928.

47. F. Scott Fitzgerald, "My Lost City," in *Fitzgerald: My Lost City; Personal Essays, 1920–1940*, ed. James L. W. West III (Cambridge: Cambridge University Press, 2005).

48. Arthur Mizener, *The Far Side of Paradise: A Biography of F. Scott Fitzgerald* (New York: Vintage, 1959).

49. Ibid.

50. Edmund Wilson, "The Delegate from Great Neck," in *The Shores of Light: A Literary Chronicle of the 20s and 30s* (New York: Farrar, Straus and Young, Inc. Publishers, 1952).

51. Curtis Gathje, *At the Plaza: An Illustrated History of the World's Most Famous Hotel* (New York: St. Martin's Press, 2000), 59.

52. Allen, *Only Yesterday*, 97.
53. "Stockingless Fad Not for The Plaza," *Women's Wear*, July 17, 1919.
54. "'Shimmy' and Its Allies in Discard as Oldtime Dance Steps Return," *New-York Tribune*, June 13, 1920.
55. Fitzgerald, "My Lost City," 112.

Chapter 5: The Big Landlord

1. "Arrest Black Again; To Press Liquor Charge," *New-York Tribune*, March 21, 1921.
2. "Jury Samples Liquor; Acquits Harry Black," *New York Herald*, March 25, 1921.
3. "Drank His Liquor, Jury Then Found Black Not Guilty," *Evening World*, March 25, 1921; and "What the Jury Swallowed," *Evening World*, March 26, 1921.
4. "U.S. Realty & Improvement Had a Prosperous Year," *Wall Street Journal*, May 26, 1921.
5. Donald L. Miller, *Supreme City: How Jazz Age Manhattan Gave Birth to Modern America* (New York: Simon & Schuster, 2014), 232.
6. "Modification of Zoning Ordinance: The Plaza Hotel," *American Architect*, December 1, 1920.
7. "Hotel Plaza Addition, New York," *Architecture and Building*, February 1922.
8. *Town Topics* 86, no. 14 (October 6, 1921).
9. "The Big Landlord," *Wall Street Journal*, June 11, 1926.
10. Hand-Book of Securities, compiled by the *Commercial and Financial Chronicle* (New York: W. B. Dana Co., 1907–1928).
11. "City Realty Value Jumps One Billion to $11,275,526,200," *New York Times*, October 2, 1923; and "U.S. Realty Earnings Show Improvement," *Wall Street Journal*, December 30, 1925.
12. "Harry Black, Genial Individualist," *Wall Street Journal*, July 23, 1930.
13. "Black Retains Domination of U.S. Realty Co.," *New York Herald*, November 26, 1924.
14. Paul Starrett, *Changing the Skyline: An Autobiography* (New York: McGraw-Hill, 1938), 69.
15. "Urges Legislation to Prevent Changing Names," *Jewish Advocate*, March 21, 1929.
16. Miller, *Supreme City*, 184.
17. Tom Shachtman, *Skyscraper Dreams: The Great Real Estate Dynasties of New York* (AuthorHouse, 2000), 111.
18. "Urges Legislation to Prevent Changing Names," *Jewish Advocate*, March 21, 1929.
19. *Town Topics*, March 23, 1922.
20. Frederick L. Allen, *Only Yesterday: An Informal History of the 1920s* (New York: Wiley, 1997), 144.
21. Ibid., 141–42.

22. Ibid., 273.

23. Starrett, *Changing the Skyline*, 115–16.

24. "The Big Landlord," *Wall Street Journal*, June 11, 1926.

25. Ibid.

26. David J. Jacobson, "What's Ahead for the Hotel Industry?" *Harvard Business Review* 24, no. 3 (1946): 339–55.

27. "Trade Upturn Seen by Hotel Leader," *New York Times*, March 21, 1931.

28. William S. Beinecke, *Bernhard Beneicke: A Memoir* (New York: Prospect Hill Press, 2005), 35.

29. John Kenneth Galbraith, *The Great Crash, 1929* (Boston: Mariner Books, 2009), 150.

30. "City Bank Men on Board of Realty & Improvement," *New York Herald Tribune*, May 16, 1928.

31. "Plan New Method of Realty Finance," *New York Times*, March 3, 1929.

32. "1929 Investment Styles," *New York Herald Tribune*, March 14, 1929.

33. "$1,253,702,357 Rise in Taxable Realty on City's 1930 Rolls," *New York Times*, October 2, 1929.

34. "U.S. Realty Cash Ample for Needs," *Wall Street Journal*, August 16, 1929.

35. Galbraith, *Great Crash, 1929*, 92.

36. Eve Brown, *The Plaza, 1907–1967: Its Life and Times* (New York: Meredith Press, 1967).

37. Galbraith, *Great Crash, 1929*, 95.

38. "Financial Markets," *New York Times*, October 19, 1929.

39. Starrett, *Changing the Skyline*, 262.

40. "H.S. Black, Stricken in Bathtub, Better," *New York Times*, October 20, 1929.

41. "Tub Victim Saved After Nine Hours," *Washington Post*, October 20, 1929.

42. Brown, *Plaza*, 71.

43. "H.S. Black Kills Self; Real Estate Magnate," *Washington Post*, July 20, 1930.

44. "H.S. Black Ends Life by Bullet in Home; No Motive Revealed," *New York Times*, July 20, 1930.

45. "Harry Black Will Disposes of $5,240,511," *New York Herald*, July 8, 1931.

46. "H.S. Black's Estate Down to $5,240,511," *New York Times*, July 8, 1931.

47. "$4,182,690 Loss Taken By H.S. Black Estate," *New York Times*, March 9, 1935.

48. Galbraith, *Great Crash, 1929*, 129.

Chapter 6: The Thirty-Nine Widows of the Plaza

1. Lucius Beebe, "This New York," *New York Herald Tribune*, April 8, 1939.

2. "Sunday Inspiration," *Washington Post*, May 19, 1917, citing the *St. Paul Pioneer Press*.

3. "Cocktails from Nursing Bottles at 'Baby Party,'" *St. Louis Post-Dispatch*, December 30, 1916; "Sunday Inspiration," *Washington Post*, May 19, 1917, citing the *St. Paul Pioneer Press*; and John Ayto, *Movers and Shakers: A Chronology of Words That Shaped Our Age* (Oxford: Oxford University Press, 1999), 61.

4. "Her Own and Hotel's Jubilee," *New York Herald Tribune*, March 10, 1957.

5. "Bells in Honor of Bride's Name," *St. Louis Post-Dispatch*, December 31, 1905.

6. "Walsh Arrested, Freed by Mayor," *St. Louis Post-Dispatch*, October 1, 1906.

7. "Society," *Detroit Free Press*, October 14, 1906.

8. "St. Louis Society's Rival Stars," *St. Louis Post-Dispatch*, November 5, 1911.

9. *Town Topics* 90, no. 17 (October 25, 1923).

10. "Obituary," *Railroad Age*, April 13, 1929; and *Town Topics* 90, no. 17 (October 25, 1923).

11. "This New York," *Atlanta Constitution*, August 25, 1940.

12. "Plaza to Fete 50-Year Tenant," *New York Times*, March 10, 1957.

13. "'Broadway' Ed Sullivan," *Washington Post*, November 28, 1935.

14. "This New York," *Atlanta Constitution*, August 4, 1940.

15. "New York Day by Day," *Austin Statesman*, Dec. 31, 1935; and "Report to the City Judge," *Austin Statesman*, February 22, 1931.

16. "On Radio," *New York Times*, March 21, 1957.

17. *New York Herald Tribune*, February 15, 1937, 6.

18. Sam Irvin, *Kay Thompson: From Funny Face to Eloise* (New York: Simon & Schuster, 2010), 190; "Dining Out," *Post Standard* (Syracuse, New York), July 18, 1949; Marie Brenner quoting Hilary Knight, *Vanity Fair*, December 1996.

19. "Hungarian Princess Travels with Menagerie of Wild Pets," *Detroit Free Press*, June 21, 1908.

20. Marquise de Fontenoy [pseudonym for Frederick Philip Lewis Cunliffe-Owen], "Artist Princess and Her Chasseur," *Washington Post*, March 18, 1909.

21. "A Protégé of Royalty," *New York Times*, July 12, 1896.

22. "It Just Looked as If Gwendolyn Had Laid an Egg," *Daily Boston Globe*, January 6, 1937; "Gives Lion to Princess," *New-York Tribune*, April 18, 1911.

23. "Princess Bars Out American Duchess," *New York Times*, April 26, 1910.

24. Ibid.

25. "Inability to Spend Million a Year Annoys Princess," *Los Angeles Times*, July 20, 1910.

26. Eve Brown, *The Plaza, 1907–1967: Its Life and Times* (New York: Meredith Press, 1967), 100; "Two Views on the $1,000 Wardrobe of Mrs. Wilson," *Washington Post*, February 26, 1913.

27. "Indict W.S. Bennet on Princess's Notes," *New York Times*, July 12, 1917.

28. "Parlaghy Horses Get a Reprieve," *New-York Tribune*, December 17, 1914.

29. "Care Free, Princess Entertains 'At Home,'" *New-York Tribune*, March 2, 1916.

30. "Princess So Ill Sheriff Orders His Picket Away," *New-York Tribune*, August 29, 1923, 7; and "Royal Honors Mark Burial of Needy Princess," *New-York Tribune*, September 2, 1923, 10.

31. "It Happened Last Night," *Newsday*, June 10, 1954.

32. Brown, *Plaza*, 155–56.

33. "Wright Revisited," *New Yorker*, June 16, 1956.

34. From Salomone's unpublished memoir. From the story titled "Plaza Sweets," in the chapter titled "Permanent Guests."

35. "Ladies' Quips Enliven Plaza's Golden Party," *New York Herald Tribune*, March 11, 1957.

36. Ira Henry Freeman, "Plaza to Fete 50-Year Tenant," *New York Times*, March 10, 1957.

37. "Mrs. Clara Bell Walsh Dies; Lived 50 Years at the Plaza," *New York Herald Tribune*, August 14, 1957.

38. "Beinecke Dies; Headed Board of Plaza Hotel: Official, 86, Helped to Found Hammond Chain, Which Included Copley-Plaza Hotel Chairman," *New York Herald Tribune*, December 21, 1932.

39. "Mrs. EA Strong Leaps to Death at Plaza Hotel," *New York Herald Tribune*, April 12, 1940.

40. "Removal of Pulitzer Fountain Considered; So Broken, It Is Held to Mar Plaza Square," *New York Times*, August 22, 1928.

41. Roy Rosenzweig and Elizabeth Blackmar, *The Park and the People: A History of Central Park* (Ithaca, NY: Cornell University Press, 1992), 439–42.

42. David J. Jacobson, "What's Ahead for the Hotel Industry?" *Harvard Business Review* 24, no. 3 (1946): 339–55.

43. Ibid.

44. Ibid.

45. United States Realty and Improvement Company consolidated company annual reports, 1911–13, 1915, and 1919–42.

46. Thomas Ewing Dabney, *The Man Who Bought the Waldorf: The Life of Conrad N. Hilton* (New York: Duell, Sloan, and Pearce, 1950).

47. Ibid., 171.

48. "A More Perfect Union," Robert Kuttner, *American Prospect*, November 28, 2011, http://prospect.org/article/more-perfect-union-1.

49. "Hotel Men Ratify Union Agreement," *New York Times*, December 28, 1938.

50. U.S. Bureau of Labor Statistics, *Handbook of Labor Statistics*, 1947 ed.; Bulletin No. 916, p. 89.

51. PBS.org, http://www.pbs.org/blackpress/news_bios/afroamerican.html; and "Urban League Forces Opening in Hotel Union," *Afro-American,* April 15, 1939.

52. John H. Thompson, "How Is the Race Faring in Union Organizations Which Have Spread Throughout Industrial Plants?" *Chicago Defender,* September 30, 1939, 13.

53. "Organize New Hotel League," *New York Amsterdam News,* July 22, 1939, 5.

54. "New York Like Atlanta; Opens Back Doors, Freight Elevators to Insult Patrons," *Afro-American,* July 29, 1933.

55. Ralph Matthews, "Looking at the Stars with Ralph Matthews," *Afro-American,* March 26, 1932.

56. "Glorified by Ziegfeld," *New Journal and Guide,* July 25, 1931.

57. *New York Herald Tribune,* September 6, 1929, 14.

58. "Prescription for Love," *New York Amsterdam News,* February 19, 1938.

59. Brown, *Plaza,* 76; and "Hotel Plaza Plans New Cocktail Room," *New York Times,* January 31, 1934.

60. Brown, *Plaza,* 79.

61. "At the Persian Room Opening—Fur Capes and Silver Lamé Gowns," *Women's Wear Daily,* September 26, 1935.

62. "New Year's Eve Dance to Aid Crippled Children," *New York Herald Tribune,* December 14, 1936.

63. "Women Get $174,297 for Needy Families," *New York Times,* March 11, 1932.

64. "U.S. Realty Reports Net Loss of $535,633 for Year to December 31," *Wall Street Journal,* January 16, 1937.

65. "Dry Law Called Hotel Bane," *New York Herald Tribune,* April 24, 1932.

66. "Beineckes Take Black Home," *New York Herald Tribune,* October 28, 1930; and "R.G. Babbage Resigns as U.S. Realty Head; Beinecke Succeeds Him," *Wall Street Journal,* June 18, 1936.

67. Stock prices from *New York Times,* June 18, 1936; and from *New York Times,* July 18, 1939.

68. "Purely Gossip," *Wall Street Journal,* November 5, 1943.

69. "U.S. Realty President," *New York Herald Tribune,* October 20, 1942.

70. "U.S. Realty Moves in Reorganization," *New York Times,* February 2, 1944.

Chapter 7: Wartime

1. Lucius M. Beebe, "The Plaza: 1947," in *The Lucius Beebe Reader,* ed. Charles Clegg and Duncan Emrich (New York: Doubleday, 1967), 123.

2. Thomas Ewing Dabney, *The Man Who Bought the Waldorf: The Life of Conrad N. Hilton* (New York: Duell, Sloan, and Pearce, 1950), 170.

3. Mason B. Williams, *City of Ambition: FDR, La Guardia, and the Making of Modern New York* (New York: W. W. Norton, 2013), 308, 327.

4. David J. Jacobson, "What's Ahead for the Hotel Industry?" *Harvard Business Review* 24, no. 3 (1946): 346.

5. Dabney, *Man Who Bought the Waldorf,* 173.

6. "Conservation in Hotels—A War Necessity," *Hotel Monthly,* July 1942.

7. "Cooking and Baking WITHOUT Sugar," *Hotel Monthly,* June 1942.

8. "Diners-Out Relish Meat of Buffalo," *New York Times,* February 3, 1945.

9. "Meatless Tuesday Goes Well in City," *New York Times,* October 21, 1942.

10. "News of Food," *New York Times,* November 12, 1942.

11. "Former Bellboy at Plaza Hotel Is Now Orderly to Eisenhower," *New York Herald Tribune,* January 12, 1943; and *Mini-Maxims,* March 1944.

12. *Hiltonitems,* April 1948.

13. "Personnel Problems," *Hotel Monthly,* April 1942.

14. "Girl Service Captains Replace Bell Boys," *Hotel Monthly,* January 1943.

15. *Hiltonitems,* July 1947.

16. "The Effect of the War on Employee-Employer," *Hotel Monthly,* June 1944.

17. "Negro Women for Hotel Work," *Hotel Monthly,* February 1943.

18. Dabney, *Man Who Bought the Waldorf,* 12.

19. Ibid., 92.

20. Ibid., 110.

21. Ibid., 116.

22. Ibid., 117.

23. Ibid., 150.

24. Conrad N. Hilton, *Be My Guest* (New York: Simon & Schuster, 1957), 195.

25. M. V. Casey, "Californian Buys Control of Roosevelt," *New York Herald Tribune,* June 6, 1943.

26. Ibid., 194.

27. Hilton, *Be My Guest,* 194–95.

28. Ibid., 197.

29. "$60,000,000 Hilton Hotel Concern Formed as Four Companies Merge," *New York Times,* June 7, 1946.

30. Dabney, *Man Who Bought the Waldorf,* 253.

31. Hilton, *Be My Guest,* 199.

32. Eve Brown, *The Plaza, 1907–1967: Its Life and Times* (New York: Meredith Press, 1967), 188.

33. "The Beautiful and the Damned," *New Yorker,* January 20, 1945.

34. Brown, *Plaza,* 188.

35. *Hiltonitems,* June 1948.

36. "Plaza Shop Finds Personalized Selling Wanted by Hotel Guests," *Women's Wear Daily*, May 17, 1945.

37. "Hotels in Action," *Wall Street Journal*, August 12, 1948.

38. "Supervisory Training Custom Made at Hotel Plaza," *Hotel Gazette*, July 3, 1948.

39. "Cecil Beaton Explores Plaza's Sub-Basement to Re-Decorate His Own Suite in the Hotel," *New York Herald Tribune*, May 14, 1946; and "The Special World of Cecil Beaton," *Good Housekeeping*, January 1958.

40. "The Beautiful and the Damned," *New Yorker*, January 20, 1945.

41. J. Randy Taraborrelli, *The Hiltons: The True Story of an American Dynasty* (New York: Grand Central, 2014).

42. Hilton, *Be My Guest*, 197–200.

43. "Trends in the Hotel Business, 1943," *Hotel Monthly*, November 1944.

44. "June Hotel Occupancy Highest Ever," *Hotel Monthly*, July 1945.

45. Brown, *Plaza*, 82.

46. Hildegarde, *Over 50—So What!* (New York: Doubleday, 1963), 73.

47. Brown, *Plaza*, 84.

48. Gabor claimed always to be winner, but she was runner-up, according to this article by George Frazier in *Cosmopolitan*, September 1950, 34–39, 124–25.

49. Hilton, *Be My Guest*.

50. Ibid., 191–92.

51. George Frazier, in *Cosmopolitan*, September 1950, 34–39, 124–25.

52. *Mini-Maxims*, November 1945.

53. "The Latest Fugitive from Sherlock Holmes," *New York Herald Tribune*, October 12, 1947.

54. "What Goes On? Hammer and Sickle Fly over Capitalistic Plaza," *Atlanta Constitution*, March 22, 1946.

55. "A Toast to the Plaza," *New York Herald Tribune*, October 3, 1947.

56. "Plaza Marks 40th Year at Brilliant Fete of 4 Decades," *New York Herald Tribune*, October 3, 1947.

57. "Plaza Observes 40 Sedate Years," *New York Times*, October 4, 1947.

Chapter 8: The Real Eloise

1. Cynthia Lindsay, "Kay Thompson," *McCall's*, January 1957.

2. *New Yorker*, May 12, 1956, 34.

3. Marie Brenner, "Kay and Eloise," *Vanity Fair*, December 1996.

4. Cynthia Lindsay, "Kay Thompson," *McCall's,* January 1957.

5. Bill Smith, "Persian Room, Plaza Hotel, New York" *Billboard*, September 28, 1951.

6. *Harper's Bazaar*, September 1952.

7. Sam Irvin, *Kay Thompson: From Funny Face to Eloise* (New York: Simon & Schuster, 2010), 182.
8. Cecil Smith, "Kay Thompson Sounds Like 'Eloise,'" *Los Angeles Times*, June 3, 1956.
9. "Authors & Editors," *Publishers Weekly*, May 12, 1969.
10. Marie Brenner, "Kay and Eloise," *Vanity Fair*, December 1996.
11. Cecil Smith, "Kay Thompson Sounds Like 'Eloise,'" *Los Angeles Times*, June 3, 1956.
12. Irvin, *Kay Thompson*, 20.
13. Cynthia Lindsay, "Kay Thompson," *McCall's*, January 1957; and Cecil Smith, "Kay Thompson Sounds Like 'Eloise,'" *Los Angeles Times*, June 3, 1956.
14. From the 2015 HBO documentary *It's Me: The Man Who Drew Eloise*.
15. Sarah Larson, "The Girl with the Eloise Tattoo," *New Yorker*, March 23, 2015.
16. Cynthia Lindsay, "Kay Thompson," *McCall's*, January 1957.
17. Irvin, *Kay Thompson*, 207.
18. Cynthia Lindsay, "Kay Thompson," *McCall's*, January 1957.
19. Kay Thompson, *Kay Thompson's Eloise: A Book for Precocious Grown Ups* (New York: Simon & Schuster, 1955).
20. Irvin, *Kay Thompson*, 207.
21. Sarah Larson, "The Girl with the Eloise Tattoo," *New Yorker*, March 23, 2015.
22. *Life*, December 12, 1955, 149.
23. Irvin, *Kay Thompson*, 211.
24. Charles Mercer, "'Eloise' Will Come to Life on Playhouse 90," *Oakland Tribune*, November 11, 1956.
25. Irvin, *Kay Thompson*, 212.
26. Ibid., 213.
27. *New Yorker*, May 12, 1956, 34.
28. *Publishers Weekly*, May 12, 1969.
29. *Hiltonitems*, December 1955.
30. *New Yorker*, May 12, 1956, 34.
31. Eugenia Sheppard, "Boom Time for Tricycles," *New York Herald Tribune*, April 9, 1956, 12.
32. Curtis Gathje, *At The Plaza: An Illustrated History of the World's Most Famous Hotel* (New York: St. Martin's Press, 2000).
33. Irvin, *Kay Thompson*, 213.
34. Rex Reed, *People Are Crazy Here* (New York: Delacorte Press, 1974).
35. Irvin, *Kay Thompson*, 215.
36. Marie Brenner, "Kay and Eloise," *Vanity Fair*, December 1996.
37. "Novel Kit," *Women's Wear Daily*, October 2, 1957; Irvin, *Kay Thompson*, 267; and "Eloise Keeps Kay Thompson on the Go," Associated Press, October 20, 1958.

38. "After Work a Time for Reading," *New York Times*, November 29, 1959.
39. Marie Brenner, "Kay and Eloise," *Vanity Fair*, December 1996.
40. "Eloise Keeps Kay Thompson on the Go," Associated Press, October 20, 1958.
41. Marie Brenner, "Kay and Eloise," *Vanity Fair*, December 1996.
42. *Pocono Record*, December 12, 1972, 9.
43. Endnotes for Irvin, *Kay Thompson*, http://www.kaythompsonwebsite.com/index_htm_files/ENDNOTES_1_2018.pdf.
44. Eric Foner, *Give Me Liberty! An American History*, vol. 2, *From 1865*, 4th ed. (New York: W. W. Norton, 2014), 933–34.
45. Craig Claiborne, "Elegance of Cuisine Is on Wane in U.S.," *New York Times*, April 13, 1959, 1.
46. "Liquid Pancakes, Plaza Waiter Controls the Formula," *Hiltonitems*, July 1950, 7.
47. According to Eve Brown.
48. Anna Boiardi, *Delicious Memories: Recipes and Stories from the Chef Boyardee Family* (New York: Stewart, Tabori and Chang, 2011), 10.
49. Eve Brown.

Chapter 9: Party of the Century

1. Phone call with Lourdes Salomone in October 2016.
2. Tom Wolfe, "Beatles Conquer New York," *Boston Globe*, February 8, 1964.
3. "With Rag-Mop Hairdos, Guitars Beatles Conquer New York," *Boston Globe*, February 8, 1964, 1.
4. "The Beatles Invade, Complete with Long Hair and Screaming Fans," *New York Times*, February 8, 1964, 25.
5. Ibid.
6. Gertrude Wilson [pseud.], "Laugh Clowns, Laugh!" *New York Amsterdam News*, February 22, 1964, 11.
7. Phone call with Lourdes Salomone in October 2016.
8. Louise Davis, "Adventures of the Happy Innkeeper," *Tennessean*, February 11, 1968.
9. Interview with Gregg Salomone at his home in Chicago in September 2016.
10. Louise Davis, "Adventures of the Happy Innkeeper," *Tennessean*, February 11, 1968.
11. Ibid.
12. Lucius Beebe, "Swank Trend in Offices Bolstered by Newcomer," *Washington Post*, December 10, 1944.
13. "New York's Plaza Hotel Sold to Boston's A.M. Sonnabend," *Daily Boston Globe*, October 15, 1953.

14. "A.M. Sonnabend Is Dead at 67; Boston Industrialist-Financier," *New York Times*, February 12, 1964, 33.

15. "Sonnabend Puts Tax Laws to Work," *Chicago Daily Tribune*, November 23, 1958, A9.

16. "The Grand Hotel: Aging but Still Elegant," *Wall Street Journal*, August 23, 1965.

17. " 'Happy Accumulator' Eying Deals," *New York Herald Tribune*, March 22, 1959, A5.

18. "Rising Costs Spur Hotels' Automation," *New York Times*, January 31, 1960, F1.

19. Franklin Whitehouse, "Hotel Business Improving Here," *New York Times*, February 12, 1967.

20. "Hilton Hotels Sells Roosevelt, Mayflower to Hotel Corp.," *Wall Street Journal*, March 1, 1956, 6.

21. Materials from the Hospitality Industry Archives from the Conrad N. Hilton College of Hotel & Restaurant Management at the University of Houston.

22. "Wet Protest Staged at Savoy Plaza," *New York Times*, October 3, 1964, 31.

23. "Women Score G.M. on Building Plan," *New York Times*, January 20, 1965, 41.

24. "Hotel Corp. Sees '64 Net More Than Doubling," *Wall Street Journal*, May 14, 1965; and "Helmsley May Buy Plaza Hotel," *New York Times*, March 1, 1973, 57.

25. "Year of the Air Conditioning," *New York Times*, July 8, 1956, 86.

26. "Plaza Pressing Expansion Drive," *New York Times*, November 17, 1964.

27. Ibid.

28. "The Grand Hotel," *Wall Street Journal*, August 23, 1965, 1.

29. Amy Fine Collins, "A Night to Remember," *Vanity Fair*, July 1996.

30. "Capote Is Cold Blooded to the Uninvited Masses," *Washington Post, Times Herald*, November 25, 1966, C1.

31. Deborah Davis, *Party of the Century: The Fabulous Story of Truman Capote and His Black and White Ball* (Hoboken, NJ: Wiley, 2006), 154.

32. Helen Markel, "The Special World of Cecil Beaton," *Good Housekeeping*, January 1958.

33. Marie Brenner, "Kay and Eloise," *Vanity Fair*, December 1996.

34. "Capote Bids to Spur Grim Social Routine," *Los Angeles Times*, October 21, 1966, C12.

35. Davis, *Party of the Century*, 176; and "Capote Is Cold Blooded to the Uninvited Masses," *Washington Post, Times Herald*, November 25, 1966.

36. "A Man of Letters Throws an A-OK Champagne Party," *Los Angeles Times*, November 30, 1966, D1.

37. Marie Brenner, "Kay and Eloise," *Vanity Fair*, December 1996.

38. Curtis Gathje, *At The Plaza: An Illustrated History of the World's Most Famous Hotel* (New York: St. Martin's Press, 2000), 133.

39. Davis, *Party of the Century*, 157.

40. Ibid., 226–27.

41. Marie Brenner, "Kay and Eloise," *Vanity Fair*, December 1996.

42. Judith A. Hennessee, *Betty Friedan: Her Life* (New York: Random House, 1999), 121–22.

43. Ibid.

Chapter 10: Prostitutes' Promenade

1. "Suspect Seized in Plaza Bomb Threat," *New York Times*, September 8, 1973, 35; and "Hotel President Pays Extortion; Man Nabbed," *Hartford Courant*, September 8, 1973.

2. "Cartman Talks Go On Uncertainly as Trash Piles Continue to Mount," *New York Times*, December 6, 1978, B4.

3. "Graft Paid to Police Here Said to Run into Millions," *New York Times*, April 25, 1970, 1.

4. "Entrance to the Plaza Hotel Is the Scene of Assassination Attempt," *New York Times*, April 25, 1970, 1.

5. "5 Thugs at Plaza Get $45,000 Gems," *New York Times*, August 1, 1972, 1.

6. "Intruder Slashes State Man at New York Hotel," *Hartford Courant*, May 27, 1974.

7. "4 Robbed in Chauffeured Limousine; 2 Gunmen Get $265,000 in Jewelry," *New York Times*, May 14, 1973, 39.

8. "German Politician Robbed of $235 in New York City," *Hartford Courant*, March 16, 1971, 35.

9. "Vendors Jam 5th Ave. on Summer Sundays," *New York Times*, July 27, 1979, B1.

10. "The Plaza's President Is Confident," *Sun*, February 9, 1973, B6.

11. Interview conducted with Stephanie Sonnabend at her home in Massachusetts, December 2016.

12. "Hotel Corp. Has a Mod President," *Boston Sunday Globe*, April 13, 1969, 106.

13. Interview with George Abrams at his office in Boston, December 2016.

14. *Lodging Hospitality*, November 1975.

15. "Persian Room Era at Definitive End," *Variety*, May 10, 1978.

16. Margaret Cousins, "Affair at the Plaza," *Good Housekeeping*, August 1956.

17. "An Edwardian Splendor or Green Tulip Modern?" *New York Times*, November 5, 1971.

18. "If It's Good, Leave It Alone," *New York Times*, October 31, 1971, D22.

19. "An Edwardian Splendor or Green Tulip Modern?" *New York Times*, November 5, 1971, 45.

20. "We Are Not 'Raping' the Plaza," *New York Times*, November 21, 1971, D27.

21. "Many Restaurants in the City Report Gains," *New York Times*, January 14, 1972, 1.

22. Roger came up with this advertising campaign with Paul Sonnabend, Roger's younger brother.

23. "Advertising: A Mood of Caution," *New York Times*, September 20, 1962.

24. Interview conducted with Gary Lavenson at his home near Boston, December 2016.

25. Interview conducted with Peter Sonnabend at the Boston Harbor Hotel, December 2016.

26. James Lavenson, "Think Strawberries," speech delivered before the American Medical Association, New York, New York, February 7, 1974.

27. According to Stephanie and Peter Sonnabend.

28. "HCA Head Sees Business Role in US Urban Crisis," *Jewish Advocate*, June 27, 1968, 10.

29. "Harlem's New Look in Building," *New York Amsterdam News*, May 18, 1968, 1.

30. "Harlem to Get 230-Room Hotel Constructed with Local Funds," *New York Times*, May 10, 1968, 1.

31. "The Jaundiced Eye," *New York Amsterdam News*, June 17, 1972, D1.

32. "New York City Is Pressing Real-Estate Concern for Upkeep Accord," *New York Times*, September 4, 1976, 18; and "4 Groups Are Key Landlords for Midtown Sex Industry," *New York Times*, July 10, 1977, A1.

33. "Alex DiLorenzo Jr. Dies; Leader in Real Estate, 58," *New York Times*, September 6, 1975, 22.

34. "The Goldman-DiLorenzo Empire and the Toss of a Coin," *New York Times*, June 3, 1979.

35. "Hilton Reports Gains," *Chicago Tribune*, August 27, 1965.

36. Sonesta's ownership of the Plaza was further complicated by a sale leaseback arrangement with the investor Lawrence Wein, which lasted from 1958 until 1972. For more on this, please read "Hotel Corp. Will Sell Hotel Plaza, New York, Under Leaseback Plan," *Wall Street Journal*, November 21, 1958; and "New York's Hotel Plaza Is Acquired by Sonesta," *Wall Street Journal*, July 6, 1972.

37. "2 New York Realty Men Seek Control of Sonesta," *Boston Globe*, May 10, 1973; "Sonesta Sought by Wellington Associates, but Such a Take-Over May Prove Difficult," *Wall Street Journal*, May 10, 1973; "Sonesta International Files Suit to Block Tender Offer from Wellington Associates," *Wall Street Journal*, May 15, 1973; "Sonesta Won't Sell the Plaza, New York, to Wellington Group," *Wall Street Journal*, May 3, 1974.

38. "Sonesta's Plaza Hotel Is Sought by Partners in New York Concern," *Wall Street Journal*, April 2, 1974.

39. "The Plaza Deal," *Seattle Times*, July 16, 1978.

40. "Aging Belasco Preens for a New Theatrical Life," *New York Times*, January 27, 1975; and "Plaza Buys Murals by Everett Shinn from Old Owners," *New York Times*, May 18, 1976.

41. "The Plaza: 'That Great Old Lady of New York City Hostelries,'" *Washington Post*, June 15, 1975, 171.

42. Carol Oppenheim, "12 rms, prk vws: For $150,000 You Can Cuddle Up in the Plaza," *Chicago Tribune*, February 16, 1977.

43. Westin Hotels earnings statements, from the Westin Hotels and Resorts archive at the Washington State University Libraries, Manuscripts, Archives, and Special Collections, Pullman, WA.

44. *New Yorker*, February 27, 1965.

Chapter 11: Trump's Mona Lisa

1. Ward Morehouse III, *Inside the Plaza: An Intimate Portrait of the Ultimate Hotel* (New York: Applause, 2001), 83–91.

2. Ibid.

3. William H. Meyers, "Stalking the Plaza," *New York Times*, September 25, 1988.

4. *New York*, September 12, 1988, 27.

5. Robert Kearns, "Allegis Selling Westin for $1.5 Billion: United Airlines' Parent Nears Goal in Restructuring," *Chicago Tribune*, October 28, 1987; Martha M. Hamilton, "Pilots and Investors Ended Allegis Dream," *Washington Post*, June 11, 1987.

6. William H. Meyers, "Stalking the Plaza," *New York Times*, September 25, 1988.

7. Ibid.

8. Lisa W. Foderaro, "Plaza Hotel May Be Sold for Co-Ops," *New York Times*, February 27, 1988.

9. During a speech at the 2016 Republican National Convention, Barrack told the crowd that Trump "played me like a Steinway piano." He said that the more experienced Trump agreed to the Plaza's high price tag so long as Barrack revealed where the hotel's problems were, and how Trump might fix them. "I will pay your boss the price that he wants and I'll close it in one week on one condition: You, Tom Barrack, tell me everything I should know that I don't know," Barrack recounted of that long-ago conversation. It was the moment, Barrack said, that the two men became close.

10. William H. Meyers, "Stalking the Plaza," *New York Times*, September 25, 1988.

11. R. L. Stern and T. Pouschine, "Can Donald Pay His Hotel Bill?" *Forbes*, July 8, 1991.

12. Wayne Barrett, *Trump: The Greatest Show on Earth; the Deals, the Downfall, the Reinvention* (New York: Simon & Schuster, 2016), 148.

13. Ivana Trump, *Raising Trump* (New York: Simon & Schuster, 2017).

14. Harry Hurt, *The Lost Tycoon: The Many Lives of Donald J. Trump* (New York: W. W. Norton, 1993), 102.

15. Charles V. Bagli, "A Trump Empire Built on Inside Connections and $885 Million in Tax Breaks," *New York Times*, September 17, 2016.

16. Barrett, *Trump*, 140.

17. "Plaza Hotel Sold to Donald Trump for $390 Million," *New York Times*, March 27, 1988.

18. Marie Brenner, "After the Gold Rush," *Vanity Fair*, September 1990.

19. Barrett, *Trump*, 418, 427.

20. Ibid., 429.

21. *Newsday*, March 30, 1988, A8.

22. Marion M. White, "Ivana Trump: Hard Work, Discipline and Self-Reliance," *St. Petersburg Times*, September 26, 1988, 2D.

23. Trump, *Raising Trump*.

24. Marie Brenner, "After the Gold Rush," *Vanity Fair*, September 1990.

25. Trump, *Raising Trump*.

26. Barrett, *Trump*, 5.

27. Marie Brenner, "After the Gold Rush," *Vanity Fair*, September 1990.

28. Michael Kranish and Marc Fisher, *Trump Revealed: The Definitive Biography of the 45th President* (New York: Scribner, 2017), 137.

29. Morehouse, *Inside the Plaza*.

30. "Ivana Trump; She's Putting the Plaza Back on New York's Map," *Ottawa Citizen*, December 8, 1988, D10.

31. Hurt, *Lost Tycoon*, 23.

32. Morehouse, *Inside the Plaza*, 83–91.

33. James A. Revson, "Social Studies: Donald and Ivana Glitz the Plaza," *Newsday*, September 21, 1989, 2.

34. "The Trump Era Begins in the Palm Court," *Newsday*, July 20, 1988, D1.

35. Carol Vogel, "The Plaza Suite: Design," *New York Times*, January 15, 1989.

36. "The Plaza Off Screen: A Real-Life Adventure," *New York Times*, December 4, 1992.

37. "Rourke Rivals Depp," *Cincinnati Post*, November 5, 1994, 12A.

38. Michael Gross, "Inside Donald Trump's One-Stop Parties: Attendees Recall Cocaine and Very Young Models," *Daily Beast*, October 24, 2016.

39. Barrett, *Trump*, 5.

40. Hurt, *Lost Tycoon*, 198–99.

41. Ibid., 196.

42. Ibid., 255–56.

43. "Ivana's New Life," *New York Magazine*, October 15, 1990.

44. Lodging Advisors Market Research, "A Concise History of the New York City Hotel Market, 1988–2016."

45. David S. Hilzenrath and Michelle Singletary, "Trump Went Broke, but Stayed on Top," *Washington Post*, November 29, 1992.

46. Marie Brenner, "After the Gold Rush," *Vanity Fair*, September 1990.

47. "Profits Within Reach for the Rejuvenated Plaza," *Crain's New York Business*, January 29, 1990, 1.

48. David Stout and Kenneth N. Gilpin, "Trump Is Selling Plaza Hotel to Saudi and Asian Investors," *New York Times*, April 12, 1995, A1.

49. Richard D. Hylton, "Debt Deal for Trump on Plaza," *New York Times*, March 19, 1992, D1.

50. Floyd Norris, "A Haze of Debt Clouds the Plaza Hotel's Gleam," *New York Times*, June 5, 1990.

51. Thomas J. Lueck, "Reaching for the Sky to Add a Room," *New York Times*, June 3, 1990.

52. "Eloise Is Alive and Well and Living at the Plaza," *Village Voice*, August 20, 1991.

53. "Trump's Plaza Plans Must Allow for, uh, Tenants," *Newsday*, December 21, 1988.

54. "The Gal Who Tamed Trump," *National Enquirer*, January 28, 1992.

55. Data from appraisal firm Miller Samuel.

56. Richard D. Hylton, "Trump Aims to Turn Most of Plaza Hotel into Condominiums" *New York Times*, April 9, 1991, A1.

57. United States Bankruptcy Court, Southern District of New York, Chapter 11 filing of Plaza Operating Partners, November 13, 1992.

58. W. Speers, "Trump Settlement Is Not a Done Deal," *Philadelphia Inquirer*, March 22, 1991.

59. Harry Berkowitz, "Finally, It's a Deal! Ivana to Get $10 Million Plus, Plus, Plus," *Newsday*, March 21, 1991, 8.

Chapter 12: The Prince and the Billionaire

1. The third-richest family in Asia, according to *Forbes*, as of November 14, 2017.

2. Interview conducted with Wallach in his home on Long Island, New York, July 2017.

3. David Henry, "Trump Says He'll Sue Post for $500M," *Newsday*, December 22, 1994, A53.

4. Interview with Kwek conducted via email, December 2017.

5. YouTube, https://www.youtube.com/watch?v=KlwCXgZwSCc; and Michael Kranish and Marc Fisher, *Trump Revealed: The Definitive Biography of the 45th President* (New York: Scribner, 2017), 296–97.

6. Jerry Useem, "Former Trump Executive Had a Penchant for Theft," *Boston Globe*, September 23, 2016.

7. Interview with Wallach conducted in July 2017.

8. Interview with Wallach conducted by phone, June 5, 2018.

9. Mitchell Pacelle, "Asian Investors Buy Up Hotels in U.S., Europe, but Move Cautiously," *Wall Street Journal*, February 19, 1997, A1.

10. Interview with Wallach conducted in July 2017.

11. Peter Grant and Alexandra Berzon, "Trump and His Debts: A Narrow Escape," *Wall Street Journal*, January 4, 2016.

12. David Stout with Kenneth N. Gilpin, "Trump Is Selling Plaza Hotel to Saudi and Asian Investors," *New York Times*, April 12, 1995, A1.

13. Mitchell Pacelle, "Asian Investors Buy Up Hotels in U.S., Europe, but Move Cautiously," *Wall Street Journal*, February 19, 1997, A1; and David Stout with Kenneth N. Gilpin, "Trump Is Selling Plaza Hotel to Saudi and Asian Investors," *New York Times*, April 12, 1995, A1.

14. Interview with Kwek conducted in December 2017.

15. David Stout with Kenneth N. Gilpin, "Trump Is Selling Plaza Hotel to Saudi and Asian Investors," *New York Times*, April 12, 1995; and James Barron, "Singapore Chain Seeks Plaza Hotel Stake," *New York Times*, January 11, 1995, D4.

16. David Stout with Kenneth N. Gilpin, "Trump Is Selling Plaza Hotel to Saudi and Asian Investors," *New York Times*, April 12, 1995, A1.

17. Ibid.

18. Nanette Asimov, "Tiny Menlo College Is Like Home for Saudi Elite," *SF Gate*, May 12, 2015.

19. Michael Quint, "Saudi Prince to Become Citicorp's Top Stockholder," *New York Times*, February 22, 1991.

20. "The Mystery of the World's Second-Richest Businessman," *Economist*, February 25, 1999.

21. Peter Truell, "A Saudi Prince Fond of High-Profile Investing," *New York Times*, April 12, 1995.

22. "The Mystery of the World's Second-Richest Businessman," *Economist*, February 25, 1999.

23. William D. Cohan, "Prince Alwaleed, Donald Trump, and the Era of Regression and Dictatorship," *Vanity Fair*, November 6, 2017.

24. Interview with Kwek conducted in December 2017.

25. Justin Doebele, "The Man with the Golden Machine Gun," *Forbes*, July 9, 2001.

26. Paul Burnham Finney, "Business Travel: The Plaza Hotel's New Owners Plan Some Changes, but They're Not About to Tamper with Success," *New York Times*, January 3, 1996.

27. Riz Khan, *Alwaleed: Businessman, Billionaire, Prince* (London: William Morrow, 2005), 4.

28. Justin Doebele, "The Man with the Golden Machine Gun," *Forbes*, July 9, 2001.

29. Riz Khan, *Alwaleed: Businessman, Billionaire, Prince* (London: William Morrow, 2005), 6.

30. Rudolph W. Giuliani and Ken Kurson, *Leadership* (New York: Time Warner, 2003), 374.

31. Jennifer Steinhauer, "Citing Comments on Attack, Giuliani Rejects Saudi's Gift," *New York Times*, October 12, 2001.

32. Lisa L. Colangelo and Corky Siemaszko, "Giuliani Nixes Saudi $10M Gift," *New York Daily News*, October 12, 2001.

33. James Barron, "Eloise Gets a New Landlord: Plaza Sells for $675 Million," *New York Times*, August 14, 2004; "New York Plaza Sold as MC Tackles Debt Pile," *Evening Standard*, August 13, 2004, 43.

34. Elizabeth Sanger, "Will New Plaza Have Old Magic?" *Newsday*, April 7, 2005, 1.

35. Edmund Conway, "Millennium Checks Out Doubled Profits," *Daily Mail*, February 22, 2005; Stephen Foley, "The Investment Column: Hold on to M&C in Hope of Better Times Ahead," *Independent*, February 20, 2004; Dominic Walsh, "M&C Considers Selling Hotels as Occupancy Falls," *The Times* (London), February 20, 2004.

36. Riz Khan, *Alwaleed: Businessman, Billionaire, Prince* (London: William Morrow, 2005), 113–14.

37. Data from the appraisal firm Miller Samuel.

38. According to the CityRealty 100 Market Report.

39. *Curbed New York*; Paul Goldberger, "The King of Central Park West," *Vanity Fair*, September 2008.

40. Adam Piore, "Scott Latham: The Art of the Commercial Deal," *Real Deal*, November 4, 2007.

41. Louis Kraar, "The Mystery Man Who Took the Plaza from Donald Trump," *Fortune*, December 25, 1995.

42. Henry Tricks and Douglas Wong, "M&C Sells New York's Plaza for $675 Million," *Financial Times*, August 14, 2004.

Chapter 13: Save the Plaza

1. "Star Memories Yule Cherish," *New York Post*, December 25, 2004.
2. Curtis Gathje, "What Would Eloise Say?" *New York Times*, January 16, 2005.
3. Alex Ulam, "What Does the Future Hold for the Plaza Hotel?" *Architectural Record* 193, no. 3 (March 2005).
4. Nicholas Confessore, "Oak Room at the Plaza Hotel Is Going the Way of the Pince-Nez," *New York Times*, December 30, 2004.
5. "Vito Pitta, Former Hotel Trades Council President, Is Dead at 78," *New York Times*, August 25, 2005.
6. PricewaterhouseCoopers data cited by Charles V. Bagli, "If They Come, Where Will They Sleep," *New York Times*, March 6, 2005; and Julie Satow, "Hotel Workers Union Protests Plaza Conversion," *New York Sun*, February 18, 2005.
7. Interview conducted with Ward at his office in October 2017.
8. "Our Members Tell New York and the World: Save the Plaza!" *Hotel Voice*, February 21, 2005, 1; and Thomas J. Lueck, "Workers Hold Rally at Plaza Against Conversion to Condos," *New York Times*, April 6, 2005.
9. "Campaign to Save the Plaza Draws Worldwide Attention," *Hotel Voice*, March 21, 2005, 1.
10. "Council Fights Hotels-to-Condos Trend," *Bloomberg News*, March 24, 2005.
11. "No Harrods at Plaza," *New York Daily News*, March 2, 2005.
12. Haim Handwerker and Anat Georgi, "I Am Eloise. I Am Six. I Live at the Plaza...In a Condo," *Haaretz*, March 28, 2005; and Julie Satow, "Battle over Plaza Becoming Costly," *New York Sun*, April 7, 2005, 1.
13. *New York Times*, March 17, 2005.
14. "Lauder's Landmark," *New York Post*, July 28, 2005, 30.
15. Robin Shulman, "Renovation of the Plaza Hotel Clears a Hurdle," *New York Times*, July 13, 2005, B3.
16. Sewell Chan, "Firms Lobbying the City Earned $36 Million in '05," *New York Times*, June 3, 2006, B2.
17. Maura Yates, "Plaza Rally to Double as Prayer Vigil," *New York Sun*, March 11, 2005.
18. "6,000 Members Meet at Radio City and Rally at the Plaza," *Hotel Voice*, April 11, 2005, 1.
19. Ben Smith, "Bloomberg Gets a Nasty Lesson: Politics Counts," *New York Observer*, March 14, 2005, 1.
20. Lloyd Grove and Hudson Morgan, "Can Plaza Bring NYC the Gold?" *New York Daily News*, February 7, 2005.
21. Interview with Ward conducted in October 2017.

22. "The Plaza Is Saved! Union Reaches Deal That Preserves Many Jobs; Mayor Bloomberg to Convene Panel on Condominium Conversions," *Hotel Voice*, April 18, 2005.

23. According to the union, as of July 2018, the current number of members employed at the Plaza stands at 472.

24. Julie Satow, "The Fate of the Plaza," *New York Sun*, April 15–17, 2005.

25. David Seifman, "Plaza Sweet Victory," *New York Post*, April 15, 2005.

26. Julie Satow, "Waldorf Astoria and Hotel Workers Union Reach $149 Million Deal for Severance Payouts," *New York Times*, June 26, 2015.

27. Rich Calder, "Bubbly Bye-Bye Good to Last Drop," *New York Post*, April 30, 2005.

28. Philip Recchia, "Last Call at Plaza for Guests & Oak Bar-Flies," *New York Post*, May 1, 2005.

29. Anthony Ramirez, "Souvenir Hunters Help Themselves to Pieces of History at the Plaza Hotel," *New York Times*, May 21, 2005.

30. *All Things Considered*, National Public Radio, March 15, 2006.

31. Christie's New York auction catalog for the Plaza Hotel, 2006.

32. Associated Press, March 16, 2006.

33. Evgenia Peretz, "Eloise Sheds a Tear," *Vanity Fair*, January 2009, 80.

34. Anthony Ramirez, "At the Plaza, Restoring Life Lived Luxuriously," *New York Times*, March 2, 2008.

35. Interview with Daly conducted by phone in September 2017.

36. Interview with Melvin conducted by phone in June 2015.

37. Interview conducted in Naftali's office in July 2017.

Chapter 14: Shell Game

1. David Chaikin and J. C. Sharman, *Corruption and Money Laundering: A Symbiotic Relationship* (New York: Palgrave Macmillan, 2009), 24; also Republic of Vanuatu Office of the Ombudsman Public Report on the Breach of Leadership Code and the Misuse of the Cyclone Betsy Account by Former Prime Minister Mr. Maxime Carlot Korman, February 26, 1998.

2. In 2011, Mascot Holdings Limited was listed in the Stolen Asset Recovery Initiative database, a partnership of the World Bank Group and the United Nations Office on Drugs and Crime. The entry was part of a database that was taken offline in 2018 due to a lack of resources to maintain it.

3. Email exchange with Dan McGarry on June 11, 2018.

4. Godwin Ligo, "Korman Looks Back, Points to the Future," *Vanuatu Daily Post*, July 30, 2015.

5. Miller Samuel data.

6. Philana Patterson, "Brokers Get Creative to Lure Bonus Money," *Real Deal*, February 1, 2006.

7. Data from *Real Deal*, https://therealdeal.com/issues_articles/the-records-of -2006/ and https://therealdeal.com/issues_articles/top-25-residential-sales-of -2005-reflect-record-market/ and https://therealdeal.com/issues_articles/ anything-but-roulette/.

8. Helen Peterson and Tracy Connor, "Loyal Despite Brothel Bust on West Side," *New York Daily News*, June 16, 2006, 8.

9. "Plaza Condo Sale Is Shrouded in Mystery," *Bloomberg News*, March 19, 2007.

10. Josh Barbanel, "(Too) Storied Hotel?" *New York Times*, September 26, 2008.

11. Alex Morrell, "A Wall Street Banker Describes the Time Donald Trump Offered to Seal a Deal with a $1 Million Coin Flip," *Business Insider*, July 12, 2017.

12. Jon Swaine, "FBI Looked into Trump Plans to Build Hotel in Latvia with Putin Supporter," *Guardian*, March 29, 2018.

13. Eileen Welsome, *Lomas del Poleo*, December 27, 2007.

14. Julia Marsh, "Ex-Wife Claims Kazakh Tycoon Faking Illness to Avoid Court," *New York Post*, November 4, 2013.

15. Dareh Gregorian, "Kaching-istan Kazakh Big: Wife Stole Plaza Pad & $75M," *New York Daily News*, August 23, 2013.

16. New York County Supreme Court, Bolat Nazarbayev v. Daniyar Kesikbayev, Maira Kurmangaliyeva.

17. U.S. Department of the Treasury FinCEN Advisory, August 22, 2017.

18. http://panama.data2www.com/e/20126809; and https://offshoreleaks.icij.org/ nodes/10148567 and https://offshoreleaks.icij.org/nodes/12104806.

19. "Since the Entry into the Prison of Díaz Ferrán His Family Does Not Stop Assembling Societies," *La Celosia*, April 6, 2016.

20. "Gerardo Díaz Ferrán, Detainee," *Cinco Días*, December 3, 2012; and "The Judge Dictates the Personal Bankruptcy of Díaz Ferrán," *El País*, November 29, 2010 (Google translation of article).

21. Evgenia Peretz, "Eloise Sheds a Tear," *Vanity Fair*, January 2009, 80.

22. Ibid.

23. Stephanie Saul and Louise Story, "At the Time Warner Center, an Enclave of Powerful Russians," *New York Times*, February 11, 2015.

24. "Moment of Luck," *Elle Man Russia*, October 2014.

25. Julie Satow, "Pied-a-Neighborhood," *New York Times*, October 24, 2014.

26. Christine Haughney, "It's Lonely at the Plaza Hotel…," *New York Times*, February 17, 2008.

27. Paul Tharp, "Horror Night at the Plaza," *New York Post*, February 28, 2008.

28. Joey Arak, "Lonely Plaza Hotel Now Proven to Be Harmful, Perhaps Deadly," *Curbed New York*, February 28, 2008.

29. Josh Barbanel, "Plaza Sweet for Repeat Buyer," *Wall Street Journal*, June 8, 2010.

30. E. B. Solomont, Katherine Clarke, "Who Earned & Who Got Burned," *Real Deal*, August 2017.

Chapter 15: The Indian Great Gatsby

1. El Ad sold 50 percent of the Plaza hotel and 25 percent of the hotel condominiums to Prince Alwaleed for $520 million. It sold out the Plaza condominiums for $1.4 billion. The commercial spaces, including the Oak Room and the Palm Court, were valued at $300 million. As part of the deal, it also acquired and converted into a condominium a small building next door to the Plaza, 22 CPS, for $50 million. All told, this brought El Ad's total revenue to $2.27 billion. Its total cost for the acquisition and renovation of the Plaza was $1.225 billion. That left it with a net profit of $1.045 billion.

2. Alex Perry, "A Tale of Two Indias," *Time*, December 6, 2004.

3. "Sahara to Launch Afternoon Soap 'Prratima' on 23 August," *Indian Television*, August 14, 2004, and http://www.sahara.in/qshop.html.

4. Eric Bellman, "Sahara Draws Indian Regulator's Eye," *Wall Street Journal*, June 17, 2008.

5. Supreme Court of India, Civil Appeal No. 9813 of 2011, pages 258 and page 26; and J. Venkatesan, "SC Orders Sahara to Refund Rs. 24,400 Crore," *Hindu*, August 31, 2012.

6. Tamal Bandyopadhyay, *Sahara: The Untold Story* (Mumbai: Jaico Publishing, 2014), 19.

7. Ibid., 226; Ashutosh Sinha and Gautam Chikermane, "India's Weirdest Worker," *Outlook*, September 8, 1997.

8. Ibid., 137; Rama Lakshmi, "Indian Tycoon Working to Sell His Iconic Hotels From Jail," *Washington Post*, September 24, 2014.

9. Kanika Gahlaut, "A-List Attendance at Sahara Chief Subrata Roy's Sons' Weddings," *India Today*, February 23, 2004.

10. Kaveree Bamzai, "The Emperor Strikes Back," *India Today*, January 17, 2011.

11. Ibid., 263.

12. Eric Bellman, "India Squeezes Influential Bank," *Wall Street Journal*, June 7, 2008.

13. Eric Bellman, "Sahara Draws Indian Regulator's Eye," *Wall Street Journal*, June 17, 2008.

14. Eric Bellman, "Sahara Draws Indian Regulator's Eye," *Wall Street Journal*, June 17, 2008; Joe Leahy, "India Freezes Sahara Financial Deposits," *Financial Times*, June 6, 2008.

15. Eric Bellman, "Indian Bank Avoids Deposit Ban," *Wall Street Journal*, June 18, 2008.

16. Supreme Court of India Civil Appeal No. 9813, pages 26–27.

17. Bandyopadhyay, *Sahara*.

18. Supreme Court of India Civil Appeal No. 9813.

19. Appu Esthose Suresh, "The Curious Case of 5,984 Kalawatis in Sahara List," *Indian Express*, May 1, 2013.

20. Supreme Court of India Civil Appeal No. 9813, pages 189–90.

21. "ED Registers Laundering Case Against 2 Sahara Group Firms," *Hindustan Times*, June 27, 2013.

22. "Sahara Victimised for Years, but Won't Give Up: Subrata Roy," *Businessline*, April 11, 2013.

23. Sundeep Jain and Tom Wright, "India's Sahara Gets Defensive After Ruling," *Wall Street Journal*, September 3, 2012.

24. Dhananjay Mahapatra, "ED Seeks Provisional Attachment of Sahara's Foreign Hotels, Files Plea in SC," *Times of India*, February 9, 2017.

25. Alex Perry, "A Tale of Two Indias," *Time*, December 6, 2004.

26. Samanwaya Rautray, "Supreme Court Grounds Subrata Roy, Bars Sahara from Selling Any Property," *The Economic Times*, November 22, 2013.

27. "SC Orders Sahara Chief Roy's Arrest," *Hindustan Times*, February 27, 2014.

28. "Tihar Prison in India: More Dovecote Than Jail," *Economist*, May 5, 2012.

29. "Unhygienic Conditions in Tihar Jail Affecting Inmates; Delhi HC Told," *DNA India*, October 15, 2014; and Neeraj Chauhan, "340 HIV Positive Prisoners in Tihar," *Times of India*, May 30, 2011.

30. N. Sundaresha Subramanian, "BoA Refused to Be Part of Sahara Deal Citing Integrity Issues: Saransh Sharma," *Business Standard*, February 12, 2015.

31. "Sahara Chief Subrata Roy Back in Special Facility at Tihar," *Live Mint*, January 13, 2015.

32. "Subrata Roy Sahara Living It Up in Tihar Jail While Employees Committing Suicide," *Tehelka*, May 29, 2015.

33. Sumeet Chatterjee and Devidutta Tripathy, "Investment Vehicle Eyes Flagship Sahara Hotels in $2 Bln Bailout for Founder Roy," Reuters, January 20, 2015.

34. Ira Dugal, "Sahara Loan Will Open Acquisition Opportunity: Mirach's Sharma," *Live Mint*, January 20, 2015.

35. Emily Flitter and Sumeet Chatterjee, "Exclusive—Subrata Roy's Get-Out-of-Jail Deal Is Mired in Mystery," Reuters, February 5, 2015.

36. "Deal Unravels as Sahara Says Mirach Forged Bank Letter," *Live Mint*, February 5, 2015.

37. "US Probing Alleged Forged Letter for Mirach in Sahara Deal," *Live Mint*, February 19, 2015.

38. "Sahara Employee Commits Suicide," *DNA*, March 25, 2015.

39. Interview conducted by Aayush Soni in Hindi and translated into English.

40. According to TC208 filings from years 2013, 2014, and 2015, provided with a FOIA filing by the NYC Department of Finance. For 2017, the $10 million figure was provided by Roy during our interview.

41. Dean Nelson, "Indian Billionaire Subrata Roy Mortgages Grosvenor House and New York's Plaza Hotel to Get Out of Jail," *Telegraph*, January 21, 2015.

42. "Plaza Hotel in Spotlight Again with Reported Bid by Sultan of Brunei," *New York Times*, August 18, 2014.

43. "Plaza Hotel Shoots Down $680 Million Offer," *New York Post*, December 4, 2014.

44. JTS Trading Ltd. v Trinity White City Ventures Ltd., Sahara India Pariwar, Aamby Valley (Mauritius) Ltd., UBS Financial Services Inc., April 18, 2017.

45. Kathryn Brenzel, "Prospective Buyer of Plaza, Dream Hotels Shakes Lawsuit Holding Up Sale," *Real Deal*, April 25, 2017.

46. *Forbes*, real-time net worth as of July 20, 2017.

47. "Pay Up or Will Auction Aamby Valley, says SC," *Hindustan Times*, March 22, 2017.

48. Dhananjay Mahapatra, "Sahara Pledges Asset Sale, 'Buyer' Surfaces," *Times of India*, March 1, 2017.

49. "U.S. Firm Backs Off from Plan to Buy Sahara's Hotel," *Hindu*, April 18, 2017.

50. Supreme Court of India Civil Appellate Jurisdiction I.A. No. 247 of 2017 In Contempt Petition (Civil) No. 412 of 2012.

51. Amit Anand Choudhary, "SC Sends Former Scribe to Jail for a Month for Contempt in Sahara Case," *Times of India*, April 27, 2017.

52. "Sahara Case: Senior Journalist Lands in Jail," *Business Standard*, April 27, 2017.

53. Will Parker, "Investors Hope Cryptocurrency Raise Will Buy Them the Plaza Hotel," *Real Deal*, March 27, 2018.

54. Lois Weiss and Steve Cuozzo, "Saudi Prince Wants to Save Embattled Plaza Hotel," *New York Post*, May 24, 2017.

55. Margherita Stancati, Summer Said, and Benoit Faucon, "The Price of Freedom for Saudi Arabia's Richest Man: $6 Billion," *Wall Street Journal*, December 23, 2017.

56. Gillian Tan, "New York Plaza Hotel Buyers Ashkenazy, Alwaleed Sue Owner," Bloomberg, May 18, 2018.

57. Dmitry Zhdannikov, "Qatar to buy New York's Plaza Hotel for $600 Million: Source," Reuters, July 3, 2018.

BIBLIOGRAPHY AND SOURCES

Newspapers and Periodicals:

"2 New York Realty Men Seek Control of Sonesta." *Boston Globe*, May 10, 1973.

"4 Groups Are Key Landlords for Midtown Sex Industry." *New York Times*, July 10, 1977.

"4 Robbed in Chauffeured Limousine; 2 Gunmen Get $265,000 in Jewelry." *New York Times*, May 14, 1973.

"5 Thugs at Plaza Get $45,000 Gems." *New York Times*, August 1, 1972.

"33 Got Christmas Rum." *New York Times*, April 8, 1921.

"1929 Investment Styles." *New York Herald Tribune*, March 14, 1929.

"6,000 Members Meet at Radio City and Rally at the Plaza." *Hotel Voice*, April 11, 2005.

"$1,253,702,357 Rise in Taxable Realty on City's 1930 Rolls." *New York Times*, October 2, 1929.

"$4,182,690 Loss Taken by H. S. Black Estate." *New York Times*, March 9, 1935.

"$60,000,000 Hilton Hotel Concern Formed as Four Companies Merge." *New York Times*, June 7, 1946.

"A Conversation with Henry Janeway Hardenbergh." *Architectural Record* 19, no. 5 (May 1906).

"A Few Facts Regarding the Plaza Hotel." *Carpentry and Building*, May 1, 1907.

"A Great Hotel Finished." *New-York Tribune*, September 30, 1890.

"A Man of Letters Throws an A-OK Champagne Party." *Los Angeles Times*, November 30, 1966.

"A Protégé of Royalty." *New York Times*, July 12, 1896.

"A Separate Peace with France Was the Object of Bolo's Plotting." *New York Times*, October 5, 1917.

"A Toast to the Plaza." *New York Herald Tribune*, October 3, 1947.

"Activities of Bolo Pasha as German Agent." *New York Times Current History*, November 1, 1917.

"Advertising: A Mood of Caution." *New York Times*, September 20, 1962.

"After Work a Time for Reading." *New York Times*, November 29, 1959.

"Aging Belasco Preens for a New Theatrical Life." *New York Times*, January 27, 1975.

"Alex DiLorenzo Jr. Dies; Leader in Real Estate, 58." *New York Times*, September 6, 1975.

"Along Fifth Avenue." *Hartford Courant*, November 11, 1923.

"A. M. Sonnabend Is Dead at 67; Boston Industrialist-Financier." *New York Times*, February 12, 1964.

"An Edwardian Splendor or Green Tulip Modern?" *New York Times*, November 5, 1971.

"Another Fine Hotel Now on the City's List." *New York Times*, September 29, 1907.

"Anti-Saloon League Inquiry Called For." *New York Times*, March 4, 1919.

"Arrest a Baron in the Plaza Lobby." *New York Times*, March 2, 1911.

"Arrest Black Again; to Press Liquor Charge." *New-York Tribune*, March 21, 1921.

"At Last Prohibition Clamps the Lid on Tight." *New-York Tribune*, November 2, 1919.

"At the Persian Room Opening—Fur Capes and Silver Lamé Gowns." *Women's Wear Daily*, September 26, 1935.

"Authors & Editors." *Publishers Weekly*, May 12, 1969.

"'Baron' Arkovy a Suicide." *New York Sun*, April 19, 1913.

"Baron Ruined on Wall Street, Attempts to Die." *St. Louis Post-Dispatch*, August 16, 1908.

"Beinecke Dies; Headed Board of Plaza Hotel: Official, 86, Helped to Found Hammond Chain, Which Included Copley-Plaza Plaza Hotel Chairman." *New York Herald Tribune*, December 21, 1932.

"Beineckes Take Black Home." *New York Herald Tribune*, October 28, 1930.

"Bells in Honor of Bride's Name." *St. Louis Post-Dispatch*, December 31, 1905.

"Black Retains Domination of U.S. Realty Co." *New York Herald*, November 26, 1924.

"Bolo Letter Named Hearst as 'My Friend.'" *New-York Tribune*, July 31, 1918.

"Bought Secrecy for Ruiz Suicide." *New York Times*, June 12, 1909.

"'Broadway' Ed Sullivan." *Washington Post*, November 28, 1935.

"Broker Kills Self Like Wife Did When Child Wedded Bogus Baron." *World*, July 25, 1913.

"Butler's Death Accident." *New York Sun*, July 27, 1906.

"Campaign to Save the Plaza Draws Worldwide Attention." *Hotel Voice*, March 21, 2005.

"Capote Bids to Spur Grim Social Routine." *Los Angeles Times*, October 21, 1966.

"Capote Is Cold Blooded to the Uninvited Masses." *Washington Post, Times Herald*, November 25, 1966.

"Care Free, Princess Entertains 'At Home.'" *New-York Tribune*, March 2, 1916.

"Cartman Talks Go On Uncertainly as Trash Piles Continue to Mount." *New York Times*, December 6, 1978.

"Cecil Beaton Explores Plaza's Sub-Basement to Re-Decorate His Own Suite in the Hotel." *New York Herald Tribune*, May 14, 1946.

"City Bank Men on Board of Realty & Improvement." *New York Herald Tribune*, May 16, 1928.

"City Realty Value Jumps One Billion to $11,275,526,200." *New York Times*, October 2, 1923.

"Cocktails from Nursing Bottles at 'Baby Party.'" *St. Louis Post-Dispatch*, December 30, 1916.

"Colored Waiters Plan National Conference." *New York Age*, April 25, 1912.

"Colored Waiters to Give Up Positions." *New York Age*, June 13, 1912.

"Coming to New York, Waiter Changes Accent." *Washington Times*, August 15, 1907.

"Conservation in Hotels—A War Necessity." *Hotel Monthly*, July 1942.

"Cooking and Baking WITHOUT Sugar." *Hotel Monthly*, June 1942.

"Costly Wedding." *Courier-Journal*, January 30, 1910.

"Council Fights Hotels-to-Condos Trend." *Bloomberg News*, March 24, 2005.

"Crush to See Brides Who'll Wear Titles." *New York Times*, January 12, 1908.

"Crushed: By Neglect of Her Son." *Cincinnati Enquirer*, April 23, 1908.

"Deal Unravels as Sahara Says Mirach Forged Bank Letter." *Live Mint*, February 5, 2015.

"Diners-Out Relish Meat of Buffalo." *New York Times*, February 3, 1945.

"Dining Out." *Post Standard* (Syracuse, New York), July 18, 1949.

"Dogs Dyed to Match Milady's Gown Even If It's 'Yaller.'" *New-York Tribune*, October 24, 1914.

"Donahue Gem Thief Is Sought in London." *New York Times*, November 12, 1925.

"Drank His Liquor, Jury Then Found Black Not Guilty." *Evening World*, March 25, 1921.

"Draught Closes Hotel." *New York Times*, January 25, 1920.

"Drops Theft Charge Against Von Arkovy." *New York Times*, March 4, 1911.

"Dry Law Called Hotel Bane." *New York Herald Tribune*, April 24, 1932.

"ED Registers Laundering Case Against 2 Sahara Group Firms." *Hindustan Times*, June 27, 2013.

"Eloise Is Alive and Well and Living at the Plaza." *Village Voice*, August 20, 1991.

"Eloise Keeps Kay Thompson on the Go." Associated Press, October 20, 1958.

"Entrance to the Plaza Hotel Is the Scene of Assassination Attempt." *New York Times*, April 25, 1970.

"Few Hansoms Now; It's All Taxicab." *New York Times*, July 3, 1910.

"Financial Markets." *New York Times*, October 19, 1929.

"'Flask Parties' Will Enhance Joy of New Year's Eve." *New-York Tribune*, December 27, 1919.

"Former Bellboy at Plaza Hotel Is Now Orderly to Eisenhower." *New York Herald Tribune*, January 12, 1943.

"Four Guests Still Remain—Furniture Auction Begins." *New-York Daily Tribune*, June 13, 1905.

"Frederick Sterry, Hotel Man, Dead." *New York Times*, July 12, 1933.

"FYI." *New York Times*, August 15, 2004.

"Gambling, Insomnia, and Morphia." *Manchester Guardian*, April 19, 1913.

"Gates Pays $46,000 Rent for His Suite." *Evening World*, April 23, 1907.

"Gerardo Díaz Ferrán, Detainee." *Cinco Días*, December 3, 2012.

"German Politician Robbed of $235 in New York City." *Hartford Courant*, March 16, 1971.

"Girl Service Captains Replace Bell Boys." *Hotel Monthly*, January 1943.

"Gives Lion to Princess." *New-York Tribune*, April 18, 1911.

"Glorified by Ziegfeld." *New Journal and Guide*, July 25, 1931.

"Graft Paid to Police Here Said to Run into Millions." *New York Times*, April 25, 1970.

"Grille Room for Dogs." *Daily People*, November 23, 1908.

"'Happy Accumulator' Eying Deals." *New York Herald Tribune*, March 22, 1959.

"Harlem to Get 230-Room Hotel Constructed with Local Funds." *New York Times*, May 10, 1968.

"Harlem's New Look in Building." *New York Amsterdam News*, May 18, 1968.

"Harry Black, Genial Individualist." *Wall Street Journal*, July 23, 1930.

"Harry Black Will Disposes of $5,240,511." *New York Herald*, July 8, 1931.

"HCA Head Sees Business Role in US Urban Crisis." *Jewish Advocate*, June 27, 1968.

"Helmsley May Buy Plaza Hotel." *New York Times*, March 1, 1973.

"Her Own and Hotel's Jubilee." *New York Herald Tribune*, March 10, 1957.

"Her Pet Dog Finds $3,000 Diamond Ring After Detectives Fail." *Washington Post*, February 11, 1915.

"High Rentals Paid in New York." *New York Times*, April 28, 1907.

"Hilton Hotels Sells Roosevelt, Mayflower to Hotel Corp." *Wall Street Journal*, March 1, 1956.

"Hilton Reports Gains." *Chicago Tribune*, August 27, 1965.

"His Wife an Heiress." *Washington Post*, March 3, 1911.

"Hotel Corp. Has a Mod President." *Boston Sunday Globe*, April 13, 1969.

"Hotel Corp. Sees '64 Net More Than Doubling." *Wall Street Journal*, May 14, 1965.

"Hotel Corp. Will Sell Hotel Plaza, New York, Under Leaseback Plan." *Wall Street Journal*, November 21, 1958.

"Hotel Men Face Grave Situation." *New York Age*, October 19, 1911.

"Hotel Men Ratify Union Agreement." *New York Times*, December 28, 1938.

"Hotel Men to Fight to Restore Liquor." *New York Times*, January 24, 1919.

"Hotel Plaza Addition, New York." *Architecture and Building*, February 1922.

"Hotel Plaza Plans New Cocktail Room." *New York Times*, January 31, 1934.

"Hotel President Pays Extortion; Man Nabbed." *Hartford Courant*, September 8, 1973.

"Hotel Santa Claus Ran Out of Cash." *New York Times*, December 26, 1907.

"Hotels in Action." *Wall Street Journal*, August 12, 1948.

"Housesmiths to Work." *New-York Daily Tribune*, February 11, 1906.

"H. S. Black Ends Life by Bullet in Home; No Motive Revealed." *New York Times*, July 20, 1930.

"H. S. Black Kills Self; Real Estate Magnate." *Washington Post*, July 20, 1930.

"H. S. Black, Stricken in Bathtub, Better." *New York Times*, October 20, 1929.

"H. S. Black's Estate Down to $5,240,511." *New York Times*, July 8, 1931.

"Hungarian 'Baron' Held for Larceny." *New-York Tribune*, March 2, 1911.

"Hungarian Princess Travels with Menagerie of Wild Pets." *Detroit Free Press*, June 21, 1908.

"If It's Good, Leave It Alone." *New York Times*, October 31, 1971.

"Ill Luck at Tables." *Bismarck Daily Tribune*, August 18, 1911.

"In the Hotel Field: National Hotelmen's Exposition." *Bonfort's Circular*, June 15, 1917.

"Inability to Spend Million a Year Annoys Princess." *Los Angeles Times*, July 20, 1910.

"Indict W. S. Bennet on Princess's Notes." *New York Times*, July 12, 1917.

"Intruder Slashes State Man at New York Hotel." *Hartford Courant*, May 27, 1974.

"Ironworkers' Memory Weak." *New York Sun*, July 25, 1906.

"It Happened Last Night." *Newsday*, June 10, 1954.

"It Just Looked as If Gwendolyn Had Laid an Egg." *Daily Boston Globe*, January 6, 1937.

"Ivana Trump; She's Putting the Plaza Back on New York's Map." *Ottawa Citizen*, December 8, 1988.

"Ivana's New Life." *New York Magazine*, October 15, 1990.

"Jewels Outside Your Furs." *New York Times*, February 12, 1908.

"June Hotel Occupancy Highest Ever." *Hotel Monthly*, July 1945.

"Jury Samples Liquor; Acquits Harry Black." *New York Herald*, March 25, 1921.

"Ladies' Quips Enliven Plaza's Golden Party." *New York Herald Tribune*, March 11, 1957.

"Last Guests Leave the Plaza." *New-York Daily Tribune*, June 11, 1905.

"Lauder's Landmark." *New York Post*, July 28, 2005.

"Liquid Pancakes, Plaza Waiter Controls the Formula." *Hiltonitems*, July 1950.

"Loss of Beauty Led to Suicide." *Nashville American*, June 13, 1909.

"Lunches and Other Adjuncts." *Cincinnati Enquirer*, May 4, 1907.

"Many Restaurants in the City Report Gains." *New York Times*, January 14, 1972.

"Meatless Tuesday Goes Well in City." *New York Times*, October 21, 1942.

"Modification of Zoning Ordinance: The Plaza Hotel." *American Architect*, December 1, 1920.

"Moment of Luck." *Elle Man Russia*, October 2014.

"Motor Cars Lead Horses." *New York Times*, May 19, 1912.

"Mrs. Clara Bell Walsh Dies; Lived 50 Years at the Plaza." *New York Herald Tribune*, August 14, 1957.

"Mrs. EA Strong Leaps to Death at Plaza Hotel." *New York Herald Tribune*, April 12, 1940.

"Murder by Iron Workers." *New York Sun*, July 16, 1906.

"Murder Hearing Begun." *New-York Daily Tribune*, July 17, 1906.

"Murder in Mid-Air by Union Workers." *New York Times*, July 12, 1906.

"Murderers 'Exonerated.'" *New York Times*, July 28, 1906.

"Near-Dry New York Amends Old Drinking Customs." *New York Times*, July 20, 1919.

"Negro Waiters in Best Hotels." *New York Age*, June 6, 1912.

"Negro Women for Hotel Work." *Hotel Monthly*, February 1943.

"New Accusers Face 'Baron' Von Arkovy." *New York Times*, March 3, 1911.

"New Plaza Hotel." *Architecture*, November 15, 1907.

"New Year's Eve Dance to Aid Crippled Children." *New York Herald Tribune*, December 14, 1936.

"New York City Is Pressing Real-Estate Concern for Upkeep Accord." *New York Times*, September 4, 1976.

"New York Day by Day." *Austin Statesman*, December 31, 1935.

"New York Hotel Finest in World." *East Oregonian*, September 19, 1907.

"New York Like Atlanta; Opens Back Doors, Freight Elevators to Insult Patrons." *Afro-American*, July 29, 1933.

"New York Plaza Sold as MC Tackles Debt Pile." *Evening Standard*, August 13, 2004.

"New York's Hotel Plaza Is Acquired by Sonesta." *Wall Street Journal*, July 6, 1972.

"New York's Plaza Hotel Sold to Boston's A. M. Sonnabend." *Daily Boston Globe*, October 15, 1953.

"News of Food." *New York Times*, November 12, 1942.

"No Harrods at Plaza." *New York Daily News*, March 2, 2005.

"No Ironworker Saw Watchman Murdered." *New York Times*, July 25, 1906.

"Novel Kit." *Women's Wear Daily*, October 2, 1957.

"Obituary." *Railroad Age*, April 13, 1929.

"Oh, Dear! War Luncheon Is Frugal at $10 a Plate." *Brotherhood of Locomotive Firemen and Enginemen's Magazine*, January 15, 1917.

"On Radio." *New York Times*, March 21, 1957.

"Organize New Hotel League." *New York Amsterdam News*, July 22, 1939.

"Our Members Tell New York and the World: Save the Plaza!" *Hotel Voice*, February 21, 2005.

"Parlaghy Horses Get a Reprieve." *New-York Tribune*, December 17, 1914.

"Patrons Offer to Help." *New York Times*, November 11, 1918.

"Pay Up or Will Auction Aamby Valley, Says SC." *Hindustan Times*, March 22, 2017.

"Penalize Big Hotels for Sugar Hoarding." *New York Times*, August 4, 1918.

"Persian Room Era at Definitive End." *Variety*, May 10, 1978.

"Personnel Problems." *Hotel Monthly*, April 1942.

"Plan New Method of Realty Finance." *New York Times*, March 3, 1929.

"Plaza Buys Murals by Everett Shinn from Old Owners." *New York Times*, May 18, 1976.

"Plaza Condo Sale Is Shrouded in Mystery." *Bloomberg News*, March 19, 2007.

"Plaza Hotel in Spotlight Again with Reported Bid by Sultan of Brunei." *New York Times*, August 18, 2014.

"Plaza Hotel Reconstruction." *New York Times*, June 3, 1902.

"Plaza Hotel Shoots Down $680 Million Offer." *New York Post*, December 4, 2014.

"Plaza Hotel Sold to Donald Trump for $390 Million." *New York Times*, March 27, 1988.

"Plaza Marks 40th Year at Brilliant Fete of 4 Decades." *New York Herald Tribune*, October 3, 1947.

"Plaza Observes 40 Sedate Years." *New York Times*, October 4, 1947.

"Plaza Pressing Expansion Drive." *New York Times*, November 17, 1964.

"Plaza Shop Finds Personalized Selling Wanted by Hotel Guests." *Women's Wear Daily*, May 17, 1945.

"Plaza to Fete 50-Year Tenant." *New York Times*, March 10, 1957.

"Plaza Waiter Arrested." *New York Times*, June 1, 1921.

"Police Draw Guns on Rioting Waiters." *New-York Tribune*, June 2, 1912.

"Prescription for Love." *New York Amsterdam News*, February 19, 1938.

"Princess Bars Out American Duchess." *New York Times*, April 26, 1910.

"Princess So Ill Sheriff Orders His Picket Away." *New-York Tribune*, August 29, 1923.

"Profits Within Reach for the Rejuvenated Plaza." *Crain's New York Business*, January 29, 1990.

"Purely Gossip." *Wall Street Journal*, November 5, 1943.

"Removal of Pulitzer Fountain Considered; So Broken, It Is Held to Mar Plaza Square." *New York Times*, August 22, 1928.

"Report to the City Judge." *Austin Statesman*, February 22, 1931.

"R. G. Babbage Resigns as U.S. Realty Head; Beinecke Succeeds Him." *Wall Street Journal*, June 18, 1936.

"Rising Costs Spur Hotels' Automation." *New York Times*, January 31, 1960.

"Rourke Rivals Depp." *Cincinnati Post*, November 5, 1994.

"Royal Honors Mark Burial of Needy Princess." *New-York Tribune*, September 2, 1923.

"Sahara Case: Senior Journalist Lands in Jail." *Business Standard*, April 27, 2017.

"Sahara Chief Subrata Roy Back in Special Facility at Tihar." *Live Mint*, January 13, 2015.

"Sahara Employee Commits Suicide." *DNA*, March 25, 2015.

"Sahara to Launch Afternoon Soap 'Prratima' on 23 August." *Indian Television*, August 14, 2004.

"Sahara Victimised for Years, but Won't Give Up: Subrata Roy." *Businessline*, April 11, 2013.

"Sam Parks Men Now Say a Fall Killed Butler." *World*, July 20, 1906.

"Says Fuller Company Brought on Trouble." *New York Times*, July 26, 1906.

"SC Orders Sahara Chief Roy's Arrest." *Hindustan Times*, February 27, 2014.

"'Shimmy' and Its Allies in Discard as Old Time Dance Steps Return." *New-York Tribune*, June 13, 1920.

"Since the Entry into the Prison of Díaz Ferrán His Family Does Not Stop Assembling Societies." *La Celosia*, April 6, 2016.

"Smiles Cost $1 Each." *Washington Post*, May 10, 1912.

"Society." *Detroit Free Press*, October 14, 1906.

"Sonesta International Files Suit to Block Tender Offer from Wellington Associates." *Wall Street Journal*, May 15, 1973.

"Sonesta Sought by Wellington Associates, but Such a Take-Over May Prove Difficult." *Wall Street Journal*, May 10, 1973.

"Sonesta Won't Sell the Plaza, New York, to Wellington Group." *Wall Street Journal*, May 3, 1974.

"Sonesta's Plaza Hotel Is Sought by Partners in New York Concern." *Wall Street Journal*, April 2, 1974.

"Songs of Winter." *Town Topics* 61, no. 7 (February 18, 1909).

"Sonnabend Puts Tax Laws to Work." *Chicago Daily Tribune*, November 23, 1958.

"St. Louis Society's of Rivals of 'Eleo' Sears." *St. Louis Post-Dispatch*, November 5, 1911.

"Star Memories Yule Cherish." *New York Post*, December 25, 2004.

"Stockingless Fad Not for the Plaza." *Women's Wear*, July 17, 1919.

"Subrata Roy Sahara Living It Up in Tihar Jail While Employees Committing Suicide." *Tehelka*, May 29, 2015.

"Sunday Inspiration." *Washington Post*, May 1917, citing the *St. Paul Pioneer Press*.

"Supervisory Training Custom Made at Hotel Plaza." *Hotel Gazette*, July 3, 1948.

"Suspect Seized in Plaza Bomb Threat." *New York Times*, September 8, 1973.

"The Beatles Invade, Complete with Long Hair and Screaming Fans." *New York Times*, February 8, 1964.

"The Beautiful and the Damned." *New Yorker*, January 20, 1945.

"The Big Landlord." *Wall Street Journal*, June 11, 1926.

"The Dry Fashion." *New York Times*, January 16, 1919.

"The Effect of the War on Employee-Employer." *Hotel Monthly*, June 1944.

"The Gal Who Tamed Trump." *National Enquirer*, January 28, 1992.

"The Goldman-DiLorenzo Empire and the Toss of a Coin." *New York Times*, June 3, 1979.

"The Grand Hotel." *Wall Street Journal*, August 23, 1965.

"The Grand Hotel: Aging but Still Elegant." *Wall Street Journal*, August 23, 1965.

"The Hotel Under Prohibition." *Saturday Evening Post*, October 14, 1922.

"The Jaundiced Eye." *New York Amsterdam News*, June 17, 1972.

"The Judge Dictates the Personal Bankruptcy of Díaz Ferrán." *El País*, November 29, 2010.

"The Latest Fugitive from Sherlock Holmes." *New York Herald Tribune*, October 12, 1947.

"The Lure of Life at a Modern Hotel." *Vogue*, April 16, 1908.

"The Mystery of the World's Second-Richest Businessman." *Economist*, February 25, 1999.

"The Plaza Deal." *Seattle Times*, July 16, 1978.

"The Plaza Hotel Dining-Rooms." *American Architect and Building News*, October 26, 1907.

"The Plaza Is Saved! Union Reaches Deal That Preserves Many Jobs; Mayor Bloomberg to Convene Panel on Condominium Conversions." *Hotel Voice*, April 18, 2005.

"The Plaza Loses 'Baron' Von Arkovy." *New York Times*, March 5, 1911.

"The Plaza of New York." *Hotel Monthly*, November 1907.

"The Plaza Off Screen: A Real-Life Adventure." *New York Times*, December 4, 1992.

"The Plaza: 'That Great Old Lady of New York City Hostelries.'" *Washington Post*, June 15, 1975.

"The Plaza's President Is Confident." *Sun*, February 9, 1973.

"The Special World of Cecil Beaton." *Good Housekeeping*, January 1958.

"The Taxi 'Invasion' of 1907." *Cosmopolitan*, October 1947.

"Third Suicide in Wake of Girl's Elopement." *New-York Tribune*, July 26, 1913.

"This New York." *Atlanta Constitution*, August 25, 1940.

"Three Suicides in Arkovy Romance." *San Francisco Call*, August 25, 1913.

"Tihar Prison in India: More Dovecote Than Jail." *Economist*, May 5, 2012.

"Time Halts for Caruso." *Baltimore Sun*, December 3, 1907.

"Trade Upturn Seen by Hotel Leader." *New York Times*, March 21, 1931.

"Trends in the Hotel Business, 1943." *Hotel Monthly*, November 1944.

"Trump's Plaza Plans Must Allow for, uh, Tenants." *Newsday*, December 21, 1988.

"Tub Victim Saved After Nine Hours." *Washington Post*, October 20, 1929.

"Two Miles of Millionaires." *Munsey's Magazine*, June 3, 1902.

"Two Views on the $1,000 Wardrobe of Mrs. Wilson." *Washington Post*, February 26, 1913.

"Unhygienic Conditions in Tihar Jail Affecting Inmates; Delhi HC Told." *DNA India*, October 15, 2014.

"Union Killing Not Murder." *New York Sun*, July 21, 1906.

"United States Realty: A Pioneer in Realty." *Wall Street Journal*, August 12, 1902.

"Urban League Forces Opening in Hotel Union." *Afro-American*, April 15, 1939.

"Urges Legislation to Prevent Changing Names." *Jewish Advocate*, March 21, 1929.

"U.S. Firm Backs Off from Plan to Buy Sahara's Hotel." *Hindu*, April 18, 2017.

"US Probing Alleged Forged Letter for Mirach in Sahara Deal." *Live Mint*, February 19, 2015.

"U.S. Realty & Improvement Had a Prosperous Year." *Wall Street Journal*, May 26, 1921.

"U.S. Realty Cash Ample for Needs." *Wall Street Journal*, August 16, 1929.

"U.S. Realty Earnings Show Improvement." *Wall Street Journal*, December 30, 1925.

"U.S. Realty Moves in Reorganization." *New York Times*, February 2, 1944.

"U.S. Realty President." *New York Herald Tribune*, October 20, 1942.

"U.S. Realty Reports Net Loss of $535,633 for Year to December 31." *Wall Street Journal*, January 16, 1937.

"Vendors Jam 5th Ave. on Summer Sundays." *New York Times*, July 27, 1979.

"Vito Pitta, Former Hotel Trades Council President, Is Dead at 78." *New York Times*, August 25, 2005.

"Von Arkovy Has Departed." *New York Times*, March 15, 1911.

"Waiters Don't Want to Take Your Tips." *New York Times*, October 31, 1911.

"Waiters Out in 17 More Places." *New York Times*, June 1, 1912.

"Waiters Quitting Hotel After Hotel." *New-York Tribune*, May 31, 1912.

"Waiters Strike Spreading Fast." *New York Times*, May 31, 1912.

"Walsh Arrested, Freed by Mayor." *St. Louis Post-Dispatch*, December 31, 1905.

"War-Bread Menu for All Hotels Here." *New York Times*, July 11, 1917.

"Was President of Hotels Plaza and Savoy Place in N.Y.C., and National in Havana." *Hotel Monthly*, 1933.

"We Are Not 'Raping' the Plaza." *New York Times*, November 21, 1971.

"Wet Protest Staged at Savoy Plaza." *New York Times*, October 3, 1964.

"What Goes On? Hammer and Sickle Fly over Capitalistic Plaza." *Atlanta Constitution*, March 22, 1946.

"What Is Your Room Cost per Day?" *Hotel World*, February 5, 1921.

"What the Jury Swallowed." *Evening World*, March 26, 1921.

"What Will New York Hotels Do Without Bars?" *New-York Tribune*, April 13, 1919.

"When Hotels Mirrored New York's Life." *New York Times Magazine*, March 6, 1932.

"With Rag-Mop Hairdos, Guitars Beatles Conquer New York." *Boston Globe*, February 8, 1964.

"Women Drivers in Endurance Auto Run." *Farmer*, January 11, 1909.

"Women Get $174,297 for Needy Families." *New York Times*, March 11, 1932.

"Women Score G.M. on Building Plan." *New York Times*, January 20, 1965.

"Won't Leave Plaza." *New-York Tribune*, June 13, 1905.

"Won't Take Back Waiters Who Struck." *New York Times*, June 27, 1912.

"Woolworth Heiress Robbed at the Plaza of $750,000 in Gems." *New York Times*, October 2, 1925.

"Wright Revisited." *New Yorker*, June 16, 1956.

"Year of the Air Conditioning." *New York Times*, July 8, 1956.

Arak, Joey. "Lonely Plaza Hotel Now Proven to Be Harmful, Perhaps Deadly." *Curbed New York*, February 28, 2008.

Architectural Record 44 (July 1918).

Asimov, Nanette. "Tiny Menlo College Is Like Home for Saudi Elite." *SF Gate*, May 12, 2015.

Associated Press, March 16, 2006.

Bagli, Charles V. "A Trump Empire Built on Inside Connections and $885 Million in Tax Breaks." *New York Times*, September 17, 2016.

———. "If They Come, Where Will They Sleep." *New York Times*, March 6, 2005.

Bamzai, Kaveree. "The Emperor Strikes Back." *India Today*, January 17, 2011.

Barbanel, Josh. "Plaza Sweet for Repeat Buyer." *Wall Street Journal*, June 8, 2010.

———. "(Too) Storied Hotel?" *New York Times*, September 26, 2008.

Barron, James, "Eloise Gets a New Landlord: Plaza Sells for $675 Million." *New York Times*, August 14, 2004.

———. "Singapore Chain Seeks Plaza Hotel Stake." *New York Times*, January 11, 1995.

Beebe, Lucius. "Swank Trend in Offices Bolstered by Newcomer." *Washington Post*, December 10, 1944.

———. "This New York." *New York Herald Tribune*, April 8, 1939.

Bellman, Eric. "India Squeezes Influential Bank." *Wall Street Journal*, June 7, 2008.

———. "Indian Bank Avoids Deposit Ban." *Wall Street Journal*, June 18, 2008.

———. "Sahara Draws Indian Regulator's Eye." *Wall Street Journal*, June 17, 2008.

Berkowitz, Harry. "Finally, It's a Deal! Ivana to Get $10 Million Plus, Plus, Plus." *Newsday*, March 21, 1991.

Brenner, Marie. "After the Gold Rush." *Vanity Fair*, September 1990.

———. "Kay and Eloise." *Vanity Fair*, December 1996.

Brenzel, Kathryn. "Prospective Buyer of Plaza, Dream Hotels Shakes Lawsuit Holding Up Sale." *Real Deal*, April 25, 2017.

Bridgemen's Magazine, January 1907.

Brock, H. I. "New York's Cocktail Hour." *New Republic*, January 11, 1922.

Building Trades Employers Association Bulletin 7, no. 8 (August 1906).

Calder, Rich. "Bubbly Bye-Bye Good to Last Drop." *New York Post*, April 30, 2005.

Casey, M. V. "Californian Buys Control of Roosevelt." *New York Herald Tribune*, June 6, 1943.

Chan, Sewell. "Firms Lobbying the City Earned $36 Million in '05." *New York Times*, June 3, 2006.

Chatterjee, Sumeet, and Devidutta Tripathy. "Investment Vehicle Eyes Flagship Sahara Hotels in $2 Bln Bailout for Founder Roy." Reuters, January 20, 2015.

Chauhan, Neeraj. "340 HIV Positive Prisoners in Tihar." *Times of India*, May 30, 2011.

Choudhary, Amit Anand. "SC Sends Former Scribe to Jail for a Month for Contempt in Sahara Case." *Times of India*, April 27, 2017.

Claiborne, Craig. "Elegance of Cuisine Is on Wane in U.S." *New York Times*, April 13, 1959.

Cohan, William D. "Prince Alwaleed, Donald Trump, and the Era of Regression and Dictatorship." *Vanity Fair*, November 6, 2017.

Colangelo, Lisa L., and Corky Siemaszko. "Giuliani Nixes Saudi $10M Gift." *New York Daily News*, October 12, 2001.

Collins, Amy Fine. "A Night to Remember." *Vanity Fair*, July 1996.

Confessore, Nicholas. "Oak Room at the Plaza Hotel Is Going the Way of the Pince-Nez." *New York Times*, December 30, 2004.

Conway, Edmund. "Millennium Checks Out Doubled Profits." *Daily Mail*, February 22, 2005.

Cosmopolitan, September 1950.

Coughlin, Gene. Heartbreaks of Society (column). *American Weekly*, n.d.

Cousins, Margaret. "Affair at the Plaza." *Good Housekeeping*, August 1956.

Davis, Louise. "Adventures of the Happy Innkeeper." *Tennessean*, February 11, 1968.

Doebele, Justin. "The Man with the Golden Machine Gun." *Forbes*, July 9, 2001.

Dugal, Ira. "Sahara Loan Will Open Acquisition Opportunity: Mirach's Sharma." *Live Mint*, January 20, 2015.

Finney, Paul Burnham. "Business Travel: The Plaza Hotel's New Owners Plan Some Changes, but They're Not About to Tamper with Success." *New York Times*, January 3, 1996.

Flitter, Emily, and Sumeet Chatterjee. "Exclusive—Subrata Roy's Get-Out-of-Jail Deal Is Mired in Mystery." Reuters, February 5, 2015.

Foderaro, Lisa W. "Plaza Hotel May Be Sold for Co-Ops." *New York Times*, February 27, 1988.

Foley, Stephen. "The Investment Column: Hold on to M&C in Hope of Better Times Ahead." *Independent*, February 20, 2004.

Freeman, Ira Henry. "Plaza to Fete 50-Year Tenant." *New York Times*, March 10, 1957.

Gahlaut, Kanika. "A-List Attendance at Sahara Chief Subrata Roy's Sons' Weddings." *India Today*, February 23, 2004.

Gathje, Curtis. "What Would Eloise Say?" *New York Times*, January 16, 2005.

Goldberger, Paul. "A Spot of Paint Won't Hurt This Lily." *New York Times*, January 22, 1989.

———. "The King of Central Park West." *Vanity Fair*, September 2008.

Grant, Peter, and Alexandra Berzon. "Trump and His Debts: A Narrow Escape." *Wall Street Journal*, January 4, 2016.

Gregorian, Dareh. "Kaching-istan Kazakh Big: Wife Stole Plaza Pad & $75M." *New York Daily News*, August 23, 2013.

Gross, Michael. "Inside Donald Trump's One-Stop Parties: Attendees Recall Cocaine and Very Young Models." *Daily Beast*, October 24, 2016.

Grove, Lloyd, and Hudson Morgan. "Can Plaza Bring NYC the Gold?" *New York Daily News*, February 7, 2005.

Hamilton, Martha M. "Pilots and Investors Ended Allegis Dream." *Washington Post*, June 11, 1987.

Handwerker, Haim, and Anat Georgi. "I Am Eloise. I Am Six. I Live at the Plaza...In a Condo." *Haaretz*, March 28, 2005.

Harper's Bazaar, September 1952.

Haughney, Christine. "It's Lonely at the Plaza Hotel..." *New York Times*, February 17, 2008.

Henry, David. "Trump Says He'll Sue Post for $500M." *Newsday*, December 22, 1994.

Hiltonitems, July 1947; April 1948; June 1948; December 1955.

Hilzenrath, David S., and Michelle Singletary. "Trump Went Broke, but Stayed on Top." *Washington Post*, November 29, 1992.

Hotel Monthly 15, no. 176 (November 1907).

Hylton, Richard D. "Debt Deal for Trump on Plaza." *New York Times*, March 19, 1992.

————. "Trump Aims to Turn Most of Plaza Hotel into Condominiums." *New York Times*, April 9, 1991.

Jacobson, David J. "What's Ahead for the Hotel Industry?" *Harvard Business Review* 24, no. 3 (1946).

Jagendorf, M. "The Rich Lore of a Rich Hotel: The Plaza." *New York Folklore Quarterly* (Spring 1953): 176–82.

Jain, Sundeep, and Tom Wright. "India's Sahara Gets Defensive After Ruling." *Wall Street Journal*, September 3, 2012.

Kearns, Robert. "Allegis Selling Westin for $1.5 Billion: United Airlines' Parent Nears Goal in Restructuring." *Chicago Tribune*, October 28, 1987.

Kraar, Louis. "The Mystery Man Who Took the Plaza from Donald Trump." *Fortune*, December 25, 1995.

Kuttner, Robert. "A More Perfect Union." *American Prospect*, November 28, 2011.

Lakshmi, Rama. "Indian Tycoon Working to Sell His Iconic Hotels from Jail." *Washington Post*, September 24, 2014.

Larson, Sarah. "The Girl with the Eloise Tattoo." *New Yorker*, March 23, 2015.

Leahy, Joe. "India Freezes Sahara Financial Deposits." *Financial Times*, June 6, 2008.

Life, December 12, 1955.

Ligo, Godwin. "Korman Looks Back, Points to the Future." *Vanuatu Daily Post*, July 30, 2015.

Lindsay, Cynthia. "Kay Thompson." *McCall's*, January 1957.

Lodging Advisors Market Research. "A Concise History of the New York City Hotel Market, 1988–2016."

Lodging Hospitality, November 1975.

Lueck, Thomas J. "Reaching for the Sky to Add a Room." *New York Times*, June 3, 1990.

————. "Workers Hold Rally at Plaza Against Conversion to Condos." *New York Times*, April 6, 2005.

Mahapatra, Dhananjay. "ED Seeks Provisional Attachment of Sahara's Foreign Hotels, Files Plea in SC." *Times of India*, February 9, 2017.

————. "Sahara Pledges Asset Sale, 'Buyer' Surfaces." *Times of India*, March 1, 2017.

Markel, Helen. "The Special World of Cecil Beaton." *Good Housekeeping*, January 1958.

Marquise de Fontenoy [pseud. for Frederick Philip Lewis Cunliffe-Owen]. "Artist Princess and Her Chasseur." *Washington Post*, March 18, 1909.

Marsh, Julia. "Ex-Wife Claims Kazakh Tycoon Faking Illness to Avoid Court." *New York Post*, November 4, 2013.

Matthews, Ralph. "Looking at the Stars with Ralph Matthews." *Afro-American*, March 26, 1932.

Mercer, Charles. "'Eloise' Will Come to Life on Playhouse 90." *Oakland Tribune*, November 11, 1956.

Meyers, William H. "Stalking the Plaza." *New York Times*, September 25, 1988.

Mini-Maxims, March 1944; November 1945.

Morrell, Alex. "A Wall Street Banker Describes the Time Donald Trump Offered to Seal a Deal with a $1 Million Coin Flip." *Business Insider*, July 12, 2017.

Nelson, Dean. "Indian Billionaire Subrata Roy Mortgages Grosvenor House and New York's Plaza Hotel to Get Out of Jail." *Telegraph*, January 21, 2015.

New York Herald Tribune, September 6, 1929; February 15, 1937.

New York Times, September 12, 1988; March 17, 2005.

New Yorker, May 12, 1956; February 27, 1965.

Newsday, March 30, 1988.

Norris, Floyd. "A Haze of Debt Clouds the Plaza Hotel's Gleam." *New York Times*, June 5, 1990.

Oppenheim, Carol. "12 rms, prk vws: For $150,000 You Can Cuddle Up in the Plaza." *Chicago Tribune*, February 16, 1977.

Pacelle, Mitchell. "Asian Investors Buy Up Hotels in U.S., Europe, but Move Cautiously." *Wall Street Journal*, February 19, 1997.

Parker, Will. "Investors Hope Cryptocurrency Raise Will Buy Them the Plaza Hotel." *Real Deal*, March 27, 2018.

Patterson, Philana. "Brokers Get Creative to Lure Bonus Money." *Real Deal*, February 1, 2006.

Peretz, Evgenia. "Eloise Sheds a Tear." *Vanity Fair*, January 2009.

Perry, Alex. "A Tale of Two Indias." *Time*, December 6, 2004.

Peterson, Helen, and Tracy Connor. "Loyal Despite Brothel Bust on West Side." *New York Daily News*, June 16, 2006.

Piore, Adam. "Scott Latham: The Art of the Commercial Deal." *Real Deal*, November 4, 2007.

Pocono Record, December 21, 1972.

Poole, Ernest. "Cowboys of the Sky." *Everybody's Magazine*, November 1908.

Publishers Weekly, May 12, 1969.

Quint, Michael. "Saudi Prince to Become Citicorp's Top Stockholder." *New York Times*, February 22, 1991.

Ramirez, Anthony. "At the Plaza, Restoring Life Lived Luxuriously." *New York Times*, March 2, 2008.

———. "Souvenir Hunters Help Themselves to Pieces of History at the Plaza Hotel." *New York Times*, May 21, 2005.

Rautray, Samanwaya. "Supreme Court Grounds Subrata Roy, Bars Sahara from Selling Any Property." *Economic Times*, November 22, 2013.

Recchia, Philip. "Last Call at Plaza for Guests & Oak Bar-Flies." *New York Post*, May 1, 2005.

Revson, James A. "Social Studies: Donald and Ivana Glitz the Plaza." *Newsday*, September 21, 1989.

Sanger, Elizabeth. "Will New Plaza Have Old Magic?" *Newsday*, April 7, 2005.

Satow, Julie. "Battle Over Plaza Becoming Costly." *New York Sun*, April 7, 2005.

———. "Hotel Workers Union Protests Plaza Conversion." *New York Sun*, February 18, 2005.

———. "Pied-a-Neighborhood." *New York Times*, October 24, 2014.

———. "The Fate of the Plaza." *New York Sun*, April 15–17, 2005.

———. "Waldorf Astoria and Hotel Workers Union Reach $149 Million Deal for Severance Payouts." *New York Times*, June 26, 2015.

Saul, Stephanie, and Louise Story. "At the Time Warner Center, an Enclave of Powerful Russians." *New York Times*, February 11, 2015.

Seifman, David. "Plaza Sweet Victory." *New York Post*, April 15, 2005.

Sheppard, Eugenia. "Boom Time for Tricycles." *New York Herald Tribune*, April 9, 1956.

Shulman, Robin. "Renovation of the Plaza Hotel Clears a Hurdle." *New York Times*, July 13, 2005.

Sinha, Ashutosh, and Gautam Chikermane. "India's Weirdest Worker." *Outlook*, September 8, 1997.

Smith, Ben. "Bloomberg Gets a Nasty Lesson: Politics Counts." *New York Observer*, March 14, 2005.

Smith, Bill. "Persian Room, Plaza Hotel, New York." *Billboard*, September 28, 1951.

Smith, Cecil. "Kay Thompson Sounds Like 'Eloise.'" *Los Angeles Times*, June 3, 1956.

Solomont, E. B., and Katherine Clarke. "Who Earned & Who Got Burned." *Real Deal*, August 2017.

Speers, W. "Trump Settlement Is Not a Done Deal." *Philadelphia Inquirer*, March 22, 1991.

Stancati, Margherita, Summer Said, and Benoit Faucon. "The Price of Freedom for Saudi Arabia's Richest Man: $6 Billion." *Wall Street Journal*, December 23, 2017.

Steinhauer, Jennifer. "Citing Comments on Attack, Giuliani Rejects Saudi's Gift." *New York Times*, October 12, 2001.

Stern, R. L., and T. Pouschine. "Can Donald Pay His Hotel Bill?" *Forbes*, July 8, 1991.

Stout, David, and Kenneth N. Gilpin. "Trump Is Selling Plaza Hotel to Saudi and Asian Investors." *New York Times*, April 12, 1995.

Subramanian, N. Sundaresha. "BoA Refused to Be Part of Sahara Deal Citing Integrity Issues: Saransh Sharma." *Business Standard*, February 12, 2015.

Suresh, Appu Esthose. "The Curious Case of 5,984 Kalawatis in Sahara List." *Indian Express*, May 1, 2013.

Swaine, Jon. "FBI Looked into Trump Plans to Build Hotel in Latvia with Putin Supporter." *Guardian*, March 29, 2018.

Tharp, Paul. "Horror Night at the Plaza." *New York Post*, February 28, 2008.

Thirani, Neha. "Indian Conglomerate Buys New York's Plaza Hotel." *New York Times*, August 1, 2010.

Thompson, John H. "How Is the Race Faring in Union Organizations Which Have Spread Throughout Industrial Plants?" *Chicago Defender*, September 30, 1939.

Town Topics, March 9, 1905; 57 (January–June 1907); 69 (January–June 1913); 86, no. 14 (October 6, 1921); March 23, 1922; 90, no. 17 (October 25, 1923).

Tricks, Henry, and Douglas Wong. "M&C Sells New York's Plaza for $675 Million." *Financial Times*, August 14, 2004.

Truell, Peter. "A Saudi Prince Fond of High-Profile Investing." *New York Times*, April 12, 1995.

Ulam, Alex. "What Does the Future Hold for the Plaza Hotel?" *Architectural Record* 193, no. 3 (March 2005).

Useem, Jerry. "Former Trump Executive Had a Penchant for Theft." *Boston Globe*, September 23, 2016.

Venkatesan, J. "SC Orders Sahara to Refund Rs. 24,400 Crore." *Hindu*, August 31, 2012.

Vogel, Carol. "The Plaza Suite: Design." *New York Times*, January 15, 1989.

Walsh, Dominic. "M&C Considers Selling Hotels as Occupancy Falls." *Times* (London), February 20, 2004.

Weiss, Lois, and Steve Cuozzo. "Saudi Prince Wants to Save Embattled Plaza Hotel." *New York Post*, May 24, 2017.

Welsome, Eileen. *Lomas del Poleo*, December 27, 2007.

White, Marion M. "Ivana Trump: Hard Work, Discipline and Self-Reliance." *St. Petersburg Times*, September 26, 1988.

Whitehouse, Franklin. "Hotel Business Improving Here." *New York Times*, February 12, 1967.

Wilson, Gertrude [pseud.]. "Laugh Clowns, Laugh!" *New York Amsterdam News*, February 22, 1964.

Wolfe, Tom. "Beatles Conquer New York." *Boston Globe*, February 8, 1964.

Yates, Maura. "Plaza Rally to Double as Prayer Vigil." *New York Sun*, March 11, 2005.

Zhdannikov, Dmitry. "Qatar to Buy New York's Plaza Hotel for $600 Million: Source." *Reuters*, July 3, 2018.

Books:

Alexiou, Alice Sparberg. *The Flatiron: The New York Landmark and the Incomparable City That Arose with It*. New York: Thomas Dunne Books, 2010.

Allen, Frederick Lewis. *Only Yesterday: An Informal History of the 1920s*. New York: Harper & Row, 1931.

———. *The 1930s in America: Since Yesterday*. New York: Harper & Row, 1939.

Alpern, Andrew. *The Dakota: A History of the World's Best-Known Apartment Building*. Hudson, NY: Princeton Architectural Press, 2015.

Ayto, John. *Movers and Shakers: A Chronology of Words That Shaped Our Age*. Oxford: Oxford University Press, 1999.

Bandyopadhyay, Tamal. *Sahara: The Untold Story*. Mumbai: Jaico, 2014.

Barrett, Wayne. *Trump: The Greatest Show on Earth; the Deals, the Downfall, the Reinvention*. New York: Simon & Schuster, 2016.

Beebe, Lucius M. *The Lucius Beebe Reader*. Edited by Charles Clegg and Duncan Emrich. Garden City, NY: Doubleday, 1967.

Beinecke, William S. *Bernhard Beinecke: A Memoir*. New York: Prospect Hill Press, 2005.

Boiardi, Anna. *Delicious Memories: Recipes and Stories from the Chef Boyardee Family*. New York: Stewart, Tabori and Chang, 2011.

Bolton, Whitney. *The Silver Spade: The Conrad Hilton Story*. New York: Farrar, Straus and Young, 1954.

Brown, Eve. *Champagne Cholly: The Life and Times of Maury Paul*. New York: E. P. Dutton, 1947.

———. *The Plaza, 1907–1967: Its Life and Times*. New York: Meredith Press, 1967.

Bruner, Robert F., and Sean D. Carr. *The Panic of 1907: Lessons Learned from the Market's Perfect Storm*. Hoboken, NJ: Wiley, 2007.

Burns, Ric, and James Sanders, with Lisa Ades. *New York: An Illustrated History*. New York: Knopf, 2003.

Chaikin, David, and J. C. Sharman. *Corruption and Money Laundering: A Symbiotic Relationship*. New York: Palgrave Macmillan, 2009.

Comfort, Mildred Houghton. *Conrad N. Hilton, Hotelier*. Minneapolis: T. S. Denison, 1964.

Cromley, Elizabeth Collins. *Alone Together: A History of New York's Early Apartments*. Ithaca, NY: Cornell University Press, 1990.

Dabney, Thomas Ewing. *The Man Who Bought the Waldorf: The Life of Conrad N. Hilton*. New York: Duell, Sloan, and Pearce, 1950.

Davis, Deborah. *Party of the Century: The Fabulous Story of Truman Capote and His Black and White Ball*. Hoboken, NJ: Wiley, 2006.

Dorsey, Leslie, and Janice Devine. *Fare Thee Well: A Backward Look at Two Centuries of Historic American Hostelries, Fashionable Spas & Seaside Resorts*. New York: Crown, 1964.

Doyle, Mary. *Life Was Like That*. Boston: Houghton Mifflin, 1936.

Farmer, Patty. *The Persian Room Presents: An Oral History of New York's Most Magical Night Spot*. San Clemente, CA: Ballymaloe, 2012.

Fitzgerald, F. Scott. *My Lost City: Personal Essays, 1920–1940*. Edited by James L. W. West III. Cambridge: Cambridge University Press, 2005.

Foner, Eric. *Give Me Liberty! An American History*. Vol. 2, *From 1865*. 4th ed. New York: W. W. Norton, 2014.

Galbraith, John Kenneth. *The Great Crash, 1929*. Boston: Mariner Books, 2009.

Gathje, Curtis. *At the Plaza: An Illustrated History of the World's Most Famous Hotel*. New York: St. Martin's Press, 2000.

Giuliani, Rudolph W., and Ken Kurson. *Leadership*. New York: Time Warner, 2003.

Graham, Stephen. *New York Nights*. New York: Doran, 1927.

Groth, Paul. *Living Downtown: The History of Residential Hotels in the United States*. Berkeley: University of California Press, 1994.

Hamilton, W. L. *Promoting New Hotels: When Does It Pay?* New York: Harper & Brothers, 1930.

Hawes, Elizabeth. *New York, New York: How the Apartment House Transformed the Life of the City (1869–1930)*. New York: Knopf, 1993.

Hayner, Norman S. *Hotel Life*. Chapel Hill: University of North Carolina Press, 1936.

Hennessee, Judith A. *Betty Friedan: Her Life*. New York: Random House, 1999.

Hession, Jane King, and Debra Pickrel. *Frank Lloyd Wright in New York: The Plaza Years, 1954–1959*. Layton, UT: Gibbs Smith, 2007.

Hilton, Conrad N. *Be My Guest*. New York: Simon & Schuster, 1957.

Homberger, Eric. *The Historical Atlas of New York City: A Visual Celebration of 400 Years of New York City's History*. New York: Henry Holt, 2005.

Hurt, Harry. *The Lost Tycoon: The Many Lives of Donald J. Trump*. New York: W. W. Norton, 1993.

Irvin, Sam. *Kay Thompson: From Funny Face to Eloise*. New York: Simon & Schuster, 2010.

James, Henry. *The American Scene*. London: Chapman & Hall, 1907.

Khan, Riz. *Alwaleed: Businessman, Billionaire, Prince*. London: William Morrow, 2005.

King, Moses. *King's Handbook of New York City: An Outline History and Description of the American Metropolis*. Boston: Moses King, 1892.

Kleinfield, Sonny. *The Hotel: A Week in the Life of the Plaza*. New York: Simon & Schuster, 1989.

Kranish, Michael, and Marc Fisher. *Trump Revealed: The Definitive Biography of the 45th President*. New York: Scribner, 2016.

Larson, Eric. *Dead Wake: The Last Crossing of the Lusitania*. New York: Penguin, 2015.

Lerner, Michael A. *Dry Manhattan: Prohibition in New York City*. Cambridge, MA: Harvard University Press, 2007.

Mangun, Bryant, ed. *F. Scott Fitzgerald in Context*. Cambridge: Cambridge University Press, 2013.

Miller, Donald L. *Supreme City: How Jazz Age Manhattan Gave Birth to Modern America*. New York: Simon & Schuster, 2014.

Mizener, Arthur. *The Far Side of Paradise: A Biography of F. Scott Fitzgerald*. New York: Vintage, 1959.

Morehouse, Ward, III. *Inside the Plaza: An Intimate Portrait of the Ultimate Hotel*. New York: Applause, 2001.

Mower, Henry S. *Reminiscences of a Hotel Man: Of Forty Years' Service*. Boston: Worcester, 1912.

Obolensky, Serge. *One Man in His Time: The Memoirs of Serge Obolensky*. New York: American Book-Stratford Press, 1958.

Okrent, Daniel. *Last Call: The Rise and Fall of Prohibition*. New York: Scribner, 2010.

Preston, Diana: *Lusitania: An Epic Tragedy*. New York: Bloomsbury, 2002.

Rasenberger, Jim. *High Steel: The Daring Men Who Built the World's Greatest Skyline*. New York: HarperCollins, 2004.

Reed, Rex: *People Are Crazy Here*. New York: Delacorte Press, 1974.

Rosenzweig, Roy, and Elizabeth Blackmar. *The Park and the People: A History of Central Park*. Ithaca, NY: Cornell University Press, 1992.

Sacks, Marcy S. *Before Harlem: The Black Experience in New York City Before World War I*. Philadelphia: University of Pennsylvania Press, 2006.

Sell, Hildegarde Loretta. *Over 50—So What!* New York: Doubleday, 1963.

Shachtman, Tom. *Skyscraper Dreams: The Great Real Estate Dynasties of New York*. AuthorHouse, 2000.

Sonnabend, Roger P. *Your Future in Hotel Management*. New York: Richards Rosen Press, 1964.

Starrett, Paul. *Changing the Skyline: An Autobiography*. New York: McGraw Hill, 1938.

Stern, Robert A. M., Gregory Gilmartin, and John Montague Massengale. *New York 1900: Metropolitan Architecture and Urbanism, 1890–1915*. New York: Rizzoli, 1983.

Taraborrelli, Randy J. *The Hiltons: The True Story of an American Dynasty*. New York: Grand Central, 2014.

Terkel, Studs. *Hard Times: An Oral History of the Great Depression*. New York: Pantheon Books, 1970.

Thompson, Kay. *Kay Thompson's Eloise: A Book for Precocious Grown Ups*. New York: Simon & Schuster, 1955.

Trease, Howard Van, ed. *Melanesian Politics: Stael Blong Vanuatu*. Christchurch: Macmillan Brown Centre for Pacific Studies at University of Canterbury and Institute of Pacific Studies at University of the South Pacific, 1995.

Trump, Ivana. *Raising Trump*. New York: Simon & Schuster, 2017.

Veblen, Thorstein. *The Theory of the Leisure Class*. New York: Penguin, 1994.

Walker, Stanley. *The Night Club Era*. New York: Blue Ribbon Books, 1933.

Weitzman, David. *Skywalkers: Mohawk Ironworkers Build the City*. New York: Roaring Brook Press, 2010.

Wendt, Lloyd, and Herman Kogan. *Bet a Million! The Story of John W. Gates*. New York: Bobbs-Merrill, 1948.

Williams, Mason B. *City of Ambition: FDR, La Guardia, and the Making of Modern New York*. New York: W. W. Norton, 2013.

Williamson, Jefferson. *The American Hotel: An Anecdotal History*. New York: Knopf, 1930.

Wilson, Edmund. *The Shores of Light: A Literary Chronicle of the 20s and 30s*. New York: Farrar, Straus and Young, 1952.

Interviews:

George Abrams, in-person interview, December 21, 2016.

Patrick Amiano, in-person interview, November 1, 2016.

Gautam Awasthi, in-person interview, June 15, 2017.

Tamal Bandyopadhyay, in-person interview, May 13, 2017.

Francesca Barra, via telephone, February 20, 2017.

Kwek Leng Beng, via email, December 3, 2017.

Victoria Brewer, in-person interview, October 25, 2017.

Didier Le Calvez, via telephone, April 11, 2017.

Marisa Recuero Carbonell, via email, January 9, 2018.

Sant Chatwal, in-person interview, May 30, 2017; June 26, 2017.

Amit Anand Choudhary, via email, April 28, 2017.

Sharon F. Corey, via email, November 17, 2015.

George Cozonis, in-person interview, October 4, 2016; June 1, 2017.

Barry Cregan, in-person interview, April 28, 2017.

Joanna Cutler, in-person interview, September 6, 2017.

Kevin Daly, via telephone, September 22, 2017.

Yvette Edwards, in-person interview, August 4, 2016.

Patty Farmer, in-person interview, September 17, 2016.

Tony Fortuna, in-person interview, April 18, 2017.

Kristin Franzese, in-person interview, August 4, 2016.

Joe Freia, in-person interview, April 26, 2017.

Daniel Jiménez García, via telephone, January 12, 2018; subsequently via email.

Curt Gathje, in-person interview, July 23, 2015; February 12, 2018.

Paul Goldberger, in-person interview, June 8, 2016.

Kent Gross, via telephone, October 21, 2017.

Sean Hennessey, in-person interview, September 6, 2017.

Celyta Jackson, via telephone, April 17, 2107.

Kenneth Jackson, in-person interview, August 20, 2015.

David Cay Johnson, via telephone, March 27, 2017.

Neil Johnson, in-person interview, April 7, 2016.

Shahal Kahn, via telephone and email, April 2017 through June 2018.

Suri Kasirer, via telephone, October 10, 2017.

Lisa Keller, in-person interview, February 2, 2016.

Sonny Kleinfeld, in-person interview, February 23, 2017.

Christopher Knable, via telephone, April 12, 2017.

Bob Kraft, via telephone, August 22, 2017.

Alexa Lambert, in-person interview, April 22, 2015; November 17, 2017.

Scott Latham, via telephone, September 25, 2017.

Gary Lavenson, in-person interview, December 21, 2016.

Joel Lavenson, via telephone, October 31, 2016.

Elizabeth Leahy, in-person interview, April 22, 2015.

Barry LePatner, in-person interview, April 14, 2017.

Nicola Lercara, in-person interview, May 17, 2016.

Kevin P. Lilles, in-person interview, April 13, 2017.

Elizabeth Lorenzo, in-person interview, April 22, 2015.

Gary Lyman, in-person interview, September 12, 2017.

Michael Maggiore, via telephone, October 17, 2016.

Francis Marrone, in-person interview, September 20, 2016.

Jon Mechanic, in-person interview, September 7, 2017.

Walter Melvin, via telephone, August 17, 2017.

Edward Mermelstein, in-person interview, July 10, 2017.

Grace Murphy, in-person interview, August 4, 2016.

Miki Naftali, in-person interview, March 25, 2015; July 26, 2017.

Dinesh Narayanan, via telephone, email, June 19, 2017.

Russ M. Nazrisho, via telephone, November 22, 2017.

Jay Neveloff, in-person interview, November 28, 2017.

Paul Nicaj, in-person interview, April 26, 2017.

Luigi Norrito, in-person interview, May 5, 2016.

Tim O'Brien, in-person interview, August 24, 2017.

Jeffrey Poirot, in-person interview, November 8, 2017.

Alan J. Pomerantz, via telephone, September 8, 2017.

Lee Harris Pomeroy, in-person interview, April 12, 2017.

Sharat Pradhan, via telephone, May 23, 2017.

Barbara Res, in-person interview, January 24, 2017.

Subrata Roy, in-person interview, June 16, 2017.

Jessdev Sagar, via telephone, May 2, 2017.

Alain Sailhac, in-person interview, May 1, 2017.

Gregg Salomone, in-person interview, September 29, 2016.

Lourdes Salomone, via telephone, October 18, 2016.

Y. David Scharf, in-person interview, September 5, 2017.

Aaron Schmulewitz, via telephone, November 10, 2017.

Saransh Sharma, via telephone, May 12, 2017.

Joshua Sirefman, in-person interview, May 18, 2017.

Edner Smith, in-person interview, March 24 2015.

John H. Snyder, via telephone, November 10, 2017.

Susan Song, in-person interview, April 22, 2015.

Peter Sonnabend, in-person interview, December 21, 2016.

Stephanie Sonnabend, in-person interview, December 20, 2016.

Charles Stewart-Smith, via email, May through July 2017.

Louise Sunshine, via telephone, April 4, 2017.

Prakash Swamy, via telephone, June 22, 2017; July 26, 2018; August 8, 2018.

Eric Trump, via telephone, October 26, 2017.

A. Vaidyanathan, via telephone, June 19, 2017.

Howard Van Trease, via email, June 11, 2018.

J. Venkatesan, via email, June 20, 2017.

Sandeep Wadhwa, in-person interview, August 26, 2017, subsequently via telephone.

Abe Wallach, in-person interview, July 28, 2017.

Peter Ward, in-person interview, June 18, 2015; October 4, 2017.

Suzanne Wenz, in-person interview, August 4, 2016.

Anton Werner, via telephone, July 19, 2017.

Andy Young, via telephone, April 23 2018.

Original Documents:

Hand-Book of Securities, compiled by the *Commercial and Financial Chronicle* (New York: W. B. Dana Co., 1907–1928).

JTS Trading Ltd. v Trinity White City Ventures Ltd., Sahara India Pariwar, Aamby Valley (Mauritius) Ltd., UBS Financial Services Inc., April 18, 2017.

Materials from the Hospitality Industry Archives of the Conrad N. Hilton College of Hotel & Restaurant Management at the University of Houston.

Materials from the Westin Hotels and Resorts Archive at the Washington State University Libraries, Manuscripts, Archives, and Special Collections, Pullman, Washington.

National Archives of Boston.

New York County Supreme Court, Bolat Nazarbayev v. Daniyar Kesikbayev, Maira Kurmangaliyeva.

Partial unpublished memoir by Alphonse Salomone.

Plaza Hotel financial statements from proprietary sources, and FOIA filings for forms TC208 via the New York City Department of Finance.

Republic of Vanuatu Office of the Ombudsman Public Report on the Breach of Leadership Code and the Misuse of the Cyclone Betsy Account by Former Prime Minister Mr. Maxime Carlot Korman, February 26, 1998.

State of New York Department of Labor Bulletin 14, nos. 50–53 (1912): 275–77.

Supreme Court of India Civil Appellate Jurisdiction I.A. No. 247 of 2017 In Contempt Petition (Civil) No. 412 of 2012 and Supreme Court of India Civil Appeal No. 9813 of 2011.

The Beinecke Family Papers at the Beinecke Rare Book and Manuscript Library at Yale University.

The Plaza, a commemorative book published by Westin Hotels for its seventy-fifth anniversary. Secaucus, NJ: Poplar Books, 1981.

United States Bankruptcy Court, Southern District of New York, Chapter 11 filing of Plaza Operating Partners, November 13, 1992.

United States Realty & Improvement Company consolidated company annual reports, 1911–1942.

U.S. Bureau of Labor Statistics, *Handbook of Labor Statistics*, 1947 ed.; Bulletin No. 916, p. 89.

Television, Video, Radio, and Film:

All Things Considered, National Public Radio, March 15, 2006.

HBO documentary, *It's Me: The Man Who Drew Eloise*, 2015.

YouTube, https://www.youtube.com/watch?v=KlwCXgZwSCc.

INDEX